POWER AND PARANOIA

Power and Paranoia

HISTORY, NARRATIVE, AND THE AMERICAN CINEMA, 1940–1950

Dana Polan

Columbia University Press

New York   1986

The Andrew W. Mellon Foundation, through a special grant,
has assisted the Press in publishing this volume.

Columbia University Press
New York   Guildford, Surrey

Printed in the United States of America

Library of Congress Cataloging-in-Publication Data

Polan, Dana, B.,
    Power and paranoia.

    Bibliography: p.
    Includes index.
    1. Moving-pictures—Social aspects—United States—
History.   2. Moving-picture plays—History and
criticism.   I. Title.
PN1995.9.S6P65   1986   302.2'343'0973   86-4144
ISBN 0-231-06284-2

This book is Smyth-sewn.
Book design by J.S. Roberts

FOR ALICE DURIEU

Contents

Acknowledgments

One of the joys for any scholar working within film history and, more specifically, within the period of the American forties is the amazingly high degree to which he/she quickly discovers the presence of what is so often only a myth in the humanities: an intellectual community devoted to dialogue, interaction, and an open sharing of ideas, perspectives, and, perhaps best of all, criticisms. From beginning to end, this work has benefited from the material and intellectual assistance of a number of giving persons.

First, I wish to thank those figures in American history who answered queries, provided references, offered copies of work in progress: Professors Susan M. Hartmann, Leila Rupp, Frank Fox, and, most especially, Paul Koistinen.

Professor John Belton at Columbia was the first film scholar to read part of the manuscript and offer reactions; his perceptive early guidance suggested initial ways to sort out openings from dead-ends in investigations of postwar cinema. I also wish to thank the following professors who read parts of the manuscript and offered advice and encouragement: Christian Metz, Jacques Aumont, Jean Franco, William M. Todd III, Bill Nichols, Tim Lyons, Scott Nygren, Judith Mayne, Maureen Turim.

Loren Shumway of Yale deserves special recognition for first suggesting to me the narrative importance of the concept of "conversion"—a concept central to my investigation of war narrative.

My work is also in great debt to that specific community of scholars producing major work on American cinema in the forties. Each of these persons was wonderfully ready to share ideas and essays: Michael Renov, Diane Waldman, Mary Ann Doane, Deborah Linderman.

Perhaps no community was as important as that of the critical theorists assembled in the English department at the University of Pittsburgh. At every moment, I rediscover the joy of having such colleagues as Lucy Fischer, Marcia Landy, Paul Bové, and James Knapp. A special thank you, also, to my chairperson, Mary Louise Briscoe, who always does more than would seem possible to build a space in which work that might not always seem to fit into the traditional goals of an English department can find a sustaining and driving support. My gratitude also goes to Phil Smith, who spent a summer taping films for me and answering queries about science fiction.

This project was aided financially by grants from the Office of Research at the University of Pittsburgh.

Several institutions helped me to discover the pleasures of archival research as they graciously opened up their doors and often dust-covered boxes to a scholar who wasn't always sure in advance of the exact sorts of things he wished to discover. In particular, I would acknowledge the openness to scholars of the film section of the Library of Congress; the Suitland, Maryland, branch of the National Archives; the Harry S. Truman Library in Independence, Missouri.

No one worked harder in building the research material for this study than Sean Monagle, my research assistant in the summer of 1983, and Suzanne Crosby, interlibrary loan librarian at the University of Pittsburgh, always ready and able to scramble after one more obscure forties text.

Fragments of this study were published as a short essay in the excellent journal *The Velvet Light Trap*. My deep gratitude goes to the editorial staff for a demanding reading that always pushed me to interrogate the implications of my argument.

The work, energy, and personality of four scholars have determined my study of film from its beginnings to such a degree that a simple thank you can never be anything but inadequate. I owe so much to David Rodowick (who constantly radiates the productive pleasures of scholarly endeavor in a contagious search for a method—for ideas, essays, and rare book titles hidden away in used bookshops); to Lea Jacobs (who was an energetic dialogic partner for inspiring discussions lasting late into the night on topics in history, ideology, textuality); to Tania Modleski for a friendship and intellectual interaction that is truly wondrous.

Ed Lowry died suddenly and tragically while I was reviewing the copyedited manuscript. It was Ed who first introduced me to the pleasures and importance of sustained study of American film narrative and with whom each new conversation seemed wonderfully to start that introduction all over again. I shall miss him deeply.

A special thank you to Don Fredericksen at Cornell for starting me on the road to film study.

My emotional and intellectual life is so interwined with Donie Durieu and her two sons, Raphaël and Gérard Frémiot, that I see them in every word and idea of this study. Book acknowledgments always seem to have trouble verbalizing their appreciation to the person closest to the author. In trying to express my gratitude to Donie, I find myself feeling the same difficulty with mere words; here, I simply say "Thank you" knowing she will know all that those words can only ever so slightly indicate.

A NOTE ON THE FILMS

Much of the research in the following pages comes from a study of approximately 700 feature films released between 1940 and 1950. The first time I mention a film, I provide the release date; thereafter, I give the release date only when it seems important to the immediate context.

POWER AND PARANOIA

Introduction

Two contiguous pages from *Life* magazine just at the end of the Second World War (August 13, 1945, pp. 34–5) can demonstrate many of the conflicts and confluences of representation in the cultural and ideological space of the American forties. On the left-hand page, a series of black-and-white photograph panels, proceeding from left to right and from top to bottom, chronicle the flame-thrower killing of a Japanese by an Australian, America's ally. A *narrative*, then—the pictures form a ministory of victory and death, the victory represented according to a dominant wartime ideology, represented for an audience back home so it can follow and situate itself in relation to the man's narrative. The narrative might seem to sum up the war, to show it as a kind of participatory drama even for those persons who can participate only through the pages of the magazine. Furthermore, this is a narrative controlled by a grounding caption that not merely describes but, also, gives the narrative a necessity, that of a grim pragmatism: "The flame-thrower is easily the most cruel, most terrifying weapon ever developed. If it does not suffocate the enemy in his hiding place, its quickly licking flames sear his body to a black crisp. But so long as the Jap refuses to come out of his hole and keeps killing, this is the only way." The simplicity of that last "is" also functions as a *surety;* the caption represents a war of necessity, a war without ambiguity.

A JAP BURNS

He refuses to leave Borneo hiding place so flamethrower kills him

When the 7th Australian Division landed near Balikpapan on the island of Borneo last month they found the town strongly defended by Japanese. As usual, the enemy fought from caves, from pillboxes, from every available hiding place. And, as usual, there was only one way to advance against them: burn them out. Men of the 7th, who had fought the Japs before, quickly applied their flamethrowers, soon convinced some Japs that it was time to quit. Others,

like the one shown here, refused. So they had to be burned out.

Although men have fought one another with fire from time immemorial, the flamethrower is easily the most cruel, the most terrifying weapon ever developed. If it does not suffocate the enemy in his hiding place, its quickly licking tongues of flame sear his body to a black crisp. But so long as the Jap refuses to come out of his holes and keeps killing, this is the only way.

AUSTRALIAN SOLDIER ON BORNEO USES FLAMETHROWER ON JAP HIDING PLACE

MOMENT LATER JAP WHO WOULDN'T QUIT DUCKS OUT ENVELOPED IN FLAMES

WITH LIQUID FIRE EATING AT HIS SKIN JAP SKITTERS THROUGH UNDERBRUSH

BLIND AND STILL BURNING HE MAKES AGONIZED REACH FOR SUPPORT, FALLS

HE TRIES TO CRAWL, FALLS AGAIN. FLAMES HAVE ALREADY CONSUMED CLOTHING

AFTER ONE LAST EFFORT, THE JAP SLUMPS IN HIS OWN GRISLY FUNERAL PYRE

Narratives of the Forties: War and Commitment

MUSHROOMS *fresh from the hothouse*

—make a truly wonderful soup

From the first spoonful you know this is going to be delicious soup . . . that you'll enjoy it straight down to the bottom of the plate. For Campbell's Cream of Mushroom Soup is a happy combination of mushrooms and cream.

The fact is, the mushrooms are actually rushed from the hothouses to Campbell's Kitchens so that all their freshness, tenderness and delicate flavor go into the soup. And the cream, added for smoothness and richness, is poured in generously. Blending the two is a soup-making art—eating the soup is a real joy! Fine for company and everyday family meals.

Campbell's
CREAM OF MUSHROOM SOUP

LOOK FOR THE
RED-AND-WHITE LABEL

21 KINDS TO CHOOSE FROM: Asparagus · Bean with Bacon · Beef · Beef Noodle (new!) · Black Bean · Bouillon · Chicken · Chicken Gumbo · Chicken Noodle · Clam Chowder · Consommé · Green Pea · Mock Turtle · Cream of Mushroom · Ox Tail · Pepper Pot · Scotch Broth · Cream of Spinach (new!) · Tomato · Vegetable · Vegetarian Vegetable · Vegetable-Beef

Campbell's
CONDENSED
CREAM OF
MUSHROOM
SOUP

Narratives of the Forties: Postwar possibilities

On the right-hand page, an ad for Campbell's soup—
again, a narrative as from top to bottom we see mushrooms, a
can of Campbell's mushroom soup, and finally a plate of soup.
The narrative here seems as tight and coherent as its left-side
counterpart; as much as the technology of the flame-thrower, the
soup here derives its being from what commentators on the war
years will sum up as America's "miracle of production." Indeed,
to make what might almost be the worst of sick jokes, we could
say that both narratives are demonstrations of Claude Lévi-
Strauss' argument that culture exists in the mediation of the "raw
and the cooked." For both stories, the advance of Western civilization is tied to a technologically perfected application of heat to
objects in the world: both narratives celebrate our ability to transform a resistant world through the tools of modernity. And yet
from page to page significant differences appear—significant variations in narrative form and narrative sense. From the start, the
ad's color (reserved primarily at this moment in *Life's* career for
advertisements and fashion photos)—that is, the fact of color, and
the fact of this particular kind of color (not photographic exacti-
tude, but a painterly approximation)—separates this story from
the other. Both narratives inscribe themselves into a certain representation of everyday forties life (as the magazine's all-inclusive
title suggests), but the advertisement avoids the claim to blunt
immediacy of the black-and-white photography; the commodity
(here, soup) takes on a certain imaginariness, the object of fantasy,
the status of a wish (and, indeed, throughout the immediate war
reconversion period, commodities are frequently presented in the
form of a promise, a gratification somewhere in the future of
something that has so long been done without; the very fact that
many of the products—for example, the ultra-modern kitchen
with its many marvels—are being offered to consumers for the
first time makes the promise doubly unreal). In the present, then,
the two narratives respectively give representation of the past and
the future. The killing is what "we" are trying to get away from
to create a world of the future centered in the ability of commodities to meet, and indeed anticipate, our every need.

Moreover, as if to amplify the ostensible magic of the

commodity, the temporal structure of the ad emphasizes a vastness of narrative sweep; where the flame-thrower scene is represented as an event of short duration slowed down by the collection of images which almost mimic the twenty-four frames per second of film, the ad in contrast gives an event of greater duration taking place in an instantaneity of narrative time. The ad presents the magic of a single narrative that passes from nature (raw mushrooms) to human production to human consumption all in the space of a single page. If the war is supposed to be the big event, significantly, the flame-thrower killing represents war as nothing glamorous—an anonymous killing, a job one has to do (and the page resolutely refuses to heroize the Australian, preferring to leave him unnamed, viewed only from a distance); in contrast, the ad can take on the qualities of an epic: human triumph over the world, the reconciliation of culture and nature. As with the killing, there is a seeming inevitability to the advertising narrative; once the process has begun, it is propelled forward with a force that vanquishes any potential resistance. But the inevitability here has nothing begrudging about it. It is not stoic duty but bountiful freedom that the ad imagines.

And yet, significantly, it is a narrative with little human agency. Fantasizing the production-consumption process as quasi-miraculous, the ad presents a narrative with no visible human figure. Rather, it is the food itself that seems to be the agent, engendering its own existence and transformations by a force of willed self-evidence. This story is self-sufficient. By a curious reversal, it renders insufficient and unspectacular the war story, which ends up as a mere reportage (like so many that dot the pages of *Life*) of a distant event (geographically distant but also, with the end of the war, temporally distant—an anachronism), an event that its audience observes from a safe distance (the camera is pulled away from the scene: while the viewer's angle is not far from the Australian's, the viewer is not there with him, but rather is observing him, watching a story). On the other hand, the soup ad has a spatial immediacy: large on the page, the mushrooms, can, and soup present themselves outward, asking the viewer to enter this process of consumption. We might even read this one ad as an allegory of the whole commodity system of postwar America. With the reification that so many scholars have seen as endemic to the process of commodification, the individual subject—the buyer or even the seller—loses any sense of agency and becomes no more than an after-effect or absent piece of a gigantic mechanism, the world of transnationals, a postmodernist labyrinth. If the flamethrowing Australian is still somewhat a heroic agent, there is little heroic about entering into the new market economy in which even specific products are coming to be replaced by services and bits of information.

But in another sense, the human *is* still all too mythically present, for the viewer *is* called into place: despite the self-engendering process that leads mushrooms "naturally" to become Campbell's soup, it is obvious that someone does after all have to enter into the process. Someone has to buy, produce, and consume; someone has to take up a necessary role. This ad only keeps implicit what other ads of the period will try to make quite explicit: it is woman—a particular representation of woman—who is to take "her" place within this magic, automatic, inevitable process of postwar commodification (and, indeed, most of the other Campbell's ads from the moment represent a serving woman). That here the position can be implicit may imply that the assurance as to the real subject of the ad is so great that direct representation can seem redundant. If the narrative of the killing tells the story of *how* "we" are fighting, this narrative of the commodity tells the story of *what* "we" are fighting for: the home, the building of healthy families, the consumption of products. Indeed, as historian John Morton Blum notes, when asked about their reasons for fighting, G.I.'s rarely spoke of principles, and referred instead to everyday objects, activities, and products—ones they remembered from the past, ones that ads promised them for the future.[1]

No doubt it is coincidental (but for practical decisions about layout, etc.) that these two stories should come together here, but even in their coincidence, it is possible to find the construction of a certain *montage,* a significant juxtaposition that signals more than either piece alone. Between the two images, within their differences, we can read an attempt to represent a certain social positioning, the fixities of a system, the delegation of roles, the assignation of goals within an ideologically defined space. This space may not be unlike that space of the social that Michel Foucault has analyzed in his work: social space as a kind of engridding where potentially separate(d) social elements find a position, a connection, a sense. For Foucault, we are never in contact with a pristine reality that would exist outside our griddings. The stabilities of our social languages work to cut up space in precise ways to govern our behavior, to calculate which things (practices, ideas, speech-acts, etc.) we can produce and which ones we can't. Our perception is an effect of our social place, and everything we do is readable in relation to a system of inclusions and exclusions that work to make up our social reality.

But Foucault also argues that social griddings are never *faits accomplis*—purely efficient and entirely successful impositions of social power over social subjects. Even if Foucault's argument, as numerous critics have shown, tends at times to imply the nightmare vision of a disciplinary society that has infiltrated all walks of life, Foucault is quite alert to the possibility that there are little places, what he calls the events of a micrological sort, that can escape or challenge a dominant engridding, that can work to shape a different discourse. For Foucault, the socially structuring forces of discourse never work in the modern age as expressions of a central, sovereign power that would issue disciplinary edicts from on high but appear, rather, as effects immanent to the actualization of a discourse in whatever context, no matter where, no matter when, no matter how trivial or isolated in the social fabric. But if this implies the spread of power everywhere, it also, Foucault contends, allows all the more for there to be momentary resistances to power, little acts of subversion that respond to power's little acts of enunciation. The more power is removed from a singular expressive function, the more it is simultaneously less and more effective.

At the same time, moreover, Foucault argues that even if it shapes social perception to its own ends, social discourse is never a purely self-contained discourse that could work in ignorance or disdain of changes in reality, physical or otherwise. In other words, even as it constructs a reality for its social subjects, social discourse finds that there are realities (themselves socially constructed) that limit the powers of discourse, that show its subservience to forces that exceed its supposedly authoritative sway.

As historical reality changes, discourse changes in an attempt to adapt to new conditions; in *Discipline and Punish*, for example, Foucault notes that discourse on incarceration *did* change from the eighteenth to the nineteenth century, and he attributes this change in part to real demographic changes in population and to real compositional changes in notions of criminality and property ownership.[2] Griddings evolve, working in a kind of dialectic or, to use a Foucauldian image, a spiral, in relation to a history they aim to enclose within rules, constraints, frames, and frameworks. Discourse doesn't remain immobile, having once and for all discovered a way to structure the social realm through fixed laws of inclusion and exclusion. Discourse must move: it must change in relation to other changes in the social field; it must enter into new realms that had previously seemed irrelevent to its operations. Thus, in an interview, Foucault explains how a new historical moment "represents the application of an entirely new *grille* [*grid*], with its choices and exclusions; a new play with its own rules, decisions, and limitations, with its own inner logic, its parameters and its blind alleys."[3]

The two pages of *Life* can exemplify, then, an attempted movement from one gridding of the forties to another. The war had posed new needs for and to American representation. But the postwar moment will be represented alternately (but even within the space of a single text) as a continuation of these needs (hence, discourse about the new world that will emerge from victory) and as an abandonment of the wartime way of life (hence, among others, the return to a discourse of woman's stereotypical place in the home). The forties can demonstrate the possibilities of a moment that is trying to hold different discursive grids— different ways of representing—together in a single, volatile space. It is the nature of such grids and the movements between them that the following pages set out to analyze.

And yet it is important to note that these stories are no more than *representations,* together a proffering of positions that doesn't imply any full or necessary taking up of those positions by social subjects. That is, when one deals especially with singular representations within the larger realm of a society's whole field of discourse, one finds that nothing guarantees the local effectivity of the particular cases, nothing impels an individual's necessary investment in each and every act of discourse.[4] In the complicated field of varied discourses all vying for a power over subjectivity, social subjects themselves move in and out of varying discursive positions, not necessarily finding themselves compelled to stay in one place always. For example, as we will see in chapter 3, the official discourse of war-affirmation may present itself as a single, synoptic discourse with the same meanings and values for all Americans, but this discourse can encounter only strangely—and with curious, almost farcical results—the claims of nonsynoptic discourses like that of the zoot-suiters who argue that official declarations are not for them.

The grid of war and peace, of a successful war, a successful peace, and a successful transition from one to the other, is a grid that exists immediately as a historically specific arrangement of discourse, one version of social practices among others. Even within the space of this discourse, tensions exist. Some—like the difference between the brutality of war and the newfound joy of a product-filled home life—may not really finally be tensions after all: the two narratives can themselves become steps in a larger narrative: war as a fall into violence from which peace will rescue us. And yet other tensions are perhaps not so easily elided: for example, the very absence of a human agent in the advertisement can suggest a trepidation about the American woman's willingness or not to enter this narrative, to be or become one of its elements; indeed, various surveys near the end of the war indicate that anywhere from 80 to 90 percent of employed women have a desire to remain employed after war's cessation.[5]

The notion of social meaning as a gridding, then, needs several qualifications. Most especially, any particular grid is only one possible system of representation among others; no grid necessarily covers all aspects of any social moment nor does it cover all the modes that it does cover with the same intensity or comprehensiveness. Indeed, against criticisms that he was constructing a totalizing vision of power in the ages he examined, Foucault always insisted that he was dealing only with very specific areas of the social realm; for example, *Discipline and Punish* is not a worldview of all aspects of the modern age but only a suggestion as to certain tendencies (no matter how dominative those tendencies might be). This is to argue that in writing history, we don't write so much *the* meaning of the period as a history of some *possible* meanings: we study what was able to emerge within, and against, what seems, at first glance at least, to be a dominant field of social perception. Hence, a certain necessary reference in the following pages to the speculative fiction of the forties (especially the growing field of science fiction) or to the marginal B films of the Poverty Row studios; by working, to whatever end, to move beyond the limits of dominant representations, these texts can suggest new images of what was possible or what was beginning to emerge in the space of the forties. Such texts can thus imply the diversity of what can happen in the historical moment. And although I won't be discussing them here, we might go beyond the field of narrativity to note how the works of a nascent New American Cinema also stand as a marker of the breadth of discursive possibilities in the seemingly unified space of the wartime and then suburban forties. For example, with opening titles that announce it as a film from "Hollywood 1943", Maya Deren's experimental film, *Meshes of the Afternoon,* can seem a dramatic alternative to classic Hollywood's narration of its moment. Where the tradition of avant-garde criticism has tended to view *Meshes* as some sort of ahistorical psycho-drama, we might well argue the degree to which the film can be read in relation to its specific moment. Hence, in wartime, if classic Hollywood shows the home to be the place that we are fighting for—a place of sexuality sublimated into a supportive spirituality, a place of homey simplicity available (for the boy overseas) for all kinds of nostalgic investments—*Meshes*, in contrast, renders the home as an alien, even evil environment, ultimate site of the loss of self, a vibrant *agon* in which aggressivity and sexuality come bursting out in a virulent fashion. To be sure, like a war-affirmative Hollywood film such as *Guest in the House* (1944), *Meshes* implies that much of the danger for the sanctity of the home derives from the intrusion into the domestic space of a mysterious, even malevolent feminine force (in this case, Deren herself with her wild, flowing hair); the destruction of the women at the end of both films may imply a certain return to stability, a doing away with all enigma and disturbances. But, in *Guest in the House,* only one woman dies while others live and go on to continue happy heterosexual relationships in the service of the American way of life. In *Meshes,* on the other hand, there is no way of life after death: the last image is of Deren dead in her chair. There is no femininity other than Deren's so that her death leaves no hope for an "American way of life." If so many of the prescriptive manuals for home-front women instruct them not to write about bad news at home of any sort (with the underlying assumption that nothing happening to the woman can be as intense as that happening to the battlefront man), *Meshes of the Afternoon* might be nothing so much as a bad news report of the most intense sort; home has become a nightmarish place where women can only destroy or be destroyed and where men only come for short visits as virtual strangers.

In a sense, such a diversity of narratives represents a conflict of spaces: that different representations are set up for forties women suggests that the forties exist as a potentially conflicting *set* of grids, different ways of narrating a contingent reality, sometimes finding a balance, sometimes encountering incompatibilities. For example, that the stories of soldiers "over there" doing their necessary job will be matched by narratives of vets returning home (and in the fears of much end-of-war and postwar discourse, that these vets will bring an overall *anomie* and even an urge to kill back with them), coupled with the representation in so many postwar films of women emphatically outside the narrative of suburban domesticity, may well demonstrate the limits and incompleteness of narrative representations like those offered in the space of the two pages of *Life.* I find such juxtapositions emblematic, then, both of a drive toward what we might call dominant narrative ideology *and* of the possible fate(s) of such a drive in its interaction with the everyday life of a culture—fate(s) that can include perhaps the very impossibility of a complete or pure dominance.

Hence, what appears to be an opposition in the title of my study may be best read as a deliberate deconstruction of the opposition in the ways that deconstruction suggests that what appears to be a steady, sharp opposition actually comes to seem a mutual interference, an infiltration. By working to historicize deconstruction as I will argue later we need to do, I want to look at the ways that a dominant power and a disturbing paranoia interweave and find each to be a parodic mirror image of the other. Power here is the power of a narrative system especially—the power that narrative structure specifically possesses to write an image of life as coherent, teleological, univocal; narrative, then as a power to convert contingency into human meaning. Paranoia here will first be the fear of narrative, and the particular social representations it works to uphold, against all that threatens the unity of its logical framework. Against the horror of all that escapes its seemingly overwhelming force, narrative takes on a number of possible strategic forms.

To take two examples (suggested in the writings of Pierre Macherey), when faced with the threat of *class,* one order of dominant narrative responds by a utopian projection that imagines a social existence without class, while another form of narrative (summed up for Macherey by Balzac's *Les paysans)* responds by active attack, imagining a particular corrupt or degenerate version of the working classes.[6] In both cases, narrative projects that are fundamentally concerned to narrate the aspirations of people outside the limits of class-conflict run up against the historical presence of class as a brute fact, an essential reality whose representation might strain the limits of traditional modes of narrativity. For Macherey, then, narrative is an imaginary solution to a problem posed to literature by its social moment. To take a further example of narrative as ideological strategy, against the perceived threat of femininity in masculine postwar America, postwar narrative significantly will frequently work out a compromise position between the two poles of utopian disavowal and active aggression; at the very moment where political threat (the Cold War fear of Communism) often seems to be narrativized unambiguously, femininity will seem as frequently to be the subject of a kind of liberalist narrative which acknowledges the new woman while continuing to argue her ultimate dependence on the old male. For example, *Red River* (1948) might seem to project a solution to a perceived problem of femininity: as tensions break up the male group and turn friend against friend, the woman takes up the gun to stop the fight, to bring men back together and then to resume a role as cherished love for one of the men.

If the forties *film noir* seems to offer a malevolent image of a seductive femininity little different from the malevolence of a postwar communism (with the two frequently combined in the representation of the dark-haired, exotic Russian agent out to trap American men in such films as *The Woman on Pier 13* [a.k.a. *I Married a Communist* (1949)] or *The Red Menace* [1949]), the liberalist films imply another positioning of femininity. Here women can have force, will, energy; but in the compromise position of these films, while not all of a woman's force, will, energy need be devoted to a man, at least some of it must. Hence, in *My Dear Secretary* (1948), the heroine, who has become a successful writer, refuses to go back to being her husband-writer's secretary *but* she still goes back to being his wife.

"Paranoia" is a strong word perhaps, tied too intensely it might seem to a particularly psychoanalytic way of seeing the world. But I don't intend "paranoia," to refer to some sort of individualized property buried deep in the recesses of the mind; rather, I want to argue the possibility of paranoia as a historical activity, much in the way that American historians like Richard Hofstader have spoken of a "paranoid style in American life." But this is not to say that the social moment I will be dealing with— the 1940's—is *dominated* by paranoia, that Americans essentially live their reality through a paranoid perspective. Paranoia is only one social practice among many, only one imaginary way that the forties come up with to live the contingencies of the moment. Paranoia can easily fuel what might seem its exact opposite–an aggressive surety, a forward propulsion of the human subject into a world that it tries to make over in its own image. But in such a case, paranoia is literally the underpinning of aggressivity; as I will argue later, the late forties and fifties novels of Mickey Spillane alternate between representations of Mike Hammer as the most brutishly assertive of heroes and as a neurotic consumed by nightmares and intense fear of femininity. But paranoia is, thus, a necessary *social* concept, for it allows a mediation between the externalities of social existence—the impositions and prescriptions of a culture—and their internalization in the form of a particular ideology and psychic economy. Realizing the origins of psychoanalytic concepts in a particular ideological context with continuing ideological effects, we can still use these concepts to write aspects of our modern history. Indeed, as Juliet Mitchell suggests in *Psychoanalysis and Feminism*, the very rooting of psychoanalytic concepts in the ideology of the bourgeois moment may make these concepts particularly advantageous in the analysis of that ideology: psychoanalysis allows us to read one of the dominant ways modern society came up with for reading itself.[7] Indeed, we can find in the psychoanalytic theorization of psychoanalytic process a certain replaying of those very processes; for example, Freud's very attempt to enclose femininity within the grid of rational investigation and cool, male calculation is readable as Freud's own attempt to hold his own psychology in check against what he fearfully saw as a certain demonic quality of feminine desire.[8]

In attempting to theorize psychological processes, psychoanalysis constructs a particular sociality, one filled with all the contradictions of modernity. Not unexpectedly, psychoanalysis so often appears as a *narrative* discourse and displays the particular contradictions of narrativity as a form that attempts to enclose contingency within the constraints of a temporal logic. Freud's encounters with the young "hysteric," Dora, for example, read like nothing so much as a Victorian detective novel (complete with upstairs maids, furtive affairs, military officers). But the narrative also shows an intertwining of power and paranoia: the masculine fear of female sexuality (Freud's inability to say what

Dora's father and Frau K have really been up to; Freud's avoidance of the lesbian implications of Frau K's relationship with Dora); the immediate appeal to social clichés of the moment (the mother who is not discussed in the narrative since she is just a neurotic housewife; the military man that Freud pushes Dora toward just because he is a military man); the synoptic desire to control not only the past and present but also the future (thus, Freud imagines what will be the rest of Dora's life after she breaks off the treatment); the simultaneous desire for and fear of transference, the possibility that the analyst will be called in to join the emotional world that some part of him would like to hold at a safe, scientific distance.

Continuing, then, the deconstruction of the opposition of power and paranoia, we will suggest that power has its psychoanalytic level while paranoia has its political level. In the words of science-fiction critic Carl Freedman, describing a post-forties, intensified version of paranoia about the new world of products and information, "Paranoia, we can conclude, is no mere aberration but is structurally crucial to the way that we, as ordinary subjects of bourgeois hegemony, represent ourselves to ourselves and embark on the Cartesian project of acquiring empiricist knowledge."[9] As Freedman argues, paranoia is not a force that comes in to disturb an already stable conjunction of power and knowledge; quite the contrary, paranoia may be a condition to which power and knowledge are responses—fearful retreats to a hoped-for position of security and reestablished authority. Similarly, a concept like paranoia might seem especially relevant to the forties and especially to the postwar commodification of everyday life where the promise of suburbia is frequently registered in everyday discourse as a nightmare. Paranoia here is not an eternally abstract condition but a specifically social way of responding to new permutations in everyday perception and possibility.

Much of recent film analysis' fascination with forties American cinema may well derive from the ways that that cinema poses historical and theoretical questions of and to the representations of ideology—the ways it suggests a narrativity caught between power and paranoia. Thus, for example, Michael Renov finds in the war period the extreme moment in American film history for the coalescence of the prescription of ideological positions and the acceptance by social subjects of those positions. The war seems a disciplinary moment in which different discourses all come together to empower a particular social reality: "This period of social life, of which film production was a part, constituted a moment . . . during which a variety of disparate elements fused together to form a condensed ideological amalgamation. . . . It is this period of film history that constitutes the apogee of confluence between perpetuation of state policy and authority and the 'relatively autonomous' cinematic institution."[10] For Renov, then, the war brings about a control of the aesthetic realm by the declared political needs of the moment: culture becomes a sort of tool for state policy and authority. On the other hand, recent work on *film noir* (especially on postwar *noir*) has read *noir* as a moment of re-relativization of the cinematic institution, its distancing from any simple (or perhaps even complex) confirmation of dominant ideological practices. The *film noir* would represent a certain escape of films from any simple confirmation of dominant ways of seeing. Thus, for example, for Sylvia Harvey, "*Film noir* offers us again and again examples of abnormal or monstrous behaviour, which defy the patterns established for human social interaction and which hint at a series of radical and irresolvable contradictions buried deep within the total system of economic and social interactions that constitute the known world."[11]

Such a dualist representation—the successful hegemony of the war period as against the contradiction-ridden postwar period—has been a dominant way of understanding the forties, and the model certainly has an attractive explanatory power to it. Indeed, it was such a model that I myself employed in an initial essay on the forties, arguing that the path of the period was one that went from necessary consensus to necessary conflict.[12] The model allowed for a clear-cut simplicity and ease of approach; it had the explanatory power of a certain "common sense." I still think that we need to start from such positions; as I will argue in the following pages, the war years can reveal, as Renov well points out, one of the intense examples of an attempt to make ideology into *state* ideology. But dualism also tends to turn the forties themselves into a kind of narrative or teleology—the story of the historically necessary liberation of film from propagandistic constraints. Among other effects, this enclosing of history within such a "logical" necessity limits an ability to understand continuities across time. For example, while the despairing films of postwar *film noir* represent a narrative universe in which lone individuals wander cut off from all connections to an inspiring authority—whether an actual figure or an abstract set of beliefs— the postwar period is also the moment of reconnection, of the rise of narratives that use the very techniques of film to bring loners back under the control of an authoritative system. For example, if so many films seem to recognize criminality as a force that works to exceed social bonds and bounds, a whole series of what I will refer to as government agency films will employ a montage that cuts from each supposedly self-willed action of the criminal to the investigative actions of the government agency that is trying to bring him or her to justice. Like such war-affirmative films as *Pride of the Marines* (1945) or *Since You Went Away* (1944) in which loners either learn to join the system or are irrevocably chastized by it, the government agency films come up with an authoritative way to deal with contingency while working to promote a mythology of the natural and the necessary. We would want, then, to note both how the war period already presents certain challenges to a classic narrativity and its ties to specific representations of wartime power and ideology *and* how the postwar period continues many of the drives toward narrative classicism apparent in the wartime narrative of authority.

Such issues raise questions about power, about its effectiveness, about its spread. They show that the very ways that we write history are of consequence for the ways we understand dominance and change. The question of the forties, then, is also immediately a *theoretical* question: how do we represent power; to what extent does the representation we choose enact or refuse or guarantee the form of power; to what extent does a certain writing of power determine the ways we can write the history of power's limits?

We will find, for example, that the war period is poten- tially a quite contradictory moment. In a sense, I would argue, the period offers Hollywood its last great chance to be a narrative art of a classic sort. But the offer is, in ways that this study will stake out, an ambiguous or even contradictory one. The war offers new possibilities for narrativity while encouraging conditions which show up those possibilities as manifestly fictional. With the war, narrative finds a solution to the problems of representing history in a coherent framework *while* discovering that it can do so only at the cost of repressions and distortions that come bursting out under moments of narrative stress.

After an introductory chapter on the writing of history and the writing of film history and a first historical chapter on the drive to narrativity in the war-affirmative narrative, this study argues then a certain breakdown of the comprehensive power of American film narrative. In a sense, the later chapters "answer" the chapter on war affirmation; against the seeming coherence of war-affirmative narrative, these chapters suggest the tempo- rariness and vulnerability of the affirmative logic that nar- rative constructs. The study sets out, then, to rewrite the history evoked in chapter 2—to find ways in which the ostensible dom- inance of "dominant" narrative representation can reveal its incompleteness.

Dominant ideology, I would argue, seems to find in narrative structure a promising form for the mediation of social conflicts and their resolution through the enveloping power of narrative and through the generation of specific figures of media- tion who take up sides of a contradiction and work to neutralize such contradiction. What seems to be narrative's openness to change, to the ambiguities of a not-yet-written future, can actually turn out to be no more than a governed progression that merely solves issues (both thematic and narrative) in calculated ways. As A. J. Greimas notes in *Sémantique structurale*, ideology often func- tions through a narrative that is finally nothing but the logically controlled unfolding of possibilities contained within a limited set of initial semantic terms.[13]

    This means, though, that one can perhaps question the completeness of an ideological field both by "unpacking" the transformation—that is, by showing the basic structure that underlies a narrative flow, by showing how the initial positing of terms can work to empower only certain narratives while excluding others—*and* by imagining or historically uncovering possible or repressed units of meaning outside the initial semantic oppositions. At the very least, as the history of what in film studies has come to be called the "reading against the grain" shows, such a questioning of narrativity can come from close analysis of the narratives themselves, from a contact that examines not what narrative accomplishes but what work it engages in (repressions, containments, transformations) to achieve its aura of accomplishment.

    Here, we might even follow the suggestions of Fredric Jameson, one of the few critics to try to use Greimas' model of narrative logic for the analysis of ideological practice. In Jameson's use of the Greimasian model, the explicit pattern of a hegemonic narrative turns out to be a kind of ideological blockage (what Jameson terms "a strategy of containment") that eliminates all but one narrative resolution—a blockage, then, that makes one resolution seem necessary, inevitable, logical.[14] Jameson proposes a working back from the coherent narrative to the possibilities it "contains": "Just as every idea is true at the point at which we are able to reckon its conceptual situation, its ideological distortion back into it, so also every work is clear, provided we locate the angle from which the blur becomes so natural as to pass unnoticed."[15] While Jameson's language may be too classical here in its reliance on notions of truth and visually based metaphors of clarity and distortion, his general point would seem to be an important one: reading as an active process of rewriting. One looks for an alternate narrative or series of narratives within a narrative that has previously claimed exclusive representation of a particular situation. For example, Jameson matches his call for a return to narrative's initial conceptual situation with a call for analysis of the other narratives that such a situation could have generated: a chosen narrative line turns out to be only one possibility among many—only one way of seeing.[16]

Along these lines, the third chapter sets out the historical stakes of such a rewriting for the forties and prepares the way for a different reading of the moment of war narrativity—a reading that looks at ties of the contradictions in wartime narrativity to contradictions in the social, aesthetic, and psychical economy of the war moment. Veering toward the postwar period, the fourth chapter suggests how one development of the war period— the rise of new positive sciences and new forms of rationality— might seem to promise a new stability to fuel a classic narrativity. For example, the forties horror film seems to undergo a secularization in which figures of menace lose their ties to forms of irrationality and become accessible to an all-too-earthy and earthly discipline and control: horror narrative becomes the successful narration of a successful cure. But, again, this stability of reason and narrative may be only superficial. Forties science may make the unknown all too secular and rational; yet, simultaneously, by a sort of curious reversal, the known—the realm of everyday life, for example—becomes itself irrational and generates forces that narrative theme and style can't always easily contain. In the chaotic films of *film noir*, especially, the ordinary world undergoes a defamiliarization in which the confidence of human projects— above all, that centrally human project of giving narrative form to experience—comes undone. The last two chapters trace some of the forms of this defamiliarization in the forties film representation of space and time; the last of these chapters ultimately argues possible ties of the defamiliarization of human coordinates to the commodification of everyday life and the rise of a nonnarrative spectacle from within the heart of classic narrativity.

Chapter One

Writing the Space
of the Forties

Toward the end of the 1945 Hollywood film *Don Juan Quilligan* (directed by Frank Tuttle, starring William Bendix), its central character (we can't call him a "hero" since the film's opening title has told us emphatically that he's not a hero and never will be) is on trial for murder and awaiting the jury's decision. Trials, the critic Mikhail Bakhtin tells us, are a historically central element in the development of narrative: not only does a trial link narrative to the juridical and ideological interests of a society, but, more to the immediate point for the telling of a tale, the trial possesses a certain specifically *narrative* power—an assured source of suspense and, more than that, an assured source of narrative resolution, a way to disambiguate narrative complexity through the univocal decision of an authoritative law.[1] A trial, then, empowers an end to hesitation and justifies this empowering through an appeal to an ostensible neutrality of the law. Moreover, as Bakhtin suggests, the trial can add a fundamental aura to narrative development. The situations that the hero faces become ultimate tests—symbolically loaded encounters by which the hero and a society set out equally to discover what the other is made of. A trial turns narrative movements into occurrences of an ultimately epochal sort.

But *Don Juan Quilligan's* trial isn't any simple murder trial with simple origins and simple motivations and simple solutions. Under two different names (Pat and Mike—his first and middle names), Quilligan had accidentally found himself married to two different women he was in love with and, after a number of strategies failed, saw no way out of his polygamous predicament other than to fake the suicide of one of his two identities. Finding the body of a murdered gangster, Quilligan put his own papers in the cadaver's pockets and dropped it into the New York harbor. But then, as if this weren't confusing enough, things turned even worse: the authorities became convinced that the suicide was a fake but one staged to cover up a murder, and they arrested Quilligan. Since Quilligan had lived out two separate lives—Pat and Mike, the Quilligan "twins"—the police assumed from the papers on the body that one Quilligan brother had killed the other. Like so many forties film characters, Quilligan finds himself in a nightmarish situation that seems some sort of weird parody or permutation of a family romance: he is on trial for killing someone he knows to be himself. He is backed into a seemingly inescapable corner: a choice between conviction for murder and conviction for polygamy. Far from a clearing up of an already complicated logic, the trial here becomes one further source of complication, one further overloading of the film's telling of a simple story—the story of the life of its nondescript title character.

The announcement comes: the jury has reached a decision. At the judge's request, the jury foreman begins to read the decision, but before he can reach the decisive bit of information, he begins to cough severely. Each time he tries to resume his reading, the coughs return. Only after several long moments of suspense and suspension is he able to announce what now is only an anticlimax—that Quilligan is innocent of murder—a verdict that still leaves open the question of Quilligan's polygamy.

A few instants of coughing in a film narrative may

seem the merest of trivialities, and yet here they can appear to have the greatest of symbolic importance. The cough that stops the flow of information turns *Don Juan Quilligan* for a moment from just a story of a life into a story about storytelling. For a moment, we find that what is central to the nature of the fiction film is not so much the fictional world it presents as the act of presenting itself, the fashion by which it brings a world into play and can, at a desired moment, signal the contructed form of what might have seemed to be the internally driven nature of a narrative logic. The cough makes *Don Juan Quilligan* into more than just a narrative; or, more precisely, it makes manifest what the film has always been, while seeming to just be a rendition of a life: with the cough, the film signals the way that its narrative is also a meditation on the nature of narrative, a reflection on the patterns of narrative construction and constitution. A story is told from somewhere, from someone, but only as long as that source is in a condition to tell. Suggesting the ways that the clarity of a narrative logic is easily prey to all sorts of complications, *Don Juan Quilligan* doesn't so much create a fictional universe as announce the strategies by which films frequently work to build up such a universe.

To be sure, in the ways that, as Roland Barthes in *S/Z* most especially analyzes, a narrative can allow all sorts of delays between the institution of a problem and its "logical resolution,"[2] *Don Juan Quilligan* might seem to be encouraging complexity only to dissipate it in the surety of a final moment. However, the film resolutely refuses the plenitude of what Frank Kermode calls "the sense of an ending"—the movement of narrative to a final point that makes sense of all that has gone before and is implicit and even necessary in all that has gone before.[3] Quite simply, *Don Juan Quilligan* finishes without ending. Cleared of murder and polygamy, Quilligan ends the film still unable to decide between the two women in his life.

Something appears to happen in the conditions for film narrative in the American forties. Seeming at first to be the most marginal of eccentricities, with its drive to make the simple narration and resolution of a story progressively impossible *Don Juan Quilligan* can ultimately come to seem centrally emblematic of shifts in the shape of film narration in the period of the forties. Most especially, I would contend that *Don Juan Quilligan* suggests limitations of a purely *narrative* understanding of the Hollywood film of the 1940s and implies instead that the period figures a certain breakdown of narrative, a play on its constitutive features.

Significantly, the strangeness of *Don Juan Quilligan's* narrative structure corresponds to a certain strangeness in the story it tells. Here, perhaps, a comparison of *Don Juan Quilligan* with some of the films that scholars have analyzed as "classic narrative" can help pinpoint what is at stake. For example, *Don Juan Quilligan's* narrative complexity seems quite different from the classic Western narratives at the beginning of the decade—narratives whose logic critics have well staked out through a combination of narratological methods with other theories on the logic of meaning: psychoanalysis, social anthropology, speech-act theory, etc. Thus, for Raymond Bellour on the 1940 film *The Westerner* and for Daniel Dayan on the 1939 film *Stagecoach*, the Western narrative seems classically American in the ways it forges a coincidence of personal story and national destiny through the elaboration of a systematic style of filming and narrating.[4]

For example, in an essay that announces its own modesty in the face of film's narrative plenitude, Bellour actually manages in a few pages to well suggest the rigor of *The Westerner's* narrative logic, its seeming ability to lock all elements into the overwhelming force of a single structure. For Bellour, this structure is simultaneously psychoanalytic, sociological, and narratological. Concerned to eliminate a figure (Judge Roy Bean) whose rampant egoism makes him aberrant in this structure, *The Westerner* links the exclusion of Bean—an exclusion represented visually by a fade and a shift out of focus as Bean dies—to the new building up of the American system in a post-Bean world. From the fade that forces Bean out of the picture—that shows his hold on the vision of the film disappearing—the film shifts to a close-up of a map of the new Texas, a Texas where, as a traveling-back shows us, the new couple finds its necessary place: in Bellour's words, "In this conjugal room . . . their shadows projected on the map underline again, as if it was necessary, the relation of reciprocity between the State and the family, which endlessly divides up representation between social law and conjugal law, through an effect of enframing. *The Westerner:* how, under what conditions, the man of the West, the man who made the West, wins a woman, a territory, becomes an American citizen" (p. 183). For Bellour, then, the film narrates through the literality of its techniques the exclusions by which an old, eccentric, nonproductive way of life gives way, in a new age of national domesticity, to the formation of the bourgeois family of the future.

Similarly, for Daniel Dayan in his book *Western Graffiti,* the 1939 *Stagecoach* is a film about the building up of a new community—the Western as the narrative of the formation of a utopia of human reciprocity and social transparency. The stagecoach literally becomes a narrative "vehicle" by which a representative group of social figures have a chance—even if a fleeting one—to participate in a new order of social relations. Again, like Bellour, Dayan suggests how this journey is as much psychoanalytic and narratological as social. Most especially, *Stagecoach* tells the story of the West through the story of one Westerner—the Ringo Kid— and his symbolic growth from "Kid" into a man able to start a new life with the ex-prostitute, Dallas. As Dayan's careful textual analysis suggests, the film systematically builds up the narrative centrality of Ringo and Dallas; for example, the famous dining-room scene may show Dallas to be the object and not the agent of the camera's look, but the imbalance between emotional and literal points of view creates a moral breach into which the Ringo Kid will step and out of which he will progressively be allocated the point of view of the camera's look. Ringo's offering of respect to Dallas merges with the film's own increasing ability to grant visibility and agency to Dallas. Thus, when Dallas waits for the end of Ringo's gunfight with the Plummers, a tracking-in toward Dallas will suddenly reveal itself to be the unharmed Ringo's movement toward her: Ringo and the tracking-in move together, suggesting an identity of their values in and for the film. Again, like *The Westerner,* with aberration banished the film's next step will be to end with an affirmation of the couple and their tie to a geography approved of by a dominant law. Under the benign

regard of the law officer who frees Ringo, Ringo and Dallas set off
into the desert to build their life together.

Now to compare the seriousness of the project of the
Western genre to a crazy comedy like *Don Juan Quilligan* and find
in the latter a disavowal of many of the attributes of the Western
may seem to be loading the case. But, at the very least, the presence
of comedy might make us wonder about the comprehensiveness
of the very construction of form and ideology that Bellour, and
others, claim to find not only in the Western but in the American
cinema as a whole. Indeed, in an essay that treats not only the
Western but also the "open fantasm of the fantastic narrative" (in
this case, the 1933 film *The Mystery of the Wax Museum*), and makes
reference to the applicability of the analysis to the films of Hawks,
Hitchcock, and Minnelli, *The Westerner* serves for Bellour as a
condensation of classic cinema itself. For Bellour, the Western is
not more "American" than other genres; at most it simply shows
the source of Hollywood genres, with their emphasis on narrating
the formation of the couple in a stable space, in some of the
strongest mythologies of land, home, and bourgeois heterosexuality. Not a privileged film, but simply a symptomatic one, *The
Westerner* suggests for Bellour "the obsession that the cinema that
is born out of this History [of the West, of the conquest of woman
and territory] must obey, and endlessly reproduce, as in a kind of
buckling, the scene that it pretends to escape from and which
constitutes it . . . the couple, the family."

Significantly, what Bellour finds specifically at work
in the Western seems not so different from the ideology of the
crazy comedy as Stanley Cavell analyzes it in his book *Pursuits of
Happiness: The Hollywood Comedy of Remarriage.*[5] Despite the fact of
coming from opposed ideological directions—Bellour intends a
critique of the socialization at work in Hollywood narrative, while
Cavell applauds the screwball comedy as a filmic realization of
the American dream of nineteeth-century romanticism—both
critics would seem to see Hollywood genres as Comic forms in the
oldest sense of the term: forms that narrate the move to festivity
on the part of people separated initially by forces of adversity. Just
as for Bellour the Western is an essentially American genre, so for

Cavell the screwball comedy is too: in its chronicling of the remarriage of the special couple in a special place (usually Con-
necticut, figured as a sort of mythic place, outside the material
debasements of a work-dominated New York), the screwball comedy is, like the Western, about the ties of place and people, about
the interconnections of America as a geography and a social
meaning.

   To be sure, the screwball comedy is set in a later moment than the Western, a moment the genre will treat as much
less innocent, much more vulnerable to a potential loosening of
familial bonds. Yet, though concerned with the mores of a new,
potentially sexualized age, the screwball comedy, in Cavell's analysis, would still work to enclose desire within the insistent and
univocal framework of the family as center of the American dream.
That the screwball comedy is a comedy of *re*marriage allows the
modern man and woman a sexual knowingness that is unavailable
to the characters in the classic Western—even if Dallas is an ex-
prostitute, the Ringo Kid is still a kid. But that the comedy is to
lead to re*marriage* enables the narratives to render newly innocent
the sexual knowledge that the couple possesses. The game playing
of Nick (Cary Grant) in a Santa Claus outfit with his wife at the
end of *My Favorite Wife* (1940) can almost seem a condensation of
the genre of the screwball comedy, where sexuality is turned into
a joke *within* the stability of marriage.

   Significantly, then, *Don Juan Quilligan* will seem like
nothing so much as a vast and systematic parody of all this classical
narrativity. For example, we might well argue that *Don Juan Quilligan* doesn't fit the Oedipal narrative that Raymond Bellour has
argued underlies the structure of American film narrative. For
Bellour, the classic film's social meaning—the formation of a new
America through the formation of a new couple—is also a psychoanalytic meaning as the films narrate the growth of questing
characters away from the conservative security of primal bonds
with the mother (or with a "mother country," the older way of
doing things) to a new life in which characters work to become
agents of their own destiny. Narrative, then, is about growth, a
projection away from roots to an open space, a vibrant future, the

past becoming no more than a source of nostalgia, an inspiring image to lead one on in future actions. In this sense, the initiating quest of *Don Juan Quilligan*—Quilligan's attempts to keep his beloved mother's image alive—may initially seem to be one more playing out of the oedipal trajectory, but quickly the film takes a distance from the oedipal pattern. If the oedipalism that Bellour sees in classic cinema means that the destiny of domesticity is a way for men to rework their most primal attachment, *Don Juan Quilligan* disavows such a destiny and turns narrative into a certain play on its own symbolic narrativity. To be sure, the film emphatically posits the memory-image of a maternal plenitude that Quilligan is now lacking and that will drive him on in the world. And yet the film will treat Quilligan's "momism"—to use a term that is coming into play in the forties—with a certain degree of bemused distance. That Quilligan at the beginning of the film buys flowers for his "dear departed mother" signals a certain infantile fixation that the film will suggest accounts for his nonheroic nature. Indeed, despite all he does for his mother's memory, there is an essential passivity to Quilligan. Caught as he is in a devotion to the past, he is a vulnerable prey for the forces of the present. One waits (with a certain inevitable disappointment) for the moment when Quilligan will take his destiny into his own hands.

But as Quilligan first meets a woman with his mother's laugh and another with his mother's talent for cooking and finds himself in equal admiration for both, *Don Juan Quilligan* constructs the impossibility of the oedipal trajectory and its forward propulsion even at the very moment that the film seems to acknowledge oedipalism as a motor force behind narrative. Here, in *Don Juan Quilligan,* the reconstruction in the present of the mother's imaginary body is broken up, dispersed among several women, fragmented into a series of individual features that no single activity, no single narrative line, could hold together. No one woman can simply revive the force of the mother. By arguing the necessary value for Quilligan of each of his mother's functions and by simultaneously arguing that no one woman combines these features, *Don Juan Quilligan* forces its narrative into an impossible situation; there is no sufficient logic for such a problem. If the past exists only as the memory of an irretrievable reality, the present exists as the presence of too much reality, too many reembodiments of the traces of the past.

Significantly, then, this fragmentation of femininity is paralleled by a corresponding fragmentation of geography. Unlike, say, *The Westerner*, where the initially vagrant hero's passing through town becomes a permanent stay as he and his newfound love build the Texas of the future, *Don Juan Quilligan* presents no one space where the fully constituted couple could find the stability of a symbolic geography and build a comic version of America together. Captain of a small freight boat, Quilligan alternates between the New York that is his nominal point of departure and the Albany that will be his recurrent point of call. But even this slight priority of terms—Quilligan as initially a New Yorker, a man at home in the big city—will become relativized through the course of the film. For example, New York may be "home" for Quilligan but it is a place of constant threat and unhomey excitement, the hustle and bustle of an unstable urban life: New York here is murderous gangsters, fast nightclubs, all the energy of a world without a firm point. Indeed, Quilligan is not really at home in this city world. He lacks the worldly talent to succeed in most social interactions and spends the greater part of his time in the safe space of his boat in the harbor. On the other hand, Albany begins as a place of alienating aggressivity—the first experience Quilligan has there is to get drawn into a fight—but it soon becomes a home-away-from-home as the wounded Quilligan is brought back to health through the ministrations of a woman with his mom's cooking skills. Not coincidentally, it seems, Quilligan's New York love has a social skill—the wonderful laugh that Quilligan hears as he walks past a saloon one night—while his Albany love has a domestic skill—cooking. The film sets up a certain symbolic structure based on mythologies of big and little cities. But the film then moves to a point where no one term has priority, where all places, all choices, are equally important and, therefore, equally impossible. Quilligan cannot do without laughter or good cooking.

Of course, in a Hollywood under the sway of the production code, it is impossible for the narrative to leave things in complete suspension, in polygamy. But, curiously, the film seems not very much to be bothered by what might seem the moral scandal of its subject. Indeed, in an America that has gone through the war years with their simultaneous renunciation and intensification of sexual desire and that is now three years away from the first volume of the Kinsey Report, *Don Juan Quilligan* can seem quite nonplussed about the morality of its situation. Indeed, it almost seems as if the film is flirting with scandal. When Quilligan first meets and falls in love with the second woman, the film immediately holds out the possibility that there is really no problem at all; Quilligan falls in love with the woman after being knocked unconscious in a fight and it might well be likely that he has amnesia and has forgotten that he has already pledged his love to another. But the film never entertains this possibility, and quite quickly, we learn that Quilligan has made the decision to fall in love with the second woman in full awareness of the pledge he has already made back in New York. The film treats all of this with a matter-of-factness that makes its force seem all the stranger in comparison with what we might assume to be the conditions of classic narrative. The film seems willingly to encourage its narrative difficulties.

Indeed, if the film seems impelled to work toward a narrative resolution, it does so only after substituting a second problem for the one of polygamy: with his two identities (New York and Albany), Quilligan suddenly finds himself called to the service of both the army and the navy. Simultaneously, this new occurrence will both further complicate Quilligan's life and create the only real moral scandal of the film—in wartime America, you must serve one service and one service only—*and* provide the possibility for a kind of phantasmtic quasi-resolution of the problem of the romance of the couple. With Quilligan freed of murder charges, the judge benificently accepts Quilligan's declaration that he can't choose between the two women and dissolves both of the accidental marriages. No longer married but still unable to choose between the two women, Quilligan ends the film by going out the door of the courtroom having chosen to join the navy.

Don Juan Quilligan works, then, by a kind of narrative derouting or detouring in which initial terms are continually displaced until the final point of a war commitment that allows the narrative to end. Like the classic narrative, this ending occurs under the sway of a Law—the confluence of the judge and the navy that the judge's decision allows Quilligan to go off to join. But the role of the Law here only emphasizes how far we've come from the classicism of a film like *The Westerner*. In *The Westerner*, the Law has a unifying effect—the forming of personal and political destiny into one logic. In contrast, in *Don Juan Quilligan*, the Law works to suspend a univocal logic, to hold personal choices instead in an endless abeyance—to resolve by leaving issues unresolved or by substituting one logic for another, rather than by finding a common ground between them. As narrative, *Don Juan Quilligan* has the fortune of being made under the influence of the war moment; like so many other comedies of the moment (for example, *You'll Never Get Rich* [1941], which I will discuss later), *Don Juan Quilligan* is able to use the war as a device that *forces* narrative resolution. But to call this a "fortune" is already to signal the problem of forties narrative: it is only able to sustain the possibility of narrative logic, of the sense of an ending, at the price of showing up the very fictitiousness of this logic, the fact that nothing guarantees a story but the authoritative and forceful force of its telling. In the forties, this authority can seem all the more mythic, all the more fictional. What historians have described as the breakdown of the classic studio system may also be the breakdown of that system's ability to confidently tell its stories. Indeed, in the moment of victory and after, where even the forcing of narrative resolution through commitment to the war effort will be lacking, narrative can seem to turn fundamentally unstable, fundamentally unable to move forward. Narrative here becomes a virtual antinarrative: nonstories dominated by an endless cyclicity or a predictable and inevitable descent into the stasis of death or unchanging passivity. Indeed, a *film noir* like *Detour* (1945) can become nothing so much as a vast bad-joke version of the classic narrative: Al Roberts' westward quest for the golden-haired Sue is a nightmare parody of the American romance where a kind of (self-willed) inability to refind innocence locks the antihero into an eternal errancy and a recurrent vulnerability to forces of evil and death.[6]

Certainly, as formal analysis of film style and technique has shown, there is a strong degree of *stylistic* regularity in much of the feature film production of the forties (although some of the production in the B units or B studios, especially, suggests a nonadherence to the classic rules). More specifically, statistical analysis (such as that conducted by Barry Salt) has argued a close adherence of forties films to classic norms for the construction of space and time in storytelling.[7] Moreover, at least one scholar, Janet Staiger, has gone on to suggest the ties of stylistic regularity to the regularity of a certain organization in the production of films—what Staiger refers to as the "Hollywood mode of production," a term that crosses between the structure of the industry and the structure of the films.[8]

But a statistical analysis of form is not in itself enough to establish the predominance (or not) of classicism. Indeed, while *at the level of style*, a film like *Don Juan Quilligan* seems a quite typical example of a Hollywood mode of production, the broad narrative moves and the articulation of these moves with the psychosocial force of the story suggest an unclassical strangeness that formal analysis alone might not account for. The avowed disinterest of empiricists like Salt in theories of symbolism like psychoanalysis or cultural semiotics can have as an effect the divorcing of formal analysis from other analytic methods *and* a consequent promotion of formal traits as the source of filmic meaning alone. I would suggest that formal analysis needs to link up with other forms of analysis before it can talk about classicism or not.

Indeed, at least one initially formalist analyst, Marie-Claire Ropars, has argued, in recent work on the stylistic constraints of specific periods in film history, that analysis of no single code or simple set of formal codes can account for the possible variations *and* regularities in style *and* ideology in narrative films of a single period.[9] Where her earlier formalist analysis had emphasized single codes—for example, the construction of space through montage in Eisenstein's *October*—Ropars now suggests the need to grasp the variable interplays of a larger group of codes, filmic *and* cultural. Instead of two-factor charts like Barry Salt's that tend to trace one technique over the length of a film or through the years of a decade or whatever, Ropars' approach expands geometrically in an attempt to coordinate a large number of variables and so suggest the variety of narrational options *within* the constraints of a historical moment. In a sense, Ropars' approach here resembles Wittgenstein's theorization of the "family-resemblance"— the idea that identity is best defined not by the presence of a single term or group of fixed terms but, rather, by the presence or absence of terms from a larger field out of which no single term necessarily always needs to be present. To be sure, Ropars' approach is not without its specific problems (and it is significant that a sequel to the work on a period's codes announces an abandonment of the larger socio-stylistic analysis for the more codifiable arena of formal analysis).[10] Most especially, the multiplication of factors leads to a certain inability of the critical discourse to find an overall perspective that can hold all variables together. There seems no easy way to hold all the signifying factors of film in one single, critical space. Yet while formal analysis works to solve this problem by an analytic specialization, it tends, as I've suggested, to forget the fact of its own specialization and to argue instead its ostensible comprehensiveness as a full method of analysis.

　　　　Against a unitary formalist method, then, the alternative is not to fall for some sort of a total history based in the totalizing power of some other singular method. It is an openness and expansiveness of method that I have tried to respect here. Most especially, I intend not *a* truth of forties film, but simply some suggestions as to ways in which forties film can seem to reject certain of the traits that scholars have come to associate with narrativity.

　　　　But in talking about the forties, I don't mean to suggest that history occurs here as some kind of *punctual* event by which a previously stable logic suddenly and irrevocably comes undone. Decades are no more than fictional constructs by which we cut a slice out of time to endow it with a human significance. Indeed, despite Dayan's claim that *"Stagecoach* is an exemplary illustration of a *norm* that the American cinema of the *Forties* proposes to the spectators of the whole world . . . [and which] imposes on students of cinema respect for the rules of 'classic' montage" *(Western Graffiti,* p. 13; my emphasis), part of the interest of Dayan's analysis lies in the ways it shows moments in which the fictionality of *Stagecoach's* nationalist-domestic myth becomes evident—moments in which the film can make manifest the logic it would prefer to hide beneath a veneer of the seemingly natural. For example, Dallas and Ringo can ride off at the end of the film only if the film has magically eliminated Indians as a threat. To be able to present its classic image of a newly formed couple breaking away from all pasts to build a new life together, the film simply has to forget that the last image it had showed us of the desert was of a desert still inhabited by Indians (even if the cavalry had chased them off into the hills). The film simply elides the danger of Indian attack in the buoyant optimism of its happy ending. The coherence of *Stagecoach's* narrative reveals itself, for Dayan, to be riddled by marks of illogic that break through the narrative logic in such privileged moments as the ending.

Furthermore, we would probably want to note that narrative in every moment is a potentially fragile construct, held in place only by the social and aesthetic conditions of that moment. Indeed, as theorists and historians of what is commonly, if perhaps somewhat inappropriately, called "primitive cinema" have argued, from the very beginning, film history is readable as a battle over forms, as the continual staging of narrative against all the forces that threaten its tenuous stability.[11] In Raymond Williams' terms, we can say that every period, and every social practice of that period, is a blend of residual and emergent artistic practices, combining in historically variable and specific ways.[12] If I concentrate here on the forties, it is not to privilege that decade as somehow a special one. Nonetheless, we would want to argue that certain developments—its specific forms of residualism and emergence, and their possible interaction—are particular to the forties; indeed, I will suggest that, in the forties, narrative becomes an increasingly residual form (which is not to say that we can't find elements of classic narrativity in and beyond the decade) while spectacle and a nonnarrativized flow of performances serve as markers of a newly emergent aesthetic possibility (which is not to say that we can't find strong moments of spectacle or nonnarrativity before the forties.)

All this means that we have a fundamental choice in our writing of film history: to write the history of the institution of classicism or, quite the contrary, to write the history of the moments and ways in which this classicism can show signs of breaking down. But Bellour's argument that a particularly classical narrativity characterizes *the* American cinema suggests that for many critics the choice is not always between two complementary methods. Too much of the work on American cinema shows that there is the temptation in analyzing classicism to find classicism everywhere and to thereby potentially further its dominance.[13] For example, this temptation seems to occur in the case of Dayan's analysis, which, against *Stagecoach's* overall classicism, calls at the beginning of the book for an analysis of those "images [that] exist in a sometimes subversive manner [and] murmur against the silence that is imposed upon them, and interrupt the regular progression of the story with zones of turbulence [and] inscribe on the same screen parasitic discourses, discourses of graffiti" (p. 12), *but* ends with an analysis of what Dayan argues is the "programmation" of the spectator—the spectator's being pushed into a position tht obscures the subversive discourses of graffiti for the sake of the discourse of the narrative. Dayan begins with a margin of freedom—on the part of the film, on the part of the analyst— that the rest of the analysis progressively closes off.

Of course, a converse temptation is equally possible: to find markers of the disturbance of narrative everywhere and so assume the full ineffectivity of narrative as a social model. This temptation seems most apparent in that area of modern criticism known as deconstruction, especially in its American variants (Paul de Man and the Yale School, Joseph Riddel, Jonathan Culler, etc.). Deconstruction argues that every human practice is double-edged, caught between a myth of referentiality and the differential qualities that means that language is never grounded in any ultimate, transcendental values. The goal of a deconstructive reading will be to make this duality emerge from beneath its repression by the seeming evidence of reference. Deconstruction performs an initially necessary analysis. It implies how every act is readable as split between teleology and a disturbing difference. But, disavowing a reference to the historical field which it views as only one more form of teleology, deconstruction can only insist endlessly on the dual nature of practices without showing how, why, when, and where one side of the duality can triumph. As a consequence, deconstruction ends up minimizing the pressures of history—the ways that history works to constrain meaning within prescribed ways of seeing. Superficially, deconstruction bears a certain resemblance to the kind of reading implied in Fredric Jameson's Marxist notion of a "political unconscious" (and, indeed, Jameson's analyses tend to stay at the level of textual logic rather than the social logic in which the texts operate). In the same way that Jameson assumes other narrative possibilities beneath the manifest narrative so that any one narrative becomes an allegory for all the possibilities of history, deconstruction works to refuse manifest or dominant references in order to find in a text another scene. But deconstruction (especially in America) works almost exclusively to bring this other level out, to make it operative; in contrast, it gives little attention to analyzing those forces that repressed the other scene and made one version appear dominant, authoritative, unique, imperial. This can lead to a static understanding of history—each and every moment as the same duality of manifest and latent. But it is necessary to see how dominant and dominated interact in historically variable ways, the former sometimes repressing the latter, the latter sometimes forcing itself onto the historical scene in an act of discursive vibrancy. There is no one political conscious and no one political unconscious. Against the deconstructive emphasis on endless interplay, I have tried to outline some of the historical forces in the forties that work to solidify cultural meanings around the force of narrativity as well as the forces that have troubled this solidification.

One consequence of deconstruction's lack of interest in the historical forces that can enable or disable dominance or subversion will be an emphasis in deconstruction on the ingenious or clever reading. Instead of understanding that history itself bears moments in which a dominant way of seeing interacts with disturbances that can take on any number of forms, American deconstruction tends to conceive of history as a closed-book in which reference and realism have always dominated language; such a tendency is already present in Derrida (however much he is frequently more historically aware than his American disseminators) in his reference to *a* "Western metaphysical tradition." But the understanding of history as a closed tradition leads the deconstructionist to assume that subversion and challenge can come only in the act of reading, in a dramatic activity by which the critic refuses the face-value of the past and works to alter it in a present reading. Not so far from the existentialists as they might imagine, the deconstructionists offer the clever reading as a proof that there still remains the possibilities for subjective critical freedom in a world of historical necessity.

Freed, or so he/she imagines, from historical constraints, the critic turns his/her own act of reading into a supposedly subversive act: for example, against readings of *Madame Bovary* as realist or romantic text, Jonathan Culler notes the impossibly large number of times characters eat veal in the book to argue that *Madame Bovary* is not a work of realism, but of "vealism," a vast joke on language in which words get so out of control that they simply become arbitrary signifiers.[14] Yet what such a reading—as interesting as it might be—misses is the fact of its own privilege as against the pressures—social and aesthetic—that led previous readers to read *Madame Bovary* for meaning and teleology. Culler never theorizes either the historical forces (for example, the institutional legitimation of a deconstructive approach like Culler's) that enable his "vealist" reading *or* those forces that so solidify the previous tradition of realist approaches. Significantly, some of the most seemingly eccentric reading in the deconstructive canon will try to argue that their readings *are* the text's own "true" or "intended" or "unconscious" meaning: for example, in his analysis of Marx's writing, Jeffrey Mehlman will find in that writing a form of the "uncanny"—"For Marx as analyst—as for us as readers of Marx—reading entails endeavoring to affirm a tertiary instance breaking with the registers of specularity and representation"[15]—and he will even try to ground this reading of Marx in an appeal to Marx's "lived" experience: "Marx must have lived the history of France from 1848 to 1852—the revolution careening backwards—as resembling nothing so much as a latrine backing up" (pp. 24–25). Mehlman tries, then, to make his own fanciful reading be *the* true reading of the text, the reading that Marx assumed; curiously, authorial intention returns to a philosophy that had so proudly announced a death of the author.

One possible manner by which one can begin to write the history of aesthetic practice in their contradictions would be to understand narrative, then, as one way open to a social moment to write a version of its history and of its present (which is not to suggest that nonnarrative would necessarily give a truth of the moment in opposition to narrative's ostensible fictions). No doubt one of the most influential theorizations of such an approach has been conducted by Pierre Macherey in such works as *Pour une théorie de la production littéraire*, although Macherey's approach is sometimes limited by his valorization of the aesthetic realm per se to a realm privileged in the unveiling of ideology.[16] That is, Macherey tends in the book to reify aesthetic practice as an *essentially* critical force. Indeed, Macherey's book seems caught between two very different theories of literary production. On the one hand, with a certain antihistorical idealism, he will try to define literary production as such and so hypostatize literary production, ideology, and the general mode of production alike as three fixed realms of the social moment.[17]

On the other hand, far more valuable will be Macherey's suggestion that each literary text be read as historically specific answer to the ideological questions of its historically specific moment, its conditions of production: here, Macherey's method demands a simultaneous attention to the specificity of an act of literary production *and* to the specificity of a historical moment. This is the approach that Macherey stakes out most carefully in an interesting little essay, "Queneau, scribe et lecteur de Kojève."[18] In this essay, Macherey suggests how the novelist Raymond Queneau became a kind of apologist in the literary realm for the philosopher Kojève's version of Hegelian philosophy; Kojève's notion that the movement of the absolute subject was a movement toward a pure vantage point from which knowledge could understand all of history was particularly attractive to Queneau, who narrativized this philosophy in such fictions as *Le dimanche de la vie* with its absolute hero. But, at the same time, the mutual attraction of Kojève and Queneau in the thirties especially suggests that each allowed the other a way to construct a particularly coherent version of the incoherent history they were living through (or perceived themselves as living through). The *philosophic* notion of a pure vantage point for an absolute subject offers *narrative* a way to engage in the sense of an ending, to find a place through and by which a story can be confidently told: "The doctrine of the end of history, insofar as it takes itself seriously and we too take it seriously, is terrifying—Kojève was in fact a terrorist of thought . . . did French intellectuals of the 1930's really believe that they were living after the end of history, and that such a situation conditioned all their intellectual and practical activity? . . . [Queneau's writing] brings the vision of universal history proposed by Kojève back to its real dimensions which are those of a determined actuality in which vibrate the menaces of a new world conflict" (p. 90).

In Macherey's reading, then, Queneau's fiction and Kojève's philosophy are both ways of imagining a version of their historical moment in quite specific and loaded ways. Hegelianized philosophy and narrativized fiction both stand as ways to represent in imagination a stability that is lacking in the perceived reality of history. As Macherey's reference in the Queneau essay to the context of the thirties suggests, it is necessary, then, to relate specific narratives to other forms, such as the discourses of philosophy, in the historical moment. Yet this does not mean treating narratives as simple or univocal or exclusive reflections of the moment. Instead, we can treat narrative as a particular version of its moment, a particular shaping of available forms and available materials. Thus, in the following pages, the continued reference to nonfilm forties texts (for example, novels, prescriptive guides, the discourses of science, the symbolisms of the commodity) does not set out to suggest an inevitable or univocal influence of any one form on another but, rather, the *complementary* investments of a variety of discourses in their social moment. More specifically, I want to argue a certain complementariness both in the ways a number of discourses of the forties attempt to construct a classical narrativity, *and* the ways a number of discourses together show up the limitations of that attempt and that construction.

The seeming simplicity of the forties becomes itself a strong invitation to such theoretical investigation: for example, the very possibility in the forties that Michael Renov refers to as a "confluence between perpetuation of state policy and authority and the 'relatively autonomous' cinematic institution" raises questions about the status of culture (and of a concept of autonomy—relative or not) and, indeed, of the status of governance. What, for example, would it mean to understand culture univocally as an effective tool of governance? For example, while Paul Hirst has attacked Louis Althusser's notion of ideology as *state* apparatus and as reproduction of production with the claim that such a notion defeats Althusser's own theoretical framework—based on a relative autonomy of specific practices—and reinscribes him in a Hegelianism in which all social practices express, serve, and function for a dominant core,[19] the war years might almost seem made for an Althusserian analysis, a moment in which the exigencies of history triumph over theoretical argument—a moment, it might seem, of the state, a moment in which art emphatically and triumphantly expresses social need. Yet it is precisely the possibility of such triumphs that we now need to interrogate.

Faced with the story of the affirmative ideology of the war years, historians have long repeated the self-advertisements of that would-be dominant ideology and have thereby perhaps even solidified that ideology. That is, following what has come to be called a *necessitarian* argument—the war *necessarily* forced a unity that overrode pluralism and sacrificed a diversity of social goals for the needs of winning—historians have tended to assume that necessity became actuality, that the war moment was a kind of virtually Hegelian "expressive totality" in which all practices worked together to one common end. The historians have passed down a particularly bearable or acceptable image of one of the supposedly last great moments of American consensus.[20] Thus, to take only one example, while Richard Polenberg's *One Nation Divisible: Class, Race, and Ethnicity in the United States Since 1938* goes a long way in dismantling representations of *postwar* America as a consensus society (as in Daniel Bell's [in]famous vision of fifties America as the "end of ideology"), Polenberg rarely takes a lesson from his own reading of postwar tensions to read similar tensions *in the war period.* Indeed, at moments, his book seems to echo that long-running argument that sees the war years as a miracle of American unity and production: for example, "The attack on Pearl Harbor clearly demonstrated war's potential as a unifying force in society."[21] And yet the increasing interest of new revisionist historians in the roots of postwar American domestic and foreign policy has led them to read in the war years themselves struggles of force, clashes of power. They have argued that the domestic scene was a site of disagreements, of oppressions, and, often, of the careful and carefully hidden deployment of new modes of power and power-alliances. Thus, despite what might seem to be the postwar emphasis of its title, George Lipsitz's *Class and Culture in Cold War America* actually begins its story in the war years, understanding those years to be far from that miracle of consensus and tolerance that has come down to us in dominant histories.[22] Similarly, historians of postwar American imperialism have suggested how military and business forces were already planning on such imperialism during the war; indeed, war strategies were planned not merely for victory, but for a very particular monopoly capitalist kind of victory.[23]

The opening of Alan Clive's *State of War: Michigan in World War II* is simple and direct in its necessitarian representation of a war effort: "The Second World War was a total war" (p. 1). Yet that simplicity only partially conceals an ambiguity that extended contact with forties history increasingly questions (and, to be fair to Clive, that the rest of his book not infrequently discusses). What is a total war? Is total war the same as total participation in a war? Was total war a desire or an actuality? Following chapters of my study will suggest certain answers to such questions; here I want only to note how Clive's phrase functions less as an *énoncé* (a denotative statement) than as an act of *énonciation*—a statement in context, transmitted from someone to someone. What does it mean for a history to make such a confident statement? Why do historians make such statements? Why the authority (the use of the emphatic verb "was")? What grounds the assurance of the historical statement? The work of new historians would seem to make much less confident the enunciation of such statements as Clive's. For example, labor historians like Nelson Lichtenstein have demonstrated the extreme intensity of labor opposition during the war peroid.[24] To be sure, much of this opposition itself participates in an ideology of affirmation; indeed, as I will suggest later, much of the labor unrest came from feelings that the so-called warlords of Washington were not running the fighting of the war in the best possible way. And yet, as Lichtenstein suggests, there was also opposition to the consequences that war affirmation had on labor; members of the working class seemed to perceive that such strategies as the no-strike pledge between bosses and the unions were as much a way of continuing prewar measures against labor as of developing specific strategies for tailoring labor for the war effort.

But there's a problem with most of the historical work on the forties, even that of the revisionists. It lacks any complex sense of the specificity of cultural practice and so either ignores this practice or treats it within the strict limits of a documentary reading—the cultural text as direct indicator of the times.[25] Furthermore, in the absence of extended reflection on culture, historical work tends not so much to follow simply its own specializations in political or economic analysis; rather, in a kind of slippage, it tends to extend its specific areas of analysis and claim the primacy of the political or the economic over the cultural. It tends to understand culture as a noncomplex, ultimately political or economic force. Forties history, in particular, is too frequently dominated by an institutions and agencies approach which sees the patterns and meanings of everyday life (when, indeed, it descends to talk about everyday life) as imposed through political moves made from on high. Even as culturally centered an analysis as Michael Renov's work on wartime film representations of women will tend to enclose its textual analysis within a notion of the film text's obedience to government agencies and their wartime needs and demands. To be sure, we *can* well posit the force and effect of institutions in the forties—both public ones and more hidden ones (like the Committee for Economic Development, a coalition of government and businessmen planning for a postwar monopolization of commodity production). But we also need to posit spaces and practices that exist outside the immediate sway of political institutions. This would not be to suggest that these spaces or practices would necessarily be subversive. Indeed, part of the importance of the Foucauldian approach has been the ways it refines a theory of power away from central authorities to acts of individual subjectivity; most recently, with the notion of "le souci de soi" (the care of the self), Foucault has argued that socialization frequently operates through a self-guided internalization by which one turns one's own body into a body politic to be governed through a complicated array of personal practices.[26] Indeed, in the next chapter we will find a similar practice at work in the promotion of the wartime individual as an object of self-scrutiny and routine.

At the same time, we would want to note that the diffusion of power through a realm of individuals allows for nodal points of contradiction. Without arguing, à la the idealist side of Macherey, that culture is inherently the space of ideology's unveiling, I would suggest that the pressures of the forties specifically tear narrative art between opposed goals and that this tearing leads to particularly intense contradictions. To take a small example, Peter Filene's retrospective declaration of a miracle of war unity—"No hysterical cries of 'slacker,' just a dogged determination to get the job done"[27]—seems curiously contradicted by at least one film of the period, the big production of *Since You Went Away* (1944), with a major scene centered on the virulent castigation of a slacker. Understanding cultural texts, then, as neither inevitable apologies for a central power nor as a concerted subversion of that power, an emphasis on contradiction allows an open and variable approach to the processes of social production.

Chapter Two

Wartime Unity:
The Representation of Institutions and the Institutions of Representation

By 1944, a new stridency makes its way into the publicity of U.S. War Bond drives. From at least 1943 or so on, public discourse on the war has included a frequent assurance of the war's end, and government agencies now begin to announce that, while such a feeling is not unjustified, it must not lead to a lessening of the war effort. War publicity must try to straddle a position between optimism and gritty pragmatism. One ad, suggested by the Office of War Information for the Fifth Bond Drive, can suggest the bluntness with which the Treasury Department hopes to now capture the American public: on a battle-scarred field, a soldier has been struck and is falling in death. The caption reads: "I died today. What did you do?"[1]

    Again, like the two pages of *Life* magazine that I dis-

cussed in the introduction, this image tells several stories—that of
men in battle; that of the people at home. But, perhaps unlike the
Life pages, this ad works explicitly to set up a system of exchange
between the two places. These are not different stories, but variations on a single story: what happens on the home front affects
instantly what happens on the battlefront. War here is a singular
and closed economy of meaning, a homeostatic system where a
severe linkage means that weakness at any one point leads to
weaknesses at other points. And though the driving presence
behind such exchange is the continued threat of death—as another ad says, "Do you expect to be alive by dinner time? A
number of Americans will not be"—the equivalence can be less
extreme, not always founded on the threat of death: in the bluntness of another ad, "Lend a hand; he gave one." What finally
matters is not so much the content of exchange but the very fact
of exchange: everything must link up, must have a dependence
upon some other part of the system. The motives behind any
linkage within the system become of lesser importance than the
overall organization; indeed, in its advice to advertisers, the Office
of War Information will go so far as to suggest that the fact of
linkage justifies whatever means lead to that linkage: "While the
patriotic emotional approach should receive major emphasis . . .
self-interest appeals should by no means be neglected." Not
merely a system of equivalences, the war-affirmative ideology tries
to set up a system of regulated transformations: so much violence
over there is readable in terms of so much self-interest here. There
is the institution of an overwhelming calculus of meaning that
implies that no element in the society exists on its own; rather,
each element gains force from its articulation with other elements.
The discourse of war affirmation works, then, to write reality
within the monocular framework of a singular, closed set of
values.

     That any one single meaning here takes its value from
its place in the overall system does not imply, though, that specific
contents are completely irrelevant to the construction of a wartime
ideology. Rather, the war ideology constitutes what structuralism
calls a *combinatoire:* a fixed number of terms or elements that can

enter into sets of permutations, different arrays of relation and connection. Such a system works here according to patterns of exclusion—a willed disregarding of aberrant discourses—or patterns of incorporation—a willed rewriting of the aberrant until it ends up as the ordinary, "normal." Meaning, then, is doubly constrained: first, by what the system accepts as meaningful elements, and second, by what the system accepts as meaningful permutations of those elements.

One especially strong wartime permutation involves the connection of an ambiguous present to a clear and precise future. The appeal here is that of a *narrative* in which the seemingly unknown future is always already written. Narrative becomes the privileged site of a meaningful closure: the beginning presupposes and even determines the end. War ideology constructs, then, a specific kind of story; in the retrospective words of pop historian Archie Satterfield, "Like a short story from almost any popular magazine of that period, the war had a dramatic beginning, a middle fraught with conflict, and a happy ending."[2] Against uncertainty, against a narrative begun by others (the Japanese attack), wartime America will write its own story, will control temporality, will govern narration. At the extreme, the future is not difference, a potential ambiguation of present situations, but rather the Same, a continual and *logically* determined extension of the present; thus, engaging in a certain punnery, the 1943 war bond campaign will adopt as a slogan "War Bonds—the present with a future."

It is a very specific kind of narrative, then, that represents the war-affirmative ideology of the American war years: a narrative of equivalence and exchange, but also ultimately a narrative of nontemporality. Narrative here is not an opening up of beginnings into the ambiguities of an unwritten future, but the controlled deployment of all temporalities according to one overarching schema. Further, in such a narrative, there will be an equation not only of present and future, but also of future and past: wartime advertising, for example, will mobilize a particular vision of the past as the quality that a successful future will lead America back to. There is most especially a particular mythology of small-town America, summed up for example in a famous ad of a soldier on leave: "The taste of hamburger, the feeling of driving a roadster, a dog named Shucks or Spot. There is a lump in his throat and maybe a tear fills his eye. It doesn't matter, kid. Nobody will see it. It's too dark." As narrative figure, small-town America offers the possibility of a system of interchangeable bits; that is, in the wartime narrative, where any element is to be equated with some other element, small-town American functions formally as a vast source of semantic elements, a seemingly endless wealth of semantic bits: hamburger tastes, roadsters, family pets, "the girl he left behind," and so on. In *V Was for Victory*, John Morton Blum calls such networks a "jumble", but if so, such a jumble has a narrative efficiency, allowing the same narrative structure to be mobilized again and again with different narrative contents.[3]

This is not to suggest, though, that the elements of "small-town America" are neutral until combined in the meaningfulness of an overall pattern. Actually, what I referred to above as the double constraint of meaning (choice of elements, permutation of elements) does not occur in two separate steps but in a simultaneity. In articulating the limits of how combinations can occur, the social system also defines and constitutes the very meaning of the elements that will be able to enter into combination. If we are to analyze what Roland Barthes calls the *mythologies* of a society, we need to engage in the very kind of critique that Barthes directed against the first versions of his own mythological analysis. Where, in the early *Mythologies*, Barthes had understood myth to be a secondary modeling system, a parasitic field of connotation that took over and redirected the innocence of denotation, Barthes later (especially in *S/Z*) felt that a lingering faith in denotation constructed a utopian notion of a meaning untouched by sociality; thus, according to *S/Z*, "denotation is only the last of connotations." There is no reality that can exist outside an ideological framing; those elements of reality that an ideology ignores become nonrealities with no force or substance. Denotation is simply a society's naturalization of its particular modeling of reality.

Thus, with a mythology like "small-town America," one has to analyze not only the positive messages of the mythology but, also, the various rhetorical strategies that work to make those meanings appear as the inevitable sense of things. For example, the Office of War Information's booklet "Small Town, U.S.A." works by the logic of appearing to have no overriding logic at all; there is no explicit enunciation of a message of propaganda here, just the chronicling of everyday life in a small town (Alexandria, Indiana).[4] Naturalization exists first of all in the use of photographs to give a certain reality effect to the text of the booklet. According to the rhetoric of the image, the image will appear to be natural, and the text will be no more than nature's dependent but reliable transmitter. Hence, in the words of the text, one photograph shows *"admiring* boys talk[ing] with Police Chief Daniels and a state policeman" (my emphasis). Such a caption assumes the admiration as given and assumes an evident and immediate meaning in the image. All through the booklet, the mythology of a small-town America is constructed by a rhetoric of clear and direct but ostensibly casual statement that works to bolster a quite specific representation of American life. Thus, there is the image of America as natural equalizer; a photo of a quaint street is accompanied by the statement that "few houses stand out among the others as indicating either poverty or wealth." This equality is then replayed in the work realm: "Delco-Remy [the town's central industry] has a contract with the Automobile Worker's Union. A shop-management committee settles grievances and helps maintain top efficiency."[5] Finally, there is a universal equality for which Alexandria is only a mediate case: "The story of a typical American town is in one sense the story of small towns in Great Britian, Russia, China, and the other United Nations. For Alexandria is at war, and its people are fighting for precisely the same reasons for which the people of these other towns are fighting."[6]

As much as it works with regulated transformations, the war narrative also functions by an appeal to clarity and sharp division, a drawing of boundaries between the realm of narrative and all the obscurities that it feels might fall outside its sway. Two successive issues from *Life* early in the decade and before America's official entry into the war can suggest how such a process works. On the one hand, an ad for a Nash car (January 8, 1940) makes the alluring promise "You'll find yourself on a road of mystery [in a Nash]." Here, before the war has begun, we're still in a moment of the attainable commodity—the product presented as the key to a wonderfully *un*predictable story: the future has not yet been written, but the commodity writes the limits of what that future can be. The world's mysteries are mediated by the becalming force of the commodity: "The scene outside is hauntingly familiar—but what's happening? Suddenly, you realize why [everyday familiarity has become mysterious]. You're in a Nash." Life here is the controlled blend of a reassuring closure (we can travel only on roads that others have already passed over—the mystery is determined in advance) and openness (we don't know this particular road so we can invest it with mystery). The commodity is a promise but it is a promise left in deliberate, alluring semi-obscurity. Indeed, as Walter Benjamin suggests, reading off of Baudelaire's interest in Poe, there may be a historical tie between the concretization of the commodity system and the development of classic detective and mystery fiction: in classic detective fiction, the world of commodities and objects comes to the detective not as a threat but as a promise or invitation—the object as a sign that will lead to a successful end. Thus, the ostentatiousness of the commodity-filled bourgeois home becomes an exciting story in which every element reveals a trace of adventure.[7] With his leisurely life, the aristocrat has the time to imagine the ordinary objects of his surrounding world as signs that speak to him of promising adventures.

It is perhaps suggestive, then, to note that another issue of *Life*, one week earlier, presents a very different understanding of mystery in relation to war: an article on "War-time London" tells us that "[in London] life is too uncertain to read detective stories. Instead, he ["the home-loving Englishman"] reads reassuring books by Dickens and Austen." In this moment of transition between an America still at peace (although discursively invested more and more in stories of war) and a world at war, this juxtaposition can help pinpoint qualities of that kind of storytelling that a war-affirming America will try to construct for itself: stories of reassurance and clarity against the uncertainties of an open future. For war discourse, there can be few "roads of mystery."

At the extreme, the affirmative narratives will try to construct a *determined logic of the future* by making a distinction between two narrative times: a fleeting, unpredictable narrative that is at the limit of narrativity—a narrative governed by the force of chaotic or contingent events—and an organized, preordained narrative in which the force of a logic governs events. Through this strategy of two times, the war-affirmative narrative is able to acknowledge contingency only to write it away within the non-contingent stability of a larger, successful narrativity. Emblematic in this respect are the end titles of the film *Flight for Freedom* (1943): "This story has a conclusion, but not an end—for its real end will be the victory for which Americans—on land, on sea and in the air—have fought, are fighting now, and will continue to fight until peace has been won." The titles begin by suggesting an uncertain future—the instability of ends against the fixities of mere conclusions—but then the ending itself is reestablished, fixed within a promise made natural by the passive grammar of the last words (the peace inevitably wins itself through the intercession of a human agency that marries itself to that inevitability). There simultaneously is and is not a sense of the meaningful ending in such a narrative. In other words, at a moment when the flux of history leaves the desired inevitability of an ending in a certain suspension, narrative will work out a compromise in which it admits the unpredictability of the end while nonetheless empowering the certainty of that end.

To take a further example, the end narration of *Wake Island* (1942) enacts the promise of a desired end by writing the future as a closure that fully answers a move set out by the beginning. Opening with a text that connects the massacre on Wake Island to such "heroic" defeats as Custer's Last Stand, the film argues that defeat is no more than a negative (and temporary) moment of a larger positivity: as the end narration declares, "These Marines fought a great fight. They wrote history. But this is not the end. There are other leathernecks who will enact a just and terrible vengeance." Defeat here is, on the one hand, a closure, the "writing" of a fully past history. But, on the other hand, defeat also writes its own conditions of openness: as long as vengeance has not taken place, the narrative will lack its logic. Vengeance here is not a mere afterthought but, rather, the necessary answer to defeat, an end point that retrospectively confers meaning on defeat and rewrites it as an essential part of victory.

In discussing the narrative logic of the war-affirmative representation, I have thus far been concentrating essentially on what, following linguistics, we might call the *énoncé* (the *enounced*) of the discourse, rather than on its conditions of *enunciation*, the situation in which a message takes place. For narrative, this is close to the difference that narrative theory sums up in the distinction between story and discourse, tale and telling. The *énoncé/* enunciation distinction—proposed to linguistics by Emile Benveniste[8]—reminds us of the necessary existence of linguistic elements as *events*—occurrences that take place in specific situations, rather than as simple denotations of events; a theory of linguistic enunciation has enabled a move away from a formal linguistics devoted to the atemporal fixing of language within a catalogue of rules and semantic regularities, and a move toward a new sociolinguistics that links communication *and* history. Theory of enunciation examines what a discourse hopes to do in being enounced. The theory suggests that any study of social meaning needs to examine not only the referential claim of the language but the force of the claiming—the force with which reference is promoted, rewritten, constructed, and, perhaps, even challenged. What we specifically need to do, then, is to examine the function of what Roland Barthes, in a self-critical analysis of his own *S/Z*, referred to as the *rhetorical code*, the code that concerns a communication's markers of its desire (for whatever reason) to communicate.[9] Where *S/Z* had concentrated essentially on the structure of the narrated level of the text, Barthes now suggests the need to examine more closely those moments where a narrative can be read to reflect upon its motives for narrating.

Recently, analysts of ideology have become interested in the theory of enunciation as a way of examining what seems to be ideology's drive toward self-naturalization, toward its self-advertisement as true, inevitable, exclusive, authoritative.[10] Thus, some analysts engage in a certain assimilation of *énoncé* and enunciation to ideology and deconstruction respectively: the discourse of dominant ideology will be one that hides marks of enunciation beneath the apparent naturalness of an *énoncé*. As ideology would have it, ideology does not speak from a specific point (for that would make it relative and, so, potentially transitory). In this view, ideology speaks from no place, or, rather, it speaks from reality itself which generates its own representing discourse. And yet the theory of enunciation ironically encourages a certain critique of the ways the theory has generally been applied in the analysis of ideology. That is, close application of enunciation theory can enable us to examine how the most ideological discourse frequently explicitly marks its conditions of enunciation; language can acknowledge those conditions while still, or even thereby, functioning ideologically. Even ideologically effective discourse may make use of modernist processes of self-reflexive enunciation.[11]

What is significant, then, about the would-be discourse of dominance during the war is its constant effort to focus on its enunciative markers, to speak in a context that it marks as a context. The affirmative discourse is not *histoire*—a narrative of a past that masks its connection to the present and is told in a third person that puts emphasis on message content. Rather, the war-supporting discourse is avowedly *discursive*, announcing and enouncing itself as a message from somewhere (for example, a government agency, a star or starlet making a war bond plea) to someone (the American people, often addressed in first person — "What did you do today?") in a particular context of space and time ("I died *today*"), for motives other than the simple representation of a reality or the letting of reality speak for itself.

Indeed, as enunciation approaches the condition of propaganda, it increasingly tends to speak of a gap between "truth" and everyday reality. That is, it suggests that everyday reality itself has now become an ideology that has seduced people away from their true self-interest. Any sort of "documentary realism" will be impossible in propaganda's view, for it is precisely

the stereotypes of the real that propaganda sees the need to pro-
agandize against. Paradoxically, even when it claims to speak as
the voice of a dominant authority, propaganda assumes a certain
adversarial position vis-à-vis the people it sets out to convince. It
simultaneously suggests that people are reasonable enough to
follow the "correct" view but unreasonable enough to have allowed falsehoods to sway them temporarily.[12] Going against any
simple assimilation of ideology and realism, propaganda frequently works by arguing that adversaries have possession of the
clichés of the real, while the propagandist has possession of a
higher, less commonsensical truth. Such a constitution of discourse as propaganda has no necessary connection to a referential
function of discourse; its truth is not the semantic truth of what it
speaks about but, rather, the rhetorical or performative truth of
the ways it speaks. Not insignificantly, the major government
agency for communication to the civilian realm will begin as the
Office of Facts and Figures—its announced goal merely to present
facts without comment or bias—but, then, will undergo so many
attacks for that goal that it will be reconstituted as the Office of
War Information (and, as if to signal the parallels between propaganda and the enunciative strategies of advertising, the position
of bureau chief for graphics and printing will go to Price Gilbert,
a former vice-president of Coca-Cola).[13]

   "There are no atheists in foxholes." Again, it is necessary to read such a statement less as a referential comment than
as an act of enunciation, a declaration made to further specific
ends: the naturalness of the comment coupled with its authority
(it comes from a Minister; it is grammatically emphatic) works
not to describe a state of affairs but to empower one. The Reverend
Mr. Cumming's statement (to which we'll see a reply in the next
chapter's discussion of anti-affirmative discourse) is the kind of
statement whose enactment will reappear throughout the war
years. Indeed, if, as Susan Suleiman has suggested, one of the
central rhetorical strategies of propaganda is redundancy,[14] it is
important to note how semantic bits—such as the theme of war
as a triumph over atheism—repeat not only in the space of a single
text but from text to text in the constitution of one vast intertext

that turns individual stories into component parts of the whole. Thus, for example, in the male-bonded group of the men in the submarine in *Destination: Tokyo* (1943), one of the few aberrations that assails the unity and coherence of the crew from within will be the atheism of the sub's doctor (Bruce Bennett). With the Japanese enemy pictured as an *easily beatable* foe (so much so that, as Robert Fyne points out, the film portrays a spectacular bombing run on Tokyo that in historical fact never took place),[15] in contrast, the film suggests that the doctor's atheism is the real foe, and the major turning point of the film will be his turning to God during dangerous surgery as the ship lies in wait. Not surprisingly, the script treatment for the film makes all the connections clear: "There are no atheists in submarines . . . at least not in this one."

All through the war, discourse announces itself in an affirmative mode. For example, as war approaches and then be- gins, the White House constantly issues proclamations of unity in which state, religion, and personal destiny come together: for example, "I Am an American" Day (May 1940); a National Day of Prayer (January 1, 1942). The importance of *narrative,* then, for the war effort lies in its resilient ability to allow conflict or contra- diction but to then enclose such tension within a higher order of unity, "the sense of an ending." For the historical moment, nar- rative is a particularly effective representational form in the ways that it substitutes for the declaration of immediate triumph a different sort of triumph, one gained after chaos and discordance. To be sure, statements like "There are no atheists in foxholes" or "I Am an American" can have a seductive power, but their lyric stasis, in which they describe a single moment in time or a state of affairs that could change, leaves them open to the possibility of contradiction. For example, an "I Am an American" Day implies that affirmation and adherence to the affirmative mode last only the length of a punctual moment; the next day, one slips back into a nonaffirmative attitude. In contrast, narrative allows an embedding of contradiction within an inevitability of solution, a final coherence. Narrative temporalizes affirmation and so allows it to anticipate and cover over countering situations. Where some theorists of narrative's politics have suggested that narrative is *the*

form of ideology in that ideology is ostensibly "the central function
or *instance* of the human mind,"[16] I would suggest rather that we
might do better to understand narrative as a historically rooted
force, a symbolic response in a specific situation to specific narrative raw material. Narrative comes into play for the war, for
example, as an especially effective discourse (although, paradoxically, as I will suggest in the next chapter, its increased effectivity
brings with it an increased vulnerability to forces of contradiction).
Narrative's advantage comes from its scope and its resilience.

In this respect, the war years take on a particularly
strong form *as a narrative moment* where ideology deals with historical variability by enframing it within the limits of a tale. For
example, many of the guides to the role of everyday life in the
war effort work not just by demonstration, explication, analysis,
argumentation, etc., but, rather, by rewriting of such discursive
strategies within the form of a storytelling. To take one example,
Evelyn Steele, in *Wartime Opportunities for Women*, allegorizes her
survey of war jobs for women through narrative fictions. Thus,
she begins a chapter on nursing with a tale:

> The big U.S. hospital ship floated calmly over the smooth
> blue surface of the Pacific . . . Nurse Helen Morse, which isn't her right
> name, sat watching over [the exposure cases]. They were, she thought,
> so little trouble . . . Beyond the portholes of the war room, she heard the
> sounds of sudden activity . . . An orderly came in. "Twenty-three fresh
> cases coming up," he said. "Some of them lulus, too." Nurse Morse had
> no more time for thinking then. She got busy.[17]

Significantly, the story will end not by enclosing the narrative
within the limits of a history—a closed, third-person, past-tense
unit of no more than anecdotal interest. Quite the contrary, in a
way that seems to blur fiction and nonfiction, *history* becomes a
discourse of and in the present: "For Helen Morse, this was literally
a baptism of fire. If you complete your nursing studies while the
war is still on, you may be that nurse." Trying to hold past, present,
and future together, the writing engages in the paradox of trying
to make its present readers coincide with a fiction set in a past.
The ambiguities of tense in that last sentence are revealing of a

new form of narrativity poised between the classically historical function of the *énoncé* and the new demands of an active *enunciation:* "you may be" hovers between present and future but also gives sense to the past by making it a component of the reader's investment in the narrative.

In several essays on film narrative (but which, I would suggest, can have extrafilmic applications), Stephen Heath suggests that "classical narrative" is that construct one of whose primary characteristics is a holding of process with an *ordered* temporality.[18] "Classical narrative" will be that ordering of events according to a logic of motivation and action, the events gaining a sense, their space converted, in Heath's words, into place. Where a kind of existentialist-inspired criticism (as in the theory of allegory of Paul de Man) valorizes temporality as the undoing of fixities, the breakdown of predictable necessity, Heath will argue in contrast that "classical narrative" undoes an initial stability *but only to recontain the resultant instabilities through a narrative closure:* "A narrative action is a series of elements held in a relation of transformation such as their consecution . . . determines a state S' different from an initial state S . . . A beginning, therefore, is always a violence, the interruption of the homogeneity of S . . . The task of narrative—the point of the transformation—is to resolve the violence, to replace it in a new unity."[19]

The war narrative (and here I mean specifically that narrative whose *énoncé* concerns our participation in the war) would seem to conform explicitly to Heath's description of a steady state followed by a disruptive violence followed by some sort of restoration. Throughout the war, there is an attempt to merge different narrative stories, to find in them a single story. Moreover, separate historical events themselves will be presented as parts of a single narrative. For example, numerous films and books present Pearl Harbor as not merely a violence, but as a *narrative* violence, a disruption of America's slow story of grappling with and recovering from the Depression.[20] As an element within a narrative structure, "Pearl Harbor" opens up several narrative possibilities. First of all, it allows the construction of a narrative of illogic recontained within a higher logic: Pearl Harbor is first a surprise, but then becomes something Americans should have expected, something in keeping with "the Japanese character." Indeed, the film *Wake Island* includes a scene where the Japanese delegates stop at the island on their way to their December 7 nonmeeting with the U.S. government. Showing here a prewar moment, this war film retrospectively invests the prewar scenes with a kind of proleptic force as the American soldiers see through the evident hypocrisies of the Japanese who assert a nonaggressive philosophy and propose a toast to peaceful coexistence.

Similarly, the very fact of the surprise attack allows the representation of America as capable and strong: that the Japanese had to attack in such a way only confirms American prowess (and many stories will emphasize as much the number of Japanese planes downed—the resilient ability of Americans to fight back—as the damage to the American fleet). Such a representation further suggests that the next time the outcome will be quite different. A forewarned America won't be so strongly hit. Thus, in the film *Gung Ho!* (1943), a ship of crack American troops passes by the wreckage of Pearl Harbor. At first, the only response would seem to be passivity; indeed, the narrator suggests that the soldiers' quiet is "mute testimony to the power of Japan." But, quickly, passivity turns into will, and silence into speech. When an officer asks a crying soldier, "Anything I can do for you?" the soldier replies, "Yeah, tell me . . . when do we go to Tokyo?" The continued representation of Pearl Harbor long after the event (as in so many films where the camera pans down knowingly to a calendar page that reveals "Dec. 7, 1941") allows the audience for these narratives after the fact a certain complicity with narrative, a certain control over history: the past is a given, the viewer is in a position of authoritative knowledge, Pearl Harbor becomes the object of a certain psychical disavowal (a violence, but one that we must and can move beyond—a violence that we can assimilate). That is, by knowing the meaning of a date that characters in the narrative don't recognize, the audience participates in an ironic view of history that paradoxically makes history all the less ironic: the realization that Pearl Harbor could have been averted (as in *China Girl* [1942], where Johnny Williams [George

Montgomery] finds plans for the Japanese invasion but doesn't know it) leads beyond irony to the belief that in the future, history will be more controllable. Indeed, a number of films—for example, *Five Graves to Cairo* (1943), *Sherlock Holmes and the Voice of Terror* (1942), *Foreign Correspondent* (1940), *Berlin Correspondent* (1942)— will chronicle the successful uncovering and defeat of other Axis plots as if to suggest that the disaster of Pearl Harbor was only an aberrant mistake.[21] Significantly, Johnny Williams doesn't know Japanese and so can't read the Pearl Harbor plans; there is the implication here that the problem was not that America as a whole didn't know but that a single and solitary American had his chance and muffed it.

      "Pearl Harbor" functions according to the operations of what Roland Barthes calls the *gnomic* code, the stereotypes of cultural knowledge that a society uses as specific points of obvious reference.[22] "December 7, 1941" will become a linguistic unit whose use unites all people who employ it; it provides the force that, in Jean-Paul Sartre's terms, turns the serial dispersion of social subjects into a group-in-fusion.[23] In Sartre's suggestion, a newly created group comes into being not out of a clear reciprocity of unambiguous communication, but rather through the mediation of any two group members by what Sartre calls "le tiers" (the third party), a system of references, interdictions, motivations, and commands that unites group members just as it really keeps them separate. In this way, "Pearl Harbor" becomes a bit in a symbolic code that unites Americans in a shared space. Thus, a frequent representation of Pearl Harbor is of the "Where were you on December 7, 1941?" variety; the answer begins in dispersion— people at the ball game, people waking up, U.S. officials getting ready for a meeting with Japanese diplomats—but then suggests a field of equivalence through Pearl Harbor as mediating unity. For example, in many films, Pearl Harbor exists as a radio message, as in *Air Force* (1943), which each of the crew members, including the dissident Winocki (John Garfield), listens in to; soon after, the aural message becomes visual as the bomber arrives in Hawaii, and, almost as in a visit to the cinema, the aircrew look out at the image of Pearl Harbor displayed out below them. The camera frames Pear Harbor to fill the screen; the soldiers' scene becomes a scene that the spectator can share with them.

But it is important to note that "Pearl Harbor" is not experienced "really" but only discursively. That is, it comes to Americans already shaped as a representation. It has little reality to interfere with its symbolic rewriting. Except for a few people with relatives in the battle (as suggested in *Air Force*, where one of the crew members loses his wife in the attack on Pearl Harbor), Pearl Harbor takes place as a symbol that quickly gains further symbolic overtones. In Richard Polenberg's words, "The attack seemed likely to unify a divided nation and heal the scars of a long, bitter conflict over foreign policy."[24] Again, what seems significant about Polenberg's words is their emphasis on temporality: an event in the past continues to live on as a unifying force in the present and future. Moreover, the symbolic force works rhetorically rather than referentially; nothing makes a divided nation into a unity except the discursive declaration that this is occurring—that it seems likely to occur.

Sartre suggests that if a group first forms in reaction to an external danger, the group all too often finds itself facing an internal danger: a dispersive fear, an unguarded laziness, the sense that the external danger is either too strong or too weak to really be fought against. Here, a second narrative move becomes necessary: not the originary violence of a single, external attack, but a subsequent narrative that represents the violence of continued attack. This narrative continuation can occur in several ways. First, the narrative can imply that external danger has not disappeared; thus, American war stories combat a public sense that victory has already been won; the war stories try to show the continued need for further victories (again, *Flight for Freedom's* distinction between conclusions and ends is emblematic here). Significantly, it is precisely as *victories* that these as yet unfought battles are represented; there is a simultaneous sense that battles have to be fought but that fighting automatically brings winning. Thus, a number of films "conclude" with the soldiers confidently on their way to another battle: for example, *Air Force, Casablanca* (1942), *Objective Burma!* (1945), *Desperate Journey* (1942), etc. The films are cyclical but this cyclicity works within the framework of a known and controllable temporality.

A second narrative option revolves around what Sartre calls Terror; in the absence of immediate dangers, a group will create its own representation of dangers (and will even make group loyalty revolve around an internally generated danger; thus, desertion from the enemy's fire can bring one under disciplinary fire). Such terror, Sartre suggests, is mediated through the group by what he calls "le serment."[25] The "serment" is an activity—not necessarily thought out by its participants—in which a group member agrees (by actions or by words) to stay within the group and to serve its needs at all costs. This internalization can become so strong that external danger proportionally ceases to be perceived as the fundamental danger. For example, as I suggested in the case of *Destination: Tokyo*, the real threat is not the Japanese, but the internal dissonances that atheism poses. Paradoxically, Roosevelt's "We have nothing to fear but fear itself," seemingly intended to banish fear, catches the necessary reliance of group adhesion on fear, on a fear that binds, a fear that each member internalizes. Part of the war narrative, then, will frequently revolve around questions of discipline, of figures who haven't sufficiently felt the terror: for example, Woody Jason (John Carroll) in *Flying Tigers* (1942), who begins by viewing war as a jolly game or as no more than a source of easy money and so causes the death of a fellow soldier. The film will then chronicle Woody's growth into a figure of responsibility. Or, rather, it will suggest that Woody can find a mediating point between his rampant egoism and the communal demands of war commitment: Woody separates himself off from the team once more but this time to crash into a Japanese bridge that couldn't be reached by a straight bombing run.

The initiating violence of the narrative works, then, to center Americans around a single goal, a shared ideological vision. If, as theorists of scapegoating (such as René Girard in *Violence and the Sacred*) have suggested, scapegoating has a community-building function by pressuring people to share a common ideological space by sharing in the expulsion of a socially defined aberration, then the war period can seem to provide America with a well-defined space of scapegoating: that which one defends against that which aggresses all defenses. Where the late thirties had often evidenced a growing discontent with Rooseveltian New Deal politics and with Rooseveltian interventionism, the war can seem a catalyst that works to minimize difference, that rewrites American social life within the limits of an ideology of unity and commitment that a number of discourses (ads, radio, some films, the internalization of media in everyday psychology) work to prescribe sharply: to cite one example, government, industry, and union officials will join together in asking workers to honor no-strike pledges for the war's duration. Significantly, Roosevelt will try to present himself as above the divisiveness of party politics; he will frequently prefer "Commander in Chief" to "President," and he will, by 1943, ask that "Dr. New Deal" be forgotten in favor of "Dr. Win-the-War." To be sure, as I will suggest in the next chapter, all this is not to suggest that this representation succeeds or that it is without contradiction. But many institutions of the war years will hold up commitment as a goal, and significantly, many film studios will try to meet that goal (for example, Warner Brothers, which had committed itself to anti-Fascism ever since Nazis had beaten the studio's representative in Germany to death in the 1930s).[26]

To be sure, fiction films don't always make the transition to propaganda easily. Even if the narrative *énoncé* of the classic narrative seems consonant with the representation of war as a story, classic narrative cinema would not seem to share propaganda's form of enunciation. For Christian Metz, for example, cinema classically presents itself not as *discursive* but as historical, collapsing signs of its communicational situation onto a narrative in third person, past tense.[27] Moreover, as I have argued elsewhere, even in moments of self-reflexivity where classic narrative makes reference to its conditions of production, these conditions tend to remain generalized—an appeal to abstract notions of *entertainment* or *spectacle;* in other words, the enunciation makes little mention of a here-and-now, of a possible historical situation, but instead suggests that the engendering context of art is art, not the needs of the social moment.[28] The audiences that, in the 1930s, would clap when the M.G.M. logo would flash on the screen to promise films of high quality were well realizing classic cinema's use of explicit enunciation as a way of directing attention to an entertainment machine. In other words, while even classical narrative may be more discursive, more able to admit that it is a production, and not a natural entity, than recent critiques of illusionism might lead us to expect, this discursivity may be as abstract and as antisituational as narrative that works to essentially illusionist ends. But such self-reflexivity may be historically more abstract than the war film's specific references to its origins in specific conditions of war. The war engages in a quite specific use of markers of enunciation.

Certainly, the war film frequently disavows an explicit propaganda function and remains instead within the enunciative mode of classic film. This explains the ease with which war as a subject matter can be mapped onto classic narrative. Thus, for example, many thrillers of the war years represent Nazism according to the conventions of the gangster film: the Nazis are referred to as a gang (and there's even a film called *The Hitler Gang* [1944]). A film like *All Through the Night* (1942) is stylistically close to previous Warner gangster films; there is little attempt to enunciate a war politics or to address the spectator as a spectator-in-a-war-situation. Indeed, the endurance of fixed forms is so strong that even those films that try initially to separate gangsterism and Nazism often seem to tend finally to blur the two: thus, while the opening of *All Through the Night* shows one of Gloves Donaghue's gang mocked because he suggests that Nazis can be bumped off just like other gangsters, the course of the film suggests that anti-gangster tactics are more than sufficient to deal with the Nazi threat: attacks with pistols and fists, escapes, and chases in speeding cars, infiltration—all these suffice to beat the Nazis.[29]

Nonetheless, such an encoding of the war within existing paradigms of narrative fiction may well aid the representability of the war within everyday America. Indeed, government and the film industry only seem vaguely to support any direct notion of film as propaganda. To be sure, the government recognizes an importance of the cinema (and so declares film an essential industry); in a revealing but typical event, Roosevelt will make fireside chats in the presence of his mother, Secretary of State Cordell Hull, and Gable and Lombard. The government seems to regard the cinema as useful simply as a source of buoyant emotions, and their estimation pays off financially: although only 10 percent of all war bond outlets are in movie theaters, 20 percent of all bonds sold are purchased there.

Yet we do find ways in which films try to be historically enunciative and try to reinscribe the context of a contemporary history and a group-binding function into their very textual strategies. First of all, there is an emphasis on voice-over narration: frequently, a voice (usually male) will initiate the story, giving it a sense of authority, a sense of authorship—for example, *Flight for Freedom, Casablanca, Back to Bataan* (1945). The voice will not only initiate the action to come but will also provide "documentary" information on the historical reality that has come before. Frequently, the voice will be doubled by other marks of authorship: credits to the assistance of the armed forces; an appeal to a book that inspired the scenario (for example, *Guadalcanal Diary* [1943], a film rushed into production to catch some of the book's success; *Since You Went Away* [1944], based on Margaret Wilder's epistolary novel); a use of props of authority such as maps *(Casablanca,* whose opening aural narration is combined with maps that situate Casablanca); frequent use of exhortation by characters often filmed in close-up and thus creating a sort of direct address (Jane Hilton's attack on slacker Emily Hawkins in *Since You Went Away* or Ambassador Davies' speeches about the need to work with the Russians in *Mission to Moscow* [1943]); inclusion of historical figures (not merely actors playing historical figures as with Erich von Stroheim as Rommel in *Five Graves to Cairo,* but also figures playing themselves—for example, Ambassador Davies appearing in the prologue to *Mission to Moscow);* and, as a variant on address by characters, address to the audience by media within the film *(Pillow to Post* [1945], where a shot at the beginning of the film shows a close-up of a radio with a voice-over asking what are "YOU" doing for the war effort; connected to this, we might note within the visuals of such films the embedding of posters, signs, placards, about the war effort—for example, war bond posters in the public library of *Shadow of a Doubt* [1943]). At the same time, many films will try to situate themselves in a spatial-temporal immediacy: films that make extensive use of the *gnomic* code of wartime knowledge (for example, the numerous references in war-front movies to the Brooklyn Dodgers), films based on news events (*Back to Bataan, Guadalcanal Diary, Thirty Seconds Over Tokyo* [1944], *In Our Time* [1944]). In *Wake Island,* the function of media becomes an explicit component of the narrative. Over montages of the soldiers fighting the Japanese are superimposed newspaper front pages extolling the marines' fortitude. Based on a real event that existed for home-front Americans only as media event, the film becomes a further relay in the media transmission of history.

The presence of specific propagandizing figures in the films suggests a more concerted way in which war narrative and film narrative can come together in a common ideological project: through the role of *enunciators.* Recently, Raymond Bellour has offered a way to read the embedding of enunciation in the *énoncé* by following characters who initiate narrative moves, through whom the narrative passes, who take up and convey the look of the camera.[30] Such characters are not only forces of the story but of its telling (a possibility made quite explicit in *The Ape Man* [1943], where one unidentified character mysteriously wanders through the film, advising and directing the other characters; at the end, he reveals that he is the film's screenwriter). As Bellour suggests, the enunciator is a general figure of classic narrative, a kind of inscribing and mediating relay of the spectator's desire(s), but it is possible, I think to historicize the use of enunciation and understand the ways that it can become a particularly attractive technique for the mobilization of identification toward the goal of commitment. Concretizing commitment through narratives centered on specific characters can encourage the spectator's own inscription into narrative. In the war-affirmative narrative especially, it is not so much psychological desire (as Bellour would have it) as national responsibility that drives enunciation.[31]

Philosophers of history have suggested that historical

narrative (that is, narrative claiming to represent "real" events of the past) traditionally relies on the unifying force of a "central subject," a narrative center, to hold the narrative together. Indeed, philosopher David Hull goes so far as to argue that without such a subject, fictive though its function may be, narrative can become chaotic, incoherent: "The notion of central subjects is crucial to the logical structure of historical narrative. Assuming for the moment that history could be analyzed completely into a single set of atomistic elements, there are indefinitely many ways in which these elements can be organized into historical sequence. The role of the central subject is to form the main strand around which the historical narrative is woven."[32] If, as Hull argues, any element can serve in history writing as a central subject (so that we have "history of ideas," "history of thinkers," etc.), the war period builds a representation of itself as a moment where disparate forces become interchangeable as central subjects all: Roosevelt, small-town America, the G.I., the army officers, are all ultimate and often equivalent signifiers that wartime America will tell its stories around.

Roosevelt, for example, serves as a figure of narrative inevitability; his endurance in office functions as a kind of paean to stability, the transmission of tradition, a conquest against endangering forces (both external *and* internal: Roosevelt is the Commander in Chief who can lead the country to victory while triumphing over his own illness).[33] As Jim Taylor (Bob Hope) says in *The Louisiana Purchase* (1941) when someone refers to Hoover, "You mean there were Presidents before Roosevelt?" To be sure, a representation of Roosevelt as unifying force is called on before the war: to take a famous example, historians of film have noted how *The Grapes of Wrath's* benevolent camp leader seems closely modeled on Roosevelt.[34] But the war continues and amplifies this mythology, playing on images of Rooseveltian endurance and resilience and the supposed naturalness and inevitability of the Roosevelt presidency (again, in *The Louisiana Purchase*, Jim Taylor announces that it's illegal to have Republican Presidents). Indeed, many films present Roosevelt as the ultimate enunciator—source and guarantor of narration: he is the narrative voice that opens or closes the film (or, in the case of *Flying Tigers*, that brings American soldiers in China the news that they are at war), or he functions to initiate the major narrative moves. For example, in *Mission to Moscow*, a directive from Roosevelt pulls Joseph Davis away from a fishing-camping trip with his family and leads him on the path toward becoming Ambassador to Russia. Similarly, in *The Princess O'Rourke* (1943), Roosevelt serves as the witness to the marriage of commoner Joe O'Rourke (Robert Cummings) and the princess Maria (Olivia de Havilland), a marriage that transcends class and cultural boundaries. That Joe confuses Roosevelt for one of the White House servants and tips him for his services only further underscores the image of Roosevelt as a unifier who can symbolically travel at ease through all walks of life.

Yet Roosevelt as figure seems to hover over many films while remaining just beyond full representation. Thus, for example, *Mission to Moscow* shows us Stalin and Churchill (played by Manart Kippen and Dudley Field Malone respectively) but keeps Roosevelt as a presence just offscreen, no more than a sleeve that juts into frame.[35] Roosevelt is here a godly figure, not representable but merely alluded to—a mediation between earthly and higher meanings (as a character in *Action in the North Atlantic* [1943] says, "I believe in God, President Roosevelt, and the Brooklyn Dodgers").

If Roosevelt is frequently at the limit of representability—an implied but unviewed presence—war narrative will increasingly discover other central subjects that it can represent: most especially, against the authority of commanders, there will evolve a mythology of the strength of the ordinary person, the average American (a mythology summed up in the title of one film, *Joe Smith, American* [1942]). Indeed, Roosevelt himself will try to participate in such a mythology by a deliberate cultivation of an image of unassuming modesty, unpretentiousness: not for nothing are his addresses to the people called "fireside *chats.*" But, simultaneously, with the Roosevelt image, there will be an increasing investment in the Willys and Joes (Bill Mauldin's famous cartoon characters) of the war, an image that sings the ostensible quiet virtues of everyday people, people who are special because they are typical. Indeed, the discourse will be so prevalent that the liberal politician Henry Wallace will eventually build his political campaign around the concept of the "people's century." The representation of the war fighter (both on the battlefront and on the home front) will often be mapped onto an already extant discourse of populism: thus, for example, in *All Through the Night*, various gangs and toughs of the city come together to fight Nazis infiltrators; when one of the toughs is asked who broke up the Nazi meeting, he gleefully replies, "The people did!"

The discourse of the common person has several important contributions to make to the narrativization of the war affirmation. First of all, it acts as a continuation of the scapegoating and excluding function so central to the narrative of commitment and unity. According to one version of this representation, not everyone in America is an average American, and it is in this "fact" that potential problems lie, as the title of one film, *The War Against Mrs. Hadley* (1942), suggests. Here again, the problem is not the nominal enemy—the countries that America is fighting against—but the aberrant internal force (in this case, a snobbish, stubborn, selfish Republican) that slows up America's constitution into a fighting machine that is most efficient when all its parts are average and subservient. Similarly, Carolyn Ware on the last page of her book *The Consumer Goes to War* will declare that "we are not fighting this war for the captains of industry, for the movie stars, for the big league baseball players, or the great cotton planters. We are fighting the war for John Q. Citizen and his wife and children."[36] But such a representation runs the risk of splitting the war constituency too sharply; for example, Bill Mauldin's cartoons will be surrounded by a debate over their potential danger to soldier morale.[37] In other words, by making too much criticism of the ways that some Americans don't match the image of the average—an image that is quite political (for example, to be average, it is best to be Democrat)—the war affirmation runs the risk of offending or excluding figures who might be necessary to the war effort.

An alternate tactic, then will be the rewriting of initially nonaverage citizens as finally average after all, or the discovery that through the very fact of their nonaverageness, certain figures can make their best efforts. Here, narratives can follow several strategies: on the one hand, a discovery of a basic humility in the heart of people who initially seemed arrogant, or, on the other hand, a deliberate humbling, by external forces, of pretentious or vain people (as happens in *The War Against Mrs. Hadley*). For example, a booklet from the Office of War Information will present rationing not as hardship, but as a welcome equalizer of social difference: "The Colonel's lady and Judy O'Grady become sisters under the ration. A large income puts no more sugar coupons in the ration book than does the factory worker wage."[38]

The emphasis on the importance of the average also further contributes to the possibility of narrative as the endless retelling of a single story. That is, by equalizing people under a banner of "averageness," narrative creates a large pool of narrative raw material to draw from: everyone's story can be a war story, everyone has something to contribute. Thus, for example, one representation will argue the importance of the elderly (as in the film *The Pied Piper* [1942], where Mr. Howard [Monty Woolley] rescues children from the Nazis),[39] while another will emphasize the necessary role of children (and even pets as in *Blondie for Victory* [1942], where Baby Dumpling and the dog, Daisy, go around the neighborhood soliciting money for the war effort). Such a discourse installs heroism everywhere, and makes everyone part of a vast story; in the words of the O.W.I.'s *Government Information Manual for the Motion Picture Industry:* "It is relatively easy to glorify the Air Corps, the Parachute Corps, or the Tank Corps. More difficult, but just as necessary, is the dramatization of the humble Infantryman, the mud-slogger whose lot is the grim combination of danger and discomfort."

The mediation of all Americans by a shared quality of averageness thus paradoxically allows the possibility of hierarchy and a division of labor in the narrative: if everyone becomes important through a particular talent, it becomes necessary to maintain social stratifications while claiming that these stratifications make no value judgment on specific roles. Thus, in an airplane like *Air Force's* Mary Ann, each soldier has an assigned role; inadequacy at one point will rebound on the operation of the whole.[40] The notion of equivalence also allows for the possibility of exchange between different points in the overall process: exchange of knowledge (thus, in the film *Fighting Seabees* [1944], Wedge Donovan [John Wayne] learns the importance of fighting according to the manuals while his superiors learn the importance of a noncivilian engineering corps) but also exchange of function (in the film *Action in the North Atlantic,* second-in-command Joe Rossi [Humphrey Bogart] can easily take over the ship when the skipper is wounded). Carolyn Ware's *The Consumer Goes to War* sums up this exchange in a chapter on "Democracy at Home":

> Under stress of war, we are rediscovering our communities as places in which to live. For many of us, they had become mere places where we hung our hats. Our neighbors were "those people" named Jones or Spinelli, whom we might greet on the street . . . but whose lives and ours were almost wholly unconnected. Now we find that we must depend on the Spinellis to look out for our children in case of emergency . . . We join with Mr. Spinelli, Mr. Jones and two others to drive to work . . . In short, we are rearranging our lives in terms of people and things right here at home. In this way we are discovering resources in our community of which we had never known . . . The garage repairman has been drafted—but Mrs. Smith's Johnnie is really a whiz at tinkering with a car. Mrs. Costa taught home economics before she was married and is willing to conduct a study group on how to get the most for your clothes money . . . A man who works at the local munitions plant can answer Susie's question, "Just how *does* the bacon fat that we save and take to the butcher shop help make bombs?" (pp. 187–89)

There is here, of course, another important narrative construction for the forties: the notion of America as a melting pot where all groups can find a welcome place; the combat-team film will provide the strongest representation of this mythology.

And yet the very sort of virulence that will frequently strike out against Wallace's "people's century" suggests an ideological limit to the discourse of commonality: it can veer dangerously close to an American fear of working-class communism, the mythology of a populism that disavows any notion of hierarchy. The association of populism and a working class threat intensifies after the war; thus, in *Red Treason in Hollywood,* Myron Fagan explains, "Some of you who read this may not know who Henry Wallace is. Well, for your information, Henry is a Soviet farmer who . . . runs around the country crooning a torch song for Joe Stalin."[41] Yet even during the war, a widespread discourse will draw a line between "community" and "communism" (and, as Katherine Archibald notes, it will frequently be workers themselves who most virulently draw this line).[42] Even a pro-Soviet film like *Mission to Moscow* will emphasize "special" Russians: the politicians, the politician's wife who is participating in war production, the young woman who is part of a crack troop of expert paratroopers. Indeed, one way that narrative can represent communality while disavowing the working class is through an emphasis on figures who are ordinary and yet somehow special, distinguished by a potential forward mobility that according to the narrative has nothing to do with class privilege; significantly, as Richard Polenberg has noted, a common sociological discourse of the forties distinguishes Americans by *status,* frequently a quantitative evaluation that looks only at income and not position in the system of production.[43] In other words, while acknowledging inequalities, the concept of status allows for a mythology of potential social mobility.

Frequently, narratives of the forties will even emphasize how figures rise in the ranks not because of unique qualities but out of pure chance: for example, a number of films about the home front or not about war at all show social ascension to be a matter of being in the right place at the right time (for example, *Rebecca* [1940], *In Our Time* [1944], *Hail the Conquering Hero* [1944]; or films about sudden inheritance like *Brewster's Millions* [1945], while a number of films about the military show men becoming heroes without having intended to (for example, *Caught in the Draft* [1941]; *Buck Privates* [1941]; *Sahara* [1943], where a whole troop of German soldiers surrender, without being asked, to two Allied soldiers; and, as a kind of extreme example, *Up in Arms* [1944], where Danny Weems [Danny Kaye] captures a whole regiment of Japanese soldiers through the accident of nearsightedness). Such a representation of unintended but lucky individualism allows a certain disavowal of human agency and collectivity. That is, it suggests that no special or necessarily advanced talents make one into a hero or a heroine. For example, in the film *In Our Time*, Jennifer Whittredge (Ida Lupino) is a governess who marries into the Polish aristocracy and leads the aristocrats and workers alike in a fight against the Nazis: if *In Our Time* attacks the cowardice and treachery and self-interest of certain members of the aristocracy (but disavows the class nature of that attack by also applauding good and benevolent aristocrats), the film will equally attack the workers who are represented (without exception) as backward peasants unable to understand the blessings of farming by machine.

One narrative figure that especially reconciles commonality and special qualities is the "second-in-command," most frequently a sergeant. The second-in-command is here a narrative construction, a mythology, rather than any sort of reference to actual seconds-in-command; indeed, although the sergeant is the most common form, the sergeant as narrative figure can be changed into some other figure as long as the qualities of simultaneous earthiness, averageness, special powers, and authority are maintained.[44] The sergeant works in such representation because of his mediating role; more than a private, he stands above the crowd, but less than a commissioned officer, he shares the common soldiers' distrust of, and run-ins with, authority. The sergeant is a seemingly endlessly reusable figure: indeed, one film's title is *The Immortal Sergeant* (1943); in *Sahara*, one character (not a sergeant) declares that "a sergeant is the same in every language." The sergeant also functions as a sign of a possible elevation in the ranks; where only special training can create a commissioned officer, promotion to the rank of sergeant comes in the heat of battle, the result of a chance necessity. At the same time, the sergeant or the second-in-command can also rise in the ranks: films will simultaneously note the uniqueness of officers but then suggest that, if need be, anyone can lead (thus, in films like *Action in the North Atlantic* or *Desperate Journey*, seconds-in-command easily assume command when their officers are killed or wounded).

Finally, the second-in-command figure allows a replaying of scapegoating and the threat of internal violence. On the one hand, even in cases where the sergeant is held up as an object of mockery (especially in comedies of camp life), the mocking functions to bring the sergeant down to earth. He is mocked not for his power but for the fact that, in his intermediate position, nothing really sustains his power except his place in the hierarchy. Thus, for example, in *Hillbilly Blitzkrieg*, (1943) it is the sergeant who is blamed when uncooperative soldiers make a mess of his uniform. A sergeant is what he is because the system is necessarily what it is. In the words of a dialogue in *Wake Island:* "Trouble with that guy [the sergeant] is that he ain't got no finer instincts." "Well, that's how you get to be a sergeant. The dumber them guys are, the more stripes they give 'em."

On the other hand, the second-in-command figure is frequently pitted, as good figure, against higher officers who don't know what the war is about and who are to be blamed for military snafus. Thus, the highly popular novel *A Bell for Adano*, by John Hersey, represents the problems of war as residing ultimately not in battles but in the sheer incompetence of generals. Although the novel's hero is nominally a major (that is, a commissioned officer), he is presented as an ordinary, unassuming figure—heroic precisely because he is nothing special (back home, the novel emphasizes, Major Joppolo was simply a civil servant, one of the period's symbols for the anonymous but efficient and therefore laudable American). As the novel's forward declares emphatically, "I beg you yet to know this man Joppolo well. We have need of him. He is our future in the world. Neither the eloquence of Churchill nor the humaneness of Roosevelt, no Charter, no Four Freedoms or fourteen points . . . none of these things can guarantee anything. Only men can guarantee, only the behaviour of men under pressure, only our Joppolos."

Significantly, although it is set in the war, no battles occur in *A Bell for Adano;* war exists only as a faint rumor, an easily dispensed with nuisance (as when the citizens of Adano mistakenly believe poison gas has been dropped on their village, and Joppolo has to assuage their fears by going out into the streets and sniffing around). The de-emphasis on war allows a scapegoating reemphasis on the danger of bureaucracy, officialdom, and authority, all condensed here around the figure of "General Marvin" (based on Patton). In Hersey's words: "I don't know how much you know about General Marvin. Probably you just know what has been in the Sunday supplements. Probably you think of him as one of the heroes of the invasion; the genial, pipe-smoking, history-quoting, snappy-looking, map-carrying, adjective-defying divisional commander. . . . You couldn't be blamed for having this picture. You can't get the truth except from the boys who come home and finally limp out of the hospitals and even then the truth is bent by their anger. But I can tell you perfectly calmly that General Marvin showed himself during the invasion to be a bad man, something worse than what our troops were trying to throw out."

Such critique of authority suggests that despite certain references to an all-pervasive unity, to an image of complete and unambiguous reciprocity and community, the discourse of war commitment is based as much on disunity with that which is constituted as different as on unity with that which is constituted as the same. Narrative here achieves a kind of generalizing power in which opposition is not necessarily a specific warring enemy but, rather, anything that can be represented as a resistant other: external forces but also internal ones. Where external others can be managed by violence, by transformation (for example, the Nazi secretary in *Berlin Correspondent* or the Vichy official in *Casablanca* who eventually come over to the Allied cause and help freedom fighters escape the Nazis), or by a discovery of qualities of the same beneath the exterior otherness (as with the Nazi general in *The Pied Piper* who maintains his Nazi evil but simultaneously asks the British gentleman to make sure his niece gets to the safety of the United States), in contrast, the internal other is combated through appreciably different means. Again, fitting Sartre's discussion of the group as an internalization of external threats, one way the war group holds itself together is by admitting threat and then, through a kind of dialectical incorporation, making that threat a source of higher strength. Thus, if one internal danger is the psychological one of cowardice, rather than simply disavowing that cowardice, a strong narrative strategy will see cowardice as something that can be rewritten and viewed in a positive light: in *Action in the North Atlantic,* Joe Rossi (Humphrey Bogart) responds to a lower officer's admission of fear with the declaration "Let me tell you something about my iron nerve, son. It's made of rubber just like everybody else's so it'll stretch when you need it to. . . . I always figured if you weren't scared, there was nothing to be brave about." Such a moment demonstrates a generalizing quality of wartime representation—its enveloping ability to take any element, even one that would seem oppositional or resistant, and represent it in terms of an overall master plot, to transcode it in a discourse of affirmation.

One pattern of such affirmation over the forces of internal resistance revolves around what we might call the "conversion narrative." If, as the war discourse will often argue, an individual gets out of place because he/she has internalized incorrect beliefs and values, then a potent narrative recovery from the violence of this bad internalization will be one in which an individual converts to a new and proper set of values and beliefs.[45] Conversion underlies a large number of wartime films: for example, *Mr. Lucky* (1943), *China Girl, Flying Tigers, For Me and My Gal* (1942), *Casablanca, Air Force,* and, with a specifically religious dimension, *Sergeant York* (1941). The conversion may be slow or fast (and the latter case gives the narrative the advantage of a certain religious aura, as in the literal case of *Sergeant York,* but also the disadvantage of seeming too sudden, "unrealistic"), but in either case, conversion is usually total, a conversion not only of mind but also of body. For example, Alvin York stops his existential brooding and becomes a man of action. As such, conversion is very close to what Sartre at the same historical moment (in *Being and Nothingness,* 1943) will define as the *project,* an individual's commitment to and engagement in a being-in-the-world, a commitment that makes every action (no matter how minute) significant.[46] Indeed, the war will so demand an engagement on the part of Americans that it will virtually write a grammar of acceptable and unacceptable human actions; discourse will argue that nothing that an individual does is without significance for or against dominant war-affirming practices of everyday life. Conversion must be complete, total, an all-consuming adoption of a prescribed way of being. Thus, *Casablanca* can end in fog, its next scene unshown, since the rest of the story seems already written; Rick has made his choice.

Further, as a kind of narrative overdetermination, the conversion plot suggests immediate rewards for conversion: the winning of respect *(Air Force)*, the thrill of accomplishment, love *(For Me and My Gal,* where slacker Harry Palmer [Gene Kelly] redeems himself in the eyes of Jo Hayden [Judy Garland] by performing heroic deeds), the conquest of guilt *(Flying Tigers),* and the nomination to the realm of an elect group. All these motives come together in *Flying Tigers,* which, in addition, amplifies the auratic nature of conversion by providing it with a special imagery: the film will constantly show close-ups of Japanese fliers bleeding when they're hit (to emphasize the finality of the American victory over them) but will show no American blood until Woody Jason is fatally wounded in the sacrifice mission that he intends as atonement for his previous egoism and disinterest in the community; the blood here suggests the enormity of Jason's sacrifice— the irreversibility, the complete offer not only of spirit, but also of body, to the war effort.

The external violence in representations of the war front finds a parallel moral and emotional violence in narratives about the home front which read that front as a similar site for a similar story of a disruptive violence counteracted by a counterattack. Between the two spheres, narrative will come up with a series of transformations, a set of rules of rewriting that transform the interests of home front into battlefront and vice versa. Thus, government, media, and private citizens together will come up with a whole "science" of home front "fighting," a grid of exchange and transformation for connecting the two fronts so that, for example, so much kitchen fat lost in the home will be equivalent to so many fewer cannon shells for the boys overseas. At the broadest level, the two fronts will be represented as one; the war is equally everywhere, as Carolyn Ware, for example, declares unambiguously in *The Consumer Goes to War:* "No one of us can escape his wartime duty. We must be at our battle stations twenty-four hours a day. . . . This is a battle which each of us fights. . . . We cannot rely on the generals. . . . On the consumer front, initiative lies in our hands—we, the privates of the civilian army back home" (p. 2).

Indeed, the home front literally becomes a war zone in films about infiltration (for example, *All Through the Night*), invasion *(Northern Pursuit* [1943]), or other forms of intrusion (as in *Mrs. Miniver* [1942], where one sequence involves the capture of a downed German flier). Through the mediation of shared concern, the home front becomes another version of the war: as the wife in *Since You Went Away* says of war, it is "the greatest adventure we ever had even though we had it separately"). Increasingly, this representation of the home front will become ever more detailed, finding no action without direct linkage to, and consequence for, the war effort. For example clothing conservation is represented as "Outfitting the Outfit", meal management as "Manoeuvres with Meat." In one of the most extreme confluences of narrative structure and a specific content, the discourse will even suggest a "natural" identity of war and a *market* economy: thus, an ad by the Bowery Savings Bank in support of the Seventh War Bond Drive (1945) shows a dictionary entry for the verb "invest": "Invest—to lay out money or capital with the view of obtaining an income. Invest—to lay siege, to attack." Here, at the pivotal (although publicly obscured) moment of the concretization of the modern military-industrial complex, war is not merely a boost to a capitalist economy but the very form of that economy. Such a transcoding can then easily lead to the plea for the acceptance of all the twists and turns of capitalism: thus, for Carolyn Ware in *The Consumer Goes to War,* "Prices which move up and down are . . . a sort of crude rationing arrangement" (p. 47). What such moments demonstrate is something very important for historical analyses of the war effort: namely, that the question to analyze is not so much whether there should have been an effort to fight, but, quite differently, what are the particular consequences—socially, ideologically, politically, psychically—of the *particular ways* dominant discourse chose to figure the fighting of the war.

Beyond a representation of external violence, then, the home-front narrative is also a representation of internal unities and their threatening disunities. Many home-front narratives revolve around the threats of individuals (especially slackers of one sort or another) who refuse to do their part in the war effort. Like the combat stories, the narratives of the home-front will bring to bear a number of different tactics (which can blur into one another) to resolve this threat, or to put it in its proper place. First, the narratives can suggest an outright disciplining of aberration; in a virtually Foucauldian sense, the discourse of war effort encourages a microphysics of power in which citizen spies on citizen, where everyone lives under the scrutiny of a relentless look. In a first stage, such scrutiny leads to condemnation and harsh criticism of others (note, for example, the scene in the film, *Since You Went Away* where Jane Hilton [Jennifer Jones] severly castigates Emily Hawkins [Agnes Moorehead] for being a slacker). Here, it becomes everyone's duty to see everyone else as a potential Other; the drive toward community and reciprocity is matched by an equally strong drive toward separation and suspicion. Thus, Carolyn Ware, in *The Consumer Goes to War*, suggests that shoppers clock the prices of their neighborhood markets, and she triumphantly reports on a case in which "after the announcement of tire rationing, a New York newspaper posted a cameraman in front of a delicatessen in the early morning and printed a photographic record of ten separate trucks that drew up to deliver milk at the store" (p. 135).

In a second move, however, discipline is internalized by the individual as a self-analyzing interrogation—the self turned into an-other for one's own critical gaze (in *Since You went Away*, Ann Hilton [Claudette Colbert] wonders if she herself is doing enough for the war effort). The war-affirmative discourse of the period seems, then, to conform closely to Foucault's sense of modern (postfeudal and postroyal) power as something that gains in effectivity the further it moves away from a central power source; against, say, Bruce Catton or John Morton Blum, who see the absence of an articulated domestic policy as a failure of wartime power,[47] I would suggest that it is in such an absence that power can come closest to achieving its greatest success, eschewing authoritative fiat for a dispersive process in which the individual becomes a sort of relay for, and embodiment of, an authorless authority. In *Punch In, Susie!*, Nell Giles notes how in the home front this internalized discipline takes on an aura of naturalness, omnipresence, and automaticness: "Since spoilage helps the Axis, everybody tries to let no mistakes get by. The other day, a girl told me she felt like a murderer every time she made a mistake."[48]

Indeed, much of the war discourse will appear not so much as direct command but as rhetorical question, an interrogation that the individual is supposed to internalize and make his/her own. For example, the O.W.I.'s *Manual for the Motion Picture Industry* suggests that instead of instructing, films can raise questions: films should lead people to internalize such questions as: "Does your home follow the instructions of the air raid warden? . . . Do you conserve on food, clothing, transportation, and health in order to help soldiers? . . . Do you salvage essential materials? . . . Do you refuse to spread rumors?" Again, this self-discipline extends itself into the little activities, the smallest events of everyday life; nothing is to be free of surveillance. For example, the O.W.I. in its booklet *Conservation of Food in the Home* will not merely make suggestions as to what one should eat, but also *how:* "An extravagant set of table manners is another cause of waste of food—not squeezing grapefruit for the last bit of juice, not tipping soup bowls for the last drop of soup, not picking up chops and chicken bones in our fingers, etc." Even the body itself becomes a target of self-discipline. Thus, an ad about faulty eyesight commands one to "Suppress that Saboteur in Your Eye."

In this respect, probably no subject is as much a site for discursive representation according to these parameters as the role of women in the war effort. If, as John Berger has suggested, ideology can create a particular divided subjectivity for women— "A woman must continually watch herself . . . from earliest childhood she has been taught and persuaded to survey herself continually"[49]—the war moment especially exploits feminine guilt and splits women between activity and a self-scrutinizing analysis of their activity. Significantly, the war discourse most frequently takes as its target here a previous representation of femininity: it is precisely representations of femininity as nonutility, as a beauty-for-beauty's-sake, as the display of seductive charms, that the war discourse seeks to transform.[50] Stereotypical femininity becomes the target of both external and internal scrutiny. External: as Katherine Archibald notes in her postwar reflection on the war years, *Wartime Shipyard*, "The women themselves formed an undeputized but effective agency for enforcement of the rules of rude and graceless dress . . . Women guards stalked vigilantly looking for the coy curl unconfined by a bandana, the bejeweled hand, and the revealing sweater" (pp. 21–22). Internal: for Howard Kitching in *Sex Problems of the Returned Vet,* "[The married woman whose husband is away] must remember that she is constantly watched and liable to be reported on . . . Probably the best thing for her is to go to occasional parties, dances, community sings, and so on, but never to permit herself to be alone with a man."[51]

In Archie Satterfield's retrospective summation, "[Wives] were usually watched with the same intensity the FBI watched suspected subversives" *(The Home Front,* p. 51). A number of strategies come together here to represent femininity as something requiring a necessary reworking. First, the discourse will insist on the inadequacies of an older feminine model: thus, according to the war discourse, such a model is corrupted by selfish narcissism ("Twelve workers who have quit worrying about 'seams in stockings' are now concentrating on the seams in the side of a Liberty Ship"),[52] by an irrelevancy to the "real" issues (as with the wife in *Pride of the Marines* [1945] who ignores the announcement of the Pearl Harbor attack because she is worried to get dinner on the table), and even by a fundamental ability to achieve its own (narcissistic) goals. The new discourse will construct a new representation of femininity that is simultaneously a complete transformation of the older model into something ostensibly more appropriate to the wartime age *and* a simple realization and perfection of the older model.

On the one hand, discourse will imply that war participation is simply an addition onto the older femininity; thus, in *Calling All Women,* Keith Ayling will end each discussion of a job that women can do with a description of the prettiness of the uniform for that job.[53] On the other hand, the discourse suggests that it is war service that will bring out the beauty and allure of women: thus, according to Nell Giles in *Punch In, Susie!,* "If your idea of a factory girl is a thin little creature who looks downtrodden and underfed, you're way off the beam, as my chums say. A factory girl in real life looks very much like Brenda Marshall, Anne Shirley, or Betty Grable" (p. 123). The film *This Gun for Hire* (1942) will even come up with the solution of seeing beauty as an expedient weapon in the war; even though her ultimate goal is to marry and settle down, the nightclub performer (Veronica Lake) agrees to continue her club spectacle in order to seduce a possible traitor and discover his secrets. The new femininity is complete and profound where the older model relied on vain, superficial, inefficient substitutes and trickeries. Again to quote Nell Giles, "I believe it is a mistake to think it impossible to be a gentlewoman on a factory bench. Women are changing, yes, but why can't a feminine CHARACTER be substituted for a FEMININE hat? . . . If we are to have less perfume and lipstick and nail polish and pink underwear, then let us have more daintiness and good grooming and gentleness and womanly character" (pp. 69–70).

Similarly, the factory is not represented in conflict with household work, but as a complement, even as its best realization: in the words of the O.W.I.'s *Women's Radio War Program Guide* (April 1944), "After months of training, no WAC will be guilty of the housewifely crime of dusty corners or messy bureau drawers or closets." And in yet another representational tactic, war work for women will be represented as symbolically exchangeable with other forms of work. On the one hand, everything a woman does influences the rest of the war effort—in the narrative of one ad:

A tired Marine lay prone on the ground. . . . A body of Japs, spearhead of an advance, moved cautiously along a trail. One Marine couldn't stop them by himself—not when he had just a single bullet left. But that was Mary Jane's bullet. It must have had a spell on it. The Marine drew a bead on the lead Jap. He squeezed the trigger. . . . He didn't miss. The Japs, confused, bewildered, leaderless . . . got out of there . . . and got out of there FAST. Later, that whole island was swept clear of Nipponese, but it would have been a far more costly fight if a single Marine with a single bullet hadn't stopped the first Japanese advance.[54]

On the other hand, war work will allow for an exchange of *understanding*; one kind of war discourse will establish a hierarchy of male activity and female activity, but will promise women a glimpse into the male realm through empathy and identification: thus, in the words of Fred Crawford, head of the National Association of Merchants, "[Women will] be better wives and homemakers [through factory work]: they'll know how tired a man is when he come home."[55] Women may not be able to enter into the male realm but they will at least have what the moment believes is the glory of knowing what the male realm is like.[56]

At the beginnning of the 1943 film *Flight for Freedom*, over images of aircraft carrier planes readying for takeoff, a male narrator announces that the success of the mission "depends on the wisdom and might of our Navy and on the spirited career of a pretty girl." The narration here condenses various aspects of war representation: the equivalence of different activities (the navy *and* the pretty girl) with a simultaneous emphasis on their different functions within that equivalence (the navy has wisdom and might while "girls" have prettiness and spirit), and the rewriting of an older feminine representation (Tony Carter [Rosalind Russell] accomplishes what she does in spite of, not because of, her prettiness). At the same time, as is suggested in the last sequence— where Tony deliberately crashes her plane in the Pacific to give the U.S. Navy the alibi of a search for her that will actually allow them to spy on Japanese military buildups—the war need not interfere with prettiness: even as she faints from oxygen loss as she pushes her plane upward in preparation for her crash dive, Tony conforms to a stereotypical image of (Hollywood) beauty. And yet "prettiness" is raised by the narrative as an issue: Tony's mission is almost thwarted because some men only treat her as an object of beauty. Thus, her boyfriend (Fred MacMurray) tries continually to remind Tony of their romantic involvement and so dissuade her from going on the mission alone. The narrative development—Tony sneaking off before her boyfriend is awake so that he won't endanger her mission—suggests that in certain cases traditional representations of woman as desiring or desired figure must undergo a stoic renunciation, a harsh pragmatism.

"From now on, virtually everything is going to be scarce" (Carolyn Ware, *The Consumer Goes to War*, p. 5). If "woman" is stereotypically a site and source of desire, war representation frequently pictures desire as a scarcity, simultaneously a precious and irrelevant commodity. On the one hand, women must maintain love for the men overseas but, on the other hand, love must not turn into an excess that would disrupt the war venture: as the bride of one day in *Action in the North Atlantic* says as she pushes her husband (Humphrey Bogart) out the door and back to his ship, "We can't sit around holding hands with all that going on." Desire, then, becomes one of the sources of narrative violence, one of the things to battle against. In a first discursive strategy, sexuality will be represented as something that most appropriately belongs to the other side, to the enemy. Thus, a War Production Board radio script presents Germany as a site of sexual manipulation:

GOEBBELS: The Nazi movement is a masculine movement. When we eliminate women from public life, it is not because we want to dispense with them, but rather because we want to give them back their essential function.
NARRATOR: Yes, the Nazis cheered. Women are to be broodmares.[57]

In a second move, desire will be represented as the province of romantic *young* women who haven't yet learned the importance of denial: for example, the misty-eyed adulation of Jane Hilton for her uncle Tony as compared with her mother's careful and thought-out platonic attitude in the film *Since You Went Away*. In a third move, desire is admitted but as something to be held in abeyance; *Since You Went Away*, for example, alternates scenes of Ann Hilton bearing up in public but admitting her love in private (in the letters to her husband), and, by a kind of narrative closure, the film rewards her patience by having her husband rescued at

the end of the film after being listed as "Missing in Action." In a
fourth move, as in *This Gun for Hire*, feminine desire is used as a
trick to seduce Axis agents: the film simultaneously acknowledges
that desire is only a superficial role under which there lies something more fundamental (the drive toward domesticity) while
suggesting a way to exploit that role temporarily.

The dominant strategy, though, will be to suggest the
possibility of desire's sublimation: in home-front service, in a
concern for the minute operations of the family (for example, *Since
You Went Away* with its detailed chronicling of the minutae of
everyday life), in a certain degree of female bonding (as in the
film *Tender Comrade* [1943], attacked in the postwar period for its
alleged radical implications), and in social work. As the narrator
of the book *Since You Went Away* declares, "If all of us spent less
time immersed in the classified ads and more time trying to read
what is in the headlines, we might be waking up faster." Such
sublimation will be generally presented not as a dismal fate to be
begrudgingly accepted but, quite the contrary, as positive joy, a
source of newfound strength and a newfound delight in social
responsibility; for example, Nell Giles declares, "I've enjoyed
working with my hands when for so long my hands have been
something to manicure and punch a typewriter with. I want to be
a more ESSENTIAL woman after this" *(Punch In, Susie!*, p. 141).

Yet such sublimation is not exclusively reserved for
women. Films of the war front suggest that male energy try to find
its place in an economy and that it be channeled to specific affirmative ends. Male and female sublimation come together in a film-
like *Prisoner of Japan* (1942). Having been a traitor to America but
having then fallen in love with an American nurse, the hero agrees
with the nurse to order a U.S. bombing of the island they're on—
which is also the island base for a Japanese strike force. In this act
of committed self-sacrifice and suicide, the man and woman admit
their newfound love but simultaneously admit the need to turn
that love into a force for a higher good. As the bombs fall on them,
they reach out to each other, and as their fingers touch, the island
explodes and the film ends with a stirring montage of U.S. planes
and ships. Virtually Freudian, the editing—from loving touch to

explosion to weapons on the march—can suggest war as a necessary answer to a potentially free-floating energy.

Indeed, the discourse on sublimation contributes to a larger, frequently non-sex-differentiated discourse of war not merely as the triumph *over* scarcity but as a kind of welcomed triumph *of* scarcity. Here, the shortages of the war will be represented as a positive good, a force that will help Americans cast off a modern decadence and rediscover their fundamental resourcefulness, a basic "know-how." For Carolyn Ware, for example,

> The war calls directly for a reversal of this attitude [of conspicuous consumption]. . . . In making this shift, we may remember that our early American ancestors cherished the ideal of "plain living and high thinking." To them, conspicuous consumption represented the aristocratic society from which they had fled in order to build a more equal way of life. The Puritans despised gaudy living, both because it represented aristocratic pretense and because it wasted the goods which God expected men to use with frugality and care. . . . It should not be hard for us to recreate the appreciation of simplicity which was a source of such pride to our forebears. The ideal of "the American Standard of Living" is something quite different from "keeping up with the Joneses." *(The Consumer Goes to War*, p. 221).

Similarly, an O.W.I. training booklet for women declares, "Women can stand a lot and actually they are workers by tradition. It is only in recent years, and mostly in the United States, that women have been allowed to fall into habits of extraordinary leisure" (quoted in Renov, p. 138). The war strips Americans down to their fundamental essence; it discovers their no-nonsense, direct-speaking pragmatism; thus, for Nell Giles, "Factory life has taught me to answer questions with 'YES' or 'NO.' The civilized world is too full of 'relative values.' Well, Munich had a relative value" *(Punch In, Susie!*, p. 141).

Moreover, the representation of American pragmatism will invoke a concurrent representation of the engineering power of American resourcefulness. That is, it will simultaneously suggest that Americans can survive with little, but also that an intensification of American industry will lead to victory over opposition. While it tells the story of war forcing citizens to rediscover joyfully the wonders of small-town life, war discourse will simultaneously sing the praises of American industry, of the conquest of resistant nature through advanced technology (see, for example, *Fighting Seabees* with its ode to the engineering corps.) Thus, Carolyn Ware in *The Consumer Goes to War* can declare equally that "the war is bringing neighborhood relationships back into cities" (p. 113) and that "a great many household tasks are still carried out in ways which fit the horse-and-buggy style of living rather than the age of assembly lines and mass production" (p. 111).

One way that the discourse works to mediate between these two representations is through a mythology of the American as essentially a *tinkerer*, a resourceful individual who can turn a negative scarcity into a positive abundance through instinct, common sense, craft, and a wry humor (one ad shows a sergeant at work on a stalled tank declaring, "You think this is bad? J'ever try to change a tire on a taxi in front of the Yankee Stadium after the 9th inning?")[58] As a narrative motif, tinkering provides first a nonauthoritarian individualism (any American has tinkering potential; the less book training the better; both men and women can tinker; hence, for women, there is advertised the Victory Dress, an outfit made up of scraps of worn-out clothing). Second, tinkering is represented as a way of meeting wartime needs: tinkerers never tinker just for the sake of tinkering but for the necessity of a job—for example, in *Air Force,* where marines and air force join to get the airplane *Mary Ann* back in operation; in contrast, in *Pride of the Marines* (1945), a husband who tinkers just to keep busy around the house is viewed as eccentric and foolish. Tinkering is so resourceful that it can even make use of uselessness, of nonsense, as in *All Through the Night, Dive Bomber* (1941), *Desperate Journey,* and *You'll Never Get Rich,* for example, where Americans get out of difficult situations through a deliberately misleading gobbledygook, a double-talk.

Tinkering more generally serves as a condensation of the overall narrative of the war effort, since tinkering can suggest an ability to make anything, even the most alien form, part of a single, overarching project; as a colonel in one ad says, "Those doggoned kids. Give 'em a screw-driver and a pair of pliers and they'll make anything run",[59] similarly, in the film *Sahara*, a captured German field truck is immediately rebuilt as a part of the oasis-fort. Tinkering is the figure of a discourse that knows no externality—a discourse to which nothing is uncannily other. Tinkering, then, stands as a form of synopticism, a narrative structuration that finds a place for everything within its totalizing system. Indeed, at the extreme, tinkering can take on virtually magical qualities; thus, Katherine Archibald recounts how the factory became a site for a kind of mental tinkering, a kind of continual superstition, for a merging of fact and fantasy in a culturally gripping blend: for example, "Manipulation of data on the various leaders of the warring nations, such as their birth dates and their years in power, led to a prediction that the European conflict would draw to its close at 2 P.M., September 7, 1944 [a prediction then revised to November 11]" *(Wartime Shipyard,* p. 190). Such astrology makes explicit the ways in which wartime discourse is not a discourse of referentiality but a narrative construction whose potential power lies in its resilient ability to rewrite everything within its single structure (and, as Archibald notes, the prediction had widespread belief; it was not isolated to a few superstitious quacks).

An exemplary case of the synoptic war-affirmative narrative is the 1945 film *Pride of the Marines,* and a close analysis of its narrative strategies can help specify the intensity and seeming comprehensiveness of wartime narrative.[60] *Pride of the Marines'* narrative is most fundamentally what I have called a conversion narrative; smug loner Al Schmidt (John Garfield) learns to convert to a cause after he is blinded in the war. Yet, though a promotion article in *Life* (August 6, 1945) suggested—through photographs paralleling the life of the real Al Schmidt (whom *Life* had reported on in its March 22, 1943, issue) and John Garfield—that the film be read in relation to the life of the real Schmidt, with blindness as the central issue, the sheer amount of time that passes before the screen Al even goes off to war can suggest that the real focus of the film lies elsewhere: indeed, the film implies that the real violence, the real threat to affirmative effort, is not what the war does to Al in rendering him blind, but, quite differently, what Al has too long done to himself—that is, refused commitment to any but the most egoistic and selfish of values. Indeed, other promotion campaigns downplayed or utterly ignored the blindness angle, and, as Roffman and Purdy suggest in *The Hollywood Social Problem Film*, the specific motif of blindness may also be displaced by the film's membership in a larger "genre": the "John Garfield film," which plays on narratives of Garfield as the man apart who must join humanity or be destroyed (for example, *Air Force*). The Garfield films as a whole concern less the specific problems that lead to isolation than the general quality of isolation. That much of *Pride of the Marines* take place even before Pearl Harbor suggests that commitment to the war cause is finally commitment to something much larger—an American dream in which war functions merely as an engendering cause. The film plays off of a mythology of American community, of American sociality as a sustaining, organizing totality. Some contemporary reviews even read the film not as entertainment story but as emphatic educational discourse, and they even became transmitters of the themes of this discourse. Thus, for *Senior Scholastic* (October 1, 1945), "The damaged pride of Marine Al Schmidt may be very like the uncertainties your brothers and friends will know when they return."

Schmidt's egoism and his refusal to be part of a stable community are violences both to the war effort and to an American tradition of family building and domesticity. The film's single narrative resolution—Al accepts the Navy Cross and simultaneously accepts the love of his fiancée, Ruth—suggests that the world of war and the world of the family do not merely coincide but have a necessary ideological bond and are part of the same space. It is for an assigned place within the social structure and not for energetic male adventure that, such a film argues, we are fighting the war. Indeed, Al seems rewarded not so much for heroism as for a newly discovered control over his drives and selfish ambition, for his ability to contain his energies within a space where necessity, not desire, controls action. Thus, Al's enlisting is initially treated as an act of gleeful hubris—not so much the fact that he enlists but that he enlists with selfish and purely hedonistic reasons—as he says, "I bet it will be more fun shooting Japs than bears." The scenes of Al at war, then, will first show that war is not fun: it is a grim, unglamorous but necessary responsibility where individual merges with the whole group. In many ways, war is unlike the hunt: the soldiers are stuck in place (and so are themselves targets); they must band together in a space of non-competition ("You'll have to watch that side!" "I'll watch it!"). Finally, there is no place for personal triumph (unlike an earlier scene of Al and Ruth out hunting with Ruth missing the prey and Al hitting it), and there is moreover no time for triumph (Al and Ruth end their hunting party with relaxation over a warm fire; in contrast, the war scene is one of constant alertness whose end is attack and then the dark of blindness).

With that synoptic optimism, then, in which all disturbance can be rewritten inside a smooth narrative that is always inexorably moving forward, *Pride of the Marines* suggests that the physical ailment of blindness is finally not the real problem; the problem is the way that Al reacts emotionally to that blindness as something he feels sets him apart from other people in a way that he can't control. With a deliberate reversal, the film ultimately reads Al's blindness as a positive good; rather than setting the blind person off from the world, blindness makes someone like Al all the more a part of humanity, a part that other people can work their cures (both medical and emotional) upon. Indeed, darkness forms a motif that runs through the film as something never really bothersome if one is part of a community. For example, Al and Ruth first meet on a "blind date"; moreover, during this date, Al is his usual cold self with Ruth until a blackout immerses them in darkness and allows Al to curb his (self-defensive) gruffness and talk to Ruth with kindness and concern.

Al's mistake, then, is to refuse community for so long. Belonging to a group, being part of a bond of communication and exchange, even seems to give one an inner sight that makes loss of physical sight less of a handicap; thus, the film constantly makes use of dialogues where "to see" slides toward its connotation of "to know," as when one of the veterans finishes a speech about the possibilities of the postwar world with the question "Can't you see it?" In the system of war affirmation, commitment gives one a special sight that triumphs over individual infirmities. At the level of enunciation, the film disavows the effect of blindness by simultaneously drawing a firm line between Al's point of view and the spectator's *and* by blurring those points of view in precise ways. On the one hand, the film deprives Al of sight only to strengthen the spectator's clarity of vision and clarity of knowledge; but for a very short sequence, after an operation, in which the spectator is in Al's point of view trying to spot a light, the point of view remains outside Al (and to a large extent, remains outside all the characters, since the spectator already knows the story; the film even plays on the audience's prior knowledge of Pearl Harbor). Even if Al goes blind, the spectator's sight is never troubled. Blindness, then, is here a local effect, not a general condition, and as such, it is one that allows the spectator a special power. Here the textual strategy of *Pride of the Marines* is not far from the technique of today's soap opera as described by Tania Modleski. In Modleski's suggestion, the soap opera offers the spectator a feeling of control by showing a series of actions that no one character in the story can have access to: it is in the spectator that there resides an ability to unify the segments and to see their interconnections and the consequences of any one action for any other.[61] Similarly, in *Pride of the Marines*, there is an alternation between Al in the hospital and Ruth back home doing everything she can to bring Al around. The spectator knows that Al is not alone, knows that tactics are in gear around him to save him.

Yet, in another sense, Al's point of view is taken up by and relayed through the overall enunciative point of view of the film. After the opening credits, the film begins with Al's narration ("Maybe you've heard of me . . . "), and it is possible to read the course of the film as a story from Al's point of view or, rather, from the retrospective point of view of an Al who has learned his lesson, who has learned to merge his perspective with that of the whole social moment. In this case, the sights that Al can't see are still narrated by him and filled in by the film which thereby acts as a relay for Al; for example, if Al departs for the war by telling Ruth, "I want one last look at that pretty face of yours. That's how I want to see you when I get back," the film provides a further look at that face, turning the spectator into a kind of continuation of Al's desire: Al can no longer see the "pretty face" but we can. Indeed, as a kind of final reversal, the general point of view collapses back onto Al's with the suggestion that Al will be regaining his sight. The film so promotes the power of community that it rewards Al with a final hope. The film seems to imply that the already minor problem of blindness will become even more minor by just fading away. Al had wrongly internalized his blindness as an ultimate problem and not as the minor setback that the film argues it is. As Ruth says, arguing with Al and trying to naturalize his handicap, "We'll have a family. . . . Sure, we'll have problems but every married couple does." But in a second move, the film overdetermines the notion of the emotional cure: once Al realizes he can live with his blindness, the blindness begins to disappear.

Oedipus acted (however blindly) on his desires, both sexual and political, through a hubris that put him above the circuit of social communication; his punishment was an incurable blindness coupled with an endless errancy, an exile from humankind, a social perversity (he can rest only in the company of his sister-daughter). If Oedipus then refuses what psychoanalysis calls oedipalization, in contrast, Al all too easily seems to accept the oedipal trajectory of renunciation, of acceptance of authority and community. Oedipus' story is a romance that leads to tragedy (the wandering figure finds that no place is his; in the pun of his name, he has no sure footing), whereas the war narrative can give us a romance that becomes a comedy (the wandering figure discovers that true strength comes not from an isolating superiority but rather from an acceptance of one's place, one's belonging). If Al begins as a kind of purely phallic figure, luxuriating in his own myths of power ("He'll probably end up married to his shotgun," is the way one character defines him early on), the course of *Pride of the Marines* suggests that self-interest has to give way to group interest and, indeed, that realizing one's place can only mean realizing one's place in a set of intersecting and complementary groups: the other vets, the military as a system, the family.

Here, though, the film sets up a definite hierarchy: while being fully human means belonging to the human community, it is in the building of the heterosexual couple that the ultimate sense of the community finds its basis, its reason. Thus, despite the uplifting help and encouragement that Al's foxhole buddy, Lee, gives him on the train as they head back east, Lee is only a kind of relay figure for Ruth's higher claim on Al; Lee remains in the story long enough to get Al in a car with Ruth (through a trick that Lee and Ruth have worked out together). Al is told that he is being driven by a W.A.V.E. and that, as per his request, Ruth didn't come to the train. Mission accomplished, Lee disappears from the narrative. Further, when Al talks to his Philadelphia friends, no one is bothered by his blindness but only by his decision to live with his brother in Chicago and not marry Ruth. The reference to the brother emphasizes that not any family will do; Al needs a woman—more specifically, a wife—in his life. Indeed, even as a loner, Al paid regular visits to his friends and joked warmly with their daughter; Al has a connection to sociality but not the right kind of connection and not the right kind of sociality. The narrative works, then, to move Al to the last line of the film where, in answer to a cab driver's "Where to?" Al can confidently reply, "Home." Not only does the line itself declare Al's assumption of a role but further, in that narrative rhyming that Raymond Bellour has suggested is so crucial to the coherence of classical narrative, the taking of the taxi to go home rhymes and brings to narrative closure a whole series of vehicle movements: the train that takes Al away, the train that brings him back, the car that Ruth drives him away from the station in.[62] Thus, where Ruth must choose, when Al comes home, between pretending to be a chauffeur (and so convey Al to a situation that she hopes will win him over) or being herself (and so probably alienating Al before she even has a chance to try to win him back), she first chooses trickery, a temporary deferment of the romantic bond. The end scene then fills in what was missing in the earlier scenes of conveyance: Al and Ruth together in the back of a car, the need for trickery gone, Al as the willing agent of the couple's future, his declaration of "Home" a bond on and of their hope.

To get to this end point, though, the film must encircle Al within a set of mutually confirming discourses where the personal and political come together in a unity. Throughout the film, Al thinks that he knows what is best for himself, but it is actually up to the people around him to do what is really right for him:

his landlord's wife makes him date Ruth even though he doesn't want to; his hospital buddies make him start thinking about the possibilities of a postwar world even though he doesn't want to; his colonel orders him back to Philadelphia (where Ruth is waiting) even though he doesn't want to go; Ruth will make him stay for Christmas dinner and rediscover love even though he doesn't want to. Family and public power link up and work together in a veritable conspiracy to discipline Al into his proper place; for example, the nurse, Virginia, writes to Ruth, "I've done my part [that is, to remind Al of Ruth's love]; now it's up to you." The interweaving of these different forces finds its fruition and confirmation in the end sequence as Al receives the Navy Cross. A close-up of a proud Ruth dissolves into the entrance of the Philadelphia navy shipyard: metonymically and metaphorically, the two images have an exchange value, both components of a centering ideology that brings Al into place. Moreover, the dissolve works to link up the awards ceremony and Ruth's love with the last moments of the film where Al begins to regain his sight; the use of the dissolve, rather than a cut, to move from the shipyard to outside leaves the difference between the two segments weakly punctuated and so suggests a certain current of causality between them. With the ceremony over, Al and Ruth must go somewhere; the dissolve naturalizes the narrative progression and depicts the move home as an expression of the love transmitted in the close-up of Ruth.

Yet, although *Pride of the Marines* is most obviously a narrative about Al, about the emotional violence(s) he brings to a stable system, the margins of the film reveal how the centering function of representation works to find a place from which it can treat all possible aberrations, all threats and violences directed at sociality and the closures of war-affirmative narrative. For example, if Al's narrative is one of renunciation—renunciation of solitude, renunciation of male hubris—the film will simultaneously figure the feminine realm as the site of a desire that also requires renunciation or even perhaps repression. Where the central sequence of Al at war shows a world dominated by capable men—and the sequence includes a number of close-ups of the men preparing their weapons as if to emphasize their calculating proficiency and their precise technical know-how—the sequences of the blinded Al back home in America show male control potentially decentered by the danger of a feminine principle that threatens to refuse its assigned place (and, significantly, even in the battlefront scene, there's a moment that shows the usually obedient technology bearing a potentially resistant mark of femininity; as the machine gun roars into action, one of the soldiers orders it, "Don't jam on me, *sweetheart*").

At several moments, the film suspends its central narrative of Al's recovery to concentrate centrifugally on anecdotes told by men about the dangers of women and of sexuality—anecdotes that suspend the literal progression of Al's story. For example, one soldier fearfully tells another about getting seduced on a date by a woman when she suddenly switched off the lights in her apartment; the anecdote contrasts significantly with Al's first meeting with Ruth where the blackout is unintentional and innocent and leads to romance, not seduction. In another sequence, disconnected from the narrative flow, one soldier shows another a picture of his "girl friend" with his best friend's arm around her; the implication is unstated but clear. Such anecdotes argue the dangers of a crossing of the socially defined limits of sexual difference, but they contain the danger by treating it with humor, by seeing the situations as lessons to learn from for the future, by judging their implications against the innocent comic triumph of Ruth and Al.

In *Pride of the Marines'* representation, the social system has determined places for women, and one sort of narrative violence can occur when women try to move beyond the limits of place. Sexual difference becomes the object of a reification, a hypostatizing of social positionings. This motif of sexual difference can find its condensation in an anecdote that Lee tells Al on the train taking them back to the East Coast (and, moreover, taking Al back to the city that Ruth lives in). Given the role of princess in the school play, Lee was forced to wear a girdle, and he describes the putting on of the girdle as an act of complete agony, concluding finally, "It was like sitting in a tight foxhole. Why do women insist on wearing those things?" In the narrative space of *Pride of the Marines*, sexual difference is something that necessitates derision, incomprehension, and especially a rigid drawing back to established positions. The film can only treat the blurring of boundaries either as something too ridiculous to be serious about (for example, in a "cute" scene, Al shows his landlord's daughter what it's like to shave by putting shaving cream on her face) or as something that one must rewrite within precise categories (as he "shaves" the daughter, Al reaffirms the rigidities of sexual difference— daughter: "When did you start liking girls?" Al: "When I discovered that they weren't boys"). Indeed, the film will continually suggest the traditional values of romantic desire and beauty in women (as when Al asks Virginia what she looks like) while disavowing the appropriateness of those values for the new responsibilities of women: for example, Virginia's name can suggest a kind of virginal purity, the "true" woman who helps every man but commits herself to no one man in particular and whose help is spiritual, not sexual.[63]

"Ever stop to wonder why Liberty is represented as a woman? Why not a man? Because in every age, women have held the torch of freedom so their men could have their hands free to work and fight" (*"Uncle Sam Speaks"* radio program, March 1, 1943). Not merely Virginia but Ruth too will be represented as above desire, as committed to the couple for some spiritual value that it ostensibly offers. Not merely is Ruth constantly associated with a nonromantic but succoring pragmatism—as when she and Virginia exchange letters of advice about Al—but she is linked with institutions of spirit and authority: the military and the church. In the church, for example, Ruth reads a cynical telegram from Al in which he tries to break off their engagement and she prays, "Dear Heavenly Father, he's got to come home." The film has such faith in the nonthreat of this woman that it even allows her a certain control of the narration: Ruth's voice is allowed to narrate parts of the film. Unlike, say, much postwar film, where first-person narration is often a narration of isolation where frequently one sex talks of threats from the other (for example, *Detour* with the man's narration; *East Side, West Side* [1949] with the woman's), *Pride of the Marines* goes back and forth between male and female narrations that work together in harmony (for example, when Al first goes off to war, Ruth talks about letters from Al while he talks of the battles he's been in). The film suggests that male and female enunciation can be part of a single discourse, a single ideological space, as long as aberration, violence, a truly disturbing difference, are dealt with, resolved.

The shot of Ruth's face at the film's end, then, takes its meaning as much from what it opposes as from what it itself represents. If, as I suggested earlier, one form of wartime sublimation will involve the imputation of sexuality to the Other, *Pride of the Marines* represents this process at work in its various visions and versions of femininity. War here centers on the *look* of the woman, and I intend a double sense here: the woman looks at her man—even when blinded, the male figure is still the figure of activity—but she is also to be looked at, admired for her ability to radiate a faith that glows on the surface of her face. To be sure, in *Pride of the Marines,* our look at this face is not yet Al's look, but as I've already suggested, the film implies an eventual real or symbolic merging of Al's and the spectator's look at Ruth's look. This perhaps is the ultimate sense of the war-affirmative narrative: the narrative not as a journey along a road of mystery as the prewar Nash ad would have it but, quite the contrary, narrative as a preordained journey through chaos to the stasis of a final vision, especially that of the woman waiting and of a government consecrating her wait.

In the 1943 film *Destination: Tokyo,* the forces of story and style all conspire to construct the possibilities for a surety and clarity of sight. Lorded over by a film title that speaks of *teleology*—the space of the Japanese city as goal, mission, target, destination—the film specifies that its narrativity is dominated by the figure of journey, a getting somewhere, and the course of the film suggests that this journey is visual as well as spatial, the journey to forge a coincidence of looking and that which is (to be) looked at. Actually, though, the film suggests that the ultimate destination is not Tokyo but the world back home: the final scene shows the submarine cruising into San Francisco bay after the successful completion of the mission as the captain (Cary Grant) scans the docks with his binoculars and finally spots his wife running up proudly to meet him. Seeming to confirm that suggestion of Raymond Bellour and others that "classic" American cinema revolves around a coinciding of narrative trajectory and oedipal trajectory, *Destination: Tokyo* suggests, in the heart of the war years, that war may only be a temporary detour to something more central: the reaffirmation of the couple but a reaffirmation controlled by lines of rigid and rigorous division—man as active agent and looker, and woman as faithful supporter and follower and *looked at figure*. Indeed, the energy of war can seem to work here to aid a particular, sublimated image of the couple. Through a kind of psychical displacement, the bombing raid on Tokyo bay—which even the submarine joins in by releasing its torpedoes in an orgiastic triumph of power—is readable as a releasing of pent-up energies: the men in the submarine get a chance to let out what they've been holding back until now. With this release out of the way, the film can construct a particularly spiritualized image of the couple (and as if to reiterate the image of the couple as one beyond physical need, they already have a child; this is a couple in its prime, not in the first moments of raw energy).

But just before he spots his wife, the captain sees nothing. More precisely, at his second-in-command's knowing request that the captain train his binoculars on the dock, the captain looks but declares that there's nothing to be seen. Only when told to look again does he spot his wife, and a smile breaks out on his face. For an instant, if only for an instant, the film suggests the excess and confusing nothingness of a noncoincidence of action and sight. Sight is always bounded and bordered by a sort of blindness.

Indeed, much of the narrative process of the film builds around the tensions that its sense of an ending (and of smaller, microsequential endings) will attempt to dissolve in a clear view (or an all-seeing "long perspective," as the original title for Frank Kermode's *The Sense of an Ending* would have it). The narrative problem of *Destination: Tokyo* is to build up sight, to make it see something. Crammed into the tight space of a submarine that is voyaging to a secret rendezvous point where sealed orders about a second, secret rendezvous point are to be opened, the sailors have little to see. In a claustrophobia that is only too evident, all too visible, the crew members look elsewhere: into the metaphoric sight of dreams, memories (for example, the captain's inspiring memory-image of his young boy in the barber's chair looking up proudly at his submarine commander father), fantasies (for example, the imaginary flashback—signaled as such—of the aptly named Wolf [John Garfield] as San Francisco "Don Juan"). Until the moment that the submarine arrives in Tokyo bay to set up the clandestine observation post whose accuracy in the sighting of sites will allow for the visually spectacular bombing by the U.S. Air Force, the film plays on oversight, mis-sight, nonsight, that will progressively be converted into clear sight and insight. For example, there is the wet-behind-the-ears kid (Robert Hutton) whose first action as officer of the watch will be to mistake a seagull for the attack of a Japanese plane but who will then redeem himself through the clarity of another action—the defusing of a bomb lodged in the frame of the sub. The final sight on the dock, then, is the film's self-reward for a whole pattern of sensory deprivation.

What's at stake, then, in the last scene is the whole apparatus of cinema as machine of the war effort. In Raymond Bellour's suggestion, the oedipal trajectory is also a social trajectory that maps interpersonal relations onto the relations of people to property, and of people to a socius, a nation, a national mission.[64] For *Destination: Tokyo*, to view the woman is to close the narrative and to close the mission—indeed, to affirm the possibility of the mission's ability to be narrated and its closure. Such an ending would seem to confirm the narrative ability of the classic form—its power to work over difference and to transcend that difference through the finality of a sensible ending. And yet, in this moment of war, the ending can seem fragile, incomplete, riddled still by a disturbing difference. The binoculars that for a moment don't see at the end of *Destination: Tokyo* can imply that nothing necessarily guarantees the right ending, the proper sight: no ultimate logic necessitates that a narrative end in affirmation or even end at all. In the war moment, for example, there's the "Dear John" fear that the woman won't show up—won't show her devotion to "her man," won't be there to be seen. More generally, we might suggest that narrative itself—as a force that tries to rewrite tension within the limits of a unitary space—is inherently open to contradiction: the sense of an ending implies that order is inevitable, but the very need to institute that order through force (the tie of the ending to the figure of apocalypse, in Frank Kermode's suggestion) implies that endings are not inevitable but need to be constructed. But this also implies the limits of any specific form of narrativity. In particular, while the physiognomy of war-affirmative narrative suggests a narrative that is highly organized, highly logical, highly coherent, that organization, logic, and coherence all have a historical relativity and vulnerability. It is these limits on the war narrative that the next chapter will set out to analyze.

Chapter Three

Narrative Limits:
The Fiction of War and the War of Fictions

In *Uncertain Glory* (1944), the narrative line around its central figure, the condemned French murderer Jean Picard (Errol Flynn), comes continually undone. Indeed, from the begininning of the film, Jean's story has been caught up in a certain imbalance. Destined for the guillotine, Jean suddenly finds himself freed by the lucky intervention of an Allied bombing raid that destroys the prison he is in. Jean is allowed a second chance, a new start.

But the story he will now begin—the narrative he will engage in—quickly becomes one in which personal desire and the ability or willingness of external realities to meet this desire move apart. Certainly, Jean begins his new life as an escapee with a strong gesture promising a directness of narrative development: seducing another crook's girlfriend, Jean plans an escape with her. Jean confidently takes the train on a direct line for Spain but suddenly finds that he has been betrayed on all sides and is once again the prisoner of his Sûreté nemesis, Bonet (Paul Lukas). There is no straight path possible for Jean; if the bombing raid brought about a lucky detour, recapture brings about a detour of a threatening sort.

But the detouring will continue. Bonet is passing through a small French town with his prisoner when they suddenly learn of a tragedy that has befallen the inhabitants; angered over the sabotaging of a railroad line, the Nazis have taken 100 of the town's menfolk prisoner and threaten to kill them unless the actual saboteurs either step forward or are informed on. Bonet suddenly has an inspired idea; since Jean is destined for execution anyway, he could pretend to be the saboteur, turn himself over to the Nazis, and thereby save many of his fellow countrymen. Having no particular feelings of patriotism, Jean is at first resistant to the idea. Eventually, however, he agrees, though it may be likely that he is simply biding his time for a new chance to escape.

Yet even this new commitment on Jean's part—however morally ambiguous it may be—is open to still a further detour. For the first time in his life, Jean finds himself in love; a young, innocent French woman has shown him the joys of commitment to a full and intense and spiritual romance. After several idyllic interludes along the banks of the river, Jean decides to flee with the young woman. Sending her to a small cottage at the edge of the woods outside of town, Jean makes his plans to escape from Bonet.

But a final detour takes place. Somewhere, somehow, Jean has discovered a commitment to the French cause; he will go through with Bonet's plan to save the 100 hostages. And yet, significantly, the film doesn't really explain the reasons for Jean's conversion. The wartime film is caught here in the limits of the ideology of affirmation. For this ideology, the goal of commitment has to be so evident, so natural, so necessary, that it needs no ulterior justification. Commitment simply happens in the instantaneity of a glow that spreads across Jean's face. As he and Bonet approach the Gestapo headquarters, Bonet tries to give the final meaning to this last, sudden turn: "It's been a long road, Jean. But you see, it's come to the right ending." In these images, commitment is literally a question of narrative—of a metaphoric movement along a metaphoric road—and a sense of the ending. Bonet's little speech works to make unambiguous what the rest of the film may make only too ambiguous: the diversity of projects to which a torn person can be committed.

Significantly, after Jean's surrender, Bonet has a second speech. Bringing word to the young woman that Jean will not be coming to their rendezvous, Bonet is asked by her, "Deep in his heart, what was he like?" to which Bonet gives a reply that will end the film in a burst of music: "He was a Frenchman."

The line is revealing in its apparent simplicity. For the narrative of war affirmation, the sense is clear: Jean was a man who realized his commitment to his fellow Frenchmen. And yet the course of the film has already implicitly questioned the notion of Frenchness as a necessarily positive value; to be French, for example, can mean being a treacherous criminal (like Jean or his criminal associate, played by Sheldon Leonard—a casting that invests Frenchness with all the connotations of forties gangsterism). Moreover, the very sort of French people that Jean's actions will help have been shown by the film to be far from the most positive of figures; a number of scenes show the families of the hostages meeting together in secret to see if they can't frame Bonet and Jean for the sabotage.

Furthermore, the declaration "He was a Frenchman" has another sense, one encouraged by the casting of dashing Errol Flynn in the role: to be French means to be a lover, a seducer, a figure of passion and desire. And far from being a mere excess, this connotation actually sums up one of the symbolic strands of the film—the way it continues the force of the "Hollywood" machine as a machine in a devotion to the powers of love and romance. Against the ambiguities of Jean's commitment to France, there is the clarity of his conversion from casual seducer to a man capable of feeling deeply the powers of personal romance. Love matters more than moral duty; or, in the terms of the Hollywood view, it is the only moral duty, the rest of humanity becoming no more than a backdrop to the joyous formation of the couple. Indeed, where the hostages remain unseen throughout the film—

mere abstractions of a notion of the French people—*Uncertain Glory* will employ all of the standard Hollywood techniques to make all too visible the forces of love: misty close-ups of the young woman, idyllic scenes with an out-of-focus background. If the stakes are love or commitment, love has an emphatic force denied to commitment. Where war commitment has a certain abstractness—and if the forces to which one commits oneself can only be rendered visible at the cost of making them unbearable (the French families who are all too willing to betray Jean)—love, in contrast, is given form, is given a body on the screen. But this embodied love can then only exist in a space other than the theoretical space of war commitment. If, in Raymond Bellour's words, the drive of classic cinema would be to construct the seeming clarity of a situation in which "the hero's fate is shaped by the feminine figure, but only to the extent that the representations organized around this figure allow for the two of them to be inscribed together in a symbolic framework,"[1] in *Uncertain Glory* there is significantly no one narrative that can hold the two commitments of love and war together—that can combine them into one. Hence, the doubts of the title: where does glory lie? What is the meaning of Jean's life? Is glory the saving of unseen Frenchmen or the loving of a woman who has only just begun to come out of her shell to discover all the joys of a (Hollywood) romance?

At precisely the historical moment where American society would seem to desire to affirm the justifiability, justness, and inevitability of what it deems the right narrative version of the war, the war moment itself can show up that desire and refuse to sustain the move toward finality, coherence, logic, a "natural" coincidence of personal and political destiny. We can well argue the possibility, then, of contradictions within the very heart of the ideology of war commitment. Of course, many of these contradictions are not new to the forties; they show up in a long tradition of sentimental romance culminating perhaps in all its intensity in those many thirties melodramas about the sacrifice of female desire to a "higher" cause (as in *Stella Dallas* [1937]). I would not want to imply the newness of narratives of self-sacrifice for the moment of the forties; quite the contrary, what strikes me as significant is the revitalization of a narrative of sacrifice at precisely *this moment* of war and commitment. *Uncertain Glory*, for example, acknowledges the strength and justifiability of two value systems (sacrifice and social commitment versus self-discovery and love) at a moment where war commitment is trying to find a way of writing all values as part of a single, monocular system.

In the 1943 *Crash Dive*, an officer announces a dangerous mission with the declaration that "I'm not going to ask for volunteers because I know that you'll all want to go." In that simultaneous interplay of blindness and insight that literary critic Paul de Man suggests characterizes statements of referentiality,[2] the officer's declaration announces the naturalness of the war effort, its seeming origin in a spontaneous willingness to fight, *but* the very fact that the statement has to be declared suggests that this natural reference to a given state is not so natural, not so given. The statement itself constructs its field of reference: if volunteering was assured, there would be no need not to ask for volunteers or, on the other hand, to mention the idea of volunteering at all. Even at its most emphatic, or perhaps because of that very emphaticness, the representation of war unity can be read as contradictory, a fictive attempt to not so much describe a state of affairs as to empower a state of affairs that it wants to have seen as already empowered. In the very act of stating, the war-affirmative statement can demonstrate the very sort of ideological work it is engaged in, the very ways in which it is not a given, but a force to be constructed.

Contradictions threaten the officer's statement in *Crash Dive* in at least two ways. On the one hand, there is the *logical* contradiction of the statement: knowing that everyone wants to go on the mission does not necessarily eliminate the possibility of asking for volunteers. It is this kind of internal contradiction—based on the very logic of the statement—that deconstruction (especially in its American variety) would be most directly concerned with: it would read the statement in such a way as to make it say two opposed or mutually interfering things. On the other hand, there is a *historical* contradiction that doesn't intervene *in* the statement and is nowhere stated *within* it. Rather, this contradiction represents the condition of the statement's possibility and impossibility: the ideological limits in which it is stated. By trying to be logically exclusive and *natural*—by trying, that is, to invoke a consensus that it already assumes is granted—the declaration signals a necessary recognition of the possibility of potential opposition: as historical event, the war effort can and may be open to various forms of historical contradiction. Of course, such a recognition is nowhere explicit *in* the statement; it is its "structuring absence," a contradiction that one can read into it in analytical retrospect but that is produced out of discourse's attempt to produce a coherent, singular form for its historical moment. We might also want to look at other discourses of the moment to understand what forms historical resistance might or can take.

We might, then, suggest that in fact the referential statement is really open to *three* kinds of contradiction: the logical, the structuring historical absence, and, as a third possibility (never stated in *Crash Dive*), the historical challenge. By this last, I mean a declared act of contradiction in which one version of history steps in to challenge another (for example—a fantasy example— if one of the men in *Crash Dive* had suddenly announced a decision not to volunteer). A critical reading of discourse can have at least three procedures open to it, then. We can read for logical contradiction, for structuring absences, and for the intrusion of emphatic challenges—an alternate voice—into the texture of the seemingly univocal text. Deconstruction's limits come from its decision to rest at the first level. The drawbacks of a purely deconstructive procedure lie significantly in its frequent inability to recognize the ways that a social context can work to make logical contradiction *seem* noncontradictory: that is, what may be structurally illogical and visible to the crafted critic may still all too easily be read by a particular group of language users as seemingly logical. Even if, as de Man would have it, every univocal reading of a declaration is a necessarily blinded reading, the fact remains that the statement was capable of being read in a particular context *as univocal* and was capable of being lived and acted upon as univocal.[3]

Deconstruction of this sort imputes to language a freedom from responsibility that it frequently does not possess in a course of events where people will act as if reference exists. The deconstructive reading needs to be balanced, then by a procedure that suggests not only how a statement could be read in a non-referential way, but, quite differently, how, when, why, and under what conditions a social moment will read statements as univocal acts of reference. In a sense, it is this sort of procedure that I tried to follow in the previous chapter; there, I suggested that the discourse of the war was a particular shaping of representation, one caught within particular ideologies of representation, ideologies that are neither natural, realistic, or universal. But if this analysis of the representational field is an analysis primarily of the field of ideology's drives to coherence, it is as possible to study the field of contradictions and incoherence. This would not be to posit such realms reworked by ideology as any sort of "truth" of the war years as against a dominant ideology's "falsehoods," but rather to suggest a limitation of a would-be dominant ideology's claim to total truth.

At this stage, history and theory rejoin since, in contrast to deconstruction's internal analysis of logical contradiction, the analyst now writes a history of active oppositions, historical events that worked outside or in contradiction to the field of dominant representations. To write a history of such opposition is not to opt for a notion of opposition as the real history of a historical moment that the historian would then transcribe passively. Such is the potential danger of a romanticism of opposition, the notion that repressed groups bear a tie to a political teleology that repression and oppression often prevent from emerging into its true historical course.[4] No doubt the most famous of such romanticisms is Gyorg Lukács' *History and Class Consciousness*, which seems to posit the working class as *the* necessary and inevitable real subject of history,[5] but it may be as apparent in postmodern thinkers who try explicitly to reject Lukács' notion of the proletariat as the new spirit of history; for example, in his preface to *I, Pierre Rivière*, Michel Foucault writes that the document left by the peasant murderer has a kind of automatic subversive beauty to it that challenges the hold of disciplinary power over Rivière.[6]

Against such romanticism—such a notion of history

as a transparency that lets the voice of true history speak out—it might be possible to imagine the *writing* of conflict as an activity itself, an active process that assails dominance by juxtaposing against it another version of the historical moment. If, in Alvin Gouldner's suggestion in *The Dialectics of Ideology and Technology,* we can only know the extent and limits of any ideological system by comparing it with another,[7] then history writing becomes a montagist writing, a process in which the historian actively brings together different interpretations of the historical field.

The importance, then, of combining theoretical reflection on narrative and its breakdown with analysis of a specific historical moment lies in the ability to acknowledge the force of both narrativity and its other *while* permitting the analyst to suggest the possible emergence or dominance of one over the other.

In the dissolve from Ruth's face to the entrance of the naval shipyard, *Pride of the Marines* works to set up an agreement between a number of different codes: sociopolitical (the centrality of the military in everyday life); narratological (the dissolve as logical act, a naturalizing connection of two sites—the personal and the political); psychoanalytic (in terms of Al's story, Ruth and the social structure are interconnected parts of a symbolic order, an oedipalization based on renunciation that is simultaneous with the assumption of a social position).

And yet we might read the film differently and suggest that it can only come to this final moment at the cost of a certain imbalance in its representational system. For example, while the dissolve initiates a certain alliance between Ruth and the military, at another level, it can signal a certain misalliance of the terms, a discontinuity between the story of the couple and the story of the would-be dominant order: more specifically, Al can only become a member of a family, at the cost of leaving active service; his blindness allows him to become a family man, but prevents him from serving as a fighting man. Significantly, the one set of photographs comparing Al and John Garfield that *Life* chose to lead off its article on the film shows Al and Garfield lounging in chairs; while the discourse of the war effort will emphasize that the handicapped person can contribute to the war effort,[8] Al's social interaction seems to lead to a life of leisure, an exclusion (self-willed or not) from the *social* production of the war effort. Indeed, a number of films suggest that a couple can only exist if it removes itself from the war (or if it is removed from the war in some way): for example, *A Yank in the R.A.F.* (1941) (with a wounded Tom Baker [Tyrone Power]), *Action in the North Atlantic, The Very Thought of You* (1944) (which by a kind of overdetermination brings its two couples together at the film's end by having *both* men [Dennis Morgan and Dane Clark] get wounded). The construction of such a narrative possibility seems a way for narrative to register a tension in the war effort between waiting and having, between having and renouncing. The very need for such a narrative possibility can make manifest the ideological nature of the discourse and further can signal its potential incompleteness.

Despite the preponderance of "service comedies," the very conditions of war can force films into a condition that seems far from classically Comic. That is, the need to go off to fight conflicts with Comedy's traditional sense of existence as huge festivity with group participation. To be sure, service films will frequently end with a moment of festivity—the celebration for the departing soldiers as in *Buck Privates* or *Reveille with Beverly* (1943)—but significantly, it is a festivity of *departure:* war means that a community of men and women together can't stay together as an inevitable, organic totality. Community celebrates its own potential fragmentation (while glossing this over through the frequent promise of an inevitable return). An alternate mode will be to displace war service into service on the home front. That is, films will try to chronicle the many ways that men fight battles in America too; this allows war and romance to find a single space. For example, in *Let's Face It* (1943), Jerry Walker (Bob Hope) manages to capture a German sub in the Long Island Sound; the film can then end with an awards ceremony where Walker's girlfriend (Betty Hutton) avows her love for him; this is a war festivity but for an already completed narrative act rather than for an ambiguous future overseas.

Similarly, other films will simply keep the men home and assert the centrality of their home-front work for the war effort. In *Blondie for Victory* (1942) for example, Dagwood's work in architecture is declared essential work—despite the fact that little building went on during the war and the film makes no attempt to claim that Dagwood is designing for the armed forces. Indeed, so caught up as it is in the comedy of married-family everyday life, the Blondie series seems to find the notion of the separation of the couple to be intolerable; to be sure, the films quite explicitly show a work realm apart from the home, but the plots interweave the two spaces through a series of plot complications. Indeed, the very repetitions of the series—for example, the films inevitably open with Dagwood rushing off to work and accidentally knocking down the postman—help to make the separation of home and office a convention-bound, predictable one— a separation that is part of the known universe of the Blondie series. Forced separations then, will become precisely the problem that initiates the narrative and that it eventually resolves; for example, in *Blondie Goes Latin* (1941), Dagwood sends Blondie off on a South American cruise only to find himself on the very same boat through a series of crazy mishaps.

Thus, in *Blondie for Victory*, the need to preserve the conventions of the series as a comedy of the couple can only enter into tension with the needs of a war-commitment narrative: indeed, the film's attempted compromise—Dagwood shows up to rescue Blondie and her Woman's Service Auxiliary from a foreign agent, and a grateful Blondie declares that she will disband the auxiliary since a woman's first wartime duty is to her family and her husband—can seem in strange contradiction with much of the discourse for women during the war, which will argue that woman's first war duty is to be everywhere and do everything. And as if to further demonstrate the separation of Dagwood's world from a war world, the film has Dagwood performing his rescue in a borrowed, obviously wrong-sized uniform (he had thought to scare Blondie back to the home by pretending he had enlisted); the inappropriateness of the uniform on Dagwood only further underscores the inappropriateness of a wartime Dagwood (as does the very notion that a uniform would scare Blondie rather than make her proud). There is little possibility for a separate tale of Dagwood in the service; indeed, in the postwar film *Blondie's Hero* (1950), where Dagwood joins the army reserves, most of the big scenes come when Blondie comes to visit. Thus, for example, Blondie and Dagwood will be caught together in a tank out of control that goes careening all over the base.

To be sure, the insistence on the couple in the tank scene here might seem contradicted by many comedy films where single individuals drive or are caught in widely careening vehicles: for example, *Keep 'Em Flying* (1941) or *Hillbilly Blitzkrieg* or, especially, *Star-Spangled Rhythm* (1942), where the heroine overenergetically and crazily drives a jeep around the base while singing, "I'm doing it for defense." The scene here becomes a double entendre of sexual sublimation, and suggests a self-directed energy outside the needs of a couple (indeed, as she drives, Polly's soldier-passengers, who include her boyfriend, go tumbling out of the back of the jeep as she continues merrily on her way). There seems to be a fundamental contrast between the adventures of the isolated individual and the couple here. And yet the Blondie films join the service comedies in eliminating what might seem to be the symbolically necessary alternative: the alternative of men and women somehow working together in a united effort for the war. Precisely, this alternative is unrepresentable: there is no one space of a united male and female commitment. The alternatives here are narcissism (the jeep scene in *Star-Spangled Rhythm*) or active removal of the family unit into the "haven" of the home (as in the Blondie films). The Blondie films seem literally unable to let Dagwood go off to war, to let him leave home in any but the most rule-bound and temporary ways.

If commitment is the desired end of a narrative of war effort, the end to which it moves, personal want can become an antinarrative, a stasis that works to assert its effort against the captivating forward motion of a conversion to commitment. The repetitive assertion of a readiness to go off to war—"And now for Australia and a crack at those Japs," as one of the flight crew of a bomber says as the men finish their narrow escape from Nazi-held Europe *(Desperate Journey)*—is sometimes matched by a repetitive desire for return. For example, Ann Hilton's letter writing to her husband is both a way of accepting his absence and of wishing for his return (and the finale of the film will reward this wish by having the husband turn out not to be missing in action). One narrative option will show the men coming back unharmed from missions and, often through the excitement of an awards ceremony, try simply to make the spectator forget that another scene—further battle—may follow. Similarly, some films will show death but have it happen to what the needs of romance will deem to be less important characters: hence, in *Four Jills in a Jeep* (1944), the crashing of a plane as Carole Landis waits for her man to return from a mission is a tragedy only so long as Carole thinks he might have been in the plane; when the man turns up, having come in safely on a different plane, the film quickly drops all reference to the crash of the other plane. But, simultaneously, other narratives will suggest the impossibility of a safe return: a number of films, for example, revolve around the death of a loved one (the male in *Passage to Marseilles* [1944]; *Since You Went Away*, which actually complicates things by saving the mother's man but killing off the daughter's; the female in *Five Graves to Cairo, Manhunt* [1941]; both members of the couple in *Prisoner of Japan; China Girl*).

        If, as Raymond Bellour argues, one narrative representation of the classic psychosexual dynamic of oedipalization occurs in the rivalry of two men for a woman—a rivalry which can be read as the combat of father and son for the mother[9]—it may not be insignificant that while a number of war films follow this pattern by having the war kill off a rival or by making a rivalry disappear in the face of a higher agreement (for example, *Crash Dive*), a number of wartime films include such a narrative moment but leave it unresolved or, to be precise, do not resolve it according to the logic of the oedipal trajectory. For example, *Buck Privates* and *Reveille with Beverly* end with a woman who is undecided in her choice of two men and watches them go off to war (in the case of *Reveille*, the woman [Ann Miller] even sings that she is "taking a rain check on love"). On the other hand, films like *Abroad with Two Yanks* (1944) and *Phantom of the Opera* (1943) end with the woman deciding she wants neither of the two men, a decision that sends them off together at the end, deciding to find comradeship in a certain degree of male bonding (and, as if to suggest a certain degree of distortion of the usual bonds of sexual affiliation, the end of *Phantom of the Opera* has the two men talk of their evening out together as a date, while *Abroad with Two Yanks* has the two men in dresses [they had been trying to crash an elegant soiree]). The formation of the couple takes on a perverse or farcical shape signaling the contradictions of male bonding. The ambiguities of romance can suggest a certain inability of the films to narrate couple formation at a moment where all the givens of romance can be called into doubt.

For the trajectory of romance, the forward move to a single-voiced ending is everything: the accomplishment of a final stasis in which the levels of psychology and sociality finally, irremediably, come together in the formation of a couple. Nothing, then, can suggest so much the troubling of the oedipal model as the problem of *endings* in the narratives of the war. To be sure, as *Air Force* suggests, many narratives will try to make *conclusions* take the place of *endings*, but the sheer variety of forms of conclusion can suggest the limitations of any unitary model of the narrative ending. Indeed, we might here invoke Frank Kermode's suggestion in *The Sense of an Ending* that the most powerful narrative structure is one based on retrospection, on what Kermode calls the stable position of a "long perspective" in which narrative elements can be ordered. In contrast, the war shows the possibility of a period in which narrative perspective can only be incomplete, in which retrospection can only fall out of alignment with history perceived as an unfolding narrative. During the war, there is no full position outside of history that would enable a complete and secure retrospection. As one character says in *Back to Bataan* (1945), "That's the worse point about war. You meet somebody. You get to know them. Wham! You never see them again. You see something but you never know how it ends. Be nice to know how all this is going to end." Similarly, in Frederick Wakeman's novel *Shore Leave*, one of the hero fliers recounts his idea for a novel of a flier's heroic efforts in the war. The response to this idea is, "The problem with that plot is that you'd never know till the war is over whether or not he actually returned" (notice how the confusion of past and present tense can signal a hesitation around the narration of an ongoing event). Significantly, the response is also a declaration about the teller of the tale: also a flier, he may not return from future missions.

Narrative here faces a problem of time: how can narrative be a closed, past-tense activity when its very actants are living through the narrative in the present? To be sure, as Kermode notes, the disjunction of retrospective narrative and contemporary history doesn't prohibit the generation of narratives; Kermode himself recounts the ventures of millennial groups whose resilient ability to continue making predictions about the future even in the face of continual disconfirmation is not that far from the wartime astrology that Katherine Archibald discusses in *Wartime Shipyard*. In both cases, the refusal of reality to correspond to narrative lines simply leads to further generation of narrative.

In other cases, wartime narrative constructs for itself a long perspective by focusing on events that have already taken place in a past (but that can seem to have allegorical relevance to the present moment); just before or at the very beginning of the war, especially, there will be a spate of films about events (real or imagined) in the American past (for example, *Belle Starr* [1941], *Kit Carson* [1940], *Young Tom Edison* [1940], *Western Union* [1941], *They Died with Their Boots On* [1941]), and as the war proceeds, recent victories (i.e., events with successful and closed endings) will quickly become subjects of narrative representation *(Guadalcanal Diary, Back to Bataan)*. There is an attempt here to avoid ambiguous or open endings by finding narratives that have already come to their necessary conclusions.

At the same time, though, a number of films will hold narrative resolution in abeyance: hence, a number of films of spectacle (especially musicals) will include a central narrative line but will frequently submerge that narrative line beneath a non-narrative display, a show. For example, in *Star-Spangled Rhythm*, Polly Judson's attempt to climb over the wall of a motion picture studio to meet a producer becomes the occasion for a lengthy, nonnarrative comedy routine. There seems to be the sense here that to tell a story—that is, to acknowledge temporality—would open representation up to all the dangers of temporal contingency: the answer, then, is a kind of refusal of narrative through an endless repetition of spectacle, an attempt to create an order out of a nonprogressive time. Indeed, as Pierre Macherey suggests in his reading of the gothic novel in *Pour une théorie de la production littéraire,* narrative may be fundamentally caught between the ambiguities of the not yet told and the plentitudes of the promise of full resolution: in a moment when full resolution is doubtful, wartime spectacle, we might suggest, works to bridge these alternatives by making every moment one of immediate plentitude.

At precisely the historical moment where American society would desire to affirm the justifiability, justness and inevitability of what it deems the right ending to the war, the moment itself shows up desire and refuses to sustain the move toward finality, coherence, logic. Indeed, the ending itself can turn from an overdetermined necessity of narrative logic into no more than a mere *fiat* that *declares* the ending and, in so doing can imply that nothing ultimately sustains an ending except the rhetorical force with which it is declared.

Significantly, one of the very forms of speech acts that speech-act theorist John Austin declares to be *infelicitous*—that is, as having no real force and no justifiable binding power—is used in war-affirmative film precisely as a way to try to end tension and bind people in the power of a successful ending:[10] where Austin suggests that marriage vows are not valid in a ceremony that not all the participants believe is real, in the film *You'll Never Get Rich,* Robert (Fred Astaire) can't convince Sheila (Rita Hayworth) to marry him so he hires a real justice of the peace for the onstage spectacle in which Robert and Sheila will act out a marriage. The dance number—"The Wedding Cake March"—works to affirm unity of love and war as the couple dance on a cake that is also a tank. Their dance is a dance of love and war together. But the resorting of the Astaire character *and of the film itself* to an evident fiction to bring about the moment of unity and reconciliation and resolution can imply the fictiveness of all endings, the actual irresolution of their resolutions.

Significantly, the notion that marriages are constructed on the basis of a certain forcing of events seems to run
through many films of the period. Most explicit perhaps about the
fictional basis of marriage is *The Miracle of Morgan's Creek* (1944),
which becomes a veritable reflection on the fictions of wartime
unity. The miracle at the film's end can suggest that little can
empower a happy ending at this moment but a miracle; there is
no necessary logic that can bring together the issues of sexuality
and commitment. Similarly, despite the emphatic clarity of its
title, a 1943 film, *This Is the Army*, suggests in at least one moment
the possibility for a sundering of national identity and couple
formation—a sundering that it will try to cover over through the
performance of an authoritative command. Readying himself to
go off to war, Corporal Johnny Jones (Ronald Reagan) refuses to
marry his childhood sweetheart, Eileen (Joan Leslie), out of the
fear that if killed, he will leave Eileen with nothing but an insubstantial image, a mere memory with no real life to it. Against
Eileen's declaration that in the nature of a couple lies the very
base of human existence—"Johnny, don't you realize that if all
men felt like you, there wouldn't be any more families, there
wouldn't be any more war"—Johnny divides the narrative unity
into two incompatible forms: "We're in a war and until it's over
our private lives just stand still." To be sure, as affirmative film,
This Is the Army finds a way to resolve the difference and rewrite it
within the framework of a single-strand narrative. Johnny's particular form of dissonance will be dissipated through the force of
an insistent affirmation. Dragging him out to meet a chaplain,
Eileen makes a speech to Johnny: "Corporal Jones, I've decided
that you don't know what the war's all about! We're free people
fighting for the right to remain free—to work and to be married
and to run a family. . . . Why do you act like we've lost the war?
Open your heart, Johnny; we're all in this fight together—women
as well as men. . . . Doggone, if we want to get married, let's get
married." Johnny is instantly convinced. They marry, and Eileen
is immediately able to watch Johnny leave for war. The couple
marries to separate: they can't have both commitments.

Farmer (to city slicker who has volunteered for the

war effort): "How come you're pitching hay?" City slicker: "I'd rather be pitching woo but war is war" (*Harvest Melody*, 1943). The war creates new narrative options for film but also brings in options that are necessary while potentially incompatible. Even when the films work to assert the couple—to end, for example, as *Destination: Tokyo* does with the look of the woman—there is a potential temporal and symbolic slippage between the elements of the representation. Love and duty belong to two different spaces and there is no automatic or necessarily natural or effective way to link them up in a single, larger space of full commitment to a single object.

Harvest Melody does suggest an option that was attempted several times in the period: since farm work was declared an essential activity, farm life would seem to allow the possibility of stories of romance that would also serve as stories of commitment. The farm was a place that could justifiably show men and women together. In *Harvest Melody*, for example, an entertainment celebrity comes to a small farm to work for the war effort in hopes of publicity; she begins in cynicism and follows her manager's encouragements to pretend she is in love with a farmer, since that sort of romance will bring her increased publicity. Eventually, the celebrity finds that her love is real and that farm love is as profound and important as the world of the city. The film suggests that both city and country worlds have a place in the war effort: for example, the greatest talent the celebrity can bring to the farm is her singing, which will inspire the farmers on to greater productivity. The war years will present the farm as a special sort of space where seemingly different goals can all find a space in which they become identical. Indeed, 1943 will be the year of the big country musical on Broadway, *Oklahoma!* which has compromise between various worlds—"The farmers and the cowboys should be friends"—as one of its major concerns.

But, for the cinema at least, the country narrative is only an incomplete solution. As a mark of this incompleteness, we might note how many of the pastoral films end with a reference back to the glories of city life: for example, in *Harvest Melody*, there are cutaways to the big fund raising event of a Madison Square

Garden boxing fight that the farmers have sponsored; similarly, in *Jive Junction* (1943), the farming youth leave the farm to participate in a radio competition. Indeed, *Jive Junction* emphatically suggests that farm life is only a transition to something more important; needing a farmer's barn so that they can set up a "jive junction" for the morale of the soldiers, the youth agree to work the farmer's land and help him get out his crop. More generally, it is possible to suggest that the representation of a country life runs into possible contradiction with the very technology of cinema itself; a force of modernity, the cinema works to advertise itself through spectacles of machinery and displays of technological possibility that are potentially incompatible with the mythology of the simplicity of country life. Indeed, it might well be that the very mythology of country life makes it potentially inappropriate for *narrative* representation, since that mythology requires a notion of the country as outside conflict, outside drama. In a film like *Jive Junction*, the country exists merely as lyric interlude: a musical sequence of slow dissolves showing kids happy at work on the farm. Country life, the films seem to suggest, is nice but the real concern of cinema lies elsewhere. It seems not coincidental that it is the B production units or the Poverty Row studios that spend the most time on representations of the country (although there are important exceptions—for example, M.G.M., with the musicals of Minnelli—that I will return to in chapter 5).

To be sure, the representation of a city-world poses problems of its own to narratives of commitment. The city precisely is the site of egoism and aggressivity—of lone figures out for the best deal for themselves. Indeed, some conversion films will take as their very goal the conversion of this city mentality into a public-spirited one. In *Mr. Lucky*, for example, Lucky (Cary Grant) is a con artist planning to fleece a women's service organization until he falls in love with its director. But here too the film can suggest the limits of its own representation. First of all, only Mr. Lucky converts; the rest of the city slickers remain as corrupt as ever. Second, Lucky's joining the war effort as a sailor is consciously registered as a kind of fleeing from the bonds of love.

When the film ends with Lucky and his love, Dorothy Bryant, meeting up again at the dock where his ship has come in for a temporary stay, the fog that envelopes the dock can seem a figure for the very insubstantiality of the ending: there is no physically existing place where love and war commitment can exist together. The two only meet in imagination, in the utopian space of a wish. The ship will come to the harbor only to part again.

Indeed, much of the problem for war narrative is that it has too many spaces to try to include in its synoptic scheme. Even the very division of the war into two fronts has the consequence of dividing up attention, fragmenting concerns. Thus, many historians report that V-J day came almost as an anticlimax after the buoyancy of V-E day; Americans had already celebrated the sense of an ending and there was little investment in a second narrative. Significantly, just after the war (but written during it), Tom Heggens' novel *Mr. Roberts* will make this division of space into the diversity of irreconcilable fronts part of the explicit premise of his book: the cargo ship *Reluctant* exists in a nether space between fronts. The comic novel of war mores can only achieve the comic stability of space by imagining a space apart from the war, elsewhere. Indeed, the moment that Roberts leaves this intermediary place to join more directly in the war effort, he is killed.

Yet even here the notion of a distance from the fronts doesn't permit a knowledgeable perspective on the war (and so, one of the running motifs in *Mr. Roberts* concerns the soldiers looking out to shore with binoculars—an image of their separation and distance from other events in their own time sphere). There is no mediating point by which one can step out of the contingency of an ongoing drama. Indeed, in novels like *A Bell for Adano* or *Mr. Roberts*, standing outside battle doesn't remove one from conflict. It simply puts one into conflicts of a different and more quotidian sort. There arise conflicts with all the personal pressures—jealousy, petty bureaucracy—that the community of war affirmation is supposed to overcome. A conversation in Frederick Wakeman's novel *Shore Leave* represents much of this sense of the period as non-totalizable series of battles:

"Well, the admiral called me in. I repeated my observations, and he said, 'Impossible. If they [an attack force of Japanese planes] were where you say they were, we'd have them picked up on the Radar.' And the aide said, 'I never thought of it, sir, but that's right. We would have picked it up on the Radar.' Jee-sus, I get tired of fighting in so many wars."

"How many are there? I'd just heard of one."

"Let's see—"Crewson counted them off on his fingers. "There's the war between the Army and the Navy. The one between the Navy and the Marines. The war between the Marines and the Army. And the great global conflict between the fighting Navy and the Paper Navy. Anything that happens to the Japs is purely coincidental."

At the same time, the home front itself can fragment into several spaces. Most explicitly, black America's Double-V campaign—no victory over there without racial victory back here—implies that the single-strand narrative of war commitment is a potentially incomplete one; there are forces that fall outside its sway. The home front is in a battle with itself.

With discourse only hesitantly able to create the conditions for successful resolution, the whole support for a single narrative of affirmation becomes difficult. No longer necessarily subtended by a narrative logic, accession to the dominant order, to a law of authority, becomes potentially awkward, incomplete, arbitrary. The debate around the advantages or not of an insertion of the self into a proffered system of dominant themes and structures is a debate that extends through the war period, sometimes quiet, sometimes virulent.

For example, there will be an active search for alternate discourses and a critique of the limits of dominant discourse at the levels of race, sex, and class. Thus, if, as I noted in the previous chapter, the master narrative of the working class tends to disavow the worker as a a possible narrative figure, preferring instead to emphasize status and the advancement out of lower classes by accidental factors, the wartime workplace itself will be the site of quite different discourses; there is literally a different grammar of the workplace, as Constance Bowman discovered: "The language my tongue wrapped itself around I shudder to recall. There might be no atheists on rubber rafts, but it was a cinch there were no Christians in the compartments where they stored them." Even more, against the government/union no-strike pledge, an attempt to create a narrative of nondissonance, workers will continually write (and enact) a discourse of dissonance: by 1944, one half of all workers are in work stoppages (an increase of 25 percent over 1943 and 40 percent over 1942). To be sure, such strikes are not necessarily projected by their participants as an active form of *class struggle;* quite the contrary, the strikes are often intended to affirm the war effort by arguing that factory authority is hampering that effort: thus, a great number of strikes are racially oriented "hate strikes" by whites protesting the hiring of blacks as an interference with their work.[11]

Equally, as Katherine Archibald notes in *Wartime Shipyard,* a suspicion of authority merged with a suspicion of communism; many workers refused involvement with union activity because they perceived unionism as communism. Instead, worker resistance tended to take on diffuse forms—especially, isolated symbolic strikes (for example, the announced one-hour strike). Insurgency, moreover, tended to take as its goal not the expression of any precise program but often quite simply a diffuse venting of anger; significantly, what worked to crystallize this anger was the figure of the *foreman,* represented in worker discourse not like the sergeant or second officer of the war film as a kind of guiding, mediating figure, but, quite the contrary, as a spy of the bosses, as a snob or wet-behind-the-ears dude too refined to understand the problems and needs of everyday work. The foreman becomes a kind of figure of tyranny or incompetence whose power seems excessive in relation to a perceived reality; even that spate of books like *Slacks and Callouses* or *Punch In! Susie* whose expressed goal is to argue the need and desirability of women to work in the factories will present the foreman as a kind of excessive figure, a terror that exceeds the needs of group binding: for example, " 'Helping Hitler again, huh?' he [the foreman] says when I tell him there's a drill on my machine that needs fixing."[12]

The narratives of war unity try to rewrite the working class as a kind of spontaneous unity—people (not members of a specific class) coming together from all walks of life to naturally form a working group; indeed books like *Slacks and Callouses* and *Punch In! Susie* go out of their way to mention the number of factory women who were not blue-collar workers or even workers at all before the war: such discussion can seem to suggest that work is not a matter of class but of individual will, of voluntary decision. (Significantly, though, a number of wartime polls suggested that many women's entrance into the factories was not a voluntary matter, but a necessity based on lowered incomes or inflationary prices.) And yet, political, racial, and sexual conflict will argue the limitations of a spontaneous, natural unity. To be sure, some affirmative discourse will try to write a place in the master narrative for nonwhite participation in the war; for example, in *All Through the Night,* as the onetime gangsters and hoods decide to turn their energy and anger against Nazi infiltrators, a close-up suddenly singles out a black man who joyously declares, "They're gonna make a war-monger out me yet!" There will be a rewriting of potentially resistant matter as ultimately a potential affirmation; thus, if one of the most violent clashes of representation will revolve around the zoot suit, *Star-Spangled Rhythm* will include a musical number where a zoot-suiter's attraction to women increases when he enlists in the military and appears on the scene in full-dress uniform.

Yet, rather than try to find a code in which to rewrite the perceived problem of social difference in affirmative terms, dominant discourse will often try to ignore it: for example, it will accept the need for blacks in the war effort, but it will simultaneously try to remove blacks from the visibility of representation (hence, the segregated fighting forces and no blacks at all in the marines or the air force). Racial protest will create a counternarrative to this discourse of the nonwhite's necessary but necessarily quiet participation in the war effort: for example, according to a 1942 Office of Facts and Figures poll, 18 percent of American Blacks imagine themselves as better off under Japanese rule. But it will also create the possibilities for the emergence of marks of protest into the dominant discourse—for example, into the news media which cannot disavow events like the Detroit race riots or

the Los Angeles zoot-suit battles (although the media can reen-
close the representation within a controlling framework; as John
Morton Blum notes, the Hearst paper *Herald and Express* ran headlines announcing "ZOOTERS THREATENED CITY").[13]

Racial difference here reactivates a social paranoia that
pushes the whites toward positions of threatened fixity. Race
becomes a limit of dominant representation, a point at which it
can only react with violent denial, a moment in which representation falters and an attempt to immediately and physically change
the situation through the exertion of power begins. The zoot suit,
for example, begins as a *semiotic* act in opposition to dominant
representation, an attempt to make style a site of what Dick
Hebdige, in reference to a later youth culture, calls "semiotic
guerilla warfare."[14]

The zoot-suit issue is an issue of meanings as much as
it is an issue of outright physical violence. The zoot suit contradicts
the sexual and social values of dominant discourse: at a moment
where the slacker is an object of official condemnation, the zoot
suit, with its emphasis on nonutility, becomes a kind of ode to a
leisure life, to effortlessness rather than effort. For example, the
watch, whose function becomes that of dangling as an ornament
on the end of a chain, can challenge the very emphasis of the
workplace on the connections of time and industrial discipline. A
contemporary article in *Newsweek* (June 21, 1943) emphatically
linked the zoot suit to a challenge to the *economy* of the war effort:
"The W.P.B. [War Productions Board] virtually banned [the zoot
suit] in March '42 when it restricted the amount of material to be
used in men's clothes, but the zoot suit has continued to thrive
mainly through the diligence of bootleg tailors." For George Lipsitz
in *Class and Culture in Cold War America,* the zoot suit condenses a
whole charged array of cultural defiances: "The zoot suit made a
virtue out of being different; it flaunted, celebrated, and exaggerated those things which prevailing social norms condemned. It
brought to male dress an ornamentation traditionally associated
only with womanly clothing, expressed an individual disdain for
convention . . . and provided a means for creating a community
out of a disdain for traditional community standards."[15] The zoot-

suiters and representatives of white culture enter into a mounting spiral of conflicting discourses that ends in action: for example, Los Angeles' mayor bans zoot suits but the zoot-suiters refuse the law; white soldiers on leave go into the Chicano sections of town, beating up zooters while the police stand by. For Lipsitz, finally, the zoot-suit riots are not an epiphenomenal eccentricity but a central moment of political contradiction in which dominant authority faces a limit to its power: "Bitter about discrimination, suspicious that the majority society might not be worth joining, and eager to affirm solidarity with their kind of people, the zoot-suiters represented not just a fad in fashion, but the politics of a spontaneous youth movement with a sophisticated understanding of the transitions and transformations of America instigated by the war" (p. 27).

"You didn't marry her; you just took out an option on her" (best friend to husband of a war couple in *The Unsuspected* [1947]). As with race, heterosexuality too is troubled, troubling, in the space of the American forties. Already during the war, the unity of the couple is assailed not merely by the fact of physical separation but as much by emotional separation—jealousy but also alienation (thus, the war encourages sudden marriages, the consequences of which will be the formation of a couple whose members don't really know each other—in the postwar period, this will lead to a rise in the divorce rate).

For example, one site of sexuality's tensions will condense around Frank Sinatra who, from 1941 on, will be a symbol of heartthrob passion. Sinatra is represented in part as a man who makes women scream and cry even at a distance and can turn them into high-spirited bobby-soxers. For soldiers away from home, Sinatra will become a sign of temptation for the home-front women, a condensation of all the fragility of the male's imagining of his home life: in the words of the narrator in Richard Brooks' novel *The Brick Foxhole*, "The crooner was singing on the radio. The little girls in the radio audience were shouting and screaming and the guys were hating the crooner and yet envying him." Significantly, part of the threat of Sinatra seems to reside in the sense that he doesn't correspond to traditional he-man norms.

At the same time that the war effort claims to be turning men into heroes, Sinatra suggests that such a conversion may be the worst path to sexual attractiveness. In the words of a contemporary article in *American Magazine* (September 1943), "A lot of square-shouldered Hollywood he-men are going to be neglected soon." Thus, the narrator in Wakeman's novel *Shore Leave* recounts his visit to a Frank Sinatra concert: "I asked a girl who sat next to Helena what Sinatra had that I didn't have, besides a voice. . . . 'Oh, you've got shoulders,' she said disgustedly 'We don't go for shoulders since Frankie came into our lives.' 'Yeah,' her boyfriend said. 'Us tall, dark and handsome guys ain't gotta chance, brother.' He was a kid of eighteen, fighting a losing battle with a mous- tache." The final observation here suggests the ironic position that Sinatra can push other men into; forced by tradition to promote a certain image of masculinity—even when their own bodies betray that image—they now find that new historical events are undercutting that image, rendering it anachronistic or irrelevant (although a defense strategy might suggest that if one isn't loved that only proves how much of a real man one is).

A further component of the threat of Sinatra will be the simultaneous breadth of his appeal and the mystery of the source of that appeal. Sinatra has the ability to appeal to all sorts of women—not just young bobby soxers—without men being able to understand how the process works. The narrator in *Shore Leave* does try to demystify the appeal through a rational dissection of Sinatra's act—"Sinatra had a lot of tricks that endeared him to the crowd. He held onto the mike, caressingly. He cocked his head and used tender little voice breaks"—but the effect of that appeal will go beyond the rational male's explanation: "I looked around at the faces of the girls. It was mass hysteria, all right. Those kids were having a mass affair with Sinatra."

Certainly, there will be a certain attempt in the media packaging of Sinatra to contain his image within more "innocent" parameters; thus, for example, in the film *Reveille with Beverly*, he sings a respectable slow song in tuxedo among baby grand pianos, candleabras, and (nonfainting) elegant women in evening gowns. There will also be a media promotion of Sinatra as a figure of goodwill in a time of turmoil and division. Significantly, though, Sinatra will come to stand for positive ethical values only by maintaining his image as seductive heartthrob. For example, in an article "written by" Sinatra for *Scholastic Magazine* (September 27, 1945), Sinatra answers the question, "What is this about races?" by promoting romance and attractiveness as two of the important qualities that transcend differences: "It would be a fine thing if people chose their associates by the color of their hair. Brother wouldn't be talking to brother, and in some families, the father and mother wouldn't even talk to each other. Imagine a guy with dark hair like me not talking to blondes."

There also seems to be a concerted effort to suggest that Sinatra's appeal only extends to vulnerable youth (note how even Brooks refers to the radio audience as composed of *"little girls"*). Thus, for example, in *Higher and Higher* (1943), Sinatra's love for Millie (Michele Morgan) is finally shown to be a kind of puppy love; she ends up with the right man, an older one (played by Jack Haley), and Sinatra ends up with a young, energetic teeny-bopper. And yet, at the same time, the image of Sinatra as seductive figure remains—and *Higher and Higher* goes so far as to keep his name Frank Sinatra even though the story is a fictional one. Significantly, the narrator of *Shore Leave* finds the mature woman who went with him out of curiosity to the concert falling for Sinatra. Where Helena's first reaction at the sight of the bobby-soxers will be to declare, "Aren't some of them awful? Golly," Helena too will fall under Sinatra's charm: "Helena whispered, 'It's just like he's telling you he loves you. He makes you feel like you're all alone with him. I forget everyone else when he sings. It makes me feel funny inside. Golly.' " The repetition of "Golly" only emphasizes how complete is the conversion: Sinatra implies that any woman can turn into a passion-filled bobby-soxer. With the end of the war, we can even find Margaret Mead having to write in a book designed to tell soldiers what home-front life was like that the soldiers should not believe all the stories of Sinatra's disruptive influence.[16] Sinatra condenses all the wartime fears of a female sexuality that is in danger of not channeling its energies in the proper direction: as a young girl tells *Time*, "My sister saw

him twice and she's afraid to go again because she's engaged"
("That Old Sweet Song," July 5, 1943).

Indeed, the affirmative discourse will have to explicitly
if begrudgingly acknowledge that life has become sexualized. For
example, the very need to alert soldiers to sexual illnesses also
means that soldiers' knowledge will have to be sexualized and
that their sexual energy must be admitted in and into the economy
of war. Between the Hollywood films of sublimation that the
soldiers are seeing for free and documentaries like the John Ford
–directed *Sex Hygiene* (1941), soldiers can witness an incompatibility between heterosexuality as spiritual love and as immediate
physical gratification. The extent to which an immediate postwar
text like Howard Kitching's *Sex Problems of the Returned Vet* repeatedly employs a rhetoric on the abnormality but also inevitability
of nonspiritualized sexuality *and* the corresponding normality of
marriage can paradoxically suggest an overdetermined need to
write away the new sexualization of relations that war encourages
in America: "Anyone who has had such experiences [i.e., sexual
contact while overseas], however solitary or rare, should be examined to exclude the possibility of venereal disease before resum-
ing sexual relations with his wife."[17] Kitching admits the presence
of sexual desire but he ultimately suggests that that desire eventually finds its (limited) place within the institution of marriage.

Hollywood Canteen (1944) will even resolve the problem
of sexuality by splitting its narrative between two soldiers, each
of whom discovers a different sort of love. If the misty-eyed hero
finds a spiritual love with movie star Joan Leslie with the promise
of marriage if he comes back from the war alive, the sidekick
(Dane Clark) will discover the powers of a carnal passion that in
its status as a direct expression of sexuality looks for no permanent
liaison. This sexualization even takes on virtually Freudian overtones as the sidekick's encounter with a passionate woman leads
him to overcome his crippling war injury: as he declares triumphantly: "It was that girl with the instinct that done it . . . . Something subconsciously primeval went on betwixt us . . . . and I
forgot my cane!"

One wartime strategy to deal with this new sexualization will be to exploit it—to use sexuality as a weapon in the war. Thus, as Zbynek Zeman suggests in *Selling the War: Art and Propaganda in World War II*, as much as it used a spiritualized image of the girl back home, American war advertising also physicalized the girl in virtually soft-core imagery of a half-dressed innocence's ravishment at the hands of a German or Japanese; as Zeman notes, the visual rhetoric of such advertising exploited its own salaciousness even as the caption tried to argue a different reading.[18]

Frederick Wakeman's *Shore Leave* even goes so far as to represent the sexualized woman as herself desirous of using her sexuality in the war effort. One of the hero Crewson's many pickups, a young woman named Ginger, comes up with a strategy for fighting the enemy:

"How can any girl be happy when they know what the men have to go through? I wanta kill those damn Japs and Germans, too. I betcha if I was a spy or sumpin', I could do it too. I betcha if I was in Germany or some place I could get Hitler to make up to me. I'd get the bastard to go to bed with me, that's what I'd do. I'd kill him in bed."

"The only weapon you'd need would be your beautiful white body, I'll bet," Mac said.

It was a subject that appealed to the girl. She kissed Mac. "When I think of you boys out there dying . . . it makes me wanta do something I just wish I could get that old Hitler in bed. I'd show that pansy. I'd kill him, that's what. . . . I wish the president'd send me over there to Germany. I'd get to Hitler. . . . If they'd only send me over there, I could do this country as much good as a whole regiment, I bet."

"You could do a regiment a lot of good, too, baby," Mac said.

And in her very attempt to use sexuality, Ginger preempts herself from the world of classic narrativity; all too carnal, she can never be a member of the classic couple. The novel must quickly abandon her: the narrator follows up Mac's last comment by wandering away from the conversation to another conversation, a more classically masculine-controlled one with an R.A.F. officer "about the ME 109E." As a chronicle of life in submarines published in *Life* (March 15, 1945) suggests, the woman of evident and open sexuality exists for wartime men in a place other than that of the woman who promises romantic sublimation: "[The men] did not pin up their own girls; those were put safely in lockers or on a shelf where they could be looked at, quietly and secretly."

More generally, it seems that the war moment can become the site for a discursive battle about sexuality and sociality. If, on the one hand, sexuality is to be rewritten into a sublimation, this sublimation is frequently inadequate, incomplete. At the extreme, female desire can set up a current of feeling in a certain excess of the norms of commitment: if *Crash Dive*'s authority figure will proudly assert the readiness of men to go to war, its woman (Anne Baxter) will lament that departure: "When you go away," she complains to Ward Stewart (Tyrone Power), "it's for several days."

Similarly, against the official ideology of war commitment, work for women will be frequently read by men as a quest of women for power, for a power over men. Although historians have emphasized again and again the massive influx of women into the labor force—for example, a 141 percent increase in the number of women working in manufacturing professions—this influx is only vaguely encouraged by government agencies[19] and is never anything more than an encouragement with precise limits and qualifications: In Karen Skold's analysis, the wartime women's labor force functioned as a classic example of a "reserve labor force," a kind of floating stopgap to be employed as mere expediency. Such an analysis even seemed evident to women workers, as Katherine Archibald noted in her recognition that the waiving of one-half of the union fee for women was not a gesture of welcome but "tacitly implied that the emergency, union affiliation, and women's jobs would terminate together."

The situation of the wartime woman is not easily accepted with women going to work, business as usual or unusual. On the one hand, there is an active movement by women to fight for rights, to report infractions; as Leila Rupp especially has noted, against the cliché in standard histories of women's ready acceptance of a role prescribed for them by affirmative ideology, the war years demonstrated the development of new forms of feminism, new attempts at women organizing to make demands that, while announcing support for the war effort, frequently conceived of that support as different in form and shape from the authoritative image.[20] On the other hand, there is an equally active move to internalize the contradictions of the dominant images of wartime femininity and accept a complicated and tension-ridden version of female desire. But, significantly, if the affirmative discourse about women workers works to show them as forces of integrative sublimation—for example, one shipyard newspaper cartoon shows two male workers' surprise when a capable co-worker removes the welding mask to reveal a woman's face beneath— home-front discourse will also figure the factory as a place of allure, a site of adventure: in the words of one ad: "I'm glad to get into war work. I've lost twenty pounds and the men are whistling at me again."[21] The drive to neutralize, to neuter, the workplace ("Like soldiers infiltrating enemy lines, women in the shipyard had to be camouflaged") will meet up against an equally insistent drive to sexualize work, to make it a site of traditional investments of a stereotypical femininity. A number of commentators go so far as to note the commonly held assumption that the government's attempts to move prostitution off the streets and away from the military bases simply moved it into the factories which were imagined to be the place of a rampant nonmarital sexual contact.

Indeed, in her war-affirmative narrative of life in the factory, *Slacks and Callouses,* Constance Bowman describes how even the factory dress code was a source of diversity and debate, agreement and separation. Here I will quote at length to capture something of the complicated interplays of desire and renunciation at work even in a seemingly minor moment of everyday life; throughout, it is important to remember that Bowman's expressed intention is not to criticize or even to neutrally describe factory work, but to promote it, to argue a necessary place for women in the war effort:

Being "in uniform" marked us as *new* to aircraft work. The girls we saw wore every type of slacks, ones that would have been more appropriate in the boudoir. . . . For blouses, they wore crepe torso affairs . . . peasant things with gay embroidery . . . and, of course, sweaters, especially a popular number, sold by the most garish stores in town and ribbed through the midriff for the best "sweater girl" effect. . . . [Hair] coverings were such in name only. . . . [A hair style was] women's crowning glory, which was usually swooped up on top of the head in a complex arrangement of combs, curls, and flowers." (p. 158)

Bowman goes on to recount what happened when the foreman told all women that they would be sent home at the gate if they came to work not wearing regulation caps:

> When we got off the bus at Gate Two, we [Bowman and her friend, C. M.] looked curiously at the other girls who were looking more curiously at us because we were the only ones wearing caps that covered *all* our hair. Most of the girls looked the way they usually did. . . . Nobody had on a cap. . . . We [Bowman and C. M.] felt rather silly, and the backs of our necks were cold. At 4:35 Mr. Billings started down the line. . . . He made all the girls wearing hair coverings other than caps cover *all* their hair, but he didn't send them home. . . . All night the excitement raged. . . . Some of the girls [without coverings at all] went home peacefully and some refused point blank. "You'll have to fire me," said one girl, "because I won't go and I won't quit." Mr. Billings backed down at that and told her to wrap her head in a towel for that night. The girls stopped work to discuss the latest developments. The leadmen said they wanted to know how they could get their ships out if the foreman was going to send all the girls home. . . . The deadline for wearing caps was pushed back to Wednesday. . . . By the time that Wednesday came, it was obvious that Mr. Billings and the other foremen had been vanquished. . . . Lindy was wearing a regulation cap but her "horns" and her "mane" were out again. Irene was wearing a bandana but her magnificent blond pompadour was uncovered. . . . Phyllis, who was now wearing her hair down over her shoulders in a mass of tiny curls, added the final touch to the farce with a triangular felt peasant cap that had a gay bunch of flowers attached to each side. The *only* woman wearing a cap that covered *all* her hair was the woman's counselor who was trying to be an example. (pp. 159–63)

Looking at the fascination with the look of women in the war-period, film scholar Jane Gaines declares, "I find something rebellious in the young women's use of cosmetics, jewelry and other devices to thwart the management rules," and indeed, the contradictions of the war period are to a large degree those of a femininity torn between a renunciation and an intensification.[22]

In part, such troublings of the war-period system of values relate to a broader troubling of the very symbolic order that would maintain and even determine wartime value. Against an older mythology of strong men alone, of women as signs of romance, the wartime situation tries to rewrite sexual differences within a larger system where each figure takes his or her place within an empowering, endowing network of meanings and positions. Governed at the top by an authority that is not so much a particular figure as the symbolic virtue of that figure (Roosevelt, Churchill, various generals)—an authority that delegates and even defines identity—the Symbolic order here would appear initially to be stable, effective, in place.

In *This Is the Army*, for example, each action refers and defers back to an interlocking grid from which it derives its sense. To be sure, there may be a certain carnivalesque playing with the hierarchy of order—as when the soldiers force their sergeant (Alan Hale) into women's clothes for the "Girls of the Chorus" number in the play they're putting on—but such moments occur always on the stage of the show within the film; such playful moments suggest no more than a feigned, fictive, fleeting disturbance of order that ultimately leaves it really undisturbed. In fact, the course of the film implies that a stable order with fixed rank and position is the ground of effective action. This order works through a series of encircling suborders that connect the minutae of everyday life to the vast nature of war as mission. Thus, at the broadest level, the symbolic order is the army itself—a complex structure of intricate relations, a comprehensive mesh of solid links as we see when a track-in to the posted announcement that the army has decided to put on a show is followed by an extended montage of soldiers at various bases and in various jobs receiving orders to participate in the show. And this general order of authority is replayed in each encounter, no matter how ostensibly individualized. Thus, Eileen debates about marriage with Johnny not with arguments from their own specific situation but, rather, from appeals to the social and military order in which Johnny and she (as a W.A.C.) are inscribed. Watched over by the authority figure of the chaplain, Eileen names Johnny as part of the order of an authoritative language (here he is "Corporal Jones"), and she presents their story as a mere echo of the broader story of a fight for freedom. Their life will have only the specificity of serving as a specific exemplum of an abstract set of values.

And yet the effective representation of authority can itself become questionable in the moment of war. The moment of the war becomes a moment of a plural society where each decision can only alienate some group. War need and the need for non-alienation of political constituencies come into potential conflict (for example, according to government analyses, blacks are needed in the armed forces to maintain desired factory output, but such a need conflicts with Southern politicians' conception of those armed forces).

Ultimately, the drive to represent Roosevelt himself as *central subject* of the war narrative becomes the sign not merely of a troubling but of an active discursive conflict. As I've already suggested Roosevelt will seem at the limit of representability, a power that can have no physical embodiment. Beyond that, though, "Roosevelt" will become a site of dispersion, another mark of arbitrariness and instability (thus joining other figures of excessive or inadequate authority such as Patton); for example, as Paul Koistinen argues, "For the President to tell the masses in December, 1943, that 'Dr. New Deal' had to give way to 'Dr. Win-the-War' was to imply that New Deal promises stood in the way of military victory or were inconsistent with it. . . . The public was left with a riddle bound to cause worry and generate resentment."[23] In such a moment, the power and desire of narrative representation to rewrite everyday life inside a coherent narrative seems to generate conflict and to create a self-deconstructive excess.

At the same time, moreover, the Rooseveltian program for war will be one that competing narratives will try to write in competing ways. For example, as Frank Fox notes in *Madison Avenue Goes to War*, American advertisers try specifically to rewrite the war effort as the effort of a free-market economy, against New

Deal notions of social assistance—in the words of the advertisers, "Charity, dole, handouts will meet with the contempt they deserve."[24] Thus, if Roosevelt speaks of the four freedoms, advertisers will add a fifth one to the list: "The U.S. system of free enterprise is the Fifth Freedom" (quoted in Fox, p. 69). The single narrative of the war effort expands its coverage but it also splits into a number of potentially incompatible narratives. Indeed, the Roosevelt image itself will become a subject for debate as Republicans argue that a promotion of Roosevelt into Commander-in-Chief can only aid the specifically political campaigns of Roosevelt as presidential candidate and party politician. One consequence will be a certain lessening of Roosevelt's authority or participation in authority situations; for example, Republicans successfully campaign to remove mention of Roosevelt from many publications for soldiers overseas (and they manage to lessen Democrat control over voting procedures).[25] Similarly, to cite another example, the Capra film *Prelude to War* (1943) will be the site for an intense debate on the relationship between politics and the war effort. As Ed Lowry explains,

> Senator Rufus C. Holman, Republican from Oregon, introduced a resolution on February 8, 1943 for the investigation of government propaganda. Having seen a private showing of *Prelude to War* at an American Legion dinner the previous January 11, Holman was upset by the political nature of the film. "At the conclusion of the picture," Holman told the Senate, "I was convinced that Mr. Roosevelt intended to seek a fourth term in the Presidency." . . . *Time* magazine [spent] the first three paragraphs of its article painting Holman as a buffoon and recalling that at one time, before the war, he had "commended the Third Reich." . . . It is interesting to note that the *New York Times* article which reported Holman's charges ended with the statement that "close associates of President Roosevelt are taking it for granted that he will run for a fourth term unless the war has been won . . . by convention time in 1944."[26]

One way to get at the consequences of all this contradiction for film narrative would be to turn to psychoanalysis and suggest that the instability of the symbolic order of authority and authoritative discourse has as a consequence a certain regression of war narrative to a sort of pre-oedipal stage. That is, the narratives can be read to respond to the complexity of the social moment through a kind of vast imagining of a drive that preexists the fall into a sublimative adult history filled with all sorts of overwhelming responsibility. In intense moments, authoritative power weakens and threatens to throw subjects into a situation of dispersion and conflict, an inability to see a single and necessary logic. In some cases, this leads to a madcap regression—all those service comedies about incompetent boobs wreaking havoc on a military base. But it as frequently leads to a reinvigoration of individualist strength, a mythology of loners who go their own way outside the constraints of a dominant system. If, for example, sexuality is becoming fearful, films of men in battle will disavow female sexuality for an image of men together fighting with a sort of unbridled boyish energy that knows little opposition or challenge. Through a kind of inversion, the more films work to affirm the triumph of the war effort, the more they can seem to move into an imaginary space governed by a fantasy of pure strength where little is affirmed but one's own prowess. And yet, not surprisingly, the very foundation of that prowess in a boyish fantasy leaves the narratives open to all sorts of sudden reversals in which strength and prowess can suddenly become weakness, in which bravery can suddenly turn into fear, in which the optimism of victory can turn into a paranoid surety of defeat.

Where a number of theorists have well suggested the complications of the symbolic order in the postwar moment,[27] similar complications can seem to have already set in within the order of the war-affirmative moment. As Mary Ann Doane suggests in her analysis of *Gilda* (1946), how hero Johnny (Glenn Ford) rises to phallic power and authority at the cost of his symbolic father's loss of representation—"Ballin [the father figure] is deprived of corporeal reality in relation to Johnny and Gilda because his structural position is that of the zero-degree of textuality, of place-holder in the narrative" (p. 20)—so too the wartime film veers between the effective representation of an oedipal situation under the sway of a father—the authority of a dominant system, the formation of couples under the sign of the benevolent, paternal system—and the perverse representation of an unbridled phallic power that knows no name-of-the-father. Indeed, as symbolic figure, Roosevelt himself is caught in a conflict of effective versus ineffective absence and/or presence. On the one hand, Roosevelt is the originary figure for the war narrative—the Law that gives all forces their position and mission (as in *Mission to Moscow* where he names Joseph Davies as Ambassador to Russia, or *The Princess O'Rourke* where he serves as witness for the marriage of commoner Joe O'Rourke [Robert Cummings] and Princess Maria [Olivia de Havilland]). In *This Is the Army*, Roosevelt comes to the last-night performance of the army play just before the boys are to be shipped overseas. But, on the other hand, in all these instances, Roosevelt is nothing but an insubstantial figure, never a full actant (at best, he is what Greimas calls the *destinateur* from whom the active hero gains a mission; at worst, as in *This Is the Army*, he does nothing but passively observe the active spectacle of others). The authority figure here is the absent cause who, like Ballin in *Gilda*, is assigned to the fate of a certain insubstantiality (a role that Roosevelt himself internalizes and encourages).

A weakly glimpsed Symbolic order throws social subjects into a potentially pre-oedipal-like state: war as game, life as immediate gratification or denial—wartime comedies, for example, become manifestly infantile, scenes of extreme accomplishment (an unbridled pre-oedipal power) alternating brusquely with scenes of extreme failure (for example, *Caught in the Draft* in which Don Bolton [Bob Hope] regains and loses and regains and loses Tony Fairbank [Dorothy Lamour]).

Closer analysis of several films that set out to represent male power can help us understand the vulnerability of war narrative to a paranoid system of sudden reversals. For example, despite its bleak title, even a noncomedy like *Desperate Journey* can seem like an infantile phantasm, a narrative of self-willed men outside commitment to a central, sense-giving authority. Indeed, many reviewers reacted to what they saw as the exaggeration of the film's narrative line, its endless celebration of men having a grand time while escaping from Nazi Germany. For example, *Time* sums up the story in this way: "[The Americans'] circuitous escape to England . . . is accomplished with more outrageous luck than even Rover Boys can count on" (August 17, 1942).

But in noting such reviews, I don't mean to imply a correctness of the reviewers' evaluation against which a film like *Desperate Journey* is to be measured. Rather, I am more interested in the fact that reviewers of the moment seemed to engage in such a measuring; something about such films seemed to exceed the limits of the clichés of wartime narrative. *Desperate Journey* suggests a certain disparity between the concept of heroism and the concept of an obedience to authority, although both are values promoted in the war moment. *Desperate Journey* resolves the disparity to the advantage of an extreme emphasis on a heroism disconnected from the proclaimed rational planning of a central and dominant authority. In this way, the film joins with a whole current of narratives in the war moment that affirm war while taking a distance from the official representation of war. For example, as the narrator of Wakeman's *Shore Leave* recounts:

[The pilots] slouched off the field as only fliers can slouch. Fliers are without doubt the most unmilitary of all fighting men. They refuse to pattern themselves to the military way of sitting, standing, walking, thinking. They'll do anything to make a uniform not uniform. I for one admire this trait in fliers, because it is a sign of rebellion against the stupidities of war that make it necessary for men to be pounded into the military mold.

I watched Crewson salute a marine. He didn't return a regulation salute. It was expert, but unique . . . a snappy stylized wave of the hand that said casually, "Hi ya, buddie."

Fliers are the only fighting men who can get by with this sort of thing. They strongly feel their importance in this war, and no superior officer is going to make them put their shoulders back, button their coat pockets, or wear their caps straight.

In the case of *Desperate Journey*, excess seems to take place at the level of the film's play with the framework of the classic narrative. Here, the death of a father figure (the flight commander killed off early in the mission) leads not to a renunciation of unbridled desires for the sake of submission to the rules but to the outburst of new desires: the soldiers can act like kids (one shoots spitballs at the Nazis; another talks gobbledygook to a Nazi general, knocks him out, and sits behind his desk; they all make wisecracks and jokes). A split occurs between the needs of authority and the desires of the individuals; the new commander, Terence Forbes (Errol Flynn), constantly wants to defer the crew's necessary return home (they've got to get back to pass on important intelligence information) to sabotage one more factory, to drop bombs on one more railroad. And, in the film's phantasm, the split is generally resolved to the benefit of the individual. Power here becomes an unbridled force that goes beyond the demands of the system.

Similarly, women here become not the objects of a sexual trajectory that would force a sublimation of infantile desires. Without a legitimating authority, the force of the couple as a goal of the war becomes less assured. Frequently, when women appear in the war narratives, they do so only as quite temporary interludes for a man who is passing on to what the films view as more important things. In *Desperate Journey*, for example, women are represented precisely as the objects of a pre-oedipal wonder—split along the lines that Melanie Klein analyzed as the "good" and "bad" object relations that the child creates with the mother. (And here, in the very ways that a film seems drawn to suggesting a bipolar image of femininity, we can perhaps see some continuities of war narrative to the paranoia of postwar *film noir.*) *Desperate Journey's* two women are, on the one hand, a woman met in a shop who at first might be a betrayer but turns out to be a nurse—that is, a succoring figure—and, on the other hand, an elderly and seemingly motherly housewife, first assumed to be a source of safety as she offers refuge and invites the pursued Americans a place to eat and rest, but then discovered to be a Nazi agent. Against the forward-moving narrative of men in control of their situation, the presence of the women sets up a kind of counternarrative: the representation of men either as passive victims (they follow the elderly woman into the trap) or passive recipients of a succoring attention.

The balancing of reversals here sets up an alternation that is not so much narrative as endlessly cyclic (perhaps like the fort/da game that Freud suggests is the child's prenarrative, pre-oedipal, phantasmatic way of dealing with the possible with-drawal but also return of the mother). Even the good woman is here not the goal of narrative—the ultimate destination of the men's mission as it is in *Destination: Tokyo*—but a mere expedient in that mission, a helper in the men's boyish fantasies of power and triumph. At the extreme, the grim pragmatism of war—the renunciation of desire and couple formation until the war is over—can turn into a sense of war itself as the real object of desire. The nonnarrativity of the boyish fantasy of endless triumph over re-sistant matter can become the desire for an endless deferment of all endings: war is really a good show where men have their best times, their greatest release. Attachment to the woman here is not the goal of war, but the disturbing disruption of it. War turns into a great show, a point made most emphatically in *This Is the Army*, where retired G.I.'s put on a show for the boys and, declaring, "It's a great show . . . and a great war," find that war allows them the best chance to turn life into an endless spectacle with no women around.

Not surprisingly, the flip side of the fantasy of power is a kind of paranoia: *Desperate Journey* alternates its crew's virtually miraculous accomplishments with a nightmarish display of the world's refusal to conform to the fantasy. Without a fully author-itative center, with only a temporary inspiration by feminine spir-ituality, the film throws the men into a kind of placeless space, an ambiguous and potentially malevolent site. Not merely femininity but all aspects of the enveloping world can become a potentially menacing other. One side of the film concerns an endless repeti-tion of disaster, from the original downing of the bomber to the death of the flight commander, to the constant ambush by Nazis and the whittling down of the crew, to the very betrayal of equip-ment and ordinary objects (the plane that crashes, the escape car that runs out of gas). The Americans move through a world that is not their own and in which there are few external aids to guide them. Away from their commanders, in a situation unexplained in their rulebooks, they must struggle without the benefit of an authoritative knowledge that could support their endeavors. Indeed, if there is a "father" figure in the film, it is the bad father represented by the German general, Major Baumeister (Raymond Massey), who decides to recapture the Americans at all costs and keeps popping up to threaten interference with their plans (a final chase sequence is a kind of microsequential condensation of this motif of endless and recurrent threat as the general's car finds them, loses them, parallels them, cuts them off, loses them again, etc.). The general becomes a sort of external projection of paranoia; significantly, he is dealt with in a manner of regressive boyish power: he is beaten up, he is mocked and spoken to with gobbledygook, and his death occurs as part of a spectacular orgy of violence as the Americans steal a German plane and turn its machine gun on German troops; immediately after, the Americans use this very plane to bomb enemy ports.

In this boyish fantasy, respectable authority only appears as a kind of last-minute afterthought; in their stolen plane, the crew members radio to England to announce their return, a "parental" recognition is established (the officers back home recognize Forbes' voice and thus no longer give him up for dead; the scene suggests the role of authority to be literally no more than a Symbolic one—a function of naming). But just as quickly, the power of individuals to go their own way outside the system reasserts itself, and fantasy once more comes in to turn the recognition of authority into nothing more than a supersedable moment in a cyclicity of fantastic power ("And now for Australia and a crack at those Japs," announces one of the crew members in the last line of the film). England remains a mere background; rampant individualism holds sway.

To be sure, there is a seemingly adult force that intrudes repetitively into the war-front fantasy: the force of death, a kind of ultimate resistance of worldly reality to the fictionalizing power of the boyish fantasy. Death puts a certain lie to the resilience of fantasy. Death is everywhere, happening to everyone. And yet even the finality of death—its status as a closing of narrative—will be rewritten in the war film as part of an antinarrative force, an endless repetition that does not die. As Alfred Appel, Jr., notes in *Signs of Life*, a commentary on American photography, the war moment even tried to disregard death: for example, the first time that *Life* tried to publish pictures of dead G.I.'s, the magazine was blocked from doing so, and the pictures only eventually came out with various intensifying marks of death—for example, maggots—airbrushed out.[28]

War narrative works to come up with a series of strategies to deal with the threat of death. First, quite literally, death becomes the mark of interchangeability; in many war films, death will simply lead to the replacement of dead soldiers by new troops and the story goes on (for example, *Guadalcanal Diary*). Another variant is to begin a narrative with what seems to be death and then exchange that first sign of death for a continuing life: for example, in *Edge of Darkness* (1943), the opening scene shows the discovery of a Scandinavian town littered with the bodies of Germans and freedom fighters alike. The film then moves into flashback to show us the freedom fighters (especially those played by stars Errol Flynn, Ann Sheridan, and Walter Huston) preparing for the battle whose results are the present time of the film's frame. But the return at the film's end to the frame shows the Flynn, Sheridan, and Huston characters having survived the battle and marching on toward their next encounter with the enemy. While the move into flashback plays on that sense of ill-fated destiny that will be so prevalent in forties film, here the flashback is a kind of deliberate trick, setting up an expectation of the worst that will then be triumphantly overturned. However, even in those cases where death is an irreversibility, a whittling down of forces—as in *Dive Bomber* (1941), where a clique of three expert pilots becomes two, then one, then zero—death is usually something that one doesn't stop to worry over; in a kind of antinarrative denial, it is passed over, quickly forgotten: in *Air Force,* for example, Crew Chief Sergeant White's discovery that his cherished son died in the earliest moments of combat is quickly repressed as a new Japanese attack leads to the need to instantly bury grief and to jump back into combat with full attention and commitment.

In other cases, death will be followed by a disavowing tone of stoic, ritual acceptance (as in *Dive Bomber,* with its passing on of a symbolic cigarette lighter to the survivors of the clique) or a tone of light comedy (for example, in *Desperate Journey*, where none of the deaths have enough influence to stop the sheer fun that the crew has in its perilous escape) or, in extreme situations, will become a source of further bravado. In *Sahara*, for example, the death of Tambul (Rex Ingram), shot down after he leaves the fort to kill a Nazi escaping with important information, is finally a positive event, a tragedy immediately turned into triumph: Tambul dies but in his death, he signals an OK to Sergeant Gunn (Humphrey Bogart) and so fortifies Gunn's own confidence. Another possibility will be to allow death, but only to secondary characters; thus, in *Since You Went Away*, young Jane Hilton's man can die in battle, but not the father of the family: the father's telephone call home at Christmas will enable the narrative to come to a sure, symbolic close.

Some films further suggest how the phantasm of the war film is a phantasm of the textual system of narrative as a whole and not just of particular characters. In *Sahara*, for example, the whittling down of the squadron coincides with a whittling down of the actors until only stars remain (Humphrey Bogart, Bruce Bennett); similarly, *Desperate Journey's* crew reduces down through the killings to just Errol Flynn, Arthur Kennedy, and Ronald Reagan. Death, then, becomes a kind of intensification of Hollywood spectacle, a reaffirmation of the dream machine; a welcomed event, death increases points of identification, and collapses the potential diffusion of character identification onto a few central figures. In this way, character and actor enter into a mutually enforcing circuit; the whittling away of a crew further encourages the prowess of the star character who must battle on alone and whose triumphant power at the film's end becomes all the more remarkable and admirable. For example, *Sahara* shows Sergeant Gunn (whose very name suggests a kind of identification with power) gaining in effectiveness the fewer men he has around him; from a single airplane with one German pilot to a scout truck with a handful of Germans to a first attack by a single wave of German troops to a final appearance of an entire German company, Gunn's adversary grows in strength as his team correspondingly diminishes in number. But each time, Gunn's ability to triumph is equal to the task before him. The phantasm is finally that of a power that derives its force miraculously: thus, in a kind of replaying of biblical mythology, Gunn will be the figure whose presence causes water to pour bountifully from the barren desert.

But in extreme cases, death leads to a certain misalignment of personal need and responsibility to a system of authority: thus, a number of films show people joining the fight not because of any sense of responsibility but because of a death that has touched them in some closely personal way. While certain films will try to realign personal tragedy and public necessity—by suggesting, for example, that the goal of commitment precisely is to uphold personal relationships—a number of films will show personal motifs as valued separately from social belonging. In *Manhunt*, for example, the hero, Thorndike, joins the war effort because a woman he felt for has been killed brutally by the Nazis.[29] The last scene explicitly shows Thorndikes's decision to undertake revenge as necessitating procedures separate from the needs of the war machine; unlike, say, *Five Graves to Cairo*, where the ending shows the hero working to avenge his loved one's death by becoming part of a regiment, *Manhunt* ends with Thorndike leaving his post (he parachutes from a plane in which he is a crew member) to pursue his lone quest. An end title that announces that Thorndike is somewhere in Germany trying to kill Hitler even seems to give a certain approval to his desire to act alone; written in the present tense, the end credit leaves the narrative open and creates the fantasy that indeed this might be a way to end the war (and, indeed, the film's opening, with Thorndike managing to aim a gun at Hitler, gives the final repetition of the manhunt a certain probability of success).

Like *Shore Leave*, with Ginger threatening to kill Hitler with sexuality, *Manhunt* creates the fantasy of an individualist, nonauthorized way of fighting the war. Significantly, both narratives suggest a certain breakdown of classic narrativity along lines of newly intensifed sexual difference: the new woman's weapon is sexuality; the man's is an uncivilized, individualized, nonobedient force driven by motives of revenge. Leaving its narrative unresolved and in a present tense, *Manhunt* suggests war not just as a narrative, but as an endless demonstration of power and vigilance. To be sure, Thorndike has a goal at the end of the film, but that goal is outside the trajectory of social desire. Thorndike has left the group, has lost the woman. His goal is to make up for a past rather than to build a new future.

In many moments of war narrative, the distance between the logic of authority and the force of the individual widens. For example, in *Manhunt*, Thorndike's ending up in a cave where, with the raw power of his wit, he confronts the Nazi Quive-Smith (George Sanders) in the ultimate battle brings to its fundamental point a narrative that all along has pulled Thorndike out of any emplacement within a social order and has moved him instead toward a primitive space of primal encounters. Despite his *nominal* membership in the aristocracy (a membership that he quickly gives up as when he discovers the delights of fish-and-chips eaten with the fingers), Thorndike is not civilized man, but a caveman. *Manhunt* suggests that the encounter with an enemy takes place in a phantasmic place outside the possibility of calm, pragmatic obedience to a central authority. Indeed, it is the Germans, not Thorndike himself, who want to label him as part of a dominant order. Where Thorndike would like to continue on in the space of pure, self-engendering individualism, Quive-Smith works to situate Thorndike, to rewrite his individuality as membership in an order. Quive-Smith tries to make Thorndike accept a naming—first, as the Thorndike who has a great reputation as a hunter, and second, as the Thorndike who acted on government orders to kill Hitler, and finally, as the Thorndike who acted on his own to kill Hitler (as Quive-Smith tells him, "From the moment that you crossed the frontier, you became an unconscious assassin").

But Thorndike's answer—his refusal to sign—pushes him toward a presymbolic space, a space where lone hunters can track down lone men as if they were a prey like any other. Thorndike's admission near the end of the film that he in fact was acting toward a socially responsible goal—that is, that he did in fact intend to kill Hitler—only inadequately answers the ambiguity of the first scene in which Thorndike's intention is undecidable (and even in admitting that he wanted to kill Hitler, Thorndike maintains that his intention had nothing to do with the wishes of his government). Indeed, the opening sequence seems to overdetermine the phantasmic structure—the image of life without responsibility or decision—by causing an external force to disrupt Thorndike's action. Having loaded his rifle, Thorndike takes aim, and then . . . a leaf falls down onto his rifle sight; Thorndike stops his action to brush away the leaf, and in that pause, a German sentry is able to jump him. An event not only in the *énoncé* (the recounted events of Thorndike's actions) but also of the *énonciation* (the narrating instance's control over the events that occur), the falling leaf allows, as Odile Bächler has noted, an ambiguation of the question of intention and leaves the film in a register where intention can never be decided.[30] We never know if war for Thorndike is ever a social, rather than personal, event.

At the same time, the space of Thorndike's adventures in *Manhunt* is frequently a space of paranoia, a space that throws Thorndike (and, with him, the film's style) into a paranoid register. That is, the film substitutes for the image of a rational, emplaced, authoritative fighting system an image of the fighter as driven by asocial needs in a place outside the centrality of a war effort: Thorndike is a kind of existential figure struggling in a wasteland that holds no teleological promise of spiritual redemption in a succoring place. The space of the paranoid register is made up of an endless pattern of aggressing and being aggressed against. The opening sequence sets up this pattern as a figure that will run through the film; if, as Jacqueline Rose has suggested, cinema bears the constant threat of the fall into paranoia through the very instability of point of view (any character can see and then become someone or something else's seen),[31] the opening of *Manhunt* shows this threat through a narrational pattern that constantly reverses point of view and exchanges the site and sight of aggression between different points of view.

Thus, the very first image has the camera tracking across the footprints in the forest floor; catching up to Thorndike, the source of those footprints, the tracking makes the hunter-hero into a hunted figure who, at the moment of obscurity, is found out (thus prefiguring the moment when the German guard catches up to him). The reversible structure condenses around the privileged moment of sight; the moment when Thorndike is able finally to capture Hitler in his rifle sight is also the moment when the German guard is able to spot Thorndike. At the moment, then, that Thorndike sees, the German sees Thorndike and prevents him from turning sight into action. From this moment on, Thorndike becomes a character who either does not see (for example, when he ventures out in the London streets to visit his lawyer, he does not spot a Nazi who spots him and sets out to trap him) or sees what he does not want to see (as in the last confrontation where Quive-Smith shows Thorndike the jewelry pin that proves that the Nazis have killed the woman, Jerry).

The opening initiates a pattern of aggressive doubling that runs through the film (and that is only partially closed off by Thorndike's final parachuting into Germany): the external world, for example, is frequently for Thorndike not a utensility that he can control to his own ends nor an authority that will grant him his proper place but a nightmare of aggressivity, based on a kind of projection of menace into all aspects of the environment: police, for example, turn out to be Nazi infiltrators; the Nazis even take over Thorndike's name; when one of their men is killed in a London metro, Thorndike is accused of the murder and pursued by the London authorities. There is little question of a world worth fighting for here, since that very world is what Thorndike ends up having to fight against. With the police turned into aggressors, with the aristocracy pictured as only able to help Thorndike up to a certain point (the government can't get too involved or the Germans will be able to claim that Thorndike *was* acting on government orders), Britain becomes pictured not as a supportive, communal place but as one more extension of a threatening surrounding. London, for example, becomes a place of shadow and obscurity, a site of omnipresent threat. On the other hand, the seemingly tranquil English countryside is also a place of ultimate menace where villagers betray Thorndike to Quive-Smith, who shows up, as in a nightmare where one cannot escape evil figures, and entraps Thorndike in a cave.

Indeed, space throughout the film has a nightmarish

quality to it: on the one hand, images of claustrophobic entrapment (the Nazi office in which Thorndike is interrogated; the secret
compartment in which he has to hide when a ship he is escaping
in is searched; the doorway he must press himself into to avoid
capture in the streets of London; the cave in which Quive-Smith
corners him and in which he is told about the death of Jerry, the
woman he has grown to love). On the other hand, there are images
of open spaces as sites of uncertainty and doubt (the streets of
London into which Nazis can pop up at any moment; the space
of the edge of a cliff where Thorndike is flung in a replay of one
of our most recurrent nightmare images—a horrifying free-fall
into an abyss).

   Space itself becomes phantasmic, charged with all the
aggressivity of a paranoia that understands geography as a menace
that is directed inward but that one can try masterfully to direct
outward. In their analysis of another Fritz Lang wartime film,
Hangmen Also Die! (1943), Jean-Louis Comolli and François Géré
suggest that that film enacts a certain displacement of the representation of a historically specific German place—that it turns
Germany from a real geographical target into a virtual nonplace
through which the film loses some of its power to condemn Nazism
as a specific force: the film is "in effect about a Germany that is
constantly *beside itself,* slipping out of its geographic limits and
losing its moral temper: unbridled."[32] *Manhunt* engages in a similar
phantasmization of historical space. Germany here is only the
swamps through which one is tracked (by the camera, by the
Nazis); the cliffs on which one is captured or thrown off; the room
in which one is questioned and taken away to be tortured. Just as
England is not a place that one fights for, Germany is not a
substantial place that one could really fight against.

   Indeed, the scene of interrogation seems a condensation of Langian style, as Raymond Bellour and others have staked
out its dimensions. First, there is a deconstruction of psychological
and dramatic depth through a deliberate flatness—for example,
the opening shot of the torture sequence which focuses on moun-
tains that are obviously a backdrop. Second, there is a deliberate
emptying of the image until it becomes a virtual blankness against

which a few objects emerge to gain a value that is emblematic, or to use Brecht's term, *gestic*. Third, despite (or because of) these obvious ways in which the "naturalistic" image is theatricalized, turned into a staging, there is a certain emphasis on the space of the frame as a potentially open space. Creating a kind of dialectic of onscreen and offscreen space, the visible image gives glimpses of another space beyond the frame: open doorways that we only get a glimpse into; windows that appear to indicate an elsewhere; entrances and exits that turn the framed area into an arbitrary cutout of space. But unlike, say Renoir, for whom openness can seem an attempt to create the reality effect of a real world in vibrant flux (as in Leo Braudy's reading of Renoir), Lang's openness seems one in which the notion of the frame as *analgon* of a real is displaced by a notion of the frame as mere element in a formal structure, a combinatory, whose value is the quasi-mathematical one of the articulation of forms, not the suggestion of human(ist) meanings of life's richness.[33] In a film that has already begun to deprive its hero of agency and turn him instead into a mere figure of the enunciative apparatus, the very composition of space deprives the "hero" of a ground in which his actions could take on a full sense.

This robbing of space's "body" extends to the representation of England, which loses the substantiality of a place worth fighting for. Indeed, the first vision of England occurs *within* the Germany part of the film: when the Nazis telephone to their embassy in England to find out if their prisoner could really be the famous Captain Thorndike, one establishing shot gives us the Thames skyline before moving into a scene inside the German embassy. The establishing shot of London seems typically Langian in its deliberate undoing of spatial richness: a bridge in silhouette with pedestrians in silhouette against a skyline that is evidently a rear projection. The very insubstantiality of this image of London is further underscored by the dissolve into the German embassy which is filmed as a vast blank wall on which one German insignia hangs emblematically and in front of which a German paces back and forth. The conjunction of shots infuses all space with a sort of metaphoric flatness and antipsychological theatricality.

The film's solution to the paranoia of aggressivity is to

respond with an equal aggressivity to the threats surrounding Thorndike. Instead of Thorndike growing out of an aggressive stage—an infinitely repeating state of attack, escape, counterattack—he rests at the level of repetition: thus, news of Jerry's death leads Thorndike not to accept authority but to strike out, killing Quive-Smith and enlisting in the R.A.F. only so he can get a chance to parachute into Germany. While Jerry is a kind of "bad object" turned good—the prostitute who shows herself capable of a nurturing love for Thorndike—Quive-Smith is a good object turned bad.[34] With a British name, and played by a British actor, Quive-Smith is a sort of double for Thorndike (and like Thorndike, he is literally and metaphorically a hunter), and, in psychoanalytic terms, he is readable as a kind of fatherly rival for Thorndike; indeed, his insistence that hunting should never be just for sport but always for a useful goal establishes him as a mark of adult utility against Thorndike's infantile invocation of a pleasure principle. But the rivalry is resolved outside an oedipal triangulation: with Jerry dead, Thorndike's quest becomes not an attempt to accept authority and renunciation but, rather, to deny it, to remain at the level of nostalgic fixation. Significantly, the cupid-arrow brooch that Thorndike gave to Jerry (and that Quive-Smith gives back to him in announcing Jerry's death) will first serve as the head of the arrow that Thorndike constructs to kill Quive-Smith and, then, as the insignia on the plane that Thorndike will parachute from at the film's end.

      More generally, actions occur in the film not as forward-moving developments but as retrospective answerings to earlier actions; where, in Raymond Bellour's analysis of *Gigi* (1958) (among other films), narrative repetition provides the basis for an essential difference—the last shot of the film is like the first but with the difference that Gaston and Gigi are now together as husband and wife[35]—*Manhunt* would seem to emphasize repetitions over difference. Rather than the synchrony by which romance and ending meet up in a film like *Gigi*, *Manhunt* suggests a nonsynchrony in which the ending occurs after romance has already been eliminated as a real force, turned into a mere memory trace of the murdered Jerry.

      In *Manhunt*, each moment of triumph is quickly reversed into a moment of paranoia: each moment of paranoia is reversed into a moment of triumph. Continually, freedom becomes entrapment, entrapment becomes escape. Each sequence becomes a microsequential embodiment of this nonadvancing procedure. The aggressor-aggressed reversals of the opening sequence are replayed at every moment: for example, in one scene Thorndike is heading down a street when Nazis suddenly appear at one end; Thorndike turns to escape in the other direction but a second Nazi appears there; Thorndike ducks into a doorway and temporarily eludes his pursuers; the Nazis figure out what has happened and begin to move in on Thorndike; Thorndike enters the house and meets Jerry who first menaces him but then helps him escape.

It may be pertinent to compare this reading to a seemingly similar reading by Raymond Bellour of a seemingly similar scene in *North by Northwest* (1959): Roger Thornhill goes to what is supposed to be a meeting at a cornfield but which actually turns out to be an ambush.[36] In Bellour's analysis, the aggressivity of the cornfield sequence occurs within a transitional moment between the pre-oedipal and oedipal phases of the oedipal trajectory: Thornhill has already had to begin renouncing his infantile desire, his hubristic sense of control over the world. On the one hand, he has had to leave his mother, and, on the other hand, he has begun to experience a certain whittling away of his phallic power through his interactions with Eve Kendall. The cornfield sequence, then, would be part of a process of growing acceptance—Thornhill accepts the fact that he is caught up in a network of intrigue whose sense eludes him; Thornhill accepts the fact that his seductive charm is not enough. Whatever the appropriateness of this reading as a model for *North by Northwest*, I would suggest that it can seem inappropriate to a contradictory film of the war period like *Manhunt*. In *Manhunt*, Thorndike begins in a world of brute power and remains there, disavowing the need for any renunciation; the ending with Thorndike brandishing his rifle repeats the opening's emphasis on prowess and stresses its continuation. The scene of ambush in the streets of London is not the discovery of a woman's independent power but a fantasy of a woman's total support, of her desire to abandon carnality to succor the male and give him justification in his quest. Moreover, where the cornfield sequence would serve to introduce Thornhill to the law of the father and so would establish the father as effective rival, *Manhunt's* narrative works to split "father" and "mother" into separate worlds, thus minimalizing the story as a story of rivalry: by making Jerry a lower-class figure and Quive-Smith an upper-class one, the film instills an incompatibility, a fundamental incommunicability, into any relationship between them. Quive-Smith's relation to Jerry becomes one of aggression, not desire. Thus, Quive-Smith can kill Jerry and turn the film into a battle of men but not a battle of men for the love of women.

But the very embodying of this aggressive force in a quite specific figure—an all-too-suave George Sanders—further changes the film from a drama of war affirmation into an enclosed, privatized, perverse drama. Indeed, more generally, the war film can be implicitly threatened by the seductive presence of the forces it explicitly wants to deem as evil. That is, it can grant a charm or substance to the enemy that it frequently takes away from the forces of good: thus, if Jerry is only an unreal memory in the last confrontation of good men and bad men, the confrontation itself is only all too real, all too physically agggressive. For example, in their article on *Hangmen Also Die!*, Comolli and Géré suggest that the affirmative project of that film autodeconstructs when, to make the stakes of the conflict high enough, it gives too much of a body to the Nazi antagonist, Gruber, and so reverses points of identification:

> Gruber is endowed with a *body:* which distinguishes him sharply from the Nazis . . . but also from the resistants as phantasms, zombies. [The film's] chief concern is that its most "positive" heroes . . . should ultimately be no more than simulacra of bodies moved by a force, an energy, a logic which they do not understand and against which they are helpless. . . . The mere physical presence of Gruber face to face with members of either group in a shot produces an effect of such violent contrast that his corporeal reality, and their unreality, is stressed and accentuated: his power, their impotence. This aggressive body denotes as such these simulacra surrounding it. There is in Gruber a healthy vampire-growth which leaves the others anaemic. (pp. 136–37)

Indeed, in her study of propaganda fiction, Susan Su-

leiman has suggested that the very drive to represent an opponent's view through an embodiment of that view in a flesh-and-
blood figure can give the opponent's view a vital force that can
create a seductive countercurrent to the narrative project of the
propaganda.[37] Propaganda is poised in a contradictory position; if
it underplays the force of the enemy, it can call into question the
very need for propaganda (who needs to be convinced to fight an
easy enemy?), but if it overplays opposition, it can either lead to
a despairing quietism or to a positive attraction to the force of the
enemy.

　　Significantly, in giving body to Quive-Smith, *Manhunt*
even gives him a certain narrative agency; it is frequently through
an identification of literal point of view with Quive-Smith's particular perspective that the spectator gains information on the
events that are transpiring. Revealingly, the figure of a camera
movement into a swamp at the beginning of the film has an almost
exact repetition later when, having thrown Thorndike off a cliff,
the Nazis go the following morning to look for the body. After
two shots of the Nazis looking, there is a cut to a shot that moves
into the swamp: what in the opening scene was a vision by the
film itself now becomes located in a particular point of view—
that of the Nazis and of Quive-Smith in particular. Quive-Smith
increasingly becomes the enunciative relay for the film's sight.
That is, he becomes the primary source of looking and so, in a
reversal that is potentially subversive of the order of war affirmation, he becomes a necessary point for a literal identification
on the spectator's part. If Thorndike's early attempt to have a full
sight by aiming at Hitler is a moment of fleeting plenitude whose
ultimate consequence is to rob him of agency, Quive-Smith becomes the agent of the look, the person who sets out to know.
The film, then, complicates identification by investing the spectator's epistemological interest in a figure from the wrong side.[38]
The lack of dialogue (or, rather, English-language dialogue) in the
two swamp sequences further encourages an identification with
forces outside or even opposed to Thorndike, the nominal hero.
With the Nazis, the spectator must learn to interpret visual signs.
By presenting voiceless images to be decoded, the sequences turn

the viewer into an active reader of the image, an interpreter not unlike Quive-Smith himself; indeed, in the second swamp sequence, the viewer receives information at the same time as the Nazis and from the same visual point of view (for example, the shot of the broken branches of a tree, suggesting that Thorndike's fall was broken and that he has escaped).

At the same time, images that are visually ambiguous to the spectator—for example, the look on Thorndike's face as he loads the bullet into his rifle and aims at Hitler—have an extreme clarity to Quive-Smith (in part, perhaps, because he was not there to witness them originally and can only unambiguously construct their meaning in the posteriority of a reflective thought). Thus, when Quive-Smith's knowledge is not concurrent with the spectator's, it is simply ahead of the spectator's, anticipating the narrative and even indeed writing it.

In the classic war-affirmative film, the hero discovers a commitment to the war through a burst of spontaneous insight and a clarity of mission that figures conversion as the ultimate subjective and heroic act—for example, Rick's commitment in *Casablanca* takes place against the Nazi's inability to comprehend which way Rick's sympathies are leaning. In contrast, Thorndike is, for Quive-Smith, perfectly readable; Thorndike's sudden declaration in the last confrontation that he had intended to kill Hitler isn't a victory of commitment but, quite the contrary, a confirmation of Nazi perception and, by that, of the Nazi perception of world politics (even if Quive-Smith never proves that Thorndike was working for the British government, he does prove that certain Britishers, however alone, were already in a war attitude before the official declaration of war).

The construction of Thorndike as a figure dispersed inside a paranoid figuration determines also the construction of the woman figure, Jerry. In Odile Bächler's words, "The image of fear, pleasure, death are delegated to Jerry as a necessary condition of the masculine phantasm, of the apprehension of his duty."[39] But in a kind of dual deconstruction of the sexual difference of classic narrativity, *Manhunt* structures this phantasm of the feminine in a perverse way. Jerry is simultaneously the available and inaccessible figure in Thorndike's narrative. Here, there can be no image of the woman waiting as in *Destination: Tokyo*. On the one hand, the representation of Jerry takes to an extreme Raymond Bellour's suggestion that "the classical American cinema is founded on a systematicity which operates very precisely at the expense of the woman, if one can put it that way, by determining her image, her images, in relation to the desire of the masculine subject."[40] Jerry is here a figure *for Thorndike* but almost excessively so; where the classic narrative would defer the formation of the couple to the final instant of an enclosing ending, here the woman is immediately available to the man from the start. There is no oedipal struggle, no need for the man to prove himself in rivalry. By making Jerry available to Thorndike so quickly, the film removes the formation of the couple as a goal of the narrative; here, there is no formation to work toward.

But, on the other hand, Jerry is ultimately unavailable to Thorndike. The film ends with Jerry killed by the Nazis; she ends up as no more than a memory-image that inspires Thorndike to repeat his initial stalking gesture. If classic cinema seems to engage in the enunciation of a male gaze, significantly, Thorndike gazes too late. Indeed, in early scenes with Jerry, Thorndike almost seems unaware of her, preferring, for example, to survey the streets outside Jerry's apartment rather than look at Jerry, dressed in a diaphanous gown. Thorndike cannot have the woman; there is no secure position for the woman within this narrative of a lone male at war. Jerry doesn't send Thorndike a "Dear John" letter but her death has a similar effect on the man; it turns Thorndike into an endlessly errant figure that the film can give no final resting place to. In this respect, this film, dismissed by so many commentators (like Lotte Eisner in her book on Lang) as nothing more than a simple war-effort film, comes to resemble nothing so much as the grim existentialism of forties *film noir:* compare, for example, the fading image of Thorndike at the end of the film with the last image of the hero (John Garfield) in *Humoresque* (1946), walking away from his friends and down a long street after the suicide of his lover (Joan Crawford).

For Reynold Humphries, such troubling of narrative

structure is specific to Fritz Lang, who would thereby take up a skewed place in relation to the classic Hollywood system: "It seems to me that the interest that Lang's cinema holds comes from the misalignment [*décalage*] between what the Hollywood machine habitually offers and what the cineaste's films offer."[41] I would suggest, however, that for the forties at least, this misalignment can be part of the "machine" itself, part of its historicity. War narrative, for example, is caught up in a misalignment between narrative instances, social goals, and the individual subject's inscription in sociality and narrativity. Some of this misalignment may come from the very difficulties of rewriting the specific dynamics of classic narrative for a war cause. For example, a combined American populism (the enemy works according to a fixed order; Americans work according to a spontaneous and native sense of right) and American spiritualism (desire is the enemy's province; Americans are fighting for something higher) can conflict potentially with the oedipal structure of classic romantic narrative where authority figures are also sexual figures—rivals—and women are the objects of desire for men.

In *Casablanca*, for example, the conversion narrative is in tension with an oedipal narrative. It may not be insignificant that the screenwriters report their confusion all through the days of production as to which ending to use (should Rick stay with Ilsa or not? Should desire or duty triumph?);[42] their hesitation is the hesitation of the Hollywood machine at this moment, the hesitation of narrativity itself at this moment. The setting of the film in the backwater locale of Casablanca sets up the filmic space as a kind of atopia, a space outside the official representation of struggle: this is not the place of war as the newspapers represent it, but an exotic space of gangsters and mysterious eccentrics. Indeed, in a skewed relation to a representation that divides war into two precise places —a European theater and a Pacific theater—a number of wartime films will move in a tangential place, literally an other scene: Martinique (*To Have and Have Not*, 1944), darkest Africa (*Tarzan Triumphs*, 1943), Casablanca, the Canadian North (*Northern Pursuit*, 1943). Such places fall somewhat outside the sway of an authoritative world. These spaces of

action are not infrequently represented as spaces bearing only
minimal links to the larger concerns of a world at war; through
the films will run motifs of broken or incomplete communication
and physical isolation. Central power is off somewhere else and,
in consequence, a space is created for a fantasy of individual,
unfettered power.

Indeed, like *Casablanca*, a number of films portray
Americans who have no military connection to the United States
in war (for example, *China Girl, To Have and Have Not, A Yank in
the R.A.F.*). In some cases, such a lack can encourage the conver-
sion-narrative pattern, suggesting that everyone everywhere must
participate in the fight (for example, as in *The Pied Piper*, where an
Englishman vacationing in France realizes that he can do his part
for the war effort). But, as much, these films will suggest that a
conversion can exist apart from the central order of an armed
forces in war; the emphasis on marginal places turns national
conversion into a private, existential struggle. From Mr. Lucky in
the fog to Rick walking away from Casablanca to Thorndike parachuting out of his plane, so many of the films of conversion
suggest that the hero converts not to a communal effort but to a
private world that exists in a skewed relationship to aspects of the
official ideology. Significantly, this existential conversion often
becomes unrepresentable; an aberration in relation to a dominant
system, the conversion occurs as a last moment, a scene in which
the character walks away or disappears, and so removes himself
from the film. There is no next scene after Rick's conversion in
Casablanca.

As if to add a further confirmation to *Manhunt's* di-
vestment of Thorndike's agency and its reinvestment of agency
and enunciation in Quive-Smith, Odile Bächler suggests how the
sequence of the Nazis' capture of Jerry is readable as a promotion
of the cinematic experience itself, an association of Nazi power
with the very running of the machine of cinema. As Jerry returns
home from the darkened scene of her final departure from Thorndike—a departure whose intense finality is signaled by a fade to
black, an emptying of the cinematic image—she enters her apartment and switches on the light only to find Quive-Smith and other

Nazis waiting for her. Jerry is in the light; Quive-Smith is in a half-obscurity. As Bächler notes, this is like cinema; the man waiting in the dark for the site to light up and turn the woman into a spectacular sight that he can safely watch from a secure point. Figuratively, the Nazis aren't a fall into darkness; quite the contrary, they are associated here with a lighting up of the scene, a rendering visible of the woman as stake of an apparatus of power. In a sense, Quive-Smith has always seen what Thorndike until too late had always missed. Thorndike didn't look at Jerry in her gown, but Quive-Smith now looks at her with all the intensity of an ultimate control.

Thus, if Thorndike's first moment of visual plenitude— the spotting of Hitler—was one that actually thrust him into a position of subjection, of the lack of agency, Thorndike's last moment (the last shot of the film) is further imaged as a final loss of vision. Where Quive-Smith enacts the coming into force of the cinematic apparatus and its enunciation, Thorndike figures the dispersion of cinema, its shutting down, its fall into emptiness. As the narrator speaks of Thorndike going to meet his "destiny," the image shows a view from overhead of Thorndike's open parachute wafting toward the ground. A shrinking circle of white against a field of darkness, the image here is the image of cinema itself moving back into the void of the nonshow. A disappearing body, Thorndike signals the ambivalence of Lang's film. When Thorndike finally becomes an agent, he becomes unrepresentable and the film stops. If Nazis have too much body in Lang films, anti-Nazis have too little. In this, in this way that a film like *Manhunt* suggests the importance of the apparatus of cinema itself for the representational enactment of ideology, we can perhaps see the fragility of cinema and, by that, the fragility of ideology itself, consigned to narrate a necessary logic of the world but simultaneously signaling the historicity of ideology and the fundamental illogic that regulates its logic.

Chapter Four

Knowledge and Human Interests:
Science, Cinema, and the Secularization of Horror

1948 . . . In his book *Cybernetics, or Control and Communication in the Animal and the Machine,* scientist Norbert Wiener imagines the possibility of a synoptic science that would have as its object nothing less than the whole of existence.[1] In many ways, the book is emblematic of a certain self-fashioning by forties science of science as expansive and heroic endeavor: Wiener's book radiates a confidence that is perhaps in contradiction with an image of the scientist as anonymous, drab worker. Wiener is more like the Hollywood image of the scientist (in a film like *Young Tom Edison*)—a strong male battling the forces of a resistant world. Wiener's cybernetics comes across as a force that knows nothing to fear.

Indeed, we can counterpose Wiener against a philosopher like Jacques Derrida, who argues that it is in the borders, the margins, the frames, of knowledge that knowledge most reveals its fragility, its vulnerability to the quicksand of a deconstructing alterity.[2] For Wiener—demonstrating a certain scientific optimism that will frequently be *the* attitude of science in the 1940s—it is precisely in the boundaries that science should and must tread, and will most show its power to conquer the unknown: "It is . . . boundary regions of science which offer the richest opportunities to the qualified investigator. They are at the same time the most refractory to the accepted techniques of mass attack and the division of labor" (pp. 8–9). Cybernetics will step in, then, as the overarching, new plan of attack, a system that finds and founds the systematicness of the world. Cybernetics writes a necessary place for itself in the modern world: "If the 17th and early 18th centuries were the age of clocks, and the latter 18th and 19th centuries the age of steam engines, the present time is the age of communication and control."[3]

Wiener's knowledge is one that wants to recognize few, if any, experiences that might be beyond the limits of a coherent rationality—experiences that might be fundamentally obscure or resistant to rationalized human inquiry. Not accidentally, Wiener's deployment of science does acknowledge one classic example of a challenge to reason but only to relegate that example to the "safe" and purely illustrative realm of a fiction, firmly designated as such:

For the existence of a science, it is necessary that there exist phenomena which do not stand isolated. [In contrast,] in a world ruled by a succession of miracles performed by an irrational God subject to sudden whims, we should be forced to await each new catastrophe in a state of perplexed passiveness. We have a picture of such a world in the croquet game in *Alice in Wonderland*. . . . The rules are the decrees of the testy, unpredictable Queen of Hearts. [Against this,] the essence of an effective rule for a game or a useful law of physics is that it be stateable in advance, and that it apply to more than one case. Ideally, it should represent a property of the system discussed which remains the same under the flux of particular circumstances. *(Cybernetics,* pp. 62–63)

Here, for a moment, Wiener represents the possibility of that kind of paranoid world which, as rendered especially in *film noir* and the American *roman noir*, is an other side and other scene of forties narrative: a world of irrationality, without God or ruled only by a purely irrational God—a world of irrevocable destiny, endless repetition (a succession of absurd nontotalizing scenes, rather than a process, a teleology, that leads somewhere), a consequent recourse to an existential brooding (what Wiener calls "perplexed passivity," not so far from the motif in *film noir* of characters, laid out on beds, hopelessly and helplessly waiting for the worst). The condensation of all this threat is in a single figure: the "bad object," the evil mother figure of the Queen of Hearts, the horror of a constant menace of loss ("Off with their heads"). But by treating all this as mere fiction, mere exemplum, Wiener's representation, then, will be one that holds the threat at a distance, writes it within the limits of a reason. The fictional world, Wiener asserts, is not our world.

Wiener's epistemology achieves a controlling perspective, a point from which it can speak, through the construction of similitude, a calculable regularity beneath a superficial flux. Such an epistemology can only see itself in an adversarial relationship to the possibility of what Julia Kristeva calls "the powers of horror": the fear in the presence of that which "disturbs identity, system, order. What does not respect borders, positions, rules. The in-between, the ambiguous, the composite . . . the culminating form of that experience of the subject [i.e., the human subject] in which it is revealed that all its objects are based merely on the inaugural *loss* that laid the foundations of its own being."[4] If it exists at all, the power of horror in Wiener's world is at best a temporary and ultimately ineffective power: here both monstrous phantasms and the potential monstrosity of an everyday world are banished, controlled. Significantly, the *demonic* can enter into the cybernetic world only if represented in a debased, reduced, safe, even cute form: in the shape of what physics calls "Maxwell's demon," virtually the opposite of that wartime demon, the gremlin, whose purpose lay in the continual disruption of purpose, in the subversion and undoing of constructions; Maxwell's demon, in contrast, is physics' fantasy of a *benign* demon, whose job it is to insure benevolently any system's ultimate homeostasis—that is, its continued possibility for, or indeed necessity of, order. With Maxwell's demon, positive science resorts to a fiction of its own. But, unlike the testy, unpredictable Queen of Hearts, the demon is a good figure—good in his effects, good in the way he allows those effects to be the predictable object of a rule-bound science.

Such a discourse of science is readable as an extreme example of an epistemological project that derives in part from what Peter Brooks, in an article on the gothic novel, has referred to as modernity's desacrailization of explanations of perceived reality.[5] Brooks provides a model for one form of desacrailization; in the gothic novel, he argues, desacrailization has led to an art of irrationality, a breakdown of explanation: "What has in fact been left after the desacrailization of the world is not its rationalization—man's capacity to understand and to manage everything in terms of a rational epistemology, and a humanist ethics—but rather a terrifying and essentially uncontrollable network of violent and primitive forces and taboos which are summoned into play by the dialectics of man's desire" (p. 262). Wiener's science would represent another possibility, another stage, in this dialectic, a turn in which the moment of the sacred and the moment of the irrational are equated as forms of dis-knowledge ("a succession of miracles performed by an irrational God subject to sudden whims"), thus necessitating, so the new science argues, a transition to a new moment in which there is instituted a new systematicity of explanation, the possibility for a knowledge that comes precisely from the scientist who is erected into the ultimate human subject. In this moment of humanist rationality, science itself can become sacralized as an *affirmative* miracle: Wiener's autobiography has the mythifying, and only partially ironic, title *Ex-Prodigy*. Such science constitutes itself as a positive epistemology that can manage irrationality, that can even effect its cure. Moreover, such a promotion of scientific positivity is figured in the very form of Wiener's writing, in which meditation and philosophic ruminations stand alongside page after page of formulae and mathematical transformations; Wiener's style is one that works to allow the different moments to glide together in a vast synthesis on the written page, the hard science seeming to arise "naturally" out of the ruminations.

So much forties science distinguishes itself not by modesty or entrenchment—a retreat into specialization—but rather by vigorous advance, a panoptic desire to gaze upon everything, to see all events as falling under its purview. To take an example complementary to Wiener, one could cite the case of Erik Erikson with *Childhood and Society,* published in 1950 (but based on research from the war and immediate postwar years). Originating in a representation of the cure of shell-shocked vets and undisciplined children—two late-war and postwar sites of a potential troubling of representation—Erikson's intellectually influential study brings together reflections on child psychology, treatment of war trauma, the origins of Fascism, an anthropology of American Indians, the ties of personal and social history, and America's quest for national identity.[6] In a kind of expanding spiral, each bit of knowledge reflects back on and informs every other; Erikson's book takes on a naturalized form as a totality that so binds all its elements together that it seems to make its own brand of totalization appear necessary and inevitable.

In a sense, such a science can only disavow or disdain what Tzvetan Todorov calls the fantastic, that space of hesitation in the presence of strangeness in which knowing is put in doubt.[7] In opposition to the fantastic, forties science itself takes on marvelous qualities: a resilient ability to find a place for any phenomenon no matter how aberrant it may initially appear to be. This is an ability, then, of the form of scientific writing: the ability, that is, to adjust discourse in such a way as to extend its claims, enlarge its promised field of application to turn threats into safe objects of scrutiny.

For example, despite its plethora of mathematic symbols, its superficial resemblance to the dryness of a classic physics text, Wiener's book is finally not that far from Borges' Chinese table, especially as analyzed by Michel Foucault, in which all sorts of seeming incompatibilities can find a calm, if surreal, togetherness in the space of a confident discourse.[8] *Cybernetics* gives us the dazzling promotion of a knowledge that can find in television scanning the solution to computer algorithms, in antiaircraft guns the origin of a theory of prediction, in the movement of ship rudders an explanation of the effects of syphilis. Wiener's text revolves around the transcoding function of certain key words like *feedback* or *oscillation* or even the newly invested word *cybernetics*, all of which function as mediations for disparate elements and which thereby allow the rewriting of difference as the same (thus, for example, feedback is a process by which an aberrant movement can stabilize itself through a kind of adjusting action, and so can reveal itself to be ultimately based on a logic of the nonaberrant).

Science here is finally not some sort of real positive knowledge in some sort of adequate relationship to a "reality" that it simply and transparently conveys; rather, it is a gripping story whose very structure works to hold its subjects in thrall. Forties science takes place as one more classic narrative form: science imagined as the sense-filled journey through chaos to the stasis of an ending, the erection of a system. Hence, for example, the widespread interest in the forties in a particular *narrativized* version of Freudian psychoanalysis as *cure* (that is, as a teleology culminating in a punctual moment of deliverance). Against Freud's own declarations of analysis' interminability, the popular American vision of psychoanalysis will see it as terminating precisely in a glorious moment of breakthrough. Hence, also, the interest of film and fiction in psychoanalysis. Beyond the specific content of psychoanalytic precepts, artists find in the new science a form whose narrativity seems ready-made and thus allows the construction of suspense and climax. In films like *Spellbound* (1945) or *The Snake Pit* (1948) or *Home of the Brave* (1949), psychoanalysis serves precisely as a force of narrative resolution. The cure occurs as a punctual moment that makes retrospective sense of all previous occurrences.

Similarly, the crime-investigation film will come increasingly to make use of certain notions of positive science as the form with which to combat crime (and, indeed, the extension of science to crime fighting will gain a special justification in a film like *Panic in the Streets* [1950], where the investigators must find a murderer not because he is a murderer but because he has an infectious disease). Just as the wartime narrative suggested a certain need for a society of scrutiny that would carefully examine and work to control all aberration, so the narratives of crime investigation come to suggest that crime is a force that must be met through a cold, calculating, encircling rationalism. On the one hand, the films will suggest that crime itself is taking on forms of rational procedure—as the gangleader (Richard Widmark) declares in *Street With No Name* (1948), "We're building an organization along scientific lines"—that only a more intense rationality can conquer. On the other hand, the films will portray crime as an aberration so intense, so irrational, that only a calm and scientific attitude can control it: for example, in *White Heat,* (1949), the perverse mother fixation of crazed arch-criminal Cody Jarrett (James Cagney) is matched by the government's careful calculation that a well-placed infiltrator could take the place of mom in Cody's emotional world and so gain his confidence. The force of science in these films is even given a specifically filmic representation: a common stylistic trait of the postwar crime investigation film will be the use of a crosscutting that jumps back and forth between the aberrant criminal and the rational forces of law and order. The cutting shows an encircling of the aberration by reason (as in *White Heat,* where scenes of the criminals going about their business give way to scenes of government agents using special, advanced methods to track down Cody's gang), but it also makes the filmic style itself participate in this encircling. Thus, in *White Heat,* the end shots of Cody madly asserting his power on top of the refinery tanks suddenly are interrupted by a shot of the government agent, Fallon, asking for "the rifle," as if he were being given one of those strangely scientistic gadgets of monster destruction that dot the science-fiction films of the fifties. (Indeed, the end of *White Heat* might bear useful comparison with the 1953 film *Beast from 20,000 Fathoms,* in their shared emphasis on special tools that kill monstrous figures perched high up on weird structures.)

Thus, forties science can itself become a kind of stabilizing raw material for other narratives. For example, Isaac Asimov's *I, Robot* (1950) finds in cybernetics the possibility for a totalizing representation of modern existence.[9] At the level of *énoncé* (the represented world of Asimov's fiction), cybernetics is precisely the science that realizes human possibility, that creates a world of endless possibility: lorded over by the robotics expert Susan Calvin (who "obtained her bachelor's degree at Columbia in 2003 and began her graduate work in cybernetics"), *I, Robot*'s world is one of homeostatic coherence, a balanced system of interlocked parts. This world is balanced synchronically (robots and humans working together, outer planets working as productive colonies of Earth) and diachronically: the narrative story represents the progressive elimination of discordant elements: immature technology ("The miles of relays and photo-cells had given way to the spongy globe of platinum-iridium about the size of a human brain"); emotionally irrational fear ("Various segments of religious opinion had their superstitious objections. It was all quite ridiculous and quite useless"); the working class as a province of dangerous regression (represented through the novel's discussion of labor's resistance to automation—in his forties science-fiction stories such as "The Roads Must Roll," Robert Heinlein also presents the struggle of labor as a historically absurd force that must and will give way to inevitable forces of progress); and female desire, portrayed as a force of unreason, a retrograde opposition to a needed progress (thus, on the one hand, "[Susan Calvin] was a frosty woman, plain and colorless, who protected herself against a world she disliked by a mask-like expression and a hypertrophy of intellect"; on the other hand, Mrs. Winston, a woman opposed in the first story to robots, is represented as a shrill and unreasonable shrew who makes "full use of every device which a clumsier and more scrupulous sex has learned, with reason and futility, to fear").

At the same time, cybernetics also gives *I, Robot* the possibility of a coherent *enunciation*—the possibility of a single narrative with a unified, overall point of view: although composed to a large extent of short stories published previously in self-contained form *before* the publication of Wiener's book, *I Robot*, as a book, blends all the stories into a single master plot, centered around Susan Calvin, who tells the stories as representative examples from the single-strand history of robotics. To be sure, with the growing legitimation of the genre in the forties, many science-fiction novels come into existence as reworked collections of stories. But, in the case of *I, Robot* at least, the reworking is itself partially constitutive of the novel's force and meaning: in bringing the stories together, *I, Robot* transforms them into a single line of signification. Cybernetics here helps construct the narrative according to a logic of exchange: each moment takes its value from every other, each moment has its necessary place in the whole. A kind of relay between *énoncé* and *énonciation*, Calvin will not merely tell the stories from a position of retrospective superiority, but she will also enter into the stories as a character of great foresight (thus, in the first story, the faltering first encounter of a little girl with a new form of robot is observed by a teenage Susan Calvin: "The girl in her mid-teens left at that point. She had enough for her Physics 1 paper on 'Practical Aspects of Robotics.' This paper was Susan Calvin's first of many on the subject"). The book *I, Robot,* then, becomes itself a cybernetic practice, a controlled universe in which moments of aberration take their necessary place inside a higher coherence in which deviation generates a restabilizing feedback. Each chapter answers the previous one, filling in its historical absences, moving its story toward a higher technological point.

The scientific representation, then, does not simply represent a magic world: it narrativizes the new world of technology as something to be accomplished in time, a process in battle with the resistant force of a violence (a violence within the story of the narrative, but also a violence on the discursive level—that which threatens narrative's successful termination in the sense of an ending). Two strategies seem particularly to be at work in the narrativization of forties science. First, as *I, Robot's* Susan Calvin figure suggests, there will be a reliance on the scientist's role as a specific enunciating figure—a figure of knowledge who can initiate and convey narrative logic. In this decade of the popular discourse of Freudianism, this role will frequently be played by a doctor figure. For example, in *Now, Voyager* (1941), the doctor works as a kind of relay between narration and narrated event: transmitting the message of the title to the sick woman, Charlotte, the doctor becomes a figure of the forward propulsion of narrative.[10] Indeed, in a kind of self-promotion of cinema, the film will justify the doctor's role by making Charlotte's conversion coincide with the emergence on the screen of that Bette Davis that audiences have come to the film to see; without Dr. Jacquith's intercession, Charlotte would have remained an inadequate Davis, not at all the image that she is supposed to have in the Hollywood mythology.

When Dr. Jacquith last sees Charlotte, she goes over plans with him for a new wing she is having built for a hospital. In the confidence of Charlotte's actions here, the narrative suggests that the psychoanalytic cure is so complete that even Charlotte's future is assured. This assumption of science's role in making the contingency of the future all too sure and predictable serves as the second strategy of scientific narrative: the confident declaration that even events to come will fall under the synoptic sway of the scientific model. Significantly, one major concern of science fiction in the forties will be a universe building, an epic narrativization of past, present, and future history into one tightly bound, single schema based on a faith in the forward advance of a definite progress. In epics like Asimov's *Foundation* or E.E. "Doc" Smith's beginning Lensman series or the short stories that Heinlein will finally collect together as the significantly named *Past Through Tomorrow*, the narratives will ambitiously work to take on all of a history, a way of dealing with all issues no matter how seemingly tangential they may first appear to be.

Thus, in a kind of Manichaean rewriting of the Cold War, Smith's *Triplanetary* will present all of human history as a working out of a battle between two ultimate superpowers; beginning its Earth tale on Atlantis and then moving the narrative up to and beyond the 1940s, *Triplanetary* suggests a link of all temporalities within a single, overriding teleology. Similarly, Pratt and De Camp's *Lest Darkness Fall* responds to the central philosophical issue behind time travel—could one change the past to rework the future?—with a simple but confident affirmation; the novel chronicles how a modern scientist who finds himself transported to ancient Rome remakes all of future history—and so eliminates such catastrophes as the fall of the Roman empire—through the careful and extensive deployment of twentieth-century technology. Even more extreme, Asimov's *Foundation* will present the future as literally already written: engaging in what he calls "psychohistory," the scientist Hari Seldin is able to combine social psychology and historical analysis to outline the broad contours of future history. Having recorded his predictions, Seldin becomes a kind of archive of the future that perplexed politicians consult whenever they wonder where history is going. Ultimately, Seldin's psychohistory turns narrative into a medium that is only superficially temporal. The figures who live out future history do so in full confidence that there is no contingency—that the seeming freedom of action is really only the necessity of a logic that is always already written down somewhere.

A conversation from *Foundation:* Gaal Dornick: "What will happen now?" Hari Seldin: "I'll be honest. I don't know. It depends on the Chief Commissioner. I have studied him for years. I have tried to analyze his workings, but you know how risky it is to introduce the vagaries of an individual in the psychohistoric equations. Yet I have hopes." In combat with temporality, there is, then, one object that cybernetic knowledge *can* admit a certain (hopefully temporary) frustration over: the object that its historical moment sums up as "mankind" (and frequently collapses onto the figure of woman as dangerous aberration, as in Lundberg and Farnham's 1947 *Modern Woman: The Lost Sex*). The human subject is here potentially an irritation, a resistant force, the scary possibility of unpredictability, scary simply in the ways its psychology threatens to resist the methods that work to know it. Synoptic science, then, ultimately must construe itself as the glorious battler *of the human*; in certain limit moments, science will even seem in danger of losing the battle. Indeed, something can seem dangerously to escape the limits of science: "There is much which we must leave, whether we like it or not, to the 'unscientific' narrative methods of the historian."[11]

And yet Wiener will constantly belie his own pessimism about the possibilities of total knowledge and, rewriting it as optimism, will argue the transferability of cybernetic "laws" even to the human realm: thus, after admitting he doesn't share Bateson's and Mead's optimism about "an appreciable therapeutic effect [of cybernetics] in the present diseases of society," three pages later he will suddenly declare the possibility, his possibility, for a whole theory of *social* economy based on cybernetic precepts: "The average human being of mediocre attainments or less has nothing to sell that is worth anyone's money to buy. The answer, of course, is to have a society based on human values other than buying or selling. . . . I thus felt it my duty to pass on my information . . . to the labor unions" (pp. 37–38).

Increasingly, science in the forties works to restrict the realm of the unknowable to the human subject alone and then increasingly tries to come up with an efficient power over that last resistant realm. One pattern of forties epistemology is that of an expanding range of objects matched by an expanding methodology overrun by an expanding optimism. Wiener, for example, will not merely present formulae but will write his own book as a series of transformations in which the human realm becomes, by the end of the book, a realm of science, a positive knowledge.[12] In a first move, Wiener claims the modesty of his venture: the theory of prediction works only in mathematical-physical space— "To predict the future of a curve is to carry out a certain operation on its past" (p. 12). But, then, a kind of enlarging operation rewrites human actions too as a form of predictability: "An aviator under the strain of combat conditions is scarcely in a mood to engage in any very complicated and untrammelled voluntary behaviour and is quite likely to follow out the pattern of activity in which he has been trained." Significantly, such a move not merely strengthens the representation of science *as science* but also science *as social planning:* obedience to authority (e.g., the pilot who follows the precepts of his trainer) is equated with obedience to unarguable laws of nature—the law, for example, of entropy in which any complicated situation can be converted into a simpler one (for

example, the "very complicated" behavior of a free-willed pilot
rewritten as the simplicity of curvilinear motion).

Moreover, the very way in which Wiener seems to
only tangentially raise issues of immediate social application for
cybernetics—for example, the rhetorical strategy by which he will
note social issues and then claim his lack of expertise in such
realms—allows the positive statements he does make to have an
air of modesty and naturalness. Here Wiener participates in what
Nadia Khouri and Marc Angenot, in an analysis of a different field
of science, have analyzed as a central ideological practice of science
writing: a practice in which "isolated fragments of scientific paradigms function as *maxims of verisimilitude.* . . . These maxims provide conditions of intelligibility for [scientific] texts and serve to
reinforce the acceptance of dominant ideologemes while further-
ing their dissemination through the social matrix."[13] The intelligibility in Wiener's science works in part at this stage by a kind of
superimposition of common cultural mythologies and scientific
precepts. Specifically, *Cybernetics* works to make the human subject
accessible to scientific investigation and control in the appeal to a
structure of "commmon sense": the notion that the individual
human being is an operational system, that the social system is an
organic body, that all this finds a source in the spontaneously
radiating truth of nature. Indeed, at its extreme, *Cybernetics* will
close its narrative in the romanticism of the pastoral community:
near the end of the book, Wiener will draw a distinction between
his scientific world and what he sees as the deviated world of a
modern reality. Cybernetics will then ironically be the advanced
science that gives us back a premodern world:

> One of the most surprising facts about the body politic is its
> extreme lack of efficient homeostatic processes. . . . There is no homeo-
> stasis whatsoever. We are involved in the business cycles of booms and
> failure, in the successions of dictatorship and revolution, in the wars
> which everyone loses, which are so much a feature of modern times. . . .
> [In contrast,] small, closely knit communities have a very considerable
> measure of homeostasis. . . . It is only in the large community where the
> Lords of Things as They Are protect themselves from hunger by wealth,

from public opinion by privacy and anonymity, from private criticism by the laws of libel and the possession of the means of communication, that ruthlessness can reach its most sublime levels. (pp. 185–87)

Cybernetics, then, functions, in Roland Barthes' term, as a mythology, a conversion of culture into nature, that denies its own cultural basis and that imputes cultural relativism and manipulation to others:

A certain precise mixture of religion, pornography, and pseudo-science will sell an illustrated newspaper. A certain blend of wheedling, bribery, and intimidation will induce a young scientist to work on guided missiles or the atom bomb. To determine these, we have our machinery of radio fan-ratings, straw votes, opinion samplings, and other psychological investigations with the common man as their object; and there are always the statisticians, sociologists, and economists available to sell their services to these undertakings. (Wiener, p. 186)

Wiener's qualification of these "ideologies" as based in *psychological* investigation is significant in the ways that it announces its own claim to be above psychology, to be a real assessment of things, rather than simply a prejudice of a limited discipline. Such a move, moreover, allows Wiener himself to engage in psychological analysis (as in his aforementioned reference to "the average human being of mediocre attainments or less") while presenting his observations as "objective" description—no longer, that is, as a discourse that approximates reality from outside but rather as a necessary mimesis generated and determined by that reality.

1944 . . . In the film *Curse of the Cat People*, Oliver Reed (Kent Smith) tries to explain to his daughter's schoolteacher that his first wife, Irena, came to a tragic end; his explanation is simple and direct: "She went mad." A simple explanation but, in comparison with the details of the earlier film *The Cat People* (1942), an obviously inadequate one. According to the plot development of *The Cat People*, Irena died from the combined force of a panther attack and a sword wound inflicted by a psychiatrist *who had himself gone mad with passion*. Moreover, *The Cat People* argued the inadequacy of any diagnosis of Irena as mad; her illness was a much more supernatural one—strong emotion turned her into a murderous panther—whose very ability to exceed psychological explanation makes a mockery of psychology and represents it as a weak science (literally so in the case of the psychiatrist, Dr. Judd, a crippled man, whose desire to cure Irena through psychoanalysis is portrayed by the film as ridiculous).

The movement from the earlier film to its sequel can suggest precisely a desire to remove from narrative that plot option that Todorov calls the *marvelous*—the moment in which fantastic hesitation resolves itself by showing events to have no natural explanation. The description of Irena's fate as a going mad shows a secularization and psychologization of horror, a conversion of something marvelous into something merely *strange* (to use Todorov's term). The problem becomes one of a human psyche assailed from within by a mere imbalance. To be sure, *Curse of the Cat People* does seem to maintain an interest in the marvelous by maintaining the figure of Irena. That is, the film does show Irena; it allows a certain credence in her existence. Yet the rigorous limitation of Irena's appearances to just those moments when the young girl, Amy, is by herself, restricts the marvelous to the realm of childhood dependency; whether real or imagined, whether the convenient fictions of a troubled young girl or the intrusion of a suppressed supernaturalism, the story of Irena never crosses the limits into an adult world of antisupernaturalism governed by a secular practicality and a faith in logic and science. Just as Irena's trace in *Curse of the Cat People* will disappear when Oliver learns through child psychology to trust his daughter and so cause her to transfer her love from the image of Irena to Oliver, so too the whole movement from film to film is one of rationalist retraction (but one that views itself as expansion—Amy is growing into a necessary adult world of reason and propriety), an enclosing of epistemological doubt within the limits of a knowing and rational system, an enframement.

"Whatever the outcome of the war, the world cannot go back to its prewar economic condition. The issue is whether modern techniques, from atom smashing to psychoanalysis to vitamins, will be used to make men free or to make them slaves."[14] Much of the epistemological discourse of the forties is not only a discourse on objects, but a discourse on scientific methods proposed to deal with those objects. Discourse is run through with discussion and debate, a reflexive analysis of ends and means. Constituted by much of its discourse as a moment of momentous possibility, a moment of pivotal cause and consequence, the decade becomes an exemplary moment of narrative, represented as the extreme possibility for projects to end well or poorly. The forties become the narrative vehicle for both paranoia as discursive event—the world pictured as a constant undoing of projects—and for the triumphant shoring up of projects within the optimistic frame of epistemological power. There is in the forties a constant dialectic of victory and defeat. Reflective discourse in the forties is both a participant in such a dialectic, and an attempt to pull representation out of the dialectic to a place and perspective of surety and security.

Hence the simultaneous generic strangeness and generic familiarity of a forties horror film, *The House of Dracula*, released late in 1945. The familiarity is there in the film's reliance on an iconographic tradition of horror as strange event: the bat that turns into a count, the Gothic house at the edge of a cliff, the laboratory with its gleaming test tubes and crackling electric waves, etc. And yet the film takes a distance from the usual thematics of the horror film—a distance summed up *in the possibility of horror's cure*. The film's narrative works around an incessant desire to familiarize horror, to move it from the realm of the marvelous to that of the strange, and thereby make it accessible as an object of science. In *House of Dracula*, a renowned doctor successively meets Dracula and Lawrence Talbot, the Wolfman, each of whom is seeking a cure for his horrific state. In the case of Dracula, the narrative resolution remains in a kind of compromise position: the cure is deemed quite possible, but Dracula's desire for evil is stronger than his desire for innocence, and he fouls up the curative process. In contrast, the doctor very quickly discovers that Talbot's case is quite simple; his problem is equally psychological and somatic—his fear of turning into a werewolf releases strange enzymes that do in fact turn him into a werewolf. The solution? A brain operation that will turn Talbot into an ordinary guy who ends the film ready to settle down in a marriage with his former nurse.

The generic strangeness of *House of Dracula's* curative conceit becomes more apparent if we compare it with an earlier Universal Studios horror film, *Frankenstein Meets the Wolfman* (1943). Here, the Wolfman is irremediably other than human, and his quest is not for a cure that will reintegrate him into everyday human life, but, rather, for one that will forever release him from contact with life— in other words, that will prevent him from being any sort of threat to humanity—by allowing him to die. The Wolfman knows that nothing could bring him back to the world of the ordinarily human; monstrosity exists in a realm that is necessarily apart. To be sure, as in *House of Dracula,* there is the confident doctor who wants to cure the Wolfman by conven- tional means such as psychology; as he says, "In order to cure this man, I have to know who he is," and he embarks on a journey to the old country to discover Talbot's past. But finding out who Lawrence Talbot is means discovering the limits of conventional frames of knowledge and their lack of extension to the realm of the fantastic. Horror and reason take place here in two separate realms with no contact between them. Conventional rationalist epistemology is inadequate, according to the film's narrative line, and the film soon has the doctor turn Faustian and emulate madly the late Dr. Frankenstein, a man first described in the film as "the doctor that could cure people that other doctors couldn't cure," but progressively revealed in the course of the film to be a creator of monsters rather than of cures for monsters. Infected by the exotic environment of Eastern Europe, the young doctor gives in to an unbridled desire.

In contrast, *House of Dracula* makes no reference to the Faustian theme (but for a brief cameo appearance by the Frank-enstein monster) and, consequently, has its doctor working in freedom from the maddening lineage of a scientific tradition gone awry. If the doctor does go mad at the end of the story, the film makes it clear that his madness was purely the result of external processes (Dracula had malevolently interfered with the doctor's metabolism), and not from any sort of extra- or nonscientific hubris lying within the heart of science. In this later film, science itself is inherently rational. In contrast, in *Frankenstein Meets the Wolfman*, the young doctor's contact with the word of Frankenstein manifested in the records of old experiments leads precisely to a hubris, to an attempt to exceed the bonds of one's initial mission; fascinated with Frankenstein's experiments, the young doctor breaks his promise to cure Talbot and instead uses his knowledge to strengthen the Frankenstein monster's monstrosity. The Wolfman is left with no option but to battle the monster and be washed away in a flood at the film's end.

The forties horror film, then, becomes a site for the narrativization of a conflict between unbridled desire and the containing of desire within the limits of a stable rationality. In certain cases, the conflict is an explicit subject of the films—for example, in *Conflict* (1945) or in *The Beast with Five Fingers* (1945), where monstrosity is revealed as an all-too-human plot to drive a man mad. Such films suggest that horror itself is a form of rationality—a carefully planned attempt to horrify along precise and predictable lines. But, in many cases, the rational cure of horror is a more complicated process. There is not a simple or immediate faith in the cure. The narrativization in the films echoes the process of the decade itself—a process by which new sciences progressively institute themselves as acceptable or even necessary or preemptory forms of knowledge.

For example, while the forties are conventionally presented as a decade of what John Seeley calls the "Americanization of the unconscious,"[15] much popular discourse of the period on psychology and psychoanalysis suggests that the constitution and distribution of those human sciences take place as a battle, a trying out of the full set of possibilities (acceptance, rejection, compromise, etc.), rather than an immediate or even easy *fait accompli*. Indeed, as a contemporary observer, Dr. C. P. Oberndorf, noted, as late as 1951, the American Psychoanalytic Association was unable to come up with a definition of psychoanalysis that would be acceptable to the members.[16] The battle occurs within psychology as a difference of representations over its possible forms: thus, frequently, each school of psychology will present alternatives not as real alternatives at all but as inadequate contenders to the throne of "truth." For example, for Karen Horney in *Self-Analysis*,

In recent times any number of books have appeared with the purpose of helping people to cope better with themselves and others. Some of these, like Dale Carnegie's *How To Win Friends and Influence People*, have little if anything to do with recognition of self but offer rather more or less good common sense advice on how to deal with personal and social problems. But some, like David Seabury's *Adventures in Self-Discovery*, definitely aim at self-analysis. If I feel the need to write another book on the subject it is because I believe that even the best of these authors, such as Seabury, do not make sufficient use of the psychoanalytic technique inaugurated by Freud and hence give insufficient instruction. Furthermore, they do not recognize the intricacies involved.[17]

Similarly, at the end of the forties especially, with the intensification of crime and juvenile delinquency, psychoanalysis and social psychology will battle for preeminence as the real explanatory model of behavior. Methods will not merely promote themselves but will try to invalidate competing methods.[18] Films of the moment regularly invoke one or the other explanation: for example, *White Heat* (1949) is explicitly psychoanalytic in its replaying of the oedipal situation as constitutive of the criminal mind, while *Fighting Father Dunne* (1948) depicts the family as a *social* institution that has the power to make or break children. Ironically, *White Heat*'s solution is predominantly social—the calculated hunting down of Jarrett by the new technologies of police enforcement—while *Fighting Father Dunne*'s is psychological—the offering of love to the youthful victims of slums and other social conditions.

Psychology is not instituted as the pluralism of an open field but as the authorization of particular narratives; as Marc Vernet has noted in an analysis of the representation of psychoanalysis in Hollywood film, the most common narrative representation constitutes psychoanalysis as a narrative of closure, a forward-propelled logic of an end making retrospective sense of a beginning. Such a representation allows the possibility of a coincidence between narrative discourse and narrative story; the film and the terminable cure seem to work together.[19]

This is not to suggest, however, that such a narrative coincidence is necessarily effective or comprehensive: for Vernet, for example, the mise-en-scène of a film inevitably allows the possibility of psychological energy not reducible to narrative line or narrative closure. Vernet proposes, then, the possibility for a psychoanalysis of film that would be quite different from the classic narrative's own presentation of the psychoanalytic process. Similarly, Maureen Turim has argued that the flashback structure of some films about psychology—for example, *The Locket* (1946)—institutes a gap between discourse and story in which the forward progression of story exists in a contradictory relationship to a complicated structure that posits the inability of a story to offer fully or adequately an explanation of psychological processes. In a film like *The Locket,* the expressed psychoanalytic solution to the problem of a woman's kleptomania seems in contradiction with the structure of the film, which suggests that no simple rational explanation could ever be fully comprehensive.[20]

The power of psychology and psychoanalysis is not automatically or naturally given to the forties but has to be progressively discovered, refined, developed, defended, instituted; significantly, even as late as the Alger Hiss trial in 1949, psychoanalysis is a site of intense debate as the presiding judge refuses to allow psychiatric testimony because of a lack of precedent. Revealingly, a number of films (especially ones early in the decade) show a suspicion of psychology and play on stereotypes of its ostensible quackery or inability to see the reality of a situation. Psychoanalysis, here, is a method that completely misses its object: in the 1941 film *Man-Made Monster,* for example, analysis is mocked when a man who kills because a mad scientist has filled him with electric rays is examined by doctors who can't see the truth of the situation and look for the source of the murderous impulses in traumatic incidents and suchlike in the killer's youth.

Even more, in a number of films, psychoanalysis is not the study of madness but itself one of madness' forms—itself a source of worldly evil. As the psychoanalyst who loses control of himself under hypnosis in *Calling Dr. Death* (1943) explains, "I was successful with everyone but myself." Indeed, the films seem

to imply that psychoanalysts don't objectively view madness from
a safe position of knowledgeable, controlled authority; rather,√
because they live with madness, they take on its forms: in the
words of *Calling Dr. Death*'s investigating detective as he arrests a
psychiatrist-turned-killer, "He wouldn't be the first one to have
gone mad studying the processes of the mind." Psychoanalysis
becomes a subject for explicit critical reflection: for example, *Calling Dr. Death*'s plot revolves around a psychiatrist who claims that,
even when under the control of unconscious forces, a person will
not do something that the ego feels is wrong: when the doctor's
wife is murdered and the doctor can't account for his movements
at the time of the crime and so becomes a suspect, he begins to
feel the limits of his own reasoned position. Then, in a kind of
narrative overdetermination, the doctor learns that he was just
hypnotized to believe that he was capable of murder; instead of
returning the doctor to a position of secure tranquillity, this discovery leads him to feel further confirmed in his newfound doubts
about human reason. Even if he proves that one can't be hypnotized into murder against one's will, the doctor learns that he
himself was an object of experimentation, despite his prior confidence that being a doctor made him too rational a man to be
vulnerable to doubts and self-recrimination.

   At the extreme, the psychiatrist and the mad scientist
become interchangeable figures, equal violators of the rules of
normality: for example, the psychiatrist and geneticist Sigmund
Walters in *Captive Wild Women* (1943), whose Crestview Sanitar-
ium becomes a laboratory for experiments in "racial improve-
ment." As an observer of desire, the psychiatrist in this stereotype
becomes a victim of desire: first of all, a desire for unbridled power
(nurse in *Captive Wild Women*: "You've lost sight of something."
Doctor: "What?" Nurse: "Yourself") but also potentially a specifically erotic desire. If, as Mary Ann Doane has suggested in
several studies of the forties "woman's film," many of these films
enact a medicalization of the sexual gaze in which desire takes on
the disguise of objective, dispassionate knowledge, then, not insignificantly, other films suggest equally a sexualization of the
medical gaze, a registering of the ways that objectivity is itself

undercut by ulterior motives, by drives and desires.[21] Indeed, *Nora Prentiss* (1947), with its happily married doctor falling in love with a sensuous woman and giving up the whole fabric of his bourgeois life for her, goes so far as to suggest that the more ostensibly rational one is, the more one will be ultimately vulnerable to a seduction: all the doctor has to do is see Nora's injured leg, and his propriety goes overboard and he embarks on a scandalous, new life.

Another film, *No Minor Vices* (1948), even overdetermines its psychologization of the medical figure through a systematic application of specific film techniques. For example, while voice-overs early in the film accompany the actions of other characters to suggest the voice of the unconscious that assists in every human activity, the doctor (Dana Andrews) is not given any voice-over until the moment when he begins to feel jealousy in his wife's interest in an avant-garde painter; the sudden utilization of the voice-over for the doctor—who earlier had denied that he had an unconscious—emphasizes the film's imputation of psychology even in cases that would deny their own psychological dimensions. The psychoanalytic encounter in particular becomes charged with a sexuality that breaks rationality (or manifests the underlying dynamics of that rationality); the doctor becomes a figure of dangerous passion as, for example, in *Whirlpool* (1949), where the mysterious Dr. Korvo (José Ferrer) tells a woman patient, "Your soul can undress in front of me," and then hypnotizes her as part of a plot to kill a former lover of his. Most explicit in this respect is *The Cat People*, where the doctor and his desire are one more cause of Irena's problems: Dr. Judd's scientific interest—seemingly legitimated by the film's opening with an authoritative quotation from the doctor—becomes interwoven with a desire that exceeds the bounds of scientific propriety. Judd, not Irena, is the figure of an energy that transgresses limits.

Nonetheless, the war years will have already worked to construct an image of psychology and psychoanalysis as effective and necessary human sciences. The war period becomes discursively a moment of psychical tension—the difficulties of home-front life and a fear of war as a source of irremediable psychological

change—and a number of writings offer themselves up as effective
cures. During the war, for example, the journal *Science Newsletter*
(which after the Detroit race riots will even try to come up with a
predictive, psychological science for dealing with unrest) will include articles on curing everything from blackout fears to the
whole world's "destructive image." Around the returning veteran,
there will be such texts as Dumas and Keen's *A Psychiatric Primer
for the Vet's Family and Friends*, Child and Van de Water's *Psychology
for the Returning Soldier*, John Mariano's *The Vet and His Marriage*,
Howard Kitching's *Sex Problems of the Returned Vet*, etc. Most of
these texts signal the inevitability of what is becoming a keyword
of the forties—adjustment—but they also write a necessary place
for psychoanalysis by seeing that adjustment as dependent on
one's turning to psychoanalysis, and psychoanalysis alone. In
cases where things are not going right for individuals, psychoanalysis steps in as the necessary solution; hence, as postwar divorce rates begin to rise, we find books like Dr. Edmund Bergler's
1946 *Unhappy Marriage and Divorce*, which argues that childhood
neurosis is the essential cause of adult problems—a cause that
only psychoanalysis can efface. At the same time, even more
purely theoretical psychological discourse that has as its ostensible
subject transhistorical notions of psychology will frame that discussion within claims of applicability to the current moment: for
example, Karen Horney, laying out in *Self-Analysis* the foundations
of an ego psychology, will argue the necessary parallel of the self-
controlled ego and the war effort: "Any help of this kind [i.e.,
psychoanalytic help] is made doubly necessary by the intricate
and difficult conditions that we all live under. . . . An integral part
of the democratic ideals for which we are fighting today is the
belief that the individual—and as many individuals as possible—
should develop to the full of his potentialities. By helping him to
do this, psychoanalysis cannot solve the ills of the world but it can
at least clarify some of the frictions and misunderstandings, the
hates, fears, hurts, and vulnerabilities, of which those ills are at
once cause and effect" (p. 9).

   The forties, then, show the rise of a positive popular
discourse of knowledge of the human mind: a fascination with

illness but also a simultaneous faith in psychoanalysis as miraculous cure. One way that narratives will resolve doubt about psychoanalysis will be to split the scientist into two figures: one authoritative and good, and one insane and bad. For example, in *Whirlpool*, the crazed Dr. Korvo is balanced by the orthodox psychoanalyst (Richard Conte).

But for the most part, the strongest solution seems to be the strong promotion of the psychoanalyst as an effective figure and a gradual elimination of images of aberrant medicine. Ultimately, there will be so much confidence in psychoanalysis that it will even be used anachronistically in narratives of the past: for example, in Westerns like *Pursued* (1947) or *The Return of Jesse James* (1950), with explicitly neurotic central figures. *The Return of Jesse James* even signals its own anachronism in a scene where a doctor hears about the man claiming to be Jesse James and declares, "It's evident from what you told us that the man who calls himself Jesse James today has become an egomaniac operating under the compulsion of a fixed idea. Now, I know that you didn't say it in quite that language. . . . Now we know very little about these things yet." Indeed, so strong will this faith in the extendability of psychoanalysis be that in film it will even inform the characterization of animals: for example, Joanna Augusta's poodle, Scheherazade, in *The Emperor Waltz* (1948), psychoanalyzed to find out why she is afraid of Virgil Smith's mutt; or Lassie in *The Hills of Home* (1948), whose plot revolves around Lassie's inability to enter water because of an early childhood trauma. Moreover, these films suggest some of the major forms that cure can take in the forties representation: on the one hand, as in *The Emperor Waltz*, the cure as an intercession of outside forces (Scheherazade needs the doctor's intervention; see also *Possessed* [1947], *The Snake Pit, Spellbound*, etc.), or, on the other hand, a kind of internal cure, a self-analysis in which the demands of the present overthrow the traumatic grip of the past and allow the epiphany of a curative moment that wells up from within (see also *Pursued*, [1947] *Somewhere in the Night* [1946], *Love Letters* [1945]).

As Mary Ann Doane has pointed out, the use of external authority figures allows not merely control but *sexual* con-

trol; the doctors are male, and their analyses bring women out of
a paranoid or masochistic space of fear, suspicion, dread, only to
enclose the women in the seeming benevolence of male power
and rightness. There are rarely female doctors or psychoanalysts
in the films of the forties. Indeed, in *Young Man with a Horn* (1950),
one of the threats of city-wise Amy North (Lauren Bacall) as
against the succoring innocence of Jo Jordan (Doris Day) is that
she has been studying psychoanalysis and treats her relationship
with Rick Martin as the object of a cold calculation. In films like
Spellbound (1945) or *Nora Prentiss* or *On the Town* (1949), female
scientists are problematic in the ways they work to close off desire;
the position for the woman is thus the converse of the man's, for
whom the danger in science (as in *The Cat People*) is that of too
much desire.

Significantly, the promotion of authority figures will
frequently aid a promotion of cinema itself, as authority figures
make use of cinematic apparati or refer to the world of Hollywood
as a point of stable reference as against the chaos of the patient's
neuroses. In other words, Hollywood cinema itself is often enlisted
as part of the treatment and cure. Thus, on the one hand, in *The
Brasher Doubloon* (1947), a woman's frigidity is cured by the showing of a film that clears her of a murder she thought she had
committed; significantly, it is the man showing the film (Philip
Marlowe, played by George Montgomery) who will also benefit
from the cure by winning the girl of his dreams. On the other
hand, in *Lady in the Dark* (1944), one sign of a woman's cure from
a childhood trauma that has closed her off from desire will be her
growing interest in a Hollywood star; in this particular case, the
woman will eventually discover that the Hollywood star is not as
manly as she expected, but desire for Hollywood manliness remains the goal, the mark that a woman has realized her necessary
femininity (and, indeed, the woman's final choice of her co-
worker [Ray Milland] rather than the star [Jon Hall] actually
represents another confirmation of the Hollywood system since
the real Milland is actually a bigger star and gets top billing over
Hall).

But self-analytic discourse offers the advantage of that

kind of dispersion of central power that Michel Foucault argues can be such an effective tactic of modern power and whose war use I discussed in chapter 2. In other words, there is in the self-analysis the possibility of an internalization of power, since each individual makes his/her own psyche a site of a self-imposed control—what Foucault refers to as the "caring of the self" *(le souci de soi)*. Typical in this respect is the representation of cure in Horney's *Self-Analysis*. Horney begins by rewriting the social field as one that generally needs psychoanalyzing, one that is dominated by what the title of her most famous book declares to be *The Neurotic Personality of Our Time*. Neurosis becomes not a specific area but a general condition: "Psychoanalysis is still and will remain a method of therapy for specific neurotic disorders. But the fact that it can be an aid to general character development has come to assume a weight of its own. To an increasing degree, people turn to analysis not because they suffer from depressions, phobias, or comparable disorders but because they feel they cannot cope with life" *(Self-Analysis)*. But in proposing the possibility of *self*-analysis, Horney will base that possibility in a reference to external curative authorities: her own authority as transmitter, scribe, for psychoanalysis' word; especially, Freud as the source of the word; and more generally, the field of humanistic culture itself as a field in which psychoanalysis will easily and appropriately find its place:

> Since Freud, unconscious motivations have been accepted as elemental facts of human psychology, and the subject need not be elaborated here, especially since everyone can enlarge his knowledge about unconscious motivations in various ways. There are, in the first place, Freud's own writings . . . and the books summarizing his theories. . . . Also worth consulting are those authors who try to develop Freud's basic findings, such as H. S. Sullivan in his *Conceptions of Modern Psychiatry*, Edward A. Strecker in *Beyond the Clinical Frontier*, Erich Fromm in *Escape from Freedom* or myself in *The Neurotic Personality of Our Time* and in *New Ways in Psychology*. . . . Philosophical books, particularly the writings of Emerson, Nietzsche, and Schopenhauer reveal psychological treasures . . . as do a few of the books on the art of living such as Charles Allen

Smart's *Wild Geese and How To Chase Them*. Shakespeare, Balzac, Dostoevski, Ibsen, and others are inexhaustible sources of psychological knowledge. And by no means least, a lot can be learned from observing the world around us. (p. 38–39)

Self-analysis becomes the application of the field of existing discourse to one's own problems. Not surprisingly, such a discourse centered on the blend of common sense and authoritative humanism works ideologically to institute a particular image of normalcy, one based on a finding of one's place in the social system. Significantly, one of Horney's first examples of a *non*neurotic personality presents that personality as the site of an unquestioning acceptance of authority: "[The adjusted employee] will more or less consciously evolve a technique for handling the boss. He will probably refrain from expressing criticism; make it a point to appreciate whatever good qualities there are; withhold praise of the boss' competitors; agree with the boss' plans, regardless of his own opinions; let suggestions of his own appear as if the boss had initiated them. . . . For an understanding of neurotic trends much depends on recognizing their difference from such *ad hoc* strategy" (pp. 47–48). As George Lipsitz points out in *Class and Culture in Cold War America*, the forties become an intensive period for the development of *industrial* psychology—the use of techniques of analysis to bind workers into the capitalist system. Normalcy becomes a normalization to the norms of an industrial system.

In the space of a psychoanalysis-dominated forties, there is little room for a conflicting discourse like that of the traditional genre of horror which suggests that certain forms are beyond cure, that something exceeds the self-declared rightness of curative discourse. Significantly, many "horror" films of the period are composite forms, mixing horror with a rationalized image of the world: for example, despite its title, the 1945 *House of Horrors* is more a murder story with the motives of the deformed killer (Rondo Hatten) given coherent explanation. Indeed, in some films, irrational horror almost seems an afterthought: in *The Bowery at Midnight* (1942), for example, the real mystery of the central character played by Bela Lugosi is not that he has discovered how to bring the dead back to life, but rather that he is a college professor by day and a master criminal by night.

Psychoanalytic discourse, then, can claim so much power in the period in part by taking on the form of epistemological investigation that characterizes positive science of the period (as in Wiener); if cybernetics, for example, rests on notions of teleology (knowledge as means to an end), of completeness, of feedback, so too will ego psychology, as in Erikson, set up a notion of analysis not as an interminable act but rather as a progressive synthesis in which contact with the individual opens up to recognition of the significations of family environment, of cultural, racial, ethnic, and national identity, all of which constitute bits of information to be turned back onto the individual subject. We can contrast such a synthesis to the representation of knowledge in a horror film like *Frankenstein Meets the Wolfman,* where the journey to find out the context of Lawrence Talbot's identity becomes a journey toward the nonsynthesizable, toward events and knowledge that don't fit the schemas of a dominant epistemology. Condensed in the image of Transylvania as a place of superstition, the old country here becomes the exotic repository of a nonscientific knowledge, a battery of beliefs and intuitions as in the case of the gypsy woman who explains the werewolf and the Frankenstein monster phenomena to the doctor. This is the opposite of Erikson's science, where the old country is also part of a weight or burden of the past but one capable of being laid to rest in the New World with its reason and its new symbolisms and cultural formations. Indeed, as biographers suggest, such a desire for control over the Old World may even be biographically the case with Erikson, who grows up in old Europe and, upon emigrating, tries to throw off a European lineage by naming himself Erik Erikson, a self-engendering eternal Adam, and by writing on the nature of American identity.[22]

If, as Robin Wood has suggested, the formula of classic horror is "Normalcy is threatened by the monster,"[23] increasingly psychoanalysis displaces the source of that menace from physically traditional monsters to the *id* as *initially* uncontrollable force or, in many cases, as in *film noir,* to a femininity or to an urban condition (or to a confluence of the two) figured as the repository of a-social or antisocial forces. Indeed, some of the horror films of the forties build such a displacement into their narrative structure—as in films like *Conflict* and *Beast with Five Fingers*, where the initially monstrous force is revealed to be the merely strange, the result of human plot—or in characterization as in *Abbott and Costello Meet Frankenstein* (1948), where, to the team of traditional Universal Studios monsters (Wolfman, Dracula, Frankenstein monster), is added the evil temptress Sandra, physically not a monster but an even greater threat in her use of all-too-human wiles to seduce Wilbur (Costello) to a mysterious island for a monstrous brain transplant.

In the rationalism of the forties, the things to wonder about are increasingly not so much alien forces or exotic other places but, quite the contrary, the places in which one lives, the "mystery" or "horror" of an everyday world. If there is at all the possibility for the representation of threat in the forties, it is not so much the threat of a world in which incurable monsters roam; rather, whatever horror appears in this new world is merely the possible horror of feeling a disjunction between ends and means *in* this world, rather than a disjunction between our world and another. As Jean-Paul Sartre suggests in his 1940s analysis of the fantastic in fiction, "The fantastic is no longer for modern man anything but a way of seeing his own reality reflected back at him."[24] And Sartre goes on to find the traces of this fantastic precisely in the resistance of everyday human objects to everyday human projects in an ordered world in which "each [tool] represents a piece of worked matter, their ensemble is controlled by a manifest order, and the signification of this order is an end, an end that is myself or, more precisely, the human in me, the consumer in me" (p. 155). Sartre speaks here of a dream of consumption that is answered by a dream of rational control of matter, rational production (of knowledge, of objects); for example, in the language of postwar suburbia, houses are not "built," but "produced."

Here again, Asimov's *I, Robot* is a significant case, for, against the resistance of tools to human ends, it narrates the return of objects to human control: *I, Robot* begins with the discovery of a new life—the life of robots who can think, who can express emotions, who have personal initiative. But the otherness of robots—their potential disruption of a *human* project—is controlled first by the First Law of Robotics, inscribed on the title page of the book: "A robot may not injure a human being, or, through inaction, allow a human being to come to harm." Second, robot alienness is controlled by the very fact that moments of robot excess are all ultimately readable in terms with human parallels: crazily whirling robots are "drunk," nonworking robots are "twiddling their fingers," robots that order other robots around are "militaristic." Robot foibles are virtual parodies of human ones: robots love to have fairy tales told to them, they worry about the nature of existence (and run to a belief in God to assuage that worry); faced with contradiction, they become neurotic or respond to the contradictory situation with aggressivity; they devour romance novels and worry about the operations of the heart. The strangeness is, like that of *House of Dracula*, the strangeness of nonhuman beings who are all too human and who are working toward an ultimate integration with a human realm. Precisely because they imitate humans, the robots can be analyzed and controlled.

To be sure, there is a cinema, especially in the late-war and postwar periods, that seems to fit Todorov's definition of the *marvelous*—that realm in which human and physical laws are suspended. Indeed, there is a whole burst of supernaturalism in such films as *The Horn Blows at Midnight* (1945), *The Ghost and Mrs. Muir* (1947), *It's a Wonderful Life!* (1946), *Portrait of Jennie* (1948), *Luck of the Irish* (1948), *Repeat Performance* (1947), *The Enchanted Cottage* (1945), *The Bishop's Wife* (1947), *Miracle on 34th Street* (1947). But, significantly, most of these films reveal the ultimate cognitive effect of the marvelous not to be uncertainty and a questioning of one's own perception and reason—a questioning that might move the marvelous toward the fantastic or toward horror. Quite the contrary, the marvelous in these films leads the human subject who is in contact with marvelous spirits or events to a new certainty, to a new faith in the psychological self. The marvelous becomes an aid that mediates the sacred and the desacralized—an aid by which humans can fulfill human ends and tasks: thus, for example, when Stephen Fitzgerald (Tyrone Power) catches a leprechaun in *Luck of the Irish,* he never asks for a magical pot of gold but makes use of the leprechaun's advice to realize goals he had had all along: to become a free-lance writer living out in the country with the love of a simple woman like Nora (Anne Baxter). Even more explicit in this respect is *The Enchanted Cottage,* where it is revealed that two people supposedly made beautiful by a magical cottage were actually made beautiful by their own psychological acceptance of each other's infirmities. Here there is a conversion of the seemingly marvelous into the merely psychological, a conversion emphasized by the point-of-view structure, similar to that in *Curse of the Cat People,* which has the two characters look beautiful only when no other characters are present to observe them.

Significantly, at least one *non-fantasy* film—*No Minor Vices*—uses the same sort of point-of-view structure to imply that ostensibly magical transformations of reality actually occur within subjective consciousness and not in any real transformation of the empirical realm. In *No Minor Vices,* each member of a childless couple looks at a portrait of the wife and sees different things there; the husband sees a daughter in the frame while the wife sees a son. Realizing that the absence of a child has been the one limitation in their marriage, the couple resolves to have a baby. Again, as with the fantasy films, a "magical" aid arises to show people the things that are missing in their lives. But *No Minor Vices* grants no special credence to magical processes; the aid has powers only in the act of a subjective perception of it. Revealingly, even the painter, whose portrait inspires the couple, sees a reflection of his own desires in the portrait; while holding the same structural position in the narrative as the marginal figure in the fantasy films—that is, the position of an intruder who teacher humans the real needs of their existence—the painter here reveals that he is all too human, all too earthly. The very similarity of *No Minor Vices* to the fantasy films can suggest that fantasy in the latter films is only an expedient for a much more secular notion of assistance in the human realm. Other films of this "genre" then, will admit the "real" existence of the marvelous but will narrativize it as a kind of expediency that helps humans toward their goals and then disappears; for example, Clarence in *It's a Wonderful Life!* only becomes embodied on the screen at the moment of George's suicide attempt; starting George off on the process of recovery, Clarence only remains until the moment that George once again admits that he is the positive agency of his own life.[25] The marvelous figure is literally a device for humans, a propitious projection of their own needs.

Regularly, the supernatural films of the forties suggest that the supernatural force is only an aid that brings out a human potential that heroes and heroines were not aware they possessed. The marvelous, then, becomes a complement of everyday existence. It turns into one more component of individual psychology, one more path toward a blending of science and subjectivity. If science sees subjectivity as its one potential stumbling block, forties supernaturalism will make itself an ally in the project to grasp that subjectivity. Horror here is not a real force but, at most, a temporary detour by human beings who haven't yet internalized a cure; in the words of David H. Fink's 1943 *Release from Nervous Tension,* "Not only do we fear things and situations that are really dangerous, but in our leisure moments we deliberately invent spooks with which to frighten ourselves." Science constructs the supernatural, then, as a force under control, itself scientific. In the words of *Portrait of Jennie's* opening credits, "Science tells us that nothing ever dies but changes, that time itself does not change but curves around us. Past and future are together at our side, together." "Science tell us . . . . "—discourse here writes a narrative in which seeming incompatibilities (those of science and fantasy) can find a new compatibility within an expansive knowledge: time, romance, the mythic conquest of death, all come "together." As Elwood P. Dowd says of his six-foot-tall rabbit in *Harvey* (1950), "Science has overcome space and time. But Harvey has not only overcome space and time, but all objections."

I would like to conclude this section by citing a film that condenses much of the fate of horror and threat in the 1940s: *Daisy Kenyon* (1947). *Daisy Kenyon's* story of a veteran who discovers that he has to be able to trust the chances of love can serve as an exemplary instance of Todorov's argument about the relation-

ship between a scientistic psychoanalysis and the fantastic: "Psychoanalysis has replaced (and thereby rendered useless) the
literature of the fantastic. Today, one doesn't need recourse to the
devil in order to speak about an excessive sexual desire, to vam-
pires in order to speak about a felt desire for cadavers . . . . The
fantastic is domesticated, like other forms, giving up the explanation of transcendental reality, resigning itself to transcribing the
human condition" (p. 126). In *Daisy Kenyon*, Peter's desire is a
virtually cadaverous one: veteran of the war and widower from
his wife's car accident, Peter sees the world as governed by what
he refers to as a "slow dying." And yet Daisy—her name itself a
mark of natural existence—will become for him a source of life,
a possibility for cure; as Peter comes to say, "The world's dead
and everybody in it *but you*." Daisy, who began her relationship
out of the duty to date a soldier on leave, now realizes her higher
mission; she must assume psychoanalytic authority and cause
Peter to internalize the psychological cure. Daisy will be the
method, Peter will be the object—"If you say so, *Doctor*," he even
says to her at one point.

Horror is here only the fear of a temporary block as
Daisy turns Peter's very complaints into excesses to be channeled
into a curative feedback structure; making the problem oscillate
into its own solution, Daisy tells Peter that if he were really and
incurably ill, he wouldn't be "sounding like a case history." The
very fact that Peter complains makes him accessible to a cure.
Classic horror makes its appearance in a throwaway line: after
their marriage doesn't immediately cure Peter, he says to Daisy:
"Look who you married: the son of Dracula." A minor line but
one that is revealing in the ways it shows horror turned into a
memory or a trace or a joke (just as the Universal monsters will,
by the end of the forties, become comic foils for Abbott and
Costello). This is much of what forties narrative tries to make of
the power of horror—no longer the classic iconography, no longer
the classic signification, but a domestication, a materialization of
its effects in an everyday realm where it can seem to menace all
the more intensely but where it can also all the more intensely
open itself up to the power of a cure.

Chapter Five

Blind Insights and Dark Passages: The Problem of Placement

"**He's no quack,**" says the friend of a low-life plastic surgeon as the doctor welcomes escaped prisoner Vincent Parry (Humphrey Bogart) for a surgical change of face in *Dark Passage* (1947). Then, through a panning shot, the doctor comes into camera view, into a direct look at the camera eye—a view that reveals him to correspond, perhaps excessively, to one's stereotypes of a quack. The first-person camera here is caught up in a moment of paranoid reversibility: on the one hand, the look of the camera delivers a confidence of sight—it ironizes the aural comment in order to ground knowledge in the surety of visual "truth"—but on the other hand, the truth that it delivers is a potentially unbearable one (the fear of being operated on by a quack), a play on the anxiety of entrapment in the grip of a supposed authority whose power is frightening and whose authority is in fact far from insured. Not the benign doctor of the rationalist and scientific tradition, the doctor figure here is himself a force of excess and menace.

If war narrative and science work equally (and sometimes together as in the case of wartime psychology) to institute a logic of temporality that would bind all moments of the social totality into one master synthesis, another side of the forties equally suggests that this dream of totality is a fragile, reversible, unstable one—a vulnerability that is figured especially in *film noir* where objects resist control, where our familiar world can turn on us, as in *Detour* where coffee cups are visually enormous, where the opening of a car door can kill, where temporal progression dilates and becomes a nightmare of coincidence and alogical repetition.

In this respect, it can be a suggestive exercise in the study of the problematic position(s) of forties culture to compare two films: *Pride of the Marines*, an investment in wartime representation, and a film that can be read as its fissuring rewriting, *Dark Passage*, a 1947 postwar *film noir*. Produced by the same studio (Warner Brothers), directed by the same man (Delmer Daves), and using some of the same character actors (for example, Tom D'Andrea and Rory Mallison), the two films have certain similarities at the level of story: both are concerned with men who return to society and try to work their way through difficulty with the help of a supportive woman. Yet the films nonetheless institute very different registers of vision and different interactions of narrative space and narrative time. While *Pride of the Marines* works to give every element (in both story and style) its "proper" place and placement, *Dark Passage* suggests a certain troubling of placement as narrative and vision break apart, constructing an incoherent and distorted narrative and narration. It is possible to juxtapose these two films not to suggest that *Dark Passage* is in any way an "answer" to *Pride of the Marines* (although certain scenes—for example, the unveiling of bandages from the face—do seem to rhyme from film to film) but rather to suggest within the forties the possibility of a mutation in the practice of "classical narrative."

The mutation occurs most strongly in the film's visual

and narrative style. Where *Pride of the Marines* reaffirms a non-aberrant (i.e., stylistically classical) narrative style (but for a dream sequence which is clearly demarcated as such and whose aberrations are held within the limits of motivation and psychological projection), *Dark Passage*'s narrative and style do not take place unproblematically. For example, the extended first-person camera style contributes to a certain nonclassicism in a number of ways: first, by intensifying the aggressiveness of the camera look *and* the aggressiveness of the outside world against that look (there is a proliferation of direct looks into the camera; further, there is also an increase in close-ups of characters—an attempt to approximate conversational distance); second, by creating a claustrophobia of sight (with more close-ups, the viewer has less of a visual field to wander in); third, by denying the star-system basis of cinematic pleasure (the credits promise "Bogart" but the first-person camera defers that promise).

Although perhaps stylistically most known for this extended attempt to create a first-person visual narration, perhaps as emblematic of the film's ambiguity is a single shot, an impossible one in terms of enunciation. As Parry discovers the dead body of his friend George, what starts as a fairly typical expository style (eye-level medium shot of Parry entering the room; cut and pan down to the body with Parry finally kneeling into frame; close-up of Parry's face) suddenly gives way to a shot of George's body shot from below floor level, his body splayed out above the lens. The shot is a short one, and of a sort that is never repeated in the film, and yet, in its very enunciative impossibility (who is seeing this?), it can stand as a figure of the film's whole narrative complication: in *Dark Passage*, the narrative and the image come apart, refusing to provide any but the most meager of certainties and centerings.

The narrative of *Dark Passage* is one in which dramatic coincidences occur so often as to break down any question of plausibility, of a narrative unity. The film seems to make explicit the essential arbitrariness of a coherent temporality. Here, I will cite just two examples (out of many possible ones). First, Parry escapes from prison on the very day that Irene (Lauren Bacall), a woman who defended him to the press during his trial even though they had never met, is near the prison doing some painting. Second, the one woman who comes to Irene's door while Parry is hiding in the apartment is Madge, a woman who knew Parry before he went to prison (and who, it will turn out, is the actual killer of Parry's wife).[1] As in *Detour*, the sheer weight of the co-incidences suggests the dominance of a logic based not on a co-herent narrativity, but a dream-logic of surprise visits, and inces-sant, insistent repetition. Of course, the *films noirs* themselves frequently encode this dream-logic within a kind of proto-exis-tentialist discourse on the domination over life of a seemingly incomprehensible, often malefic *fate*.[2] Such a discourse allows the films to acknowledge absurdity while perhaps beginning to grasp it in an act of naming: in Irene's explanation of the first coinci-dence, "I don't believe in fate or destiny or any of those things . . . I guess it was something like fate."

In a system dominated by dreamlike fate, human in-teraction becomes a further site of incoherence, each encounter posing the equally likely alternatives of threat or salvation. Within *Dark Passage*'s first-person point of view, for example, each en-counter is first registered visually as a kind of shock, as an intrusion into the screen's frame of an initially alien force (for example, the quack doctor). Interaction becomes the point of a fundamental interplay of an anxiety and a security that pivot around each other: for example, Irene first appears by moving brusquely into Parry's field of view and ordering him about but only minimally justifying her actions: on the one hand, the presence of Lauren Bacall in the role and the viewer's possible knowledge of her involvement with Bogart work against anxiety, but the filming increases anxiety by soon leaving Parry's point of view, by giving shots of Irene where her interests and next moves are fundamentally undecidable. For example, as Irene's car approaches a roadblock, the point of view turns away from Parry; at precisely the moment when Irene will have to demonstrate whether she is for or against Parry, Parry loses what little visual hold he had over the development of the narrative.

Moreover, in its representation of San Francisco, *Dark*

Passage imagines the big city as a symbolically small place, the constant possibility of agonistic threats where everyone you meet has a potentially malevolent relation to you: for example, Parry can't go to an all-night diner without the only other customer turning out to be a cop out to arrest him. In this world circumscribed in a paranoid fashion, no encounter is uncharged or without some signification. Even being asked for a light by a stranger on the street becomes a source of dread; all through the trivial encounter, Parry has to wonder if he will be recognized. It may not be irrelevant that one anecdote of the film concerns a goldfish bowl; the film pictures San Francisco as a kind of enclosed place where you can never escape bumping into someone who knows you. (Similarly, in another forties film, *Leave Her to Heaven* [1945], social life is literally described as a goldfish bowl where no one can escape the withering, crushing glance of others.) If the war-affirmative narrative applauds panopticism and calls for a willing scrutiny by all of all, the nonaffirmative film presents the figure of a horror and danger of sight. Even a seemingly comic film like *Father of the Bride* (1950) will turn its comic festivity into the nightmare of a scrutinized failure, especially in a noirish dream sequence where Stanley Banks (Spencer Tracy) sinks into the ground as guests express horror or mockery at his inability to preside over his daughter's wedding.

Significantly, the only time in *Dark Passage* that Parry is out on the street and doesn't meet anyone occurs when he boards a trolley car filmed in such a way that we do not see other passengers or even a driver; in the narrative world of *Dark Passage,* one is either completely alone or among people who can only be in some *significant* relationship to the self. Solitude or community here are equally potentially disturbing conditions.

To be sure, within the chaos of its narrative, *Dark Passage* does allow for the resolution of several narrative threads: Parry successfully has his face changed by plastic surgery; he successfully discovers his wife's murderer; he successfully escapes to South America to live happily ever after with Irene. But each of these narrative closures has little force in the forward movement of narrative resolution. Indeed, many of the film's individual events act as detours which pull Parry away from successful completion of his original quest. For example, in one long sequence, Parry is accosted by a blackmailing thug who goes with him on a literal detour as they drive through backroads of San Francisco only to end up in a kind of refuse area at the bay's edge. Parry does triumph over the blackmailer and does even learn from him an important fact (namely, the best way to escape from the country if need be), but in relation to Parry's overall goal, the sequence with the blackmailer is for Parry and for the narrative itself a kind of derouting, a loss of direction (and, significantly, the advice on how to leave the country is also advice on how to leave the narrative, not to resolve it).

The film, then, allows the answering of narrative enigmas but only by suspending other enigmas or by displacing their predictable endings into different kinds of endings. It works by a continual derouting or detouring of any single narrative strand. After his bandages come off, Parry declares the clearing of his name to be his driving force, the project that will make or break him—as he declares, "I've got the Indian sign on me. It seems I can't win. I've got to start out and prove who killed her"—but the film makes that project incapable of resolution. Parry confronts the murderer, Madge, but she refuses to go the police and then falls to her death from her apartment window. If, as Frank Kermode suggests in *The Sense of an Ending*, the successfully closed narrative is a positive apocalypse in its delivery of characters from a disturbing violence into the comforting stasis of a sense-filled ending, then Parry's confrontation with Madge is first of all nonapocalyptic—in a completely deflating moment, Parry asks Madge if she killed his wife and she says "Yes," and then he asks her if she will say that to the police and she simply and smugly answers "No"—and then, second, it is wrongly apocalyptic: the confrontation ends dramatically but not in the way that Parry intended. Parry's only chance for innocence vanishes with Madge's death. The escape to South America, then, is an ending of convenience, a *deus ex machina* conclusion that has little force of closure and can suggest the nonconformity of this film to a classic model. Suddenly entering into the story, the expedient of "Peru" allows the nar-

rative to end without resolution. Rather than an ending necessi-
tated by initial narrative premises—as in Greimas' narrative
rectangle—the escape to Peru shifts the narrative into another
mode, another register, disconnected from the previous narrative
line. Peru here functions as a utopian or atopian site, not simply
in the narrative's story but also as a force of the narrative structure
itself: literally a nonplace whose existence is phantasmically propitious. The "happy ending" exists here in an unreal register, a
suspension of narrative time that can signal the strangeness of its
own suspension.

In terms of overall narrative structure, it is useful, then,
to compare the unbandaging sequence of *Dark Passage* to that of
Pride of the Marines. In *Pride of the Marines,* with its notion that there
is a place for everyone in the dominant system, the fact of blindness
is underplayed and is presented as only a minor moment of a
narrative whose overall story is that of a generalized triumph. In
Pride of the Marines, then, the operation on Al's eyes is a de-
emphasized event; indeed, there's no hint in the previous scene
that an operation is about to occur. Although the operation fails
and might thus seem to leave the narrative of recovery unclosed,
the failure is rewritten in terms of a larger narrative closure: blind
or sighted, Al is an important man (important for Ruth; important
for his country). The blindness, the operation, its success or failure,
are all relatively insignificant to the film's narrative course: thus,
right after the failed operation, Al's doctor tells him that he can
try again in a year, but this second operation is never mentioned
again and the film's apocalyptically optimistic ending of Al going
home (plus the overdetermination that begins to give him back
his sight) makes his blindness no longer an issue.

In *Dark Passage,* on the other hand, the operation succeeds, but it is one of the few events to succeed in a narrative that
is overwhelmingly devoted to the breaking apart of narrative flow.
The operation and the unveiling of bandages are built up by the
first sixty-two minutes of the film as events of ultimate significance
(since we never see Bogart until the unveiling). But the consequences of the unveiling are strangely nonapocalyptic, insignificant. First, while *Pride of the Marines* goes immediately from

operation to unveiling (as if to get this secondary narrative out of the way), *Dark Passage* stretches out the time, delaying the payoff. And yet, in a second source of nonapocalypse, the unbandaging loses any signification, since we already know that it is Humphrey Bogart who will emerge as the face beneath the bandage. Moreover, the connotations of Bogart as an actor of crime films works against the narrative function of the surgery; Parry may be going through surgery to remove himself from a noirlike world, but the Bogart face thrusts him all the more directly back into that sort of world.[3] Finally, and most important for the logic of the narrative, Parry's face change accomplishes little; while his first public encounter after the bandages come off ends well, his next three encounters are ones in which his new face doesn't help him at all: first, he is stopped by a cop who thinks that his *behavior* is strange; next, a desk clerk treats him with suspicion because of the *name* he gives to check in a seedy hotel; finally, he is menaced by a blackmailer who has been following him even before his operation. Even though the operation is dramatically a turning point in the film, it is a particularly undramatic point, one that changes little.

In its narrative of continuous contingency, *Dark Passage* demonstrates that the centering subjects that could give narrative a full project are potentially lacking for postwar film. Thus, where Al Schmidt's authority figures keep telling him to have courage, Parry's doctor tells him/us in a full-face close-up that "there's no such thing as courage. There's only fear, the fear of getting hurt and the fear of dying. That's why human beings last so long." In this world, courage no longer has the status of a transcendent power, and it is no longer something that could inevitably hold a narrative logic together. If *Pride of the Marines* gives us the positive existentialism of commitment to a being, *Dark Passage* gives us the negative existentialism of commitment to a nothingness, the instabilities of life and narrative falling prey to the inescapabilities of a historical absurd.

But for Irene's help, Vincent Parry is alone in *Dark Passage*. His best friend dies early on; the police are against him. In this representation of a struggle lived out in a high degree of solitude, *Dark Passage* can seem emblematic of certain tendencies of forties narrative. Conditions of the postwar period particularly intensify these tendencies. For example, the death of Roosevelt in 1945 can have its effect on narrativity and on the effective representation of power. Roosevelt has been a force of narrative in two ways. On the one hand, his endurance in office suggests a long-running and successful story (and, as A. A. Hoehling suggests in *The Home Front*, in this respect, Roosevelt may be only the most important of a series of long-running authority figures—long-running big-city mayor [La Guardia], long-running boxing champion [Joe Louis], long-running cardinal [Spellman]). On the other hand, Roosevelt's power in office has led him to assume the role in narratives of an enunciator, a figure who initiates and legitimates and develops the narratives of others. The death of Roosevelt, then, can mean a certain lessening of the power of these narrative forces of continuity and enunciating authority. Although Truman eventually works himself into a position of certain authority, his regime begins surrounded by doubt and a nonconfident lack of a sense in how things might turn out. Significantly, what many scholars have focused on as the political struggle of Truman's first moments in power[4] is also a struggle of *meanings* as Truman has to work to construct an image that might approximate the force of Roosevelt.[5] Certainly, by the end of the decade, Cold War issues will allow a certain independent image for Truman. For example, against Roosevelt's East Coast intellectualism, Truman will be able to promote himself as the Midwest ordinary man who is not given over to all the dangers of a rich world and a high culture: Truman's "plain speaking" attitude works well at a moment in which East Coast intellectual Alger Hiss is on trial and leading many Americans to the assumption that East Coast intellectualism is not far from communism.

But at the beginning of his presidency especially, Truman can only fail at offering a strong central subject to the American imaginary of the moment. Truman's own choice of an attitude—the substitution of an ordinary common sense for the Roosevelt ambition, the turning of the New Deal into a Fair Deal—can suggest Truman's assumption of a sort of image of a benign calmness, an unassuming clarity. Paradoxically, this retrenched position means that Truman's acts of aggressive and assertive determination will seem contradictory or arbitrary (as in his sending the military in to end the coal miners' strike); as Bess Truman herself will jokingly say, "To err is Truman."

To be sure, one attempted solution is to keep an image of Roosevelt going strong—there is in the immediate postwar period a rash of Roosevelt emulations including the founding by high government officials of National Roosevelt Clubs. Certain speeches of Truman will even be preceded by the recorded voice of Roosevelt. In the words of Mayor La Guardia, "We cannot think of President Roosevelt as one who is gone. He is here. Every hope, yes, the peace of the world, requires his constant spiritual presence."[6]

Fictional narrative appears in a variety of ways to enact the ambiguous representation of authority. But I need to clarify here my sense of the force of this ambiguity. Although I would suggest that, in style and story, a film like *Dark Passage* demonstrates a certain distance from classic narrativity, from that narrative coincidence of social, romantic, and narratological logics, the distance of the *film noir* doesn't imply an *ideological* liberation. To be sure, there is a liberation from a certain *narrative* ideology—narrative, in Macherey's sense, as a coherent, coherency-making resolution of contradictions. But I would contend that ideology can take on forms other than the narratological alone. Indeed, as the end of the next chapter will argue, the fall into nonnarrativity becomes itself a problem for which new forms come into play as symbolic resolutions of the generated tensions: most especially, postwar commodification occurs as a kind of spectacle that assumes that it is all too necessary to throw off narrative in order to enter a show of endless, nonprogressive circulation of signs.

Similarly, we might echo Jean-François Lyotard's recent suggestions in *The Post-Modern Condition* and claim that the end of an age of master narratives can lead to control by a new and different sort of logic: the rise of an informational society governed by norms of input/output (rather than beginning/middle/end), by performativity, a limiting rationalism.[7] Indeed, if, as I argued in the previous chapter, forties scientific discourse comes increasingly to understand human psychology as the one matter most resistant to scientific norms, science itself can seem to enter into a spiral of power where each psychological excess is met by a new application of norms; for example, in *White Heat,* if the law officers first follow the criminals through a method that requires direct observation (what they call the A-B-C method, using several cars to follow one car) and so can be fouled up if the suspect's car gets out of sight, the officers end by establishing a more efficient mode of surveillance—the use of direction finders that can keep a car located even at a great distance. To be sure, the films of scientific control move to an ending where reason effectively banishes an aberration—as in the mushrooming clouds that signal Cody Jarrett's apocalyptic end in *White Heat*—but the ending here seems to matter less than the playing out of the spirals. Indeed, the films on forces of authority in contact with an aberrant *juvenile delinquency* argue that the youth condition is a force that no simple sense of an ending can control or contain: one boy may be punished (*Knock on Any Door,* 1949) or cured (*Fighting Father Dunne),* but there are always other boys ready to run riot, as the defense attorney (Humphrey Bogart) indicates in his final speech to the jury in *Knock on Any Door* (see also *The Naked City* [1948] with its end suggestion that solving a crime simply means that the homicide squad will have to get ready for the next crime to come along). In his book *The Show of Violence,* psychologist Fred Wertham goes so far as to argue that delinquency and psychosis are so widespread and so much more complex than standard criminology would imagine that rational control through disciplinary means can only misunderstand and take an inadequate, reductive attitude toward the cure.

Where, as a number of commentators have explained, narrative bears an intimate connection to desire by functioning as a logic that would work to hold desire within coordinated constraints,[8] the forties representations can suggest a condition in which desire refuses a place within narrative, splits off and becomes a seemingly independent force. Criminality and nonspiritualized sexuality turn extreme—hence, the fever-pitched acting of Cagney in *White Heat* or of Peggy Cummins in *Gun Crazy* (1949) playing a woman who wants more and more (a desire rendered in a whole series of outlandish Freudian symbols). At the same time, the forces of reason and propriety turn all the more ordinary, dull even, betraying little sign of emotion, of desire—hence, that whole spate of postwar films about coldly efficient law officers (played frequently by bland, look-alike, forgettable actors such as Mark Stevens in *Street with No Name*) going about their business; hence, too, all the scenes where the cold law officer must refuse desire (for example, the cop in *The Naked City* who leaves his bathing-suited wife to go back on the case).

With the split between desire and logic, narrative resolution becomes all the more extreme. It is easy at the end of a film like *Gun Crazy* to feel emotionally ambivalent about the ending's sense: is it good or not that the bland forces of small-town America (the sheriff whose dad was a sheriff and whose son will likely be a sheriff) have won out over all the excessive energy of a woman like Laurie? But this ambivalence catches something perhaps of the ambivalence of the forties moment itself, especially of the postwar moment: it is poised between logic and desire, reason and energy.

This contradictory state of things is not in itself progressive. Indeed, as historians and theorists of Fascism especially have suggested, it is socially ambivalent moments above all that tend to generate the social conditions for Fascism; as Ernesto Laclau suggests in *Politics and Ideology in Marxist Theory*, nihilism, a discontent with traditional master narratives as a justification of the existing state of things, can equally lead to an intensification of a savior-power mythology or to a desire for revolutionary change.[9] Thus, in the forties, the transition from the benign oedipalism of Roosevelt to the confused nonleadership of the early Truman can lead to the fifties' investment in a noncentralized, bureaucratic, informational governance—Eisenhower, Riesman's "man in the crowd," Whyte's *Organization Man*—but, as I will argue in more depth later, it can also generate the image of a savior figure in someone like Mickey Spillane's Mike Hammer, destroyer of bureaucracies; of dangerous female desire; of Communist threat; of decadent European intellect; and so on.

The forties, then, are a moment poised between various historical possibilities. There are certain complementary or parallel structures in social representations and in narrative representations of the moment. For example, in many narratives, authority figures will progressively move into the background, leaving the narratives open to the stories of loners of all sorts. On the one hand, there will be films like *Gilda,* which chronicles the rise to power of the new, common man as against the supposedly phallic force of culture, wealth, and tradition. As Mary Ann Doane's textual analysis of the film demonstrates, the elimination of the authority figure is a process carried out even at the level of stylistic details: for example, the "father figure," Ballin, is turned into a mere shadow, an insubstantial force, against the newfound power of Johnny.[10] That Ballin's absence is in part a self-intended one—based on his connections to various political and economic conspiracies of a postwar age—only further shows how authoritative power can seem in conflict with the needs of the ordinary people, the Johnnies of the world. When authority disappears, it does so as a trick or betrayal.

But if *Gilda* suggests how the diminuation of traditional authority can lead to a mythology of the new investment of power in the common person, other films will imply on the other hand that the inadequacy of a central power brings with it the loss of individual power. Many forties narrative figures move in a kind of absurd existentialist space of overwhelming solitude where no authoritative law exists to give any meaning to one's actions. At the extreme, this will lead to a brooding passivity, a sense that there's no legitimate(d) action left. In *The Killers* (1946), for example, authoritative law has so retreated from its role as a guide and support for the individual's actions that it turns into a veritable force of menace for the "hero," Swede (Burt Lancaster). With Swede's release from prison, the older man, Colfax, seems at first to offer Swede an aid and a restoration of a goal. But Colfax turns out to be part of the problem: Kitty (Ava Gardner) is his girl and not Swede's, and in a series of psychologically charged confrontations, Swede learns that dominant power exists not as the granting of benefits to its subjects but, quite the contrary, as the deliberate control and exploitation of benefits and subjects to the benefit of power itself. After a series of betrayals by Colfax, Swede becomes a man whose life has little meaning—a man who drifts from locale to locale without finding sense anywhere. The new arrival of Colfax on the scene can only further drive the Swede into a passivity; realizing that not even existential brooding saves one from the reach of power, Swede gives in to the finality of death.

At the same time, other narratives will posit a certain mediation of power and the individual by splitting the narrative universe into two planes where lone individuals struggle but against the background of an absent yet still potentially legitimating authority. In negative cases, this split seems only to incease the absurdity of the individual struggle. There will be a number of narratives about individuals buffeted around by the sheer multiplicity and anonymity of bureaucracies of the government or industry. For example, in E. E. Smith's science-fiction novel *Triplanetary*, gladiators struggling for their freedom in ancient Rome have no idea that their each and every gesture is being controlled by cosmically warring forces. If forties technology works in part to legitimate a new image of the vast corps of anonymous technicians who will build the American future—as in the large team effort of the Manhattan Project—a whole series of paranoid narratives represent the dangers of an anonymous and technicist approach to the everyday world of ordinary humanity. Thus, a film like *The Red Menace* will show an ex-G.I. so thrown around by the bureaucracy supposedly established to help the veteran that he turns to the Communist party for a new investment in manhood.

And yet other narratives will turn the very problem of vast and anonymous agencies into the very solution to the absence of a central authority. In such narratives, the loner fights precisely for such agencies; it is in the technology of bureaucracy that one's life takes on a sense. Thus, through the latter part of the forties, especially, there will be a whole series of films about government agencies and the individuals who work for them: for example, *T-Men* (1947), *Border Incident* (1949), *State Department File 649* (1949), etc. Significantly, many of the films come from the same film-makers who work in *film noir* (for example, director Anthony Mann, actor Dennis O'Keefe, photographer John Alton), and, but for an opening and closing in which the scene shows the government agency in question, the films concentrate on the individual agent's immersion in a *noirlike* world. In its most immediate situations, life here is still absurd—for example, the chance encounter with a family friend who accidentally reveals the undercover T-man's identity in *T-Men*—but these encounters take their *final* sense and justification from a sense of service to a higher cause that overcomes solitary doubt and entrapment. In *Border Incident*, the return out of the claustrophobic *noir* world back to the image of the authoritative agency will even receive a particularly marked stylistic treatment: against the stark *noir* images of the death of a best friend by machinery in an open field or of the darkened canyon where the border patrol battles it out with an illegal aliens ring, the end shots of the agency bureau in Washington are filmed with a framing symmetry and an even and bright lighting that give the image a clarity and surety that the interior narrative of the film had denied.

But the sudden break from the fallen world in which loners battle resistant forces to the epic world of a logic lorded over by authoritative forces can suggest that, for such narratives, there is no easy mediation between the two narrative worlds. Even those science-fiction epics of empire building that I discussed in the last chapter tend in the postwar moment to split the narrative line between a large narrative of empire and a series of smaller narratives about individual battles for and against the empire. A potential conflict opens up between an overall narrative line and the unpredictability of numerous individual tales. To be sure, as I argued in the last chapter, specific figures like *I, Robot's* Susan Calvin or *Foundation's* Hari Seldin will work to span these two narrative levels—to show that is, that each individual narrative is finally no more than a micrological condensation of an overall plan or process. But in another sense, the very sweep of these narratives can lead to a certain undoing of narrative unity. In Smith's *Triplanetary*, for example, certain figures are instituted as narrative subjects only to be killed off or to be pushed out of the picture by the forces of history (for example, the dedicated Ralph Kinnison, forced out of war armament service by an impossible bureaucracy). There is a virtually deliberate inability to rest with any one story, any one narrative situation. Authority becomes a static symbol which can only vaguely inspire the struggles of the individual narrative agents.

While a number of critics have argued the enactment of an existentialist attitude in forties film, it is necessary I think to emphasize that such an existentialism is primarily a negative existentialism, one in which environments, for example, don't reflect back to a character his/her personality or values—that is, his/her freedom to shape externality according to individual desire—but, quite the contrary, rather demonstrate the radical externality and even resistance of environment to the imprinting of a self upon environment. To be sure, as with forties existentialism, the forties film character can appear to find a certain freedom in necessity: a begrudging willingness to keep going despite, or even because of, the sense that worldly reality will always do its best to show up the insufficiency of human projects. But, as with existentialism, freedom implies necessity; there is little redemptive transcendence here. One is always in situation, always shut off from any full or ultimate possibility of a spiritual redemption.

The split between narrative agent and narrative authority is also the split of a hero from a grounding in a space that could give individual actions a sense. Environment is here the possibility of the significant reversibility of every object—its potential to turn against or be turned against its would-be user. In such a world, for example, even nonweapons can suddenly become sources of menace: the antlers that suddenly become the threat of eye gouging in *Raw Deal,* (1948); the gigantic coffee cup in which one can drown in *The Horn Blows at Midnight* (1945); the bannister that breaks and the anchor that impales in *The Reckless Moment* (1949); the telephone cord that strangles in *Detour* (1945).

There is a representation of a situation in which all externality can be a force and source of menace.

For folklorist Vladimir Propp, the stability of a classical narrative lies in the stability of narrative *functions*—characters, for example, represented as a finite set of narrative possibilities. Objects in Propp's schema become virtual projections of a solid stable function that moves the narrative along. For example, as Propp notes in *The Historical Roots of the Folktale*, even the ostensible threat of death becomes in the folktale not a disruption of a larger narrative teleology but one more element in that teleology's effective functioning: death is a challenge that the hero accepts and surmounts and even turns into a positive good—death as a step that leads to the rebirth of a stronger, more mature hero.[11]

In contrast, the forties narrative, then, can represent the possibility of narrative disfunction, of a disruption of narrative elements and agents. Thus, where for Propp, objects simply become aids or temporary hindrances—for example, the magic tool that one has to learn how to obtain and use—the forties object is *simultaneously* help and harm (and unpredictably so), a threat of full resistance to a character's narrative control. To put this another way, if the *project* (to use the existentialists' term) is a narrative activity through which human beings work to come to terms with an environment and make it their own, forties narrative can serve as the site of a kind of reversibility of meaning—what we might call a *symbolics* of narrative space—in which environment ceases to be a reflection or object of human projects and turns instead into a potential disruption, subversion, dispersion of projects. Not a symbolism in which each object is named and so has its place within a human scheme, a symbolics is the space of the object's permutability, its ability to pass through all possible functions.[12] Such a symbolics is, then, the measure of a gap between intention and realization—a gap that occurs first at the level of language. Language comes from others as a force that the individual must work to master but that can quickly exceed his/her attempts at mastery. For example, in forties film, fate is decided as much by words as by actions: vows, threats, promises. The opening of *The*

Killers (1946), for example, shows a kind of abstract power of the *contract* over life and death: the two killers who come after Swede are quite emphatic in their declaration that they themselves have nothing against him, that they've never even met him. Even the war-affirmative command that greets weary soldiers only to throw them immediately back into battles of war can become a kind of enforcing strangeness as in *Objective Burma!* with its intimations of a distant, arbitrary command.[13]

But language can also come from the outside not as the sense of omnipotent authority but rather as the lack of authority, the individual's immersion in a world of absurdity as, for example, in the use of private codes in crime or comedy. The tough films of the postwar period especially represent a situation in which fear of contact or combat with the other—the male faced with the force of femininity, for example—leads to a kind of erection of language into a barrier, a deliberately studied banter that hides emotion and works to project an image of self-possession. Moreover, even in those situations where an individual tries to make his/her language a force of personal energy, language can exceed intention. It will become ambiguous or meaningless: for example, Wilbur in *Abbott and Costello Meet Frankenstein* trying to tell his partner that Dracula and the Frankenstein monster are in the next room but finding himself unable to do anything but produce noises. Here language becomes a force that, far from converting the external world to personal ends, ends up as a kind of externality itself and turns against its originator.

Where a number of critics have argued the influence on forties film (and especially on *noir*) of an expressionist aesthetic, it is important to emphasize that the expressionism here is most often not the triumph of a subjectivity in which environment somehow reflects back to a character his/her own internal nature but, quite the contrary, an expressionism that demonstrates the radical externality and alterity of environment to personality.[14] Thus, when characters are willfully expressive, they will frequently find the vehicles of their expression turning against them. For example, in *Leave Her to Heaven* (1945), a growing dissonance between husband and wife is represented through a dissonance in environment: trying to please his pregnant wife, husband Richard (Cornel Wilde) secretly converts one of the rooms of their house into a nursery only to discover that this surprise holds no pleasure for his wife. Similarly, the wife, Ellen (Gene Tierney), will try to use her own body as an expressive vehicle of her love for Richard; but when she gets pregnant to regain his love, she will quickly begin to feel the very fact of her pregnancy—the ugliness that she imagines it has brought her—to be the reason for her husband's increasing interest in her adopted sister (Jeanne Crain).

Moreover, those moments that seem closest to a direct representation of character vision are not so much moments of subjectivity's triumph but of subjectivity's dispersion, its subordination to a complex structure of point of view that goes beyond the single vision. For example, although introduced by specific characters, flashbacks are not necessarily filmed in such a way as to represent the controlling point of view of the narrating character: that is, the flashback frequently exceeds the vision of its narrator or signals the invalidity of the narrator's version of events. In the extreme case of *Lydia* (1941), the same scene will be narrated twice to pinpoint the inaccuracies of one character's particular remembrances of the past. The flashback becomes a source of a sort of perspectivalism in which reality becomes no more than the individual views one has of it. Similarly, dream sequences tend to reflect not the grounded wishes of the character but a lack of control: for example, in *Pride of the Marines; Murder, My Sweet* (1944); *Getting Gertie's Garter* (1945); *Up in Mabel's Room* (1944), or *Spellbound*, dreams show bits of the subject's experience that don't add up, that have no sense (except the paranoid one of non- or countersense). One exception might be *Dr. Jekyll and Mr. Hyde* (1943), where Jekyll's deams are quite explicit sexual fantasies— volcanic eruptions, the explosive unscrewing of the cork (which has Ingrid Bergman's face on it) in a bottle of champagne, the whipping of a team of horses whose faces are that of Lana Turner and Ingrid Bergman. But one function of *Dr. Jekyll and Mr. Hyde* is precisely to show such fantasy as excessive monomania: subjective vision can have no fit in the structured reality of a Victorian

England and so must be killed off. In other words, when a vision is emphatically personal, it is emphatically aberrant. Perhaps most extreme in this respect is *No Minor Vices*, where a doctor imagines his own suicide, represented on the screen as two eyes confronting an ultimate nothingness. Indeed, even *Lady in the Lake* (1946) destabilizes the power of its first-person-point-of-view structure by enveloping it in a plot of aggression and doubt (thus, until almost the last moments of the film, Marlowe doesn't know if Adrienne Fromsett is really on his side or not; the camera sees but its look is uncertain).

In this way, every action reveals its limitation as an attempt at sense making, an attempt at impressing one's self onto the world in a significant way, constraining the world according to the dimensions of a project. Here, the gap between intentions and words can turn into a gap between intentions and actions, and this gap condenses in many films: Dix Handley's body alongside the Kentucky horses in *The Asphalt Jungle* (1950) or Harry Fabian's body tossed into the water as so much flotsam in *Night and the City* (1950) or the hero, Jeff, shot dead in *Out of the Past* (1947). Death serves here as a farcical mark not simply because it signals an end to projects but because it signals the end as inherent in the very nature of bodily materiality. No matter the grandeur of a project if the body gives way. If the project is a way of being-in-the-world, it is the body that existential phenomenologists like Sartre and Merleau-Ponty suggest is the mediation of that being and its world—the relay between mind and matter.

A mediation of world and individual, the body is an intermediate site, fraught with all the tensions of external and internal assault. A betrayal by the body, then, is the ultimate irony, the very tool of Being undercut. Death occurs in film on the one hand as an abrupt finality in excess of its cause—for example, injuries that shouldn't be fatal but suddenly are, such as the shooting of the partner in *Out of the Past,* the two deaths in *Detour,* the accidental killing of a suspect in *Where the Sidewalk Ends* (1950), the illness that no one realizes is fatal in *Caged* (1950). On the other hand, death becomes an extended affair, a long-term suffering of the body: as Lawrence Alloway notes in his book *Violent*

America: The Movies, 1946–1964, the postwar years especially become a kind of cataloging of all the wounds that can be inflicted
on bodies (Alloway connects this to the war's new demonstration
of the real force of weapons).[15] Indeed, against the wartime desire
to not acknowledge death—to airbrush it away—a postwar combat film like *Twelve O'Clock High* (1949) seems to revel in the
mentioning of gory war wounds: the first major action to show
the officer's fortitude has him taking control of the removal of a
severed body part from a wrecked plane.

Furthermore, death becomes not the instantaneity of
heroic release but a kind of slow-motion rebellion of each body
part: for example, in *Beyond the Forest* (1948), Rose Moline's final
and fatal walk to the train station is an expansion of pain into an
ultimate extreme. Death here is not the ultimate accomplishment—as in the wartime film *Fighting Seabees,* where the wounded
hero blows up dozens of Japanese in his last living gesture—but
a mark of nonaccomplishment, of a failure of all projects. The
train that Rose just misses in *Beyond the Forest* stands as a sign of
death, as a vicious cutting off of possibility. The narrative here is
not the realization of a project, but the undermining of the project
by one's own body. If one of wartime representation's ways of
dealing with death was to have it occur in a sudden burst of
explosive glory—for example, the sublimated orgasmic touch of
the two lovers in *Prisoner of Japan*—death now becomes a drawn-
out affair, an act of suffering with little glory to it.

Beyond the tool, classic narrative in Propp's analysis
also provides its protagonist with a helper, a kind of sidekick figure
who allies with the hero. In the forties narrative, though, ''help-
ers'' are not infrequently resistant or unhelpful. If the war-affirmative films represent the evolution of the group as an efficient
machine or organism, other narratives show sidekicks to be self-
willed agents in their own right who refuse subservience to the
wishes and needs of the hero: for example, in *Red River* (1948),
Groot (Walter Brennan) is a voice of (unheeded) conscience for
Tom Dunson, resisting his projects, suggesting an alternate pattern
of action. Significantly, Groot functions as the narrator of the film,
thus enclosing Dunson's agency within a narrative that is not

under Dunson's control. In other films, the splitting of the group will be even more intense: comrades become the bitterest of enemies. In *Desert Fury* (1947), for example, Eddie Bendix's decision to dump his partner, Johnny Ryan (Wendell Corey), will occasion a gigantic outburst of invective on Ryan's part, a bitter lament in which years of repressed feelings of hateful competition come bubbling to the surface and end in murder. In *film noir* generally, the conversion of the helper into an other is extreme and intense. Alliances are temporary, never completely open: a partner can turn out to be your enemy (for example, the blackmailing partner in *Out of the Past*). At best, alliance has to be coldly professional (for example, the government agents in *T-Men* and *Border Incident* who must quietly watch their partners get killed violently) or tinged with a cool, distancing surface of toughness and swagger. In *The Maltese Falcon,* (1941) for example, the partnership of Miles Archer and Sam Spade only goes so far—a relationship in which sharing or reciprocity are mediated through wisecracking one-upmanship, a desire for money and women, and even betrayal (Spade is having an affair with Archer's wife).

The moment of the forties, then turns into a moment of narrative instability, a moment in which a would-be dominant representation tries to enclose narration within a coherent logic tied to stories of romance, duty, and epistemological certainty, but where equally narrative is dispersed, broken down. For example, the very codes of narrativity that Roland Barthes reads as irreversible or only weakly reversible become in forties narrative the very site of a privileging of reversibility. Thus, what Barthes calls the *proairetic* code, the code of action, and which he describes as the very "armature" of the "readerly" text becomes in forties narrative the pivotal moment for a kind of writerly reversibility, each intended action leading not logically to its implied conclusion, but, quite the contrary, actions fissuring into isolated bits. If narrative's reason relies on a logic of the already done—that governing of the future that proairesis would work to institute—not insignificantly, forties narrative can demonstrate the possibility of an undoing of the already done, its throwing into doubt; narrative becomes no longer the place of *sequence*, but rather of interruption.

For example, so many actions in forties films are incompleted actions, broken by chance, a derouting of direction: for example, *Scarlet Street* (1945), where a decision to walk home in the rain causes Criss Cross (Edward G. Robinson)—whose very name can suggest the ways the "unitary" narrative is actually an intersection of narrative singularities—to encounter the seductive woman, Kitty.

To be sure, the derouting of narrative can create a new narrative line, a reinvesting of action, but this establishes narrative as the fundamental absence of an overall closure: narrative becomes a detour that never reaches back to its original point of departure. Indeed, the very image of the detour will become a common figure in forties films—police roadblocks (*Gun Crazy*, [1949], *They Live by Night* [1949]), construction crew barriers (*The Reckless Moment* [1948], *The Big Steal* [1949]), backroads that seem to go nowhere (*Mr. Blandings Builds His Dream House* [1948], *The Runaround* [1946]). And, of course, the film *Detour* builds its whole structure around the deferment of actions, against the trajectory of the already read future. As Tania Modleski has argued, *Detour* becomes an exemplary case of the derouted text, where loss works against completion and arrival:[16] the derouting of Al's goals is caused first by external facts (for example, the hitchhikers that he picks up) and then by Al's own internalization of incompleteness as the very condition of his existence (he tries to phone Sue and can't go through with the call). When Al does act, his actions derail: on the one hand, the simple actions that should easily found the proairetic basis of narrative lead to consequences that are in excess of their initial structure. For example, the ostensibly minor act of opening a car door causes a sleeping man to fall out and kill himself on a rock; if, as Barthes has suggested, the proairetic code depends on two moments—an initiating action and its determined completion, an ideal case of narrative, in other words—then, significantly, *Detour* here sets up a situation in which the second moment "answers" the first only farcically, a completion in defiance of the initiating intention. On the other hand, major moments when Al does decide to act become moments where outcomes turn against him: for example, his sudden will to reject Vera's control of his life becomes a moment that leads to another kind of control—Al's attempt to wrest the telephone from Vera leads unexpectedly to murder and makes Al's detour from innocence infinite.

Classical narrative is a known movement in a world of known objectivity, the clarity of known objectivity, the clarity of the Sartrean *project*. The project is a kind of predetermined monologue between character and environment—an already written freedom in which environment becomes part of the human narrative. But if, in Sartre's terms, choosing a project seems to give one transcendence from the absurdity of brute, insignificant materiality and seems then to make of life a narrative, the forties film in contrast can show the fall back into immanence, into a mockery of projects. Where the successfully classical narrative relies on a coincidence of the forward direction of narrative flow and the projective propulsion of character intention, what forties narrative can institute is a sort of disjunction between the elements of narrative. Narrative time and character time can enter into conflict in cases where the project necessarily becomes one of a need to stop time: for example, in *D.O.A.* (1949) (the man who wants to find his poisoner before the poison takes effect), or *On the Town* (sailors who have only a twenty-four-hour leave), or novels like Cornel Woolrich's *Deadline at Dawn* (where each chapter is introduced by the image of a clock that is coming closer to the deadline) or his *Phantom Lady* (where each chapter is introduced by a moment of the countdown to the execution of an innocent man). Time itself becomes here not the transcendence of history but one more reminder of history's reversible and potentially resistant materiality. This is a very different time from that of a forties science or forties supernaturalism. Scientific time and supernatural time are times that are *mythic* in the specific narratological sense that Russian semiotician Jurij Lotman has assigned to this term: a temporality that is ultimately atemporal, nothing but the predictable working out of an already known end that echoes and reflects and reinforces human goals.[17] In myth, narrative is a move toward a time that is outside of time—a moment that transcends the variabilities of historical flux. This is the kind of narrative that is given its most famous representation by Hegel: narrative as a fall into alienation that is resolved by the transcendence of alienation in a higher finality. For Hegel, ideality is never immediate, a purely romantic fusion of subject and object, but precisely a process, a Comedy by which subjects make objects theirs, for-them.[18]

And yet such a narrative is necessarily contradictory: the moment of transcendence has always to come by fiat alone, by a willful leap out of time, rather than by a "natural" move out of time: the point of transition becomes fixable precisely as a point *in history* (as those scholars suggest who note that Hegel represents himself and the Prussian state as moments of ideality).[19] In other words, there is nothing that grounds the ending of a narrative except internal claims of that narrative, deliberate exclusions of those differences that would seem to fall outside the narrative sweep and that make the moment of the ending *seem* natural. For example, by the very act of making different levels of narrative action coincide, narrative can imply the rightness of its ending. This, for example, is the comic vision of Stanely Cavell in *Pursuits of Happiness:* Cavell's story of the screwball narrative follows the Hegelian model (while casting it in an American mode): the initial moment of security turns out to be weak and superficial, leading to a fall into time (the couple breaks up; they enter into various adventures) which finally moves out of time in a utopian place, mythically figured as a site outside the endlessly mounting pro-ductivity of an urban-based capitalism. But to promote the pos-sibility of such a utopian place, the screwball films (and Cavell, in a mimetic repetition of the ideology of the films) must leap from personal story to abstract myth—that is, to notions that the indi-vidual couple is somehow the embodiment of the American dream and that the rhythm of the couple is the rhythm of nature, etc.

The possibility of "history" in Lotman's sense, then, is to show that such a leap is precisely a myth, an exertion of force that is baseless and vulnerable. It is this vulnerability that a film like *Dark Passage* can suggest: if, in myth, narratives begin by a self-engendering fiat—"In the beginning," an example of those kinds of speech acts that John Austin has shown construct a state of affairs by announcing that state—narratives also *end* by fiat, the sense of an ending as finally no more than the authoritative imposition of an ending. *Historical* time, as Lotman argues, would then be the time of accident, of difference, of a splitting of narrative lines that thereby shows up the arbitrariness of fiat. This is the time of the project not as control of the future, but as a kind of gamble, the commitment to an unrecallable gesture.

Many forties films, for example, revolve around ultimate schemes—plans that are irreversible once started but which, once started, can move in an unplanned direction, revealing not a coherence of narrative time, but its resistance to unity. For example, in *Night and the City*, Harry Fabian lives as a kind of manic arbiter of the future: his life is a constant flight from the responsibilities of his actions. Harry deals with each moment by fictionalizing it as part of a promised benefit in the future. For example, as enemies crush in on him, Harry quickly improvises an alibi of a gigantic scam that he is planning. His mistake, though, is that he starts believing his own fictions and imagines that a forward flow of narrative could take him out of the dangers of time into a mythic place of bountiful reward. Harry puts everything into an ultimate project, one which is as easily derailed as it was put into place.

Lotman argues that an exemplary figure in the representation of mythic time is the gambler. The gambler here will be that character who endlessly repeats and who leaves the time of historical change for the stasis of an endless cyclicity of loss and gain; indeed, as Walter Benjamin has noted, the gambler is like the factory worker in the constant replay of the same gestures, always staying in the same place, not an agent but an object of an endless system.[20] And yet, in a way that neither Lotman nor Benjamin fully seem to recognize, their analogies work against the supposed sanctity of a mythic time: as figures within an economy of exchange, the gambler and the worker might seem outside of time but they are all the more resolutely in it, their gestures standing as ways of fictionalizing time, of mimetically repeating some ostensibly natural cyclicity. Cyclicity here is forced (forced for the worker, for example, by a scarcity that makes him/her work and internalize scarcity as a necessary condition). This un-naturalness becomes evident in those moments when cyclicity derails (for example, the factory is shut down by layoffs or strikes; the gambler goes bankrupt): not insignificantly, gambling will be a common event in forties films as precisely an act of noncyclicity, the grip of a time that controls not because it repeats but because it has no predictability or, at most, only the predictability of the individual's inevitable defeat.

Where Benjamin's gambler is the Parisian aristocrat who seems to stand outside of history and seems literally to have time in his hands (but only "seems," since the forward move of capitalism will increasingly make that aristocrat dispensable), the forties gambler is a figure from the middle classes (or lower) for whom gambling is not simply a game, a series of losses to be written off as a source of ludic pleasure, but an earnest attempt at accumulation, a desire precisely to leave an endless cyclicity of defeat for a utopian time of wealth and power. Losing here is the possibility of a dangerous irreversibility: for example, Harry Fabian in *Night and the City*, who gambles on a gigantic venture and must pay with his life when something unpredictably defeating happens. Significantly, many of the gambling films make a point of opposing to the all-too-human hero or heroine another figure, the head of the gambling racket or boss of the crime system (Kristo in *Night and the City*, Corrigan [Steve McNally] in *The Lady Gambles* [1949]); these latter figures are the ones outside of time, the ones for whom life is a safe repetition (for example, in *The Great Sinner* [1949], the casino owner Armand is a kind of superior witness to the failings of the gamblers around him).

For such superior characters, time is precisely a source of play, to be toyed with for pleasure but to be rejected when it threatens to become too historically variable, unpredictable, or demanding (thus, in *The Lady Gambles*, the casino boss, Corrigan, takes Joan Boothe [Barbara Stanwyck] out for a ride and drops her off in the middle of nowhere when she begins to take her gambling too seriously). Although they "gamble," such figures are never literally gamblers. They never take any risks; the system is theirs and they can't lose.

But for the lower-class gambler, loss is omnipresent, not merely a possibility but a probability. Thus, *The Great Sinner* begins with Fedor (Gregory Peck) on his deathbed, reduced to poverty and illness by his failure at the gambling table. As his beloved Pauline (Ava Gardner) comes in, wind blows open Fedor's windows, extinguishes the candles in his room, and blows the pages of his autobiography across the floor. Here the film suggests one irreversibility of nonmythic history: death not as comedy nor as tragedy but, at the most, as farce and irony. In the case of *The Great Sinner,* certainly, there will be an attempt at a remythification of narrative (most especially in the religious ending of Fedor finding salvation at church). This remythification will begin to operate in the very opening of the film: Pauline picks up one of the sheets of the autobiography and the film goes into flashback recounting in chronological order the events that led up to Fedor's failure. The flashback will end with Pauline's reaffirmation of her love for Fedor—a reaffirmation that will give Fedor confidence to keep on living. And yet two excesses remain outside this mythic pattern. First, Pauline began to read the pages of Fedor's life without bothering to put the scattered pages in order: a minor detail, perhaps, but it can suggest the constructed nature of any optimistic narrative of coherence, its arbitrariness. Second, the confidence of the ending—Fedor's decision to realize his potential as a great writer, and give up gambling—ignores one of the facts established earlier in the narrative: namely, that Fedor had sold all his claims and rights to his writings for all time to Armand, the owner of the casino. Fedor's triumph is only one more subjection to a system.

Nothing, then, finally guarantees the transcendental power of narrative, and forties narratives are frequently nothing so much as a manifestation of all the alternatives to such a power. Death, for example, becomes a narrative element that can signify mythic realization, but that can as easily be a point of meaninglessness, a complete non-sense. To be sure, on the one hand, death will be a welcome escape from temporality, the possibility of release from the world and a union with a "truth" outside history: in *Portrait of Jennie* or *The Ghost and Mrs. Muir,* for example, death allows the possibility of endless romance, a romance not subject to the vagaries of material change. Similarly, a film like *Laura* (1944), with the heroine turning out not to be dead, suggests a rewriting of death as life.

But it is as frequently possible to read an element of satire into such moments: triumph undercuts itself through its very artificiality. Significantly, films that are in certain moments especially triumphant are, at other moments, especially vulnerable to the undoing of triumph: each moment then becomes a reading and rewriting of the other. Like the expedient of "Peru" in *Dark Passage*, triumph here is a miraculous force that converts death into life, loss into plentitude. Hence, a number of films condense around a nodal moment of reversibility, what Barthes in *S/Z* calls the "risky" moments of narrative. In *Laura*, for example, the moment when Mark McPherson goes to sleep in a chair in Laura's apartment becomes the magical and mythical moment of transition between life and death: a track-in followed by an immediate track-out has no function but to signal the enunciative possibility of the film's shift into another register. Indeed, it is quite possible because of this to read the rest of the film as little more than Mark's dream of fantasy (or the film's dream of a love so strong that it can rewrite the reality of death). Everything goes right for Mark from this moment on. Laura returns from the dead, Laura quickly falls in love with him, he gets to punch Shelby in the stomach, he breaks the case. Significantly, the Vera Caspary novel *Laura* suggests that the flip side of a fantasy of a power that overcomes death is a kind of loss of control, a lapse into silence. In the novel, Laura's return disturbs the control of narrative: for example, Mark begins his part of the narrative by telling us, "When Waldo Lydecker learned what happened after our dinner at Montagnino's on Wednesday night, he could write no more about the Laura Hunt case. The prose style was knocked right out of him." Yet Mark too will lose his voice in the presence of a death-become-life: "She edged toward the door. 'Are you . . . ' But I couldn't say the name. She had spoken, she was wet with rain, she had been frightened and had tried to escape. Were these real evidences of life just another set of contradictions?"

Laura's concern with portraiture suggests another way in which that film's mythic solution of death serves as an example of a general fascination with the links of death and representation in the forties. The artistic representation is a way of keeping alive the dead (for example, the photograph of the dead tuberculosis victim in *Chicago Deadline* [1949] that incites the reporter to seek out the truth of her maligned reputation). But, ironically, as a stand-in for life, the portrait can in certain cases substitute all too well for life: in *The Two Mrs. Carrolls* (1947), for example, Mr. Carroll (Humphrey Bogart) marries women only so that he can paint them and then kill them. The painting becomes a fundamental pivot between two possibilities and becomes a figure for narrative itself, a constant conflict of plenitude and loss, of each turning into the other. Significantly, the forties also witness a Hollywood production of *The Picture of Dorian Gray* (1945), ultimate demystification of the mythology of art as complete mimesis, as the continuation of a life through its image. Not only in the story but also in the form of such films, the portrait can suggest a parodic deflation of the force of the live characters: their lives are frequently only an illusion, and little prevents them from ending up as a mere memory trace, a portrait on a wall.

For Frank Kermode, the sense of an ending comes as a holding of death within the assuring coherence of a controlled structure. But the flashback structure of films like *The Great Sinner* can construct a sense of loss against narrative life flow. Similarly, in many films, the fore-sense that the story will end in disaster can, even when a happy ending tries to discount it, encourage an attention to the narrative as an accumulation of bad moments: in such cases, the "happy" ending will be read in terms of its inability to dispense with such moments. For example, *It's a Wonderful Life!* engages in a number of rhetorical strategies to affirm the possibility of its title—it sets its plot during Christmas; it gives George Bailey not one but several cute Hollywood children—and yet it is possible to read for implications against the film's optimism. For example, the solution is only temporary at best (the original $40,000 is still missing; Mr. Potter has not been vanquished). Similarly, the flashback's meaning can go against the meaning of the solution (where the ending shows that all are brethren, the flashback suggests that only the presence of George Bailey prevents a fail into chaos—not a very optimistic vision of human value: here, the film's ostensible populism shades into fascism and the suggestion that the masses are a rabble saved only by a strong individual). The preflashback Bedford Falls appears already to have some of the qualities of the flashback version (thus, George's employees look suspiciously at him when he comes out of a private meeting with Violet; later, Potter mentions rumors about George and Violet—rumors that could only have started with the employees).

In narratives less avowedly optimistic than *It's a Wonderful Life!*, loss appears as a constant undoing of transcendence: Kermode's triumphant ending can always have another antitriumphant moment added to it. Indeed, the forties will frequently engage in a rewriting of endings, an adding on or taking off of scenes, a hesitation about which option to follow. As often as it will announce a prewritten end (for example, during the war, the assurance that victory will come), representation will suggest the indefinite deferment of endings. Thus, for example, the arrival of victory over Europe and Japan can be rewritten as a possibility (often only partially begrudging) of further war: in Richard Brooks' words in *The Brick Foxhole*, "Their war was with the Japs. And after the Japs would come the Russians. And why the Russians? They couldn't tell you. It was just accepted that that would happen."

But the forties narratives refuse the unified sense not only in the retrospective stability of an end, but in the very constitution of a beginning and in the potentials for eventual closure that beginnings institute. Indeed, the openings of many forties films set up an ambiguity of actions: for example, actions that seem easily read but whose proffered interpretation turns out to be wrong (thus, *O.S.S.* [1946], where John Morton [Alan Ladd] steals plans from a U.S. armaments plant; the use already of Ladd in earlier films as ambivalent figure can encourage a reading of this scene as espionage, but it is soon revealed that Morton is simply an agent in training for the O.S.S.) Similarly, there will especially be a representation of actions that are readable in conflicting but equally probable ways (for example, the openings of *Shadow of a Doubt* or *This Gun for Hire,* which play on the undecidability of character values—are these men brooding in bed good men or bad?). Significantly, a number of actors (for example, Dick Powell, Robert Montgomery) will produce films in the forties precisely to go against type, and to create a situation in which the logic of implication between an action and its consequences becomes unpredictable. For example, it is hard to know how to read traditionally comic actor Robert Montgomery when he plays a tough guy out for revenge in a film like *Ride the Pink Horse* (1947).

     Some films explicitly figure the opening as a locus of death or loss or confusion. Even a number of titles signal the threatening quality of the narratives: *Caught* (1949), *Pursued, Possessed, Caged, Accused* (1948), *Act of Violence* (1948), *Act of Murder* (1948), *Build My Gallows High* (a.k.a. *Out of the Past,* 1947), *Desperate* (1947), *On Dangerous Ground* (1951), *Raw Deal* (1948), etc. Such titles can suggest a film's immersion in chaos or confusion from its very first moments. To be sure, such titles can become proairetic promises, working to establish a kind of contract of assurance between film and spectator. Indeed, Marc Vernet has suggested that *film noir* may finally provide the contract of a fulfilled narrativity: "The contract [of titles and credit sequences] channels the flux of fiction, gives it a sense—that is, both a direction and an ultimate signification. The narrative must infallibly lead to a truth that is already (or almost already) constituted."[21] Yet, as I've tried to suggest, the narratives don't always have *a* direction but can give in to an unfinished detour. Moreover, when the films work to establish the certainty of truth, the truth that is established is often an unbearable truth. For example, the point-of-view structure in *film noir* is one that often puts the spectator in the potentially uncomfortable position of sadism (Marlowe's aggressiveness in *Lady in the Lake*) or masochism (the flaming meal thrown at the camera in a first-person shot in *Raw Deal*) or in the perhaps even more uncomfortable transitional state *between* sadism and masochism. The clear sight is a potentially unbearable one.

     Moreover, the ambiguity of narrative contract is established in many *films noirs* from the first moment: for example, *The*

Killers' opening is a kind of continued interplay of promises of identification *and* forestallings of identification: one promise sets up Nick Adams as the story's center, the figure through whom events will pass, but Nick vanishes from the film after the first flashback. The psychical investment can seem to transfer to Swede (played by the rising star Burt Lancaster), but that contract is undercut by his immediate death. The opening of *The Killers* becomes a kind of metaphor of cinema itself, then, and of its possibilities of offer and removal; the bursts of the killers' machine guns which light up the darkness of Swede's room become a figure for the cinema, a dramatic and strobic alternation of light and shadow, a process that gives and takes away.[22]

To be sure, many of those films whose forward narrative trajectory is undone by a flashback that causes events to be read with knowledge of how they will turn out, try to forestall the loss that such a structure can entail by combining the story in the past with an open story in the present. For example, a number of films will alternate representations of the past of a dead character with the story of the investigator's investigation: *Citizen Kane* (1941), *The Mask of Dimitrios* (1944), *Chicago Deadline, Laura, The Killers.* The films try to suggest the fresh openness of a present as against the closed and ill-fated nature of a past. Yet only infrequently will the film rewrite the narratives as ultimately a single story, and when it does do so, the moment of combination or intersection becomes one of uncanniness (for example, the strangeness of Laura's return) or, more frequently, aggression (*The Killers* with Reardon set up for an attack by Swede's killers; or *The Mask of Dimitrios* with Cornelius Leyden [Peter Lorre] endangered by Dimitrios). In other words, the narrative of a present investigation of a past can threaten to either split the narrative into irreconcilable parts or to suggest that reconciliation will be perverse (Mark McPherson's love for Laura) or dangerous. As Jack Shadoian notes in his analysis of *The Killers,* insurance investigator Reardon's meeting with Kitty raises the possibility of a domination of the past over the present, the possibility that Kitty will draw Reardon into her narrative, rather than vice versa: "An image of Swede and Kitty kissing passionately fades into a shot of Kitty and

Reardon (. . .). The shots are linked by the candle on the table that burns at the center of Swede and Kitty's fading embrace. . . . Although the candle—Kitty's flame—has burnt low and is fluttering, it still works. Reardon is fascinated by her narrative, a narrative of evil and treachery, suggesting that if he were slightly less strong (. . .) he could well fall under Kitty's control."[23]

A film like *Citizen Kane* suggests one consequence of this divided narrative: in *Citizen Kane,* the investigator can become a kind of shadow figure, his story only lightly preempting the narrative force of the inner narrative. But this option troubles identification by giving it too little to identify with: like Thompson, the viewer is a reader of fragments, but rather than serving as a point of enunciation, Thompson's fleeting appearances in the film can destabilize point of view and make him also an object of investigation (one wonders what he looks like; one tries to read the emotions and motivations in his responses to various characters: for example, will he really try to sneak cigars to Jedediah in the old-age home?). Between the richness of the past and the instabilities of the present, a disturbing disjunction is once again all too possible. In *Citizen Kane,* of course, the split between investigating character and spectator culminates in the privileged look at Rosebud; and yet this look only increases the ambiguity of identification—by giving the spectator power over Thompson (the spectator sees what he misses) but also by giving Thompson a power over the spectator (just before the revelation of Rosebud, Thompson declares that no one thing could ever sum up a life). Rosebud becomes an ultimate mark of unreadability: does or doesn't it serve as an explanation of Kane's life?

More generally, we might note that the films of investigation frequently give investigators the power of a certain point of view without giving them all the powers that classically come with point of view. For example, if, in Raymond Bellour's suggestion, male characters in classic narrative are frequently relays of a spectator's desires—for a fetishizing voyeurism, for example[24]—the investigators in these films have little access to voyeurism or can only participate in a voyeurism that is signaled as such (thus, before Laura comes to life, Waldo points out the strangeness of McPherson's love for a dead woman and for her portrait). Frequently, the films play on a distinction between a viewer's sight and the investigator's lack of access to such sight: an emphasis, for example, on a woman whose charm has faded (Susan Alexander in *Citizen Kane*, Irana Preveza in *The Mask of Dimitrios*, both hardened and ruined by the time the investigators meet them). Similarly, many of the investigators themselves seem to have no existence other than that of investigating, little possibility of serving as a relay for desire (Thompson in *Citizen Kane* is only seen on the job; Ed Anders in *Chicago Deadline* goes to his new girlfriend's apartment for a chat only to fall asleep on the couch). Whatever desire occurs, then, occurs in a split between the inner story and the investigation; there is little unity.

But if some narratives disturb identification by investing narrative agency in a too insubstantial figure, other narratives trouble identification by a too strong character: for example, a too intriguing villain. Again, this becomes a problem for the war narrative: to make conflict seem strong enough, it must give evil a body—one that can be too strong or exciting. For example, *Shadow of a Doubt* (1943) creates a structure of characterological ambiguity that signals a divergence from any simple repesentation of narrative violence and the threat of evil. Appearing at times to be an allegory of war (traces of which exist in the presence of soldiers on the streets of Santa Rosa, in the war announcements posted on the walls of public places, and in a kind of allegorical generality to the speeches about the menace in today's world), *Shadow of a Doubt* will include speeches about the ultimate nature of evil. Yet the very fact of a few points of convergence with the narrative of affirmation can only emphasize all the more the nature of the divergencies. From the opening moments, the narrative diverges from the affirmative model. On the level of *énoncé*, the opening story shows a failed side of the American effort, an unglamorous American city, images of squalor and poverty. On the other hand, the enunciation sets up an instability in identification; the first camera move into Uncle Charlie on the bed sets him up as an object of knowledge, a target of probing sight (although this is offset somewhat by the choice of the generally sympathetic

Joseph Cotten for the role), but this is quickly reversed when Charlie learns that two men are waiting for him: the men become the target of enunciation, and Charlie its subject (for example, in the first person point-of-view shots on the two men as Charlie walks toward and past them on the street corner). Similarly, a shot soon after of Charlie telephoning to his relative in Santa Rosa represents an instability of character position: on the one hand, the background of men playing pool in a seedy joint confirms an identification of Charlie with a low-life milieu, a shadowy urban world, but the extreme closeness of Charlie to the foreground will separate him off from this world, and the fact that he is telephoning to announce his departure from the urban environment (plus the fact revealed to us by the call that he is not a loner but has a family) can lead to a possibly quite different investment in Charlie.

Such filming strategies can turn narrative not into a meaning to be consumed but a structure to be read actively. There is first of all a difficulty at the level of the image itself: in *noir*, for example, shadows render the image ambiguous—not only what is going to happen in a space but what that space itself is. Faces become blank surfaces on which conflicting emotions can be read: for example, Spade's look at the end of *The Maltese Falcon* when he hands Brigit to the police and tells her he knew all along that she was the murderer. Such ambiguity not only renders emotion reversible but affects the actions that emotions depend upon; thus, narrative moments will pivot around gestures or actions that can equally hold opposing significations, an ambiguity even commented on explicitly by characters, as in *Road House* (1948), where two lovers (Cornel Wilde and Ida Lupino) discuss the sudden change to what seems to be benevolence on the part of a maniacal, jealous rival (Richard Widmark).

But it is also objects that can become parts of a structure of ambiguity in the reading of a narrative. An extreme case is *Scarlet Street*, where Chris Cross' paintings remain visually the same but change their possible significations with each change in the narrative story; the characters' debate about the artistic merits or not of each painting is repeated in the spectator for whom the art comes to have no univocal sense. The twists and turns that the characters undergo—their crisscrossings—echo in the spectator who must continually revise his/her own estimation of the value of images.

In some cases, the ambiguity of reading derives from a multiplication of narrative possibilities. In other words, a would-be dominant narrative line recedes and becomes only one alternative among several. In some cases, the alternate narratives exist only as possibilities, never fully realized in the unfolding of the film (thus, it is possible to rewrite *Casablanca* with the romance ending that the screenwriters sometimes preferred). In *It's a Wonderful Life!*, for example, the alternate universe of an existence without George Bailey is intended for George as an enframed exemplum to demonstrate all the more forcefully to him the necessary rightness of his life. In certain cases, the alternative narrative will actually appear, but with markers that maintain it as imaginary or as limited to the point of view of specific characters: for example, *Lydia*, where two flashbacks of the same event reveal two characters' quite different remembrances of that event. Rather than taking place from a "long perspective" (to use Kermode's term) that gives every element an exact position, narrative at such moments becomes perspectival, a collection of individual narratives that add up to no one whole. This, of course, is the possibility that *Citizen Kane* works toward, a possibility that for some analysts moves it out of the realm of classic narrative and into the camp of modernism.[25] But *Citizen Kane* is only an extreme of what will be a general possibility for narrative in the forties. For example, forties science fiction shows a particularly intense concern with the alternate-universe narrative, the discovery that each world and its narratives are echoed in the existence of alternate worlds and alternate narratives: in Frederick Brown's novel *What Mad Universe*, for example, a pulp science-fiction writer discovers that each of his space-opera tales comes into a real existence somewhere when he writes it down and that he can enter such narratives whenever he likes.

A number of other processes suggest a dissatisfaction of forties narrative with the necessity or interest of a present and dominant univocal, exclusive narrative line. This dissatisfaction

shows up as: fascination with retrospection and nostalgic recrea-
tions of the past and a consequent sense of the rise of history as a
fall into a loss of that past; a fear-filled separation from a sustaining
innocence (as in the opening of *Gaslight* [1944], where the murder
of Paula's aunt throws the young woman into a time of mystery
and aggression); a blurring of the narrating instance between
character and noncharacter point of view (for example, the use of
lying flashbacks—flashbacks that seem to be the representation
of a character's past but which are actually the temporally and
spatially rooted lie of the character in the present—as in *Stagefright*
[1950] or *The Falcon in Danger* [1943], where in flashback, we see
a kidnapping that never occurred); an ambiguity in characterization that shows up in the representation of specific characters;
and the splitting of a single-character narrative into a set of narratives all with equally central central subjects. For example, just
as *Citizen Kane* will split identification between Kane and Jedediah
(a split represented emphatically as a relation of two characters
who are simply alternate versions of one person in the scene where
Kane finishes Jedediah's review), *This Gun for Hire* will split narrative agency between the morally ambiguous Raven (Alan Ladd)
and the morally good but narratively minimized Michael Crane
(Robert Preston). Again, like *Citizen Kane,* a number of forties films
will add tension to narrative by splitting enunciation between an
investigator and a central figure who is the object of investigation
(for example, *Passage to Marseilles, Manhunt).* Where the use of an
investigatory figure in film encourages an epistemological point
of identification for the spectator, many of the forties films of
investigation diffuse that identification and send it in potentially
mutually exclusive directions. For example, in all those postwar
films of government agencies tracking down aberrant criminals,
identification is torn between the epistemological rationality of
the investigators and the emotional vibrancy of the criminal.

        To be sure, films can show situations in which subject
and object, project and environment, can crystallize in a euphoric
moment, or series of moments, of plenitude. Even if *Gun Crazy,*
for example, is a film about splits—the cuts, for example, that
interrupt the fugitive's escape to show the government agencies

that are encircling them—the force of desire can frequently (if not inevitably) overcome splits. Thus, in *Gun Crazy*, one image literally suggests a crossing of divisive forces. Caught in a cabin during a storm, Laurie and Bart begin to doubt the nature of each other's commitment, and the composition shows them on either side of the frame dramatically separated by the black barrier of a stovepipe. But as they talk and resolve their differences, Laurie leans in toward Bart, crossing the barrier and suggesting an ability to break all disruptive blockages. Likewise, another scene ties reconciliation to a reduction of narrative options to a univocal perspective: having decided to split up after a robbery, Laurie and Bart head in opposite directions down a road—implying a certain breaking up of narrative itself into two subplots—but suddenly, simultaneously, they stop their cars, turn around, and meet in the center in an ecstatic moment of commitment and consecration.

Like *Pride of the Marines*, even a narrative of the menacing or alienating and empty city like *Dark Passage* will show its central character finding a certain stability through the aid of a number of characters (in this case, the best friend, the plastic surgeon, the cab driver, and, of course, Irene) who encircle him with authority, a streetwise knowledge that enables him to find a passage through the threatening darkness: "Count ten and then get the elevator to my apartment," commands Irene as though she's been saving fugitives all her life; even the blackmailer who is menacing Parry stops for a moment to give him information on how to escape from the country. Moreover, an explicit message of the film will argue that one can only win out if one has friends: thus, in a didactic scene that can rhyme with *Pride of the Marines'* optimistic discussion by vets of their postwar plans, Parry overhears two lonely people reaching out to each other in a bus station, and he immediately feels inspired to telephone Irene to tell her, "I'm just beginning to realize that it's better to have something to look forward to."

But the stability of this message is undone by a narrative style that continually complicates the status of image and dialogue as conveyors of a truth. The very artificiality of the scene of two lonely people connecting up in a bus station seems to signal the film's basis here in a certain fiction, the melodrama of chance romances starting in public places that runs through the forties (for example, *Woman in Hiding* [1950], *The Clock* [1945], *In the Good Old Summertime* [1949], etc). Indeed, in *On the Town*, the sailors, arrested by the shore patrol, are only reunited with their loved ones through a fiction manifestly signaled as such: to the accompaniment of old-time melodrama music played by characters within the story, each of the women tells with exaggerated emotions of the tragedy that has befallen the boys. The successful contruction of love here is no more than a staging, an artifice. Similarly, in *Dark Passage*, the moment of comic reconciliation creates a kind of clash with the film's thriller framework. At the same time, the very fact that this chance encounter can become the motivation for Parry's inviting Irene to Peru, the event that terminates the film, signals a kind of disproportion between cause and effect—a breakdown of narrative tightness, each moment as a complication of other moments.

Indeed, more generally, the notion of the new life of modernity as equally an arena for danger or romance, and the representation of romance as a fictive or miraculous solution to the problems of isolation, is the subject of a number of forties narratives. The spaces of the city or of the extensions of modernity into the countryside become ambiguous places that threaten loss as much as they promise adventure and romance. For example, the motel—that meeting up of the romance of the road (see the thirties film *It Happened One Night*) with the new alienations of endless roads all looking the same—becomes a central site for the staging of space as ambivalent force. If Gyorg Lukács (in the auto-critical 1967 preface to *History and Class Consciousness*) saw the hotel as a perfect image of an old Europe's fall into chaos and despair, the motel seems an appropriate image for a later moment where the elegant decadence of an aristocracy has given way to a mass-life run through with petty crimes, petty intrigues. The motel is the figure of furtiveness and a life dominated by the endless but transitory interaction of people all with something to hide. Significantly, the years from the thirties on witness a discourse on the motel not as adventure or romance spot, but as the place of a festering, wasteland rot: for example, for J. Edgar Hoover, "The files of the F.B.I. are loaded with instances of gangsters who have hidden out in unregulated tourist camps, while officers combed the country for them, revolvers drawn and nerves taut for the expected gun battle."[26]

Most explicit, perhaps, in showing the ambivalent possibility of the new space of modernity for the fragmentation of narrativity is Cornell Woolrich's 1944 novel *Deadline at Dawn*, where each narrative denouement exists alongside the possibility of an equally significant but opposed alternate denouement. Modernity here is the possibility of a generation of endless narratives, all equally possible expansions of initial premises. Read this way, the novel becomes a kind of meditation on novel writing, a recognition of, and playing with, the fact that any one narrative is not the "natural" telling of events, but only one option among others, a logic, not logic itself. Beginning with an epigram that will become a kind of generative model for each narrative moment, its simultaneous promise of loss or triumph—"Each hour, each minute, can hold all Hell or Heaven in it"—*Deadline at Dawn* can become a discourse *on* the structure of the thriller, on the ways that its thrill functions around the ambiguity of pivotal moments. The story of a woman and a man meeting in a dance hall and agreeing to try to solve a murder and then leave town together is structured in such a way that each action signals the possibility of some other action or consequence to have been as likely: the man wonders if he should approach the woman; the woman wonders if she should let the man approach her, and then she wonders how much commitment or credence she should give to each of his actions or declarations (such as his statement that he will be implicated the next morning in a murder that he had nothing to do with); the man and the woman wonder together how they can track down a murderer they literally know nothing about. Deciding that anything they do is as effective or ineffective as anything else they could do, the man and woman decide simply to walk in different directions from the scene of the crime and see if they spot any leads.

To emphasize that the uniqueness of any narrative lies

only in its particular embodiment of a permutational field out of which it is one, but only one, possibility, the novel then has the two characters immediately tumble upon two likely suspects (a nervous and bleeding man who may have been shot by the murder victim; a woman who acts mysteriously and admits that she shot a man). But the narrative then as quickly reasserts the fictionality of these narrative options by having both suspects turn out to be wrong leads (the nervous man is simply a nosebleeder anxious because his wife is giving birth in the hospital; the woman has indeed shot a man but not the one whose murder the hero and heroine need to solve). To the last moment, when the hero and heroine have solved the crime and are trying to leave town, the narrative maintains each moment as only one possibility among others; for example, at the very last moment, the bus driver hesitates to let them on the bus out of town because he has already left the dock and he believes in following the rules.

Deadline at Dawn may finally end well in a euphoric image of harmony and a promise for a future that will be a reinvestment of a pastoral past (since it has been revealed that the hero and heroine are originally from the same small town): "Her head had dropped to his shoulder, was rocking there gently in time with the motion of the bus. Her eyes dropped blissfully closed. 'We're going home,' she thought drowsily. 'Me and the boy next-door. We're going home at last.' " But the overall structure of the narrative relativizes this ending and suggests that its closure lies not in any natural pastoralism but only in the assertion of a desire, an optimism without inevitable ground.

"New York, New York. It's a wonderful town. The Bronx is up and the Battery's down. The people ride in a hole in the ground. New York, New York—it's a wonderful town." For the three sailors of *On the Town*, (1949), space would seem to be in place—the city as a site of geographic certainty. And yet, in the optimism of a musical that, through montage, can show all sites/ sights of New York to be a part of one big spectacle of song and dance, even here space can turn ambivalent, and become a kind of source of confusion. From the very first moments, it becomes apparent, for example, that if the song has any kind of realistic motivation in the plot, it is as a kind of aural guidebook that the sailors rehearse to keep from getting lost in the big city: significantly, despite their preparations, the first time that these sailors are in a subway station, they abandon all prior knowledge and must ask directions.

In postwar film especially, the city becomes the space for the representation of environment as a potentially or inherently ambivalent site. In the 1950 film *Once a Thief*, for example, the credits even announce "The City of Los Angeles" as one of the characters, and this seeming throwaway credit—one more mark of the postwar emphasis on on-location filming—can come to stand as a figure for the whole film. In *Once a Thief*, the "heroine" (June Havoc), a petty thief trying to turn good, finds that the only "real" power she has in an urban world is to kill the man who has most exploited her. Unlike affirmative films about enforcement agencies, *Once a Thief* pictures the Los Angeles police as part of the menace of big-city life. As the opening credit images show the technology of enforcement at work and an A.P.B. on the heroine is read out over the airwaves, a web of enclosure is set up around the heroine; her first gesture in the film—to walk into police headquarters to turn herself in and so initiate the flashback that will chronicle her increasing defeat in the big city—suggests a necessary logic by which the big bureaucracy of enforcement inevitably pulls an aberration under the sway of its modern force.

"A billion people—every one of them a stranger. Or, what's worse, maybe not a stranger" (George Taylor in *Somewhere in the Night* [1946]). The city functions in forties narrative as a place of ultimate ambiguity, a virtual infinity of stories. The city is a place where everything is possible, where every option is open, where every gesture is readable in a number of equally likely ways: for example, Crystal Shackleford's search through the streets of London at the beginning of *Three Strangers* (1946) seems to be a pickup, although the mysteriously ambiguous look on Crystal's face might suggest other (unfathomable) possibilities (and, indeed, it turns out she needs two men for a supernatural rite). The city then functions for narrative not so much as a single or fixed symbol but as a site of symbolisms, a device that allows a plethora of narrative possibilities—a plethora even made explicit at the opening of *Side Street* (1949), where the camera gazes at people in a crowd while a narrator's voice announces that each of the people could have a story told about him/her. The city is not only a subject of the films but a device for the narration of films.

One way to analyze the new narrative function of the symbolic space of the city is to note its effect on that most classic of narratives, the detective story, especially as examined by Walter Benjamin in his *Charles Baudelaire*.[27] For Benjamin, Baudelaire's Paris is the site of a *certain* reversibility of meanings—for example, the flowers that are evil, the prostitute who is a goddess, the beauty that is the rot of death. But the reversibility here occurs within the knowing subject's controlled perception of reversibility and rarely extends to a loss of epistemological control over environment. That is to say, the subject witnesses the changing nature of the city while remaining unchanged himself; the knowing subject constructs for him- or herself a stable position of knowledge before which worldly ambiguity and reversibility parades itself. Hence, for Baudelaire, the importance of the dandy—that figure who wanders within the crowd but is emotionally apart from the crowd. Hence, too, Baudelaire's interest in Poe for whom the detective or city dweller moves through a city that he questions but that rarely questions him. The city here is the city of a leisured class, an aristocracy that can seem to pull itself out of the flux of history to a point of safe, aesthetic observation.

Arising in a nineteenth century geared more and more to an economy of saving and of the "rational" conquest of nature through the controlled application of an industrial capitalism, classic detective fiction can seem a kind of attempt to make control and economy seductive. Hence, the detective as the heroic figure who wastes nothing, for whom no aspect of the human world is without interest and for whom no element in the world cannot be situated inside an explanatory narrative.

And yet what seems significant is not simply that this incorporation of alien facts inside a master-narrative occurs but that it needs to be advertised, to be talked up. In particular, the detective becomes a figure of constant self-promotion, endlessly insisting on a productive prowess. The classic detective story can become not merely the spectacle of discovery but an explicit and even desperate announcement of itself as spectacle: hence, the theatrical way in which the detective stages the final unveiling of the criminal.

Classic detective narrative, then, announces both its necessity and its fictionality, an announcement that, as Benjamin suggests, parallels the historical necessity and essential expendability of its writers, its readers, and its social functionality. Expendability, for example, shows up as a certain fetishizing of death, not only of victims or of murderers but even of the detective himself: Holmes killed off (and resurrected), Poirot giving in to the ravages of time. To be sure, in most cases, the detective rarely faces his own death but there's a sense in which the detective can become a kind of vampirish figure —an anachronistic trace of a way of life that no longer has any life-blood and takes sustenance from the follies of the new world. The detective here is like Baudelaire's aristocrat, sitting lazily but desperately in a cafe, waiting for something to happen: detective and aristocrat thrive not on society's functionings but on its disfunctionings. The detective can even become someone whose very presence on the scene seems to invite death (as in Christie's *Peril at End House* where a murderer tries to commit the perfect crime because she can plant misleading clues for Poirot). If the detective is the figure who reaffirms that everything has its proper place, he is simultaneously a figure who can show the ambiguities of place, the aggressions that lie beneath the surface of an ordered society. Indeed, part of the possible moral conclusion of classic detective fiction is that, as much as it separates a guilty party off from innocent ones, it also establishes the possibility for any one of the suspects to have been guilty.

In Dorothy Sayers' *Whose Body?*, Lord Peter Wimsey hangs up the telephone and tells his butler that a body has been found in the tub of a friend of his mother; the butler simply replies, "How gratifying, my Lord." For the classic detective, reality is a source of joy, a text to be read from the safe position of a superior, untouched enjoyment. If there are two narratives in classic detective fiction—a crime and its solution, as a number of scholars have pointed out—the fiction allows for a temporal or spatial gap between the two (as in Poe's "Marie Roget" story where the detective solves a case by reading about it in the papers); but, significantly, this gap is ultimately closed over in the discursive coherence of the detective's retrospective retelling of the original crime. The story of a crime can become literally an *object* with definite boundaries that the detective can play with in the sanctity of a secure present. The detective figure is a mythical figure in Lotman's specific sense—that is, a figure out of time, in a pure cognition of time, granted the ability of an instantaneous illumination that sees what others miss.

We might sum up the modern mutation of the form by suggesting that in the newer art of detective narrative, the two stories of the classic detective narrative—crime and its retrospective investigation—threaten to become one. The classic narrative is based on a cognitive separation of the detective from all the all-too-worldly evils of the crime he is investigating. But in the new form, the investigator is no longer someone who looks back on an already completed event and cognizes it from a safe, aestheticizing distance. With the hard-boiled mutation of the form, the detective now exists in historical time, in which the time of investigation and the time of experience can become one. If the classic detective is a kind of reader of an already finished text, the new detective is more an actor, caught in a narrative that writes him as much as he writes it. The doubts that are already clouding the sanctity of classic detection come out in fuller force in the new works.

For example, in a famous anecdote in the novel of *The Maltese Falcon*, Sam Spade explains to Brigit why he became a detective, telling a story of one of his clients, a man named Flitcraft, for whom a beam falling from a construction site became a mark of the world's unpredictability. Spade only vaguely explains the significance of the story, but that significance would seem to reside in the detective's recognition that he too lives in an unpredictable world.[28] Where Flitcraft's response was to experience momentarily a kind of ultimate existential horror but *then* to retreat back to a position of naive faith in the order of things—Spade had found him in another city living exactly the sort of life he had fled—Spade's response seems to be one of begrudging acceptance of the potential disorder of things, life lived as constant alertness for "beams falling." Although one man is the detective and the other is the detective's target, both share the experience of facing a potentially contingent world: Spade realizes that he too can become a prey of sorts.

Similarly, in the forties, we find examples of detectives turned into objects of investigation and even into the object of other detectives' investigations: for example, *Out of the Past* with Bailey (Robert Mitchum) pursued by his former partner; *The Dark Corner* (1946) with Brad Galt (Mark Stevens) pursued by the mysterious man in white (William Bendix). Indeed, *The Dark Corner* suggests that even moments when the detective feels most triumphant are in fact the moments of his greatest vulnerability: for example, Galt begins to shadow the detective shadowing him, not knowing that this is what a murderer has been expecting him to do. Galt's fate is the fate of many investigators—not only detectives specifically—who assume that the world will follow their wishes and then find out otherwise: for example, in Woolrich's novel *Waltz Into Darkness*, even the man who hires a detective to investigate his wife finds himself an object of investigation as he reconciles with his wife (thereby turning into an accomplice to murder) and finds that the detective won't call off the pursuit.

The opening of *Out of the Past* emphatically signals certain reversals of the detective tradition. Opening shots show a fast car moving into a small town; the shots are from the point of view of the car's driver. But this first narrative agency—this first figure of forward movement with whom we are offered a visual identification—turns out to be a bad guy. In this, the film splits point of view and makes ex-detective Jeff Bailey the object of a process, not its subject. Jeff spends much of the film in a virtual somnambulism—a deadened passivity in which he simply waits. This somnambulism is only vaguely interrupted by actions: in-

deed, Jeff's most authoritative gesture will be to set up the trap
that leads to his and Kathy Moffett's death. Jeff is rarely an agent,
rarely the classic detective.

In other cases, nonprofessional investigators find
themselves forced to investigate in situations where they lose
control of the world around them: for example, Bigelow (Edmund
O'Brien) in *D.O.A.*, turned into an investigator of his own murder
when a poison gives him only a little while to live. A scene in
which Bigelow runs through the city streets crazily and leans
against a magazine rack filled with issues of *Life* can suggest the
character's entrapment in an absurd situation; indeed, as Jack
Shadoian suggests in his analysis of the scene in *Dreams and Dead
Ends*, Bigelow is running from nothing specific or physical but,
rather, from his own fear of his situation.

There is frequently a maddened quest to establish one's
own innocence or guilt. In the case of narratives of amnesia, for
example, such as *Somewhere in the Night* or Woolrich's *The Black
Curtain*, the investigation takes on a somewhat oedipal twist as
investigators confront their own capacity for violence. The amnesia narrative, where an investigator finds out that he may also
be the object of his investigation, suggests a certain blurring of the
classic boundaries between knower and known, between character and a supposedly separate reality. Perhaps most extreme in
this respect is the 1946 film *So Dark the Night*, in which the Sûreté's
most famous detective investigates a bizarre double murder only
to discover that he is the murderer, committing his crimes out of
an intense schizophrenia. Significantly, the film ties the outburst
of the murderous impulse to the detective's seduction by the
newfound joys of the flesh: where Paris allowed the detective to
surround himself with all the cold, emotionless machinery of a
big agency's investigative resources, the detective's vacation to a
small town throws him into direct physical contact with a world
of vibrant emotion. Indeed, it is literally because of the fact that
he has been such a man of reason, of dry calculation, that the
detective so easily falls prey to passions—both romantic and murderous; ultimately, it is because he knows that he is really a rather
stuffy older man in comparison with the young, vibrant fiancé of

the woman he loves that the detective gives in to murder and kills the young lovers.

At the same time, confident declarations of authoritative knowledge on the part of an investigator can reveal a certain ambiguity, if not a complete fictionality. In *The Maltese Falcon*, for example, there is no way to decide univocally about Spade's declaration that he knew all along that Brigit was the murderer. Moreover, even if he did have the knowledge to solve the crime immediately as he claims, he didn't act on his knowledge; quite the contrary, he allowed himself to become a figure of a self-agonizing desire, rather than a cold, calculating "Thinking Machine."

To be sure, some detective narratives will try to solve doubt through the reinstauration of a strong hero, invulnerable to all the forces that would pull him into the decay of history's flux. In Lotman's terms, there will be a remythification of the detective figure. And yet this remythification can all too often signal its own processes, and suggest how the return to a centered power is run through with a disturbing uneasiness.

The fantasy of power becomes explicit in a 1946 combination detective and science-fiction novel, Will Jenkins' *The Murder of the U.S.A.* Here an atomic-rocket attack on the United States becomes a mystery story as the American scientists capture an unexploded enemy rocket and try to deduce the country of origin. When the solution appears, the United States retaliates and completely destroys the enemy (who is unnamed but obvious since the Americans send their rockets over the North Pole). The last scene suggests the degree of triumphant fantasy in this story of power; with the war over, the hero and heroine go up to the surface to have a picnic on the green grass, under the blue skies of a U.S.A. that seems not at all to have been at war.

But if *The Murder of the U.S.A.* can demonstrate its ideological work through the sheer utopian optimism of a triumphant America, other super-detective narratives can suggest a certain intrusion of paranoia and doubt into the very fabric of the narrative. Most important for the end of the forties and beginning of the fifties in this respect will be the Mickey Spillane/Mike

Hammer novels. The Hammer books work insistently to reinstall a forceful central subject in the detective narrative; the Hammer texts will be narratives of an intense ego; in an interview with Dick Cavett several years ago, Spillane even attributed the success of his books to the use of personal pronouns in their titles (*MY Gun Is Quick*, *Kiss ME*, *Deadly*, etc.). The novels picture a world caught between an intense evil and a crippled or vulnerable good (gimps, amputees, helpless prostitutes); Hammer is called into play as the force that will defend the latter and make up for its inadequacies by fighting the former. But the strength of Hammer is vulnerable in at least two ways typical in the representation of the postwar moment. First, there are his recurrent dreams of his first act of killing: the awake Hammer is engaged in an active process of repression of dreads and doubts that can easily come back to haunt him during sleep. Second, and more important in the movement of the late forties, Hammer will match his power over women with a paranoid flight from them, a revulsion from carnality and the flesh. The cataloguing of the physicality of destroyed flesh—for example, the faces that Hammer is always smashing in—has a complement in the physicality of a potentially destroying flesh—the seductive physicality of the woman who tempts Hammer to go all the way and reveal what he is made of: by the time of *Kiss Me, Deadly*, destroyed flesh and destroying flesh will converge in the image of the burned body of the evil woman, Lili Carver. For all his emphasis on a forceful male sexuality, Hammer seems most at "home" in a distanced realm, a separation in which women's sexuality becomes no more than the object for a voyeuristic and safe gaze on the part of the man.

At the extreme, the detective discourse on the resistance of objects and others to human projects can fuel a vast paranoia of conspiracy—the sense not so much that objects passively resist the project but quite more frighteningly that they resist quite actively. In the late forties especially, such a paranoia will link up to a specific representation in "documentary" novels and news media of crime no longer as an individual pursuit, but as a vast network of control and domination—no longer, as was the case in earlier representation, an evil limited to the biggest of the big cities and intergang warfare but now showing up everywhere and having consequences for everyone (hence, scandal books by Lait and Mortimer such as *Kansas City Confidential, New York Confidential*). Crime is no longer the effect of a specific figure of criminality but a quality potentially at work in every person and in every relationship. *Murder, Inc.*, by Burton Turkas and Sid Feder (1951) and based on the New York district attorney's investigation of crime in the 1940s, makes this new sense of crime emphatic: "The most nefarious gangs of the Prohibition era seemed apple-off-the-pushcart crooks compared to the activities of the country-wide cartel. The F.B.I.'s Public Enemy outfits in bank robbery and kidnapping looked like mischievous boys tying cans to dogs' tails against the well-oiled machine working the racket and murder of the nation."[29]

But the representation of a conspiracy that defeats all projects through the form of crime is only a localized condensation of a more abstract sense of existence as conspiracy. Significantly, where the new "documentary" representations of crime show local investigations leading to the discovery of giant systems (such as *Murder, Inc*), detective narrative will often proceed in another but complementary direction—finding that a specific and concrete crime is only a figure for a metaphoric corruption, an existential rot in the heart of human relations. The investigation becomes a journey into the nature of the human condition, a process of discovery that renders irrelevant specific guilts and instead inscribes a metaphoric guilt *everywhere*. In Raymond Chandler's novels of the forties, for example, Philip Marlowe's moments of greatest pensiveness and existential brooding come not in the heat of investigation but in moments where he temporarily pulls back from the forward propulsion of the quest. For example, *Farewell, My Lovely* portrays rest as a restless event in which one locks into all the corruptions of the universe:

> I lay on my back on a bed in a waterfront hotel and waited for it to get dark. . . . The reflection of a red neon light glared on the ceiling. When it made the whole room red it would be dark enough to go out. Outside, cars honked along the alley they called the Speedway. Feet slithered on the sidewalks below my window. There was a murmur

and mutter of coming and going in the air. The air that seeped in through the rusted screens smelled of stale frying fat. . . . I thought; and thought in my mind moved with a kind of sluggish stealthiness, as if it was being watched by bitter and sadistic eyes. I thought of dead eyes looking at a moonless sky, with black blood at the corners of the mouths beneath them. . . . I thought of lots of things. It got darker. The glare of the red neon sign spread farther and farther across the ceiling. I got up on my feet. . . . After a little while I felt a little better, but very little. I needed a drink, I needed a lot of life insurance, I needed a vacation, I needed a home in the country. What I had was a coat, a hat and a gun. I put them on and went out of the room.

In such an existential drama, any action, any event, no matter how minor, can suddenly become the occasion for malaise and doubt; if the war-affirmative narrative creates a system of interchangeability based on the centering of environment around the rightness of human aspirations, in contrast, the art of paranoia suggests a system of interchangeability based on human decenterings where every element is a mark of loss and powerlessness. In Raymond Chandler's *The little Sister*, for example, a minor run-in with an aggressive driver becomes for Marlowe the impetus for a long and bitter reflection on the wrongness of the world—a wrongness that extends from minor details to major situations.[30]

Many of the figures that in the war moment were invested with positive values now increasingly become marks of doubt and anxiety. For example, there will be an intensification of a discourse on juvenile delinquency, on the dangers of one's lovable children turning into one more set of statistics in a list of social problems. The sheer accumulation of the discourse works to argue a documentary truth in the discoveries it claims to have made about a new nature of American youth: thus, in the words of the inside blurb to the novel *Lower Part of the Sky* (renamed *Juvenile Delinquents* at the end of the forties): "Savage beatings, knives and zip-guns and slum-style sex learned in poolrooms and cheap hotels . . . youth of the slums . . . taught how to kill and hate society. The real picture of today's teenagers gone wrong. Although this story depicts the streets of New York's Greenwich

Village, it might be happening in your own home town." Even cute little Cookie in *Life with Blondie* (1946) threatens that she might "become a juvenile delinquent" when her mother leaves home to take a job in the fashion industry. While the war had already shown a concern with the latchkey children who had no parents at home, the affirmative discourse of the war had tried frequently to represent this situation as a nonproblem. Most especially, there is a whole group of wartime films in which energetic children or adolescents use their energy for the war effort in ways their parents hadn't imagined or had even discouraged: *Jive Junction* (where the kids turn a barn into a U.S.O. hall); *Miss Annie Rooney* (1942), *Since You Went Away* (1944), etc. Precociousness is here a potentially utilizable force. Certainly, there will be important exceptions. For example, Tootie (Margaret O'Brien) will, in a film like *Meet Me in St. Louis* (1944), suggest a childhood energy and potential violence which is in opposition to the narrative of technological affirmation (for example, she will try to derail the trolley). And yet, in the very way that *Since You Went Away* draws a certain distinction between the misty love of Jane and the serious sublimation engaged in by her mother, the wartime films of precocious children tend sharply to consign precociousness to a specific moment of life that children will inevitably and naturally grow out of. And, indeed, in another way, Tootie's ultimate act—going to the world's fair—affirms the new technological age and accepts modernity.

But in the postwar representations, there will frequently be a juvenile energy that cannot be assimilated; even in the many narratives that deal with the conversion of delinquents into citizens, there will usually be at least one youth who refuses conversion and remains obdurate to the end: for example, *Fighting Father Dunne* (1949), *City Across the River* (1949), *Knock on Any Door* (1949), with its youth's motto "Live fast, die young, and leave a good-looking corpse." Indeed, *Knock on Any Door* suggests a certain undoing of the classic narrative of investigation; against other forties documentary-fictions of investigations to clear someone's name (for example, *Call Northside 777* [1948]), investigator Andrew Morton's narrative becomes one in which he discovers that he has been lied to from the start by his defendant. Investigation here leads to a truth but one that is unbearable in the message it offers about new youth. While a number of advertisements during the war will suggest that children's future is the stake that "we" are fighting for, the new discourse of delinquency will argue that that future has realized itself as a nightmare where one's children don't reflect back one's place in the world but, rather, show it coming to a farcical or unbearable point of no return.

"The aftermath of war is rubble—the rubble of cities and of men. They are the casualties of a pitiless destruction" (opening title to *Kiss the Blood off My Hands* [1948]). At its extreme, the discourse of doubt and reversibility will imply that it is not merely the subject's world that is the source of doubt but the subject him/herself. There will be a representation of the self as a force that is out of its own control: for example, Louise Howell (Joan Crawford) imagining the killing of her daughter in *Possessed* (1947) and then realizing the unbearable implications of her own fantasy.

One of the most intense and massive versions of this representation of a deconstructing self will be the end-of-the-war and postwar discourse on the dangers posed by the returning veteran. Where the war-affirmative narrative will uphold the need for strong men against all assailing forces—as in *Gung Ho!*, where the young recruit from Brooklyn engages in a mad dash to blow up a Japanese pillbox—there will now be the implication that a teleology of willed masculine strength can only be the same as an unbridled, obsessive destructiveness. There will be the suggestion that the path to violence is a natural one: in the words of Willard Waller in *The Veteran Comes Home*, "That hand that does not know how to earn its owner's bread, knows how to take your bread, knows very well how to kill you, if need be, in the process. That eye that has looked at death will not quail at the sight of a policeman."[31] To be strong is to be dangerous. Thus, articles about new criminals will emphasize their origin in military discipline: "Trained to Kill" is the title of a *Newsweek* article (April 15, 1946) about one Tony Doto, a violent criminal whose violence is directly linked by the article to his training and a "head-wound at Bastogne."

Certainly, there will be attempts to write away the fears of the potential effects of what will be summed up as "war neurosis." For example, as much as it constitutes the possibility for war neurosis, forties psychology will also try to argue the restrictions of such neurosis to highly marginal cases: thus, in the confident words of A. Carpenter in *Science Digest* (June 1947) in an article entitled "Pattern for Murder," "If the act is one normal individuals can't imagine themselves committing it has probably been done by someone mentally afflicted." But this "common-sense" separation of the normal and the pathological is belied by public discourse (especially in newspapers, magazines, and self-help books) that tries to argue the neurotic personality of the entire postwar moment. In the words of *When He Comes Back*, a manual for the families of returning vets. "Almost anyone might develop a full-blown psychoneurosis if placed in circumstances with which he cannot cope, or if torn within himself by conflicting urges and emotions which he cannot reconcile. In peace-time such conflicts often arise in connection with our affections, hatreds, and ambitions." Discourse on the postwar neurotic man ends by instituting a gap between what it accepts as the awful facts and what it desires as the best alternative. Thus, even in the space of a single book like Benjamin Bowker's *Out of Uniform*, the argument will begin with an optimistic act of imagination—"Veterans *will* look back on their war experiences with proud satisfaction. The immediate little resentments will fade out, leaving a memory of full, intense years."[32] But then the book will show a compulsion to admit the insufficiency of this imagination in the face of what it assumes to be the bitter truth: "It was only after victory that the invasion of America [by the neurotic vet] became a reality" (p. 25).

In an article on one vet, a would-be Hollywood actor, Richard Tregaskis ends by noting how the vet, Jim Davis, intends to buy a house but that "he has no intention of settling down or raising a family."[33] According to the postwar discourse, the problem of the neurotic man is not necessarily only his capacity for violence but, as much, his potential refusal to form a family, to enter into the traditional patterns of domesticity and home building. While there will be postwar narratives of women on their own, frequently these narratives will suggest the incompleteness of these actions without the participation or approval of a man; for example, *The Reckless Moment* ends not with Lucia Harper's successful extrication from her problems, but with the absent husband's call to home after that success. On the one hand, the ending engages in a certain mocking of the men who are so absent that they don't know the problems that women have to live through (see also *Whirlpool*), but, on the other hand, the ending also suggests the insufficiency of a woman's narrative unmarked by a man.

"The cities can be rebuilt, but the wounds of men, whether of the mind or of the body heal slowly. This is the story of one such man; and of the girl whose path he crossed" (the continuation of the opening title to *Kiss the Blood off My Hands*). But where the man is neurotic and filled with doubt, there will be the suggestion that a man's narrative is also insufficient without another person's help—a woman's aid. Just as the war-affirmative narrative imagines femininity as a spirituality that inspires men toward narratives of heroism or rewards them for the successful return from such narratives, one postwar discourse will promote femininity as a spiritual force that can save masculinity from its fall into doubt, dread, and neurosis. In the juvenile delinquency narratives, for example, men will encounter women who are outside a life of delinquency and who thereby promise a return to a moment of innocence and purity (for example, the sweet, blonde manager of a candy shop in *Knock on Any Door*).

But the return to innocence is impossible. In *Knock on Any Door*, for example, the need for money in order to survive in the big city drives Nick back to crime and the blonde to suicide. In the novels *The Amboy Dukes* and *The Lower Part of the Sky*, growing up has meant a growing into sexual awareness; it is impossible for the men to remain on a spiritual plane with the women who offer salvation to them. In breaking the bonds of spiritualism, the men can only lose sight of salvation, and death becomes the inevitable outcome. Intriguingly, the sense of defeat in the delinquency novels has an intensity that infects their very narration: they each end with a description of the young hero's subjective perception of all that happens in his own death. The novels approach the limits of representation at such a moment and show that defeat is so omnipresent that even moments that are generally beyond rendition are not to be spared the sanctity of silence (we might compare this rendition of one's own death to the famous dead man's narration in *Sunset Boulevard* [1950]).

In the wartime film *All Through the Night*, a wisecracking nightclub owner responds to reforming gangster Gloves Donovan's desire to help a sweet, innocent woman find her mother with a direct and cynical comment: "If my customers start thinking about home and mother, I'm a dead duck." Yet the course of *All Through the Night*, as affirmative film, will suggest that family is precisely *the* real goal: the family that Gloves' investigations reunite, the surrogate family that the newfound populism of Gloves' gang creates, the family of the future that Gloves' newfound love for the young woman will lead to. But if the narrative structure of affirmation allows for a propitious (if ultimately unstable) solution of the problems of narrative asynchrony, so much of forties cinema stages the impossibility of such a solution: spiritual redemption through the forces of domesticity—through the imposition of a domestic space—is unavailable in an America for whom innocence is becoming a mark of a vanished past. Only in the "Peru" of *Dark Passage*, in a mythic place outside American reality, will any sort of escape be possible.

Chapter Six

Beyond Narrative:
The Space and Spectacle
of the Forties

In the 1950 crime film *711 Ocean Drive*, everything centers on the need to control space. From the relay-amplifier system that would-be criminal Mal Granger (Edmund O'Brien) sets up to link up all the bookie joints in California to a central information system, to the declaration by one of the "boys" back East that they want to take over Mal's local organization since "it's ridiculous that [the] syndicate has never gone past Kansas City," *711 Ocean Drive* suggests that power finds its strength in a battle over space. Mal's success crystallizes, then, in a certain ownership of geography—in the luxuriousness of the beach-house he moves into when riches begin to come his way.

And yet, curiously, in a film whose title itself signals a fixing in space, *711 Ocean Drive* makes no mention in the course of the film of the address that its title refers to. At the very center of the film, there's a certain decenteredness, an inability to make geography anything more than a fleeting, unsure, insubstantial site. Mal ultimately has no address; even if the film shows idyllic scenes of Mal gamboling on his beach, the idyll is evanescent, a faint few scenes in a film that spends much of its time chronicling Mal's movements through a space he is never at home in—for example, his feverish attempts to outrun the cops at the film's end. Indeed, in a film that emphasizes how it is simultaneously the syndicate (with headquarters in a fine old building in Cleveland) and the rationalist police force that control space (and, indeed, ultimately work together to trap Mal), Mal finds increasingly that space is a space of others, a force that turns on him, that betrays his projects and transforms them into nothingness. The only space that Mal can really come to rest in is the overpowering geography of Boulder Dam, where he is cornered by the police and shot down at the film's end. Ironically, the ending seems an answer to Mal's hopes at the beginning; if Mal began his new life in crime by using his expert background in electronics to get ahead in the criminal flow of information, the ending, in contrast, shows Mal dwarfed by the technology of electricity, trapped among "hydro-electric generators each with a total capacity of 150,000 horse-power" (as the tour guide blandly intones as Mal wonders how to get out of this maze that he is caught in).

If, in Jean-Paul Sartre's words, quoted in chapter 4, modern art is "no longer for modern man anything but a way of seeing his own reality reflected back at him," in the forties this reflection occurs as a distortion in which the human subject sees reflected not an image of control but of loss and confusion; in Sartre's words, "Objects don't have the mission of serving ends but rather of relentlessly manifesting a fleeting and unsettling finality: thus, this labyrinth of hallways, doors, and stairways that lead nowhere, innumerable signposts that dot routes and signify nothing."

The reversiblity of cinematic space is most especially a reversibility carried out in the recurrent representation of quite specific spaces, and, to a large degree, forties narrative is nothing so much as a vast meditation on place and space, on the field in which action and meaning are constituted. Such a meditation is even signaled by titles of forties narrative: *The Window*, (1949),

The High Wall, (1947) *Secret Beyond the Door,* (1948), *The Spiral Staircase,* (1946), etc. Again, what the representation of space here provides is not the stability of a symbolic system where everything has its fixed value but rather an instability where each space can have multiple functions (including some that one would not have anticipated).

One such space is the home as a site of potential narrative reversals. As I've already suggested, the imperatives of war invest themselves in a particular representation of home. At the extreme, the forties home is not simply a haven against the outside world but a separate world of its own, a vast act of imagination. In a wartime film like *White Cargo,* (1942) even the jungle outpost caught up in the war effort becomes a kind of substitute home. Lorded over by the patriarch Witzel (Walter Pidgeon), this "home" doesn't even need a mother; the new, young recruits are sent by the Home Office in an endless reengendering stream of new material.

Home becomes a self-enclosed environment (as in the novel and film *The Big Clock* [1948], where the husband's name is George, the wife's is Georgette, and their child's is Georgie) with its own rules, its own language games, its own memory (as in *Death of a Salesman* with Willy continually invoking the triumphs of the past), and its own rituals (for example, in *The Big Clock,* George must go through the exact same breakfast banter with his child every morning). Home here works rigorously to close out the world of ambiguous interaction, of ambivalent meanings. It is the mark of a certain surety and security.

But as sign, "home" is something not necessarily limited to a specific locale, a specific building. It is an attitude—a way of perceiving environment—as Bowie and Keechi discover in *They Live by Night* (1949), where they infuse each trailer court cottage with the radiance of their love. Home's values can extend outward—through the stability of a job, the camaraderie of friends, through places invested with the succoring warmth of the home. Even public places are transformed into symbolic extensions of home values: Grand Central Station in *The Clock* (1945), the Empire State Building in *On the Town* (1949), the soda fountain and movie theater in the Cornell Woolrich novel *Rendez-Vous in Black*. Even a whole neighborhood can become an extension of the home as in *Casbah* (1948), where the criminal, Pepe le Moko (Tony Martin), remains unapprehended as long as he remains in the Casbah quarter where he knows every trick, and where every person is his friend.

But as no more than a representation, "home" is grounded in nothing that assures its permanence or its invulnerability; in certain cases, a disruption can even show up the extent to which dependence on "home" is not some sort of natural activity, but a social phantasm run through with a lingering desperation. In *In a Lonely Place* (1950) when Dix (Humphrey Bogart) and Laurel (Gloria Grahame) go out to a restaurant for a quiet evening together, their intimacy is interrupted by the arrival of an antagonist on the scene: as Janey Place and J. L. Petersen have argued, the interruption is displayed not only in the events of the story, but also through film style as a series of unclassically framed close-ups of Dix and Laurel instill a visual imbalance into the scene.[1]

For the first part of the forties, indeed, "home" is often only an unstable fantasy. During the war 50 percent of the American population is renting and frequently doing so in habitations far below needs and expectations. There is a dramatic housing crisis (lack of available sites, the absence during most of the war of any sort of rent control) that is frequently represented in narratives of the time *(Since You Went Away* [1944], *Twin Beds* [1942], *The More the Merrier* [1943]). The housing problem continues on into the postwar period when a new suburbia will suddenly be offered as the necessary solution: see, for example, *It's a Wonderful Life!*, where George Bailey's great contribution to Bedford Falls will be the construction of a suburbia with easy financing.

Yet, almost as quickly, suburbia will become the target of counter-discourses: for example, the Ma and Pa Kettle films with their image of the modern, prefab home as a technology gone haywire. By the 1950s, criticism of suburbia is widespread, finding in the suburban phenomenon the cause for all American maladies and malaise. From the very beginning, suburbia will be the cause for a battle in the representations of everyday life; for example, as Saim Nalkaya explains, the Levittowns (which by 1950 provide housing for 1 out of every 200 American families) will be represented by their builders as the ultimate logical organization of everyday life (same color every eight houses; one willow, three fruit trees, twenty-eight to thirty flowers or shrubs for every house) but will quickly be perceived by their inhabitants to be the height of arbitrary and irrational authority (for example, the Levittown owner's manual prohibits wash being hung up on anything other than umbrella-type hangers) and will quickly be beset by all sorts of stylistic subversions (additional rooms, new colors, resurfacing, etc.).[2]

The space of home life can find itself interrupted in two directions—an outward move that rejects the symbolic support offered by the home, or an inward move by which external forces intrude upon a home life. On the one hand, home is surrounded by constant temptation, the desire to throw off stabilities for the promise of some other way of life. In certain cases, this desire grounds itself in the representation of home life as itself already impure, as offering nothing but a kind of moral deadness through banality, triviality, pettiness, and stultifying repetition (for example, Chris Cross' home life in *Scarlet Street*, a mark of the gap between his aspirations—to become a great, romantic painter—and his actual situation—a lowly clerk in a dark, dingy apartment with a shrewish wife). With a representation that will intensify in the 1950s with the figure of "the man in the grey flannel suit," or what David Riesman will call the life of the "lonely crowd," forties narrative can suggest that "normal" life is itself abnormal, a horror based on renunciation, blind obedience, compromise, a horror to flee from: as Don Birnam (Ray Milland) says in *The Lost Weekend* (1945), "Most people lead lives of quiet desperation. I can't stand quiet desperation." The outside world then becomes a mark of a something missing, a possibility that home life seems to close off.

And yet rarely do the narratives argue the ultimate possibility of such options of escape from the home, for to do so would be merely to substitute one stability for another. Instead, the narratives suggest that the world away from home is equally or more entrapping than the world of home. For example, there seem to be few rip-roaring adventure stories of an epic sort in forties narrative; when adventure occurs, it tends to be either tinged with regret or to be a debased, reduced kind of adventure. Thus, on the one hand, a film like *Captain China* (1949) with its two-fisted title character, will bear certain marks of seafaring excitement, but will enclose these marks in a story of self-doubt and antiheroism. Captain China (John Payne) begins the film in a drunken stupor as his ship sinks, and he is subsequently divested of his command. China will spend the rest of the film looking not for adventure but for revenge (and all his actions will be viewed with a certain disapprobation by a woman who is skeptical of the seafaring life; it is this woman who will eventually win China away from the sea and promise him a home life on land).

On the other hand, a number of films—B movies especially, marginalized to the edges of the forties film industry—do deal with adventure but an adventure lacking in epic intensity. For example, many of the Roy Rogers films from Republic Studios rewrite the pioneering adventure of the West in modern times with singing cowboys (Rogers and the significantly named *"Sons* of the Pioneers"—not epic heroes themselves but only offspring of epic heroes) defending such outposts as a Christmas tree ranch (*The Trail of Robin Hood*, 1950), or a salmon spawnery (*Susannah Pass*, 1949). Significantly, *The Trail of Robin Hood* has nothing to do with the mythic figure, not even metaphorically; there is no investment in old legends of masculine heroes of the land. Such films suggest a certain deflating resolution of a central contradiction in the Western as epic form: the sense that in bringing civilization to the West, the Westerner is bringing about his own future irrelevance. Even an "epic" film of the Old West like *Duel in the Sun* (1947) seems strangely anti-epical in this respect: the battle of rugged individualism and technological modernity is resolved to the benefit of the new world of lawyers and railroad men.

Here we might echo a point made by Henri Lefebvre in *La révolution urbaine* when he argues that in the modern world system, even the countryside's significations and values are rewritten as dependencies of urban power.[3] Thus, in *The Emperor Waltz*, the romantic values of an idyllic island rendezvous between Joanna Augusta (Joan Fontaine) and Virgil Smith (Bing Crosby) are qualified by their being enunciated in flashback from the point of view of Viennese aristocrats who enclose the memories of the past within their caustic gossip. Significantly, Virgil is able to triumph and win Joanna at the end only because he himself is a kind of force of modernization (for example, he begins the film as a traveling salesman who wants to get into the palace to sell the emperor the new technology of a phonograph); at the film's end, he argues that the emperor's code of class hierarchy is out of time, an anachronism. *The Emperor Waltz* thus reiterates the particular fate of pastoralism within American mythologies which react to the power of the aristocracy with a populism that paradoxically readily fuels a nascent industrialism.

Indeed, the very possibility of a pastoral art of cinema can enter into contradiction with cinema itself as a modern technology. For example, as Serafina Bathrick suggests in several writings, many of the films of the forties work to suggest a mediating and reinforcing interplay of technology and a supposed preindustrial innocence.[4] In many cases, the innocence of a pure life is presented as incomplete without the intercession of technology and industry. For example, in *Meet Me in St. Louis*, as Bathrick suggests, many of the women's songs take place around or in homage to works of industry; the new technology of electric lights, the trolley, the world's fair.

Similarly, in what must be one of the great oddities of forties cinema, *Bill and Coo* (1947), a narrative of small-town life acted entirely by dressed-up birds, the possible cuteness of such a conceit is intruded upon by an emphasis on the constructed nature of the cute scenes: before the story proper starts, a self-reflexive segment shows the director and bird trainer at work building this imaginary world. Similarly, the narrative itself is one that goes out of its way to announce the incompleteness of the small-town idyll: for example, when a circus comes to town, the film makes a point of noting how Bill's mother couldn't go because she had to work. At another moment, the narrator shows how the choice of idyll or evil is a choice of the narrative instance itself: "Chir-pendale [the small town of the film] seems to be a lovely feathered utopia, where the fullness of life can be enjoyed happily and fully, a place where each individual can live contentedly beside his neighbor, shaping his own destiny with freedom from fear. . . . But can he? No—the heavy footsteps of evil are ever lurking nearby, casting a dark, malignant shadow over the small metrop-olis." *The New Yorker*'s contemporary review of the film even linked it to *film noir:* "[The marauding crow] is the outstanding actor, much more menacing than Bogart or Robinson has ever been" (April 10, 1948).

The enclosing of birds within the frames of a studio production becomes, then, a kind of figure of the fate of "Nature" within a modern, technological world. More generally, it might seem that the fairy tale per se is a rarity in forties narrative. Warners cartoons, for example, show not the reconciliations of animals to a natural environment but their displacement to a world whose values are determined by needs of contemporary life: for example, Tex Avery's *Little Red Hot Riding Hood,* which starts out to tell the old story only to have the characters reject the quaintness of the fairy tale as one of the most unbearable of anachronisms in a new, urban age.)

As a number of critics have noted, one of the extreme sites of this demonstration of technology's triumph over "Nature" occurs in the musicals directed at M.G.M. by Vincente Minnelli. These musicals instill an ambiguity into the very representation of the natural, pulling it between the naive realism of the pastoral moment and the marked artificiality of the studio system. For example, the very opening images of *Yolanda and the Thief* (1945), where what seems to be a two-dimensional painting suddenly reveals itself to have depth as a man and llama walk from back-to foreground, construct screen reality as an ambiguous reality where each perception can turn into a reading that qualifies or contests other readings.[5] "Nature" ceases to be a steady value and becomes no more than one structural component in a permuta-tional field.

Similarly, as Andrew Britton has suggested, *Meet Me in*

St. Louis' narrative trajectory revolves around the power of an end moment—the visit to the fair—that is filmed precisely as a constructed moment, a scene in a studio set.[6] Here, indeed, the technique of filming doubles a signification of the story itself: if New York is figured in the story as a dangerous place of modernism (for example, the place to which the father is being transferred; the place from which the fiancé, Warren, uses the new technology of long-distance calling to *not* propose to the daughter, Rose), the force of modernism also shows up in the story in the positive image of the world's fair itself—an ode to the coming technological world created, as the film notes, by dredging up a swamp, destroying the object of grandfather's memories.[7] Indeed, the dismal fate of grandfather himself in the film—living out his life in a small second-floor room filled with marks of an eccentric hobby (hat collecting) and having as his major narrative function to pass his granddaughter on to a new generation of men—suggests a limitation to the nostalgic inclinations of the film: as Robin Wood has suggested, here *Meet Me in St. Louis* may not be that far from *The Texas Chainsaw Massacre* (1974) with its once-productive family pushed to the backwaters of American capitalism and its aged patriarch turned into a virtual mummy little different from the scraps and refuse that make up this family's home.[8] At the extreme, as such analysis suggests, *Meet Me in St. Louis* implies that by 1944, an innocent small-town America is explicitly a fiction, an aesthetic construction. While the order of scenes follows the order of the seasons and so might seem to root narrative events in a kind of naturalness, each of these scenes is introduced by a still image approximating a greeting card that then comes to life. The past can only exist if called into play by the technology of the present.

In *The Pirate* (1948), the impossibility of the natural as a pure realm of innocence is specifically linked to the possibilities of cinema.[9] Said in the story to take place in the Caribbean, but announced in the end credits as filmed "entirely in Hollywood, USA." *The Pirate* makes explicit the impossible fate of the idyllic moment, while significantly tying the desire for idyll to the desires of a woman. The young woman, Manuela, dreams of adventures on the high sea (which she's never seen) with the pirate Macoco (whom she's never met but only read about in books). From the first, nature exists for Manuela only as a construction of the tales that she reads. About to be married against her will, Manuela convinces her guardian-aunt to give her one glimpse of the sea by taking her to the port for her wedding dress. A short sequence shows how Manuela's naturalist inclination is rewritten by a force of cinema as triumphant technology (which thereby becomes a kind of spectacular relay of Serafin [Gene Kelly], the clown who feels that Manuela's real destiny lies neither with pirates nor with respectable bourgeois mayors but rather with the world of spectacle). Manuela moves toward the right of the frame, weaving her way among the crates on the shore, as the camera tracks before her. Suddenly, her face becomes illumined with rapture; she has evidently spotted the sea that she has so dreamed about. And yet, significantly, here where we might expect a corresponding reverse shot to show us that sea, the tracking shot continues by having Manuela walk off screen right as Serafin pops up behind a box and sees her (and fills with equal rapture). The specificity of the woman's look, of a woman's desire, is passed onto and decentered by another look—that of the man who knows that the enframed world of spectacle is the best one for the woman.

The next shot shows a frontal view of Manuela looking out at the sea, and then there is a quick cut to the sea, a cut back to Manuela radiant, a cut back to the sea, and then a cut back to Manuela who suddenly discovers (as we do) that Serafin is at her side. The two shots of the sea are the only nonstudio shots of the film, and they can thus have only the vaguest of epiphanous force in a film so concerned as it is to construct a fantasy universe based on masculine spectacle. The relay of Manuela's actions through Serafin's thus only further displaces the "natural" unity of subject (Manuela) and object (the sea) through the intrusion of a third term that comes increasingly to turn the female subject into a man's object (and only a few scenes later Serafin will hypnotize Manuela and cause her to perform a breathless stage spectacle). Moreover, the very way that Manuela is established as a character makes the sea images an inadequate vehicle for her adventurous desire. Manuela's first dreams of Macoco the pirate come through pages of a book; indeed, when she is told that Serafin is actually Macoco in disguise, her fantasy image of Macoco in adventures as a pirate appears manifestly as an unnatural image—filmed on a set, staged as a kind of virulent ballet. Even if "Nature" exists for Manuela, it is a nature that she reshapes according to the parameters of a nonnatural stage spectacle.

More generally in forties cinema, water, the sea, only seem to weakly bear the symbolism of a natural force, of some sort of pure adequation of representation and reality.[10] If American narrative art frequently works to represent water as an idyllic space, an escape from the crush of an artificial, modern world— for example, the romanticism of Huck Finn's voyage down the river—the forties suggest the impossibility of that space, its status as anachronism.[11] For example, Huck Finn's Mississippi becomes itself the aestheticized object of a stage spectacle in the "Old Man River" production number of *Till the Clouds Roll By* (1946). Significantly, an earlier scene of this film has Jerome Kern (Robert Walker) wandering down to the river's edge and, in an epiphany represented through montage, experiencing the radiant message of the mighty river. But the water's message as he perceives it is to commit himself to the world of show: the river becomes the source for its own enframement and domination within a constructed spectacle.

Similarly, other narratives of the river—for example, *The Naughty Nineties* (1945), *Letter to Three Wives* (1948), *The Foxes of Harrow* (1947), among others—reintroduce a signification of the river that was already in place in *Huckleberry Finn:* the recognition that the river idyll is only a temporary idyll at best, subject to constant invasion, constant overturning. In *Letter to Three Wives,* for example, the prospect of a nice afternoon on a boat trip up the Hudson is marred from the start by a letter announcing that one of the three chaperones' husbands has run off with another woman; the boat trip turns into a kind of entrapment as the women have to wait in desperate impatience for the voyage to end to know which wife has lost; the trip also becomes a cause for guilt-ridden self-appraisal and doubt, represented through flashback. In other cases, a steamboat trip on the river begins as a voyage of joy—for example, the women in *Dragonwyck* (1946) and in Cornell Woolrich's novel *Waltz Into Darkness* traveling toward what they think will be blissful marriage—but finding only that joy turn into misery or, in the case of *Waltz Into Darkness*, even death. In *Dragonwyck*, Miranda's excited viewing of the Dragon-wyck mansion at a distance from the railing of the steamboat will be undone by the agonies of her close-up, day-to-day activities in Dragonwyck in contact with its dark, fateful secrets.

The limitations of watery places lie perhaps in the fact that they are ultimately never atopias—places existing nowhere except in a rich potentiality—but all too geographically real places, easily locatable in relation to the ordinary world they stand against, and therefore prey to all the earthy forces of that world. This means first that the ordinary world can seduce the utopian voyager back to harsh reality: for example, in *Lydia*, Lydia's won-derful idyll on a northern island with a sea captain is brought to a traumatic end when the sea captain sneaks away in the middle of the night out of a feeling of responsibility to his land-based wife; Lydia will spend the rest of her life closed to any romance but the romantic memory of that idyll. On the other hand, the geographic specifiability of the utopian place means that people who have fled there can always be tracked down: the watery place is given over to scenes of continued intrusion: in *Whiplash* (1948), for example, escape and recapture against the backdrop of the peaceful sea becomes a repeated image as first the unhappy wife of a gangster flees to the seaside only to have one of her husband's thugs show up to bring her back, and then a boxer in love with the wife flees to the seaside only to have the wife bring him back to the husband for whom he is an employee. The idyllic place seems to be figured in many narratives precisely so that it can be assailed: for example, in *Out of the Past*, Jeff Bailey's repeated sojourns near a lake and waterfall in the countryside are repeatedly interrupted by the call of the city that comes out of the past to propel him into a dangerous future.

Even the controlled environment of the pool or lake will frequently become a major place of tension or aggressivity.

For example, *The Damned Don't Cry* (1950) specifically sets up the pool as a point of intersection between idyll and menace: the pool here exists in images of Ethel Whitehead (Joan Crawford) joyfully swimming in the pool of her gangster boyfriend, but the images come from a film found after the gangster's murder and projected by the police in their search for clues. The "purity" of the moment of ecstatic enjoyment is contained within the limits of a cold, dispassionate investigation—a conflict emphasized cinematically by the clash between the silent images of Ethel's fun and the policeman's cold and seemingly all-knowing aural commentary. In another way, then, the film also sets up the swim as the intersection of a lost past against a harsh present. Romantic utopia exists only as a memory, subject to a rewriting by the present. Similarly, in *King's Row* (1941), the opening skinny-dipping scene of Parris Mitchell (Robert Cummings) and Cassandra Towers (Betty Field) becomes finally only a trace of a lost memory as Parris has to grow up and deal with the pains of maturity (including the death of Cassandra).

Far from offering a refuge from the conflicts of sociality, the supposedly idyllic place becomes itself a site for such conflicts, a place of would-be adventure distorted by greed (for example, the betraying pirates in *The Black Swan* [1942], a place of life turned into death (*Humoresque* [1946]), where the romance of the sea ends as a suicide in that same sea). In the didactic *Sea Wolf* (1941), the sea even becomes the space for painful discussion of options open to human behavior; characters who escape to Wolf Larson's boat find not escape but an intensification of human aggressivities as Larson shows the world of the ship to be a world of coldness, hatred, mockery, a constant struggle for power. Ultimately, the boat itself becomes a force to try to flee from—a force of dangerous repetition as the escapees find their several-days journey bringing them back full circle to the boat and to all its threats.

If *The Damned Don't Cry* puts in conflict the ostensible naturalness of a swim and the calculated coldness of a police investigation, other narratives show the ostensibly natural environment of water to be itself a place of schemes and calculations:

for example, swims designed as seductions or incitations to jealousy *(Road House, Scudda Hoo! Scudda Hay!* (1948), *Leave Her to Heaven)*. *Leave Her to Heaven* is most extreme in this respect, picturing the pool in the middle of the New Mexico desert as the place of Ellen's scheming and conceit against the unassuming naturalness of adopted sister, Ruth, in her garden. Richard's writing table borders on both places, pool and garden, but it is Ellen's machinations that gain the upper hand: for example, Ellen's graceful glides through the water will attract Richard's attentions when he realizes that she has taken off her engagement ring in response to his presence. Ellen is always converting spontaneous action into a scheme; life for her is always a competitive sport. As her mother says as she watches Ellen race two little children across the pool, "Ellen always wins." Indeed, Ellen's calculated mastery of water will be repeated in a later, major scene where she allows Richard's brother to drown in the Maine lake so that she can have Richard to herself. Furthermore, the torment that her scheme eventually causes Richard will be figured visually by the surf pounding up against the rocks where he has come to brood in his misery.

Richard and Ellen meet in *Leave Her to Heaven* on a train taking them to a vacation spot. In part, if the pool is not a spot of idyll, this is so because it is specifically a vacation spot, a temporary place, an idyll from which one must return. Beginning in transit, the character remain in transit, no place really in place, no site a settlement. Indeed, for Ellen in *Leave Her to Heaven*, permanence too often means the permanence of a continued interruption—for example, the relatives who are always showing up. Thus, it is because she knows that she will soon be leaving the vacation spot where Richard is that Ellen feels forced to engage in her seductive tricks. There is no stable site of romance, as Ellen discovers after her marriage to Richard when an intimate scene of her waking Richard is interrupted by the greeting voice of Richard's brother in the next room.

As a number of film scholars have pointed out, forties characters are wanderers, trying to leave behind the tensions of a modern world for the clarity of another place, a place outside history. Their journeys, though, lead them to encounter the same sorts of tensions everywhere. The walk along the road is an encounter with the ambiguity and potential menace of new towns and with the extension of towns in cafés and motels (*The Postman Always Rings Twice* [1946], *Road House, Fallen Angel* [1945]). The straight journey outward becomes a circular detour, precisely because there is nothing new to discover.

Similarly, along with classic epic westerns that show the beginnings of a Western society (as in the church-raising sequence in *My Darling Clementine* [1946]), the forties also show a concern with post-Westerns or adult Westerns in which society has come and put its imprint everywhere.

A number of Westerns concern themselves *not* with the historically first moments of a lone hero epically confronting a resistant world in a glorious combat; rather, the concern is for a slightly later moment in which there is no longer a place for the individual Western spirit, and where conquest has already become tied to a monopolist ambition: for example, *Silver River* (1948) with Mike McComb (Errol Flynn) demonstrating his prowess by breaking up a strike by mine workers; *Duel in the Sun* with railroaders confronting farmers (and the film being on the railroaders' side); *The Oxbow Incident* (1943) with its image of mob rule and its critique of machismo (embodied in the ex-Confederate who demands that his son be a man at all costs). Especially interesting in this respect is *Red River* (1948), which, in a sense, is two Westerns: the first part of the film is a classic Western of pioneer conquest—condensed around a scene of attack by Indians, who are represented as malevolent, alien others—a classic story of land and propriety; while the second part of the film stands as a kind of ironic recognition of the probable outcome of such a story: a megalomania, familial discord, the transformation of friendship into antagonism.

Other films will follow this two-part structure which ultimately turns adventure into no more than the nostalgic memory for a later moment. There is the sense that there's a point (temporal as well as spatial) after which the classic Western can no longer work; hence, a number of Westerns that deal explicitly with the conversion of the original adventure into legend or even media production: *Buffalo Bill* (1944), where Bill's performing of a Wild West show is contrasted as positive event to the dangers of ending up a penny-arcade oddity; *They Died with Their Boots On* (1941), which ends not with the Little Big Horn but with Mrs. Custer's successful attempts to protect her husband's name; and most especially, the Roy Rogers films *The Trail of Robin Hood* (1949) and *The Bells of Rosarita* (1945), where the need to get a load of Christmas trees to market or to save an orphanage brings out of retirement a number of old-time Western *movie stars* (i.e., artificial cowboys) who ride up one by one to have a last chance at glory. Hence, too, a number of films of modern-day "Westerns" set in dude ranches, modern-day reconstructions of an Old West spirit: for example, *Ride 'Em, Cowboy* (1942), *Two Guys from Texas* (1948). The title of *Two Guys from Texas*, furthermore, pinpoints this homogenizing quality; actually from New Jersey, the two guys discover that in this modern age, the Westerner exists only as a kind of superficial costuming; all they have to do is dress like cowboys and people blindly accept them as cowboys. *Two Guys from Texas* even includes a song specifically about the loss of the Old West adventure through the advent of cars and transportation as the linking up of distant places into one homogenous whole: as the lyrics of the song indicate, "The problem will be great. We're gonna have a problem, because all the traffic's interstate."

"Someday I'd like to see some of this country we've been traveling through" (Bowie in *They Live by Night* [1949]). With the new world of an alienating modernity spreading its significations everywhere, the alternative for the searching hero or heroine is to keep searching, keep on moving. But where a Huckleberry Finn could always try to move out ahead of civilization, or where in the romantic hoboism of the thirties a Chaplin could always head on down the road, in the forties narrative, there's often no place to go to: the roads are blocked; one's reputation has preceded one's arrival (for example, Bowie and Keechi out for a night in a new town in *They Live by Night* are immediately spotted and told to leave at once); one is always forced back to a starting point (the failed hitchhiking in *The Postman Always Rings Twice* [1946], the failed escapes to the seashore in *Whiplash* [1948], Sullivan's failed attempts to get away from Hollywood in *Sullivan's Travels* [1941]). The possibility to keep moving is often literally presented as a wish thwarted by a reality; hence, a number of missed escapes: Rose Moline's body along the railroad tracks in *Beyond the Forest*, Ole Olson (John Wayne) delayed into missing his boat home in *The Long Voyage Home* (1940). Hence, also, the sense that escape only means a temporary respite before things catch up: *High Sierra* (1941), *Colorado Territory* (1948), *Gun Crazy*, *Out of the Past*, *The Killers*.

The ending of *Wake of the Red Witch* (1948) makes most emphatic this ultimate dependence of the questing spirit on the controls of an inescapable capitalism: Captain Rawls (John Wayne) wants to be a seafaring adventurer, but in an age of monopoly control of the shipping lines, he has only the alternatives of working for the company or working against it in an illegality. He chooses the latter option—deliberately sinking one of the company's ships so that he can later regain its treasures for himself—but he finds that even on the most remote of island hideouts, the company boss awaits him. Forced to go back to work for the company, Rawls is killed underwater in a dredging operation, and as sailors look at his severed air line, a superimposed image shows Rawls' ship, the *Red Witch*, sailing majestically with flags unfurled. Adventure here is not even a memory, but no more than an unfulfilled fantasy, the possibility for endless voyage existing only in the nonplace of death.

At the same time, though, the few places that do exist outside the increasing network of modernity take their values from this modernity; they are no longer places of an originary pastoralism but, quite the contrary, represent the unproductive places left behind in modernity's expansion. If the forties are the intensification of the big moment of modern American travel—the rise of the interstate highway system—travel here loses epical qualities and becomes little more than a fast journey through sites that one has little time to turn into sights. Indeed, French sociologist Jean Baudrillard suggests that the rise of the modern transportation system is a central force in the postindustrial breakdown of human subjectivity. For Baudrillard, it removes any ground in which human agency could take on any force or value:

> This change from human scale to a system of nuclear matrices is visible everywhere. . . . The countryside, the immense geographic countryside, seems to be a deserted body whose expanse and dimensions seem arbitrary (and which is boring even if one leaves the main highways), as soon as all events are epitomized in the towns, themselves undergoing reduction to a few miniaturized highlights.[12]

The forties narratives show an emphasis on the outside of the productive system reduced to dead ends, backwaters, marginalia to the system: thus, an iconography of a kind of nonspace: rundown boarding houses, fleabag hotels, all-night cafés or bars, etc. In the forties film, "Nature" itself will become a kind of wasteland, as, for example, in the fog-bound mountaintop of *Gun Crazy*, where the hero and heroine meet their end. Indeed, from its opening *noir* images of a rain-streaked street at night, *Gun Crazy* becomes a kind of typology of nonpastoral, wasteland sites: a carnival shot through with aggressivity and decay (the hobbled carny boss); the endless roads; the meat factory with its grotesquely hanging slabs; the cheap motels and hash joints. When Laurie gets her one glimpse of a family, it is only too obvious to her that family life represents a world she can never know (and, perhaps, would never really even care to know).

In the postwar period, to be sure, there will be an increasing investment in the countryside as a pastoral space of refuge from the city, represented in novels and autobiographies like *The Egg and I* or *Tavern in the Town* or Shirley Jackson's *Life Among the Savages*, or films like *The Egg and I* (1947), *Mr. Blandings Builds His Dream House* (1948), *Welcome, Stranger* (1947), *Mrs. Mike* (1949), *Never a Dull Moment* (1950).[13] But even here, the country will be represented as a difficult or impossible place: a place of hardship and even death (for example, *Mrs. Mike* with its hunting accidents, stillborn babies, plague); a place of suspicion and gossip *(Ma and Pa Kettle* [1949], *Mr. Blandings Builds His Dream House); a* place of retardation and insanity *(The Egg and I);* and a site of jealousy. Certainly, the films can end with a moment of reconciliation to country life, but this reconciliation is often begrudging, based on an interest in something other than the country for itself ✓ (for example, in *The Egg and I* and *Never a Dull Moment*, the women who have fled back to the city return to the country not because they really want to live in the country but because the man each loves lives there). In the case of *The Egg and I*, reconciliation with the country life occurs simultaneously with a rejection of the original parameters of that life: in her absence, Betty's husband has bought a modernized, superefficient farm that will eliminate all the problems that had previously made Betty's life hell.

Mr. Blandings Builds His Dream House may be the most extreme of the contradictory films about country life. Here each promise of wonderful pastoralism is undone in a moment of farcical reversal; even the journey to the site of the country home becomes a kind of parody of willed teleology as the father's confident sense of direction ends up leading the family to drive around and around in confusing circles. Significantly, *Mr. Blandings* ends with an affirmation of the greatness of country life: Blandings' best friend, Bill Cole (Melvyn Douglas), who has been a kind of narrating chorus for the tribulations of the Blandings family, suddenly declares to Blandings his envy of the new life that Blandings has constructed for himself. But this end declaration, which allows Blandings and the film together to feel there is a triumphant sense to all the absurd encounters with the horrors of nature, only inadequately answers all the absurdities of that life. The declaration comes unexpectedly, without any immediate cause or motivation, and seems to be less authoritative than simply extraneous (and, indeed, the film's opening scene where Cole knowingly introduces the flashback story of the Blandings' encounters shows a Cole who seems in full consonance with his city life—not at all a man who would prefer another, countrified existence). Furthermore, even if the declaration coincides with a number of solutions to physical problems in the Blandings home, a number of problems remain: most especially, nothing can change the railroad schedule that means that, no matter how wonderful the Blandings country home is, Blandings will still always have to get up in the middle of the night to get to his job in New York City on time. Like so many other films of the "country," *Mr. Blandings* emphasizes the horrors of country life to such a degree that no final optimism can fully dissipate the sense of harsh critique.

For the most part, to move away from home is to move toward danger. Such a process is explicit in the film *D.O.A.* (1949), where a man in a hotel room on a trip away from home hangs up on his fiancée as she is giving him a kiss over the phone, and goes off to a party where he will be fatally poisoned; the implication of the coincidence of the actions will be to suggest that the poisoning is a consequence of the man's journey from domesticity. Similarly, in *Woman in the Window* (1944), the vacation of his family makes a college professor prey to dangerous influences; the absence of domestic support entails instant vulnerability, even in this psychology professor who had warned his students about the dangers of giving in to the unconscious. Likewise, in *Casbah*, the limits of the neighborhood are quite emphatically the limits of security. Home here exists as a definable space; as soon as Pepe le Moko leaves the Casbah to flee with his loved one, he is shot down. The last images of Pepe sinking to the ground as the plane with his loved one flies off in the distance signal a gap between desire and its ability to be realized in an insecure, frequently malevolent world.

A number of film titles even emphasize motion, but a motion that is rarely an exciting one of rich possibilities: hence, the titles themselves suggest menace, danger, a potentially ill-fated journey: *Dark Passage, Nightmare Alley* (1947), *Street of Chance* (1942). Journeys will be descents or detours into a hellish place. As John Belton notes in an analysis of wanderers in forties film, such wanderers have little of the romantic allure that accrues to hoboes and vagabonds in earlier periods of American narrative (and even as late as the thirties for film).[14] In *Detour*, for example, Al Roberts' westward quest as he journeys toward California and the golden promise summed up by blonde-haired Susan becomes a kind of debased farcical version of the American pioneer venture. As Belton explains,

The map montages which trace with animated arrows and moving lines the wanderings of the hero in the early sequences of *I Am a Fugitive from a Chain Gang* lend geographical specificity and a sense of purpose to his journey. But *Detour's* travel montages deny specificity and purpose. The camera pans westward over a succession of maps superimposed with shots of Roberts' feet walking; there are no arrows or lines to indicate where Roberts is. Somewhere past Chicago, the maps cease to appear, eliminating even this abstract index of the hero's spatial progression. The journey has taken Roberts to an uncharted no-man's land. The journey montage continues with a shot of Roberts hitch-hiking from the wrong side of the road. Though the direction of Roberts' movement remains consistent, the logic of his actions, and that of the traffic around him, do not.

The American journey toward a supposed fulfillment becomes an entry into a wasteland. Indeed, the Los Angeles that Al finally reaches will be characterized only by marks of transitoriness: used-car lots, fleabag hotels. In such an environment, geographic closeness to Sue can still mean emotional separation, so Al hangs up the phone when Sue comes on the line.

Like Oedipus whose victorious journeys (for example, his victorious meeting up with the Sphinx) only temporarily conceal the dangers of travel (the crossroads where mastery really is loss), the journeys of so many forties characters (and of their narratives with them) are journeys not of open opportunity but of constriction and even of complicity in evil. Thus, in *Somewhere in the Night* (1946) and Cornell Woolrich's novel *The Black Curtain*, amnesia victims regaining memory quickly find that to recover an identity is also to recover all the guilt of identity, including, in both cases, the possibility of a murder. To be sure, both narratives eventually clear the hero of culpability, but the recognition that the hero *could just as well have been guilty* remains. Indeed, *Somewhere in the Night* will absolve the hero of crime only to leave open the question of moral guilt (through cruelty he may have been responsible for the half-accident, half-suicide death of a girlfriend). That the film can only have the hero and his new love go happily off at the end by her feeling *intuitively* that he's innocent of all wrongdoing can well suggest the artificiality and mere expediency of the happy ending.

Even more explicit in this respect is Cornell Woolrich's

novel *The Black Angel,* where a woman's every action makes her
realize the extent to which her marriage is built on lies and absurdity. Discovering that her husband has a mistress, the heroine
goes to the mistress' apartment for a confrontation only to find
the woman dead and her husband accused of the crime. The wife
takes on the task of clearing her husband's name, but already the
recognition that even if innocent of murder, her husband is guilty
of infidelity turns her quest from an epic or romance into an
ironically deflated duty engaged in with a grimness tinged with
regret. During her quest, indeed, the woman will discover a man
whom she could truly love, but it is too late—the necessity of her
mission and her sense of responsibility to her marriage force her
away from this new love—and the woman ends up begrudgingly
with her husband but thinking all the while of the romantic
adventures that she could have had with the other man.

   The Black Angel's ending suggests that staying within
the limits of home is no guarantee of security and surety. First of
all, the outside world can quite easily intrude into the space of the
home (or of the surrogate homes as in the restaurant scene in *In
a Lonely Place).* Each means of entry into the home can become a
source of menace: for example, the telephone becomes a way that
the external world can make its presence known within the supposedly closed space of the home, as in *Sorry, Wrong Number*
(1948), where an invalid overhears a phone conversation in which
her own murder is being plotted out. Explicit in this respect is the
opening of *Desperate* (1947), where the flat and even lighting
during the wife Sue's cute preparation of a first anniversary dinner
for her and husband, Steve, suddenly is interrupted by a cutaway
to the chiaroscuro lighting of a man calling from elsewhere to ask
about Steve's trucking experience and to pull him away from Sue
and drop him into a world of criminal evil. The cut itself enacts a
narrative vulnerability of the domestic world.

   "Home" can become itself an alien place, a geography
that turns against its inhabitants—a space of otherness, as the title
of one film, *House of Strangers* (1949), suggests. Thus, as Lucy
Fischer has argued, the shootout in the aptly named *House* of
Mirrors in *Lady from Shanghai* (1948), can seem like nothing so

much as a representation of a perverse forties home: crippled husband, ravenous and castrating wife.[15] Home is also a space of passive resistances—gadgets that don't work *(The Milkman* [1950]; the Blondie films) or even go crazy *(Ma and Pa Kettle* [1949])— but also a space of positive menace (for example, in Cornell Woolrich's novel *Rendezvous in Black*, a woman is killed by a poison-coated nail protruding ever so slightly from a floorboard of her home; in the Charlie Chan film *Charlie Chan in the Secret Service* [1944], one room of a scientist's home is booby-trapped with a trick gun). At such moments, the home confirms a second move in Freud's etymology when he suggests that the homey, the *heimlich*, is itself a potential source of the uncanny, the *unheimlich*— that it is the world of the ostensibly comfortable haven that is itself the most strange, filled with tension and the psychodrama of a "family romance." Significantly, the "strangers" in *House of Strangers* are the brothers who have become so alienated from each other that they relate to each other through suspicion, menace, and even the threat of murder.

    A number of films represent the home as a kind of intrusion of past events which recur in the present only through a kind of evil psychical return. Some films, for example, emphasize the dual existence of homes in past and present, and suggest ways in which past tensions can potentially block the free development of inhabitants in the present: *Enchantment* (1948), *Dragonwyck* (1946), *The Ghost and Mrs. Muir* (1947), *Moss Rose* (1947), *House of Strangers* (1949), *Rebecca* (1941), *House by the River* (1950). In each of these films, the home is not simply a physical environment, but an active force that encapsulates all the ups and downs of a family history and can determine actions in the present. In *Rebecca*, for example, each object of Manderley implies to the new Mrs. de Winter the continued presence of Rebecca's will and emotional might. Significantly, the burning down of Manderley doesn't bring complete release from the hold of the place; the new Mrs. de Winter will continue to live out the force of the house in her daily dreams. Other films will further emphasize the ties of home to the emotional or psychological pressures of the past. Thus, in *Moss Rose*, a mother who is afraid of her son growing up keeps his childhood room as it always was and strangles the women he becomes involved with. *Enchantment* goes so far as to have the house introduce and narrate the story of its human characters. In *House by the River*, both house and river become frightening sites of a "return of the repressed" as a murderer finds traces of his crimes coming back to haunt him: first, the sack containing the victim's body rises up from the bottom of the river, and second, the murderer is killed in a fall when he mistakes rustling curtains for his victim come back to life. The house here *is* the mark of the inescapability of the past and of destiny, a tie of past to future.

Every point of the home can become an element in a reversible signification. For example, there is in the forties film a veritable cataloguing of the variable functions of interior architecture: doors—for example, doors as escape, doors as mystery *(Rebecca, Secret Beyond the Door* [1948], *The Two Mrs. Carrolls* [1947]), doors as menace; stairways—stairways as escape, stairways as menace *(The Spiral Staircase* [1946], *Woman in Hiding* [1950]); hallways; and secret passageways *(Woman in White* [1948]). Significantly, the most ideologically interior place, bedrooms, and the most exterior ones, doors and windows that mediate between inside and outside, become equally subject to alternating senses.

Windows, for example, serve a variety of functions: marks of intrusion (thus, one of the character traits that mark Favell in *Rebecca* as shady is that he first makes his entrance through a window); the threat of falling (that is, something to commit suicide by jumping through as in *The Locket, Rebecca, The Lady Gambles);* or something to be murdered with by being thrown through as in *The Fallen Sparrow* (1943). Significantly, in several films, murder, suicide, and accidental death through windows blur (and not only for characters but also for the spectator), thereby suggesting the ambivalence of sense; thus, in *Dark Passage*, for example, it is never clear (even with motion-analyzing equipment and freeze-framing) how Madge manages to fall through her apartment window to her death. Similarly, the second Mrs. de Winter's near death by falling in *Rebecca* is fueled both by Mrs. Danvers' encouragements to jump and by Mrs. de Winter's own sense of the failures of her life with Maxim. Even as vehicles for sight, windows become invested with ambivalent possibilities. Rather than as an appreciation of the "view," the window's vision is one that shocks: the sight of a burning Pearl Harbor through the window of the airplane in *Air Force;* the witness of murder (as in *The Window* [1949]); but also the danger of being seen from without (for example, the *agricoles* scene in *Madame Bovary* [1949], where Emma and Rodolphe have to stay away from windows for fear of being seen).

The geography of the home becomes a potentially paranoid space—each familiar object turning into a possible threat, a betrayal. Significantly, as the murder-suicide window scene in *Rebecca* makes explicit, life in such a space can often only work itself under the force of a compulsion—that is, the human subjects find themselves living their lives as if under the influence of trajectories they cannot control. The subjects turn into objects of their own environments. Space speaks to them with a seductive—and sometimes dangerous—voice. Sometimes, the compulsion is revealed to have quite specifically external causes: hypnosis *(Sleep, My Love* [1948], *Whirlpool)* and/or plots to drive one crazy *(My Name Is Julia Ross* [1945], *Gaslight* [1944]). That such plots are plots revolving around the ambiguous functions of space becomes quite clear in *Whirlpool,* where the hypnotized woman's discovery of a murder is also a discovery of space, an equation rendered through an extravagant camera movement that follows the woman's motions by swinging through a balcony and craning across a living room.

But such forced compulsions are only one form of compulsions that work themselves out in an encounter with space: as frequently, the compulsions are inner-directed: a propelling curiosity tinged with fear. Here, there is an initial act of mild wonder, a desire to be curious, but this faint curiosity will quickly become caught up in a compulsive need to know. More specifically, as Mary Ann Doane has argued for that plethora of forties narratives in which women investigate an alien presence that is their own home, such narratives construct the investigation of space as a kind of potentially masochistic venture, a situation in which the space that the woman is assigned culturally—that

is, the home—becomes, through its fragmentation into places that
are seen and unseen, the site of terror and victimization, the
investigating look turned dramatically back on itself.[16] Indeed, for
men in narratives of investigation, it tends to be places outside the
home that are sites of paranoid and/or masochistic compulsion:
when it is into a home space that danger intrudes on a man, it is
registered precisely as a punctual, dramatic intrusion—for example, the compact that a seductive woman rolls across the floor
to the door of George Taylor's hotel room in *Somewhere in the Night*.
Exceptions, such as Woolrich's *Waltz Into Darkness* or Vera Caspary's *Bedelia*, where ill men are menaced in the space of their
homes by murderous wives, seem rather infrequent; and, in another sense, the scandal of these narratives is not so much that
the women are victimizers as that they are not victims (thus, in
Waltz Into Darkness, the husband's greatest shock is his discovery
that his murderous wife smokes and looks at herself in the mirror—that is, that she doesn't accept stereotypes of an innocent
and pure domesticity).

    For men, space becomes alien through a momentous,
shattering event: the war injury and the side of a building falling
in that bring on amnesia in *Somewhere in the Night* and Woolrich's
The Black Curtain respectively. For the woman, in contrast, discovery of menace is all too often a gradual process, a passage through
a series of vignettes in which women discover the strangeness of
their ordinary situation as a kind of accumulation of almost im-
perceptible changes in that situation. Indeed, in *Gaslight*, Paula's
life of slowly mounting menace from her husband takes place as
a kind of contrast to the dramatic opening with Paula taken away
from the site of her aunt's murder. Paula reacts to the violent death
of her aunt with a frozen stare, while her reactions to the little
acts that her husband perpetrates take on a hysterical, feverish
tone. Away from the punctual, intense moment of dramatic turn
or revelation, it will be the small things, the little events, that for
the women signal the transformation of home into horror.

    To be sure, there are intensely horrific moments in the
woman's film—for example, the second Mrs. de Winter's ill-fated
walk down the stairs to the costume ball, the second Mrs. Carroll's

discovery of her husband's death portrait of her, Margie's discovery in *Margie* (1946) that her teacher hasn't come to ask her to the school prom—but such incidents frequently occur not simply as singular moments but as the culmination of an accumulation of moments—the final event serving as a kind of retrospective confirmation of all previous incidents. This becomes most explicit in *Reckless Moment* (1949), where two kinds of narratives run side by side for the woman, Lucia Harper (Joan Bennett): on the one hand, there is the dramatic and eventful story of death, cover-up, blackmail, dangerous romance, but, on the other hand, there is the narrative of everyday life—which can appear as entrapping or threatening as the first. Thus, while trying to save her family from the threat of a murder investigation, Lucia must also simultaneously tend to her daughter's love life, her father's need for someone to talk to, her son's allowance, etc. Many of the punctually dramatic events occur outside Lucia's control; her function is primarily to try to pick up the pieces afterward. Hence, there is a regular recourse in the film to cutaways—cuts to the actions that Lucia can only influence in a highly mediated fashion: Martin Donnelly (James Mason) telephoning to his blackmail associate; the daughter accidentally killing the seducer; Donnelly crashing his car.

More than the male narrative of investigation—for example, the Ellery Queen Wrightsville trilogy of the 1940s which moves Queen out of the big city and into the seemingly homey space of small-town America but in which the procedure is still that of the classic detective story—the woman's investigation is frequently a discovery of the ability of every bit of knowledge to be doubled by a conflicting bit of knowledge. That is, where the detective's investigation is supposed to be a whittling down of ambivalence to a single meaning, the woman's narrative can become the source of an expansion of meanings, a multiplication of ambiguities and ambivalences. For example, in the forties gothic, the more a woman lives with her husband, the more she wonders just exactly who or what he is: perplexity increases. As Tania Modleski suggests in *Loving with a Vengeance*, the female gothic is readable as a kind of meditation for women on married life, a meditation that can function by allowing all possibilities (he loves me, he doesn't love me) to be entertained (and not only successively but simultaneously).[17] To be sure, the narratives end with a moment of disambiguation—the husband really does love her *(Suspicion, Rebecca)* or he really does hate her *(Gaslight, Sleep, My Love)*—but, as with other situations of narrative resolution in the 1940s, the ending here is only a resolution by fiat, an emphatic declaration that this is the way things must be, but also a declaration that in its very emphaticness only signals the arbitrariness of any particular choice. Indeed, the production problems over the endings of *Suspicion*—can Johnny be a murderer, if played by Cary Grant?—are a kind of mark of the ways that any one narrative line can be rewritten as its converse. More generally, the move from confusion to enlightenment occurs so punctually as to signal its miraculous qualities: Maxim's declaration that he hated Rebecca, Mark Caldwell's declaration in *Cry Wolf* (1947) that it is his brother and not he who is the madman of the family, Johnny's declaration in *Suspicion* that he has always loved Lina. Significantly, as Modleski notes in analyzing a similar process in the modern gothic and Harlequin romances, such bursts of enlightenment are most frequently used to clear a man of suspicion, as if to suggest that it is only in a utopian moment or space that men can be nondangerous for women. Nothing can *necessarily* entail the innocence of the suspected male.

Not infrequently, the female gothic will double the ambivalent male by another figure who seems to represent a clear-cut, good alternative to the potentially evil husband.[18] Often a doctor *(Caught, Dragonwyck)* or some other kind of authority figure (for example, lawyer, policeman), this male would appear to be a figure of respectability, purity, and stability. And yet, even here, it is possible to read the narratives in a different direction and find marks of ambivalence even in the representation of such seemingly positive figures. First, these characters are sometimes motivated by ulterior motives unrelated to pure romance. Thus, in *Gaslight,* the policeman (Joseph Cotten) first becomes interested in Paula because she looks like her aunt and thereby revives his love for the deceased woman. Here, the gothic "hero" becomes

part of that general figure of obsession that frequently drives investigators in forties narrative—an obsession that shows up any
pretense to dispassionate objectivity on the investigator's part (for
example, *Laura* [1944], *Chicago Deadline,* with their heroes in love
with the image of dead women). Second, the male "heroes" are
sometimes aggressive figures, deciding for themselves a woman's
fate. This becomes most explicit, as Mary Ann Doane analyzes it,
in *Caught* (1949), where Larry Quinada (James Mason) makes up
his mind about Leonora Eames (Barbara Bel Geddes) in a scene
marked by her absence: in Doane's words,

> Toward the end of the film there is a scene in which Quinada's
> empty desk is used as a pivot as the camera swings back and forth
> between the two doctors (James Mason and Frank Ferguson) discussing
> her fate. Obsessively moving across the desk from doctor to doctor, the
> camera constructs a perfect symmetry by framing both of the men in
> their office doorways. . . . The scene is a performance of one of the
> overdetermined meanings of the film's title—Leonora is "caught," spa-
> tially, between an obstetrician and a pediatrician. . . . The scene dem-
> onstrates the technical fluency of the camera in narrating the woman's
> story, extended to the point of ejecting her from the image. . . . The film
> succeeds in constructing a story about a woman which no longer requires
> even her physical presence.[19]

Furthermore, in other cases, the gothic "hero" is quite
literally himself a force of outright menace. For example, *The Spiral
Staircase* sets up the dissolute vagabond brother as the likely suspect
behind a series of strangulations of women as against the authoritative, respectable Professor Warren (George Brent), only ultimately to reveal Warren as the real murderer (thus playing not
only against the clues of the film but also playing against connotations of Brent as gentle, romantic lead). Moreover, while the
film goes so far as to create a second doctor figure (Kent Smith)
who seems a potential romantic figure for the heroine, Helen
(Dorothy McGuire), his initial way of dealing with Helen's mute-
ness is one that approximates the actions of the strangler: brusquely grabbing Helen, the doctor shakes her violently back and
forth, yelling at her. Aggression, even if finally localized in one
character, the real murderer, is a latent (or not so latent) possibility

in *all* the male characters; as one character explains at the beginning of the film, the murderer might be "somebody we all know,
somebody we see every day. Might be me. Might be you."

Similarly significant in terms of its running through
the various permutations of ambivalence in the gothic is *Notorious*
(1946), which pinpoints the dimensions of the gothic by taking a
certain distance from its generic center. Like the traditional gothic,
Notorious has the woman rushed and rushing into a marriage that
will take her to a foreboding home with mysterious chambers and
family secrets. Yet, if *Notorious* seems superficially to follow the
gothic by splitting the male into two figures, the dimensions of
this split do not follow fully the usual pattern. Significantly, from
the beginning, there is no doubt as to Alex Sebastian's love for
Alicia or to his allegiance to the Nazi cause. Romance and evil
become split into two clear camps in Alex—a split that allays any
kind of doubt or suspicion. He is a good husband and an evil Nazi.
In contrast, doubt is easily displaced onto Devlin (Cary Grant),
ostensibly a figure of stable authority but whose interactions with
Alicia are based on critical scrutiny (we first see him from the back
as a shadowy figure observing her); aggression (he punches her);
insult; and mistrust. Significantly, scenes that show Devlin's growing romantic interest in Alicia are not witnessed by her—for example, Devlin's protestations when he learns of plans to use Alicia
to infiltrate Sebastian's home—thus, Alicia lacks the evidence that
would prove Devlin's love for her. For Alicia, then, Devlin becomes the source of doubt, the figure whose love or lack thereof
is in question. In its variations on a theme, *Notorious* can suggest
the permutational openness of the gothic as symbolic form. Any
man—husband or not, Nazi or figure of benign authority—can
be a source of dread.

Another significant aspect of the forties gothic that
makes of it a kind of meditation on the dangers of an all-too-real
everyday life is its frequent localization of action in an existing
and defined geographic space: Rio *(Notorious)*, London *(Gaslight)*,
New York City *(Sleep My Love)*, the Hudson River valley *(Dragonwyck)*. As much as the modern gothic pictures an exotic and imaginary place, a scene of otherness and mystery, it will also suggest

the possibility of an otherness *in the heart of the familiar.* Indeed, in ✓
Gaslight, part of the agony for Paula is knowing how close she is
to an ordinary London scene: one of her greatest defeats occurs
when her husband lets her happily prepare for an evening out on
the town only to tell her at the last moment that they cannot go
out. There will be an emphasis in these films on a specifically
modern world—one in triumph over superstition, mystery, irrational forces. The gothic here is not *The Monk* or *The Castle of Otranto,*
those gothics of an earlier period where evil is a literal extension
of the devil and so emerges in particularly devilish places (cata-
combs, sepulchers, etc.). Rather, the menace of the modern gothic✓
is the menace of an all-too-natural world: for example, the gas-
lights carefully turned down each night by the husband in *Gaslight.*
Even gothics set in a past time often locate malevolence in precisely
definable terms: *Dragonwyck,* for example, plays on historical reference to the tenant revolt in early America to designate its story
as specifically the clash of two social groups—a decaying aristocracy and an insurgent populist agronomy.

    But such a situating of the modern gothic in a familiar
space allows the specific threats of an exotic world to infiltrate
and infuse into the familiar world itself. That is, it is the ordinary
forces of modernity or everyday life that can become marks of ✓
menace. Through a kind of contagion, it is not simply the malevolent patriarch in his stately but mysterious house that is the threat,
but rather, quite frequently, figures and elements of an ordinary
life: a car salesman (Favell in *Rebecca*), ordinary townsfolk (the
people, including a priest, who block the heroine's escape in *My
Name Is Julia Ross* [1945]), a doctor *(Sleep My Love),* a mother-in-
law *(Notorious).* Fear is displaced from a punctual event with a
single exotic agent behind it to a more diffuse sense of the ordinary
world as menacing in its constant scrutinies, constant dangerous
encounters loaded with challenge and disturbing criticism.

    In *Rebecca,* for example, the new Mrs. de Winter's ag-
ony comes as much from fears of being thought gauche, of appearing wrong, than from any direct physical aggression on the
part of others. Significantly, when the mystery of Maxim's relation
to Rebecca is cleared up, the film doesn't end but simply shifts to

invest fear in another kind of threat: the all-too-worldly menace of blackmail and a court investigation.[20] *Rebecca* will then, through a kind of alternating editing, even go on to suggest a direct parallel between the exotic world of gothic menace and the ordinary world of legal menace: as Maxim brings the investigation to a close in London, a cut back to Manderley shows Mrs. Danvers hovering over Mrs. de Winter and undoubtedly planning some sort of evil action; the two spaces are linked not only by the logic of the editing but also by Favell, a figure who mediates both worlds and is seen telephoning to Danvers when the legal investigation is resolved.

In a significant reversal, this diffusion of an originally gothic menace throughout the ordinary aspects of everyday life allows the conventions of the gothic to be mapped onto narratives in which romantic, wishful, or even exotic women find themselves married to all-too-ordinary men. The menace here is no longer that of a mysterious and unknown quality but, quite the contrary, of the too well known, the all too predictable. Here the woman worries not that her husband is mysterious but, quite the contrary, that he is too ordinary. Thus, in *Caught,* when Leonora discovers that her husband intends to break his promises of romance and plans instead to continue his old business-dominated way of life, Leonora reacts with a kind of instant, saddened recognition: she appears to know immediately that Smith would not change, that he would remain a workaholic.

If, as I suggested earlier, *Reckless Moment* shows a woman living through two kinds of potentially aggressive narratives—a dramatic one of murder and physical danger, and the other of ordinary household life as a series of repetitive, insistent demands—a number of forties narratives will concern themselves with conveying the burdensomeness of this second narrative: *Madame Bovary, Caught, Beyong the Forest, Whirlpool, That Uncertain Feeling* (1941). If the gothic menace proper is frequently the menace of an older way of life trying desperately to hang on in a modern world (as in *Dragonwyck),* menace in these "reversed" gothics will frequently come from the modern, technologized world: the nascent careerism of nineteenth-century France *(Madame Bovary)* or

Austria *(Letter from an Unknown Woman)*, the accomplished capitalism of a millionaire *(Caught)*, the unending drive of competitiveness *(That Uncertain Feeling)*. Indeed, as Mary Ann Doane has suggested, *Caught* even inscribes cinema itself as a kind of menacing sign of modernity: as Leonora tries to find a moment of enjoyment during a party of her husband's business associates, her husband shows a documentary film that represents the achievements of his industry. With her laughter in conversation sharply curtailed by her husband, the woman here exists in opposition to technology and can only assert herself at the cost of absence (from the room and, for a moment, from *Caught* itself).[21]

To be sure, other films allow the woman a presence and even announce explicitly an admiration for her struggle against the repressive structures of an ordinary life. For example, *Madame Bovary* changes Flaubert's novel in ways that work to increase sympathy for Emma: her sending her daughter away to a nursemaid is eliminated from the film; her fainting at the discovery that she has given birth to a girl is changed into her lack of reaction as Charles whispers the news while she is already unconscious. Most significantly, the film puts Flaubert (James Mason) on the witness stand during his obscenity trial and gives him the speech of a noble humanist who tried to portray realistically the plight of women.

To a certain degree, such a gesture also subordinates the plight of women to other plights: that of a man struggling to clear himself, of a novel struggling to be cleared of an improper reputation—indeed, an end title simultaneously announces Flaubert's acquittal and the book's ascension to the rank of classic. The reverse-gothic may represent the miseries of a woman's situation but it also can displace such misery onto the male figures pictured as inverse victims of the woman's aspirations: Richard (Cornel Wilde) cleared of murder but sent to prison anyway for perjury in *Leave Her to Heaven;* Charles Bovary financially ruined by Emma's improper handling of accounts; Dr. Lewis Moline (Joseph Cotten) losing his patients through his wife's greed in *Beyond the Forest.* Significantly, a number of the films are structured around flashbacks presented by men to explain the consequences of a woman's ambition: *Madame Bovary, Leave Her to Heaven, Beyond the Forest*. In such cases, the very techniques of cinema work to turn the woman into an element of a man's story. Furthermore, other films will employ other techniques as a way of representing women as a case, a symptom, an example, a threat whose existence is subordinated to, and determined by, a man's. Thus, as Deborah Linderman notes for *The Cat People*, the opening and end titles do not in any neutral way describe the action of Irena's story but put it under the marks of a male control: "For whereas the first [shot] is a 'made-up' quotation, a fabrication, *The Anatomy of Atavism* [by Dr. Judd, a character in the film] being a completely hypothetical work, the last [shot] comes from one of the Holy Sonnets of John Donne, and is 'real,' a sign that the cinema has abandoned its represented or interior frame with its inadequate methods of containment in order to effect a recontainment at a metatextual level, that of the cinematic phantasy itself."[22] In other words, in a moment of tension, the film makes an appeal to a whole range of authorities, real and fictive, blurring cinema and history.

And yet, in a way that has generally seemed to resist analysis (perhaps because our analytic concepts are traditionally geared toward specific kinds of emphatically dramatic narratives only), the woman's film in the forties can set up a countercurrent that asserts itself above and beyond the ability of techniques of narration to contain that countercurrent. The very fact that so many directors or producers decided to deal with the question of women can suggest a recognition, no matter how recontaining, of women as a force of representation; as Thomas Elsaesser notes,

Projection of sexual identity and its mechanisms of displacement and transfer is translated into a whole string of movies often involving hypnosis and playing on the ambiguity and suspense of whether the wife is merely imagining it or whether her husband really does have murderous designs on her: Hitchcock's *Notorious* and *Suspicion*, Minnelli's *Undercurrent*, Cukor's *Gaslight*, Sirk's *Sleep, My Love*, Tourneur's *Experiment Perilous*, Lang's *Secret Beyond the Door* all belong in this category as does Preminger's *Whirlpool* and in a wider sense Renoir's *Woman on the Beach*. What strikes one about this list is not only the high number of European emigres entrusted with such projects but that virtually all of the major directors of family melodrama (expect Ray) in the fifties had a (usually not entirely successful) crack at the Freudian feminist melodrama in the forties.[23]

And yet this "feminism" doesn't come out as any sort of full, expressed, intended voice: following Jacques Derrida, for whom the notion of a voice's full presence is an impossible (if constantly attempted) myth, I would suggest that the films maintain traces of a female experience that tries to assert itself in a number of ways but whose presence is frequently contained by narrative development and other structures of the cinematic representation.

As a first sort of such traces, we might note the rise of female narration in the forties, a narration that gives the woman some claim in the recounting of her own story: *Rebecca; Woman in Hiding; East Side, West Side*. To be sure, such narration usually disappears early on in the film, but it can become potentially a position of perspectival knowledge that qualifies other actions and that seems to make the woman a subject, rather than object. This becomes fairly pronounced in *East Side, West Side* (1949), which, like the gothics, shows a woman unsure of her husband, but offered the love of another man (an authority figure—namely, a hero-cop). The film bears certain qualities of the reverse-gothic; living in the heart of modern New York, Jessie Bourne's problem is not that her husband is too often mysteriously at home, engaged in nefarious plots against her, but that, quite the contrary, he is too often away from home, predictably in the arms of another woman. For the first part of the film, Jessie takes on a certain agency of action: she narrates the opening of the film, she visits a woman who helped her husband out of a jam, and ultimately, she goes to confront her husband's lover (Ava Gardner). When the lover is killed, however, the film suddenly shifts the narrative to the detective, Mark Dwyer (Van Heflin), as he decides to investigate the crime and clear Jessie's name. In this shift, the film becomes classically masculine: the strong story of the detective who is professional enough to almost immediately locate the guilty party (in this case, a jealous other woman) and is clever enough to trick her into confirming her guilt and strong enough to resist her charms and overpower her with a knockout punch. The woman here conforms to rigid stereotypes: the city-wise blonde as man-eating killer; the blonde as vulnerable fool (she allows a man to easily pick her up and never suspects that he might be a cop). And yet the film returns to a certain degree of female agency at the end: even with her husband proven innocent, Jessie decides she can no longer bear his infidelity and she sends him off. At the same time, Jessie defers the admissions of love on Dwyer's part and makes him return to Europe without any commitment for the future on her part. The heterosexual couple remains unformed, in suspension, no longer a decision of the man alone (as occurs so often in the gothic, where a woman finds herself almost unexpectedly married to a stranger and, then, as unexpectedly loved by another man).

Moreover, a certain faint paralleling of qualities in the two men in her life can suggest that neither choice would work for Jessie. Thus, where the title of the film serves as a kind of mark of class distinction to suggest that the world of wealth is not so grand for Jessie and that she might be better off with the ordinary man-of-the-street, Dwyer, one throwaway line by her husband has him pleading to hold their marriage together by making reference to the ways their marriage was a site of growth: he learned to like opera and she learned to sit through baseball games. Here, suddenly, it is the supposed symbol of an upper-crust life who marks himself as a man of the people against the feminine world of high culture. Moreover, if Jessie's husband is a man who mistreats women in the film's terms by leaving them alone, by refusing to give them the love they so emphatically want, Dwyer is equally a man who ignores one woman for another. Although his childhood sweetheart, Rosa (Cyd Charisse), has waited years for him to return home from the war, he quickly discards her when he sees Jessie. When Rosa tries to regain her self-confidence by declaring to Dwyer that she could make any man take an interest in her, Dwyer fixes her up with a date with another man. Dwyer and the film completely abandon her at this point. Dwyer and Brandon Bourne are then both characters who flee a certain fe-

male principle of homey devotion, attracted by something different. With the doubling of the two men, the film also doubles the
women and so can imply a potential inadequacy of traditions of
romance and marriage.

   "Six years ago, I committed a crime against society . . .
I married a man" (*The Unfaithful*, 1947). Verging on explicit declaration, feminine discontent in the forties can insist itself through
commentary on the fate of women: Emma Bovary's continued
expressions of discontent, Ellen's disparaging comments on pregnancy in *Leave Her to Heaven*, Ann Sutton's unleashing of invective
in *Whirlpool* against the husband who wasn't emotionally available
to give her the mental support and help she so needed. On the
one hand, films will frequently try to recontain the woman's
feeling by prescribing it as hysterical, by showing it as leading (or
as having led) to dangerous consequences (Emma Bovary ruins
her family; Ellen aborts her baby; Ann becomes a kleptomaniac).
And yet, on the other hand, moments of the films suggest a certain
rightness to the woman's charges: thus, in *Whirlpool*, the psychiatrist instantly abandons his wife when she is suspected (wrongly)
of murder; Charles Bovary cannot at all comprehend his wife's
romantic dreams; and Richard in *Leave Her to Heaven* never understands his wife's desires for time together without family
around. Again, some of the changes that *Madame Bovary* undergoes
in coming to the screen seem significant: many of the changes
work to make Charles even less of an agent than he is in the book,
turning him instead into an extreme mark of a stupid passivity.
All of Charles' past is eliminated, thereby making him less of a
full character in his own right. Similarly, the failed operation on
Hypollite, the club-footed man, is changed into Charles' sudden
decision not to operate at all; such a change turns Charles from a
failed actor to a nonactor. Moreover, the *style indirect libre* that in
the novel allows point of view to move freely between various
characters and so makes Emma's story only one among several is
reduced in the film to a point of view that, except for the opening
and closing frames, stays close to Emma. For example, in many
shots, Charles is a small figure in the background, seen through
doorways, glimpsed in his office. The moments in which the

camera approaches Charles and leaves Emma are moments in which he has no control: for example, his drunken inability to mix with the guests at the Vaubeyssard ball or his furtive tearing down of a "For Sale" sign that will soon be put back up again. Even with the framing by Flaubert's trial, most of *Madame Bovary* works resolutely to become Emma's story. Indeed even the title loses one of the ironic senses it had in the novel where it referred as much to Charles' mother as to Emma; here in the film, there is only one Madame Bovary trying to live her own desire.

The Vaubeyssard ball is further significant for its mise-en-scène in which a gliding, whirling camera movement establishes a structure of feeling—to borrow a phrase from Raymond Williams—that stands in a certain contrast to the narrative *economy* of classic narrative's forward drive. Indeed, the contrast is explicit in a match cut from Charles drunkenly smashing his wine glass on the floor to the tinkling of crystal chandeliers as dancing women sweep past them with outstretched fans. The men engage in punctual actions while women engage in movements of endearing lightness. Again, a change from the novel seems significant; in the novel, Emma rests between dances and observes a count who, according to the gossip going around the room, was once a lover of Marie Antoinette. The spectacle of the ball, then, exists in relation to specific stories of romance and adventure. In the film, on the other hand, the dancing goes on and on without interruption: narrative is diffused into a paroxysm of unnarrativized sights and sounds, or of sights and sounds that quickly exceed narrative development (for example, Emma's declaration that she can't breathe in such a stuffy room leads to a montage of windows being smashed in). Significantly, it is not the end of a tune that naturally brings the music to an end, but, rather, Charles' blundering onto the dance floor to try to dance with his wife. Spectacle and story separate and enter into conflict—spectacle here is a space of feeling opposed to the vulgar and disruptive story of male endeavor. This is not to suggest, though, that the film promotes spectacle as a sufficient way of being. Much of the "tragedy" of the film comes from the fact that Emma has to live in an empirical time. The seemingly endless whirl of the ball comes to an end and lives on only as the impossible memory of a lyrical nontemporality that Emma will never be able to retrieve. Against the inadequacy of a static memory, temporality will be the force of a forward-moving history that will crush Emma and drive her on to suicide. The end of the film—Charles forced into poverty and riding out of town—will rob death even of any grandeur of transcendence.

Men's time, women's time, enter into a nonsynchrony in so many films of the forties. There seems to be no single space in which all desires can come together in permanent and euphoric triumph. Indeed, the split that I have referred to in previous chapters between investigators and criminals, between cold rationalists and emotional rebels, suggests an inability of desire and middle-class propriety to condense in simple figures.

For example, the opening of *This Gun for Hire* shows Raven as a figure of conflicting narrative powers; on the one hand, he is the figure that the narrative begins with, and while the possible confluence of Raven and the spectator is further amplified by Raven's interest in a kitten, his immediate aggression toward women and children runs against that confluence and sets up a multiplicity of positions. Crane's insertion into the story might serve as a stabilizing force, a recentering of identification, but Crane is rarely presented as a figure of narrative agency, someone to relay narrative progression through: rather, he is emphasized as the figure who lacks agency, the figure around whom other people and forces act (for example, the train that separates him from Ellen; Raven's own ability to separate the young couple). *This Gun for Hire* shows narrative as a fragmentation: significantly, this fragmentation can only be solved by loss—by Raven's death—the elimination of the film's initiating narrative figure (just as *Citizen Kane* gives us Kane at the beginning only to immediately remove him from the narrative present). *This Gun for Hire* ends with a man and woman together, but, for a certain desire that drives the narrative, it is the wrong man and woman. Victory here is marked as compromise, an acceptance of renunciation but an acceptance that is tinged with regret—an acceptance that much of the film runs against. If Crane can't have Ellen for much of the film, Raven gets to stay a whole night with her. The sense of the ending is a forced sense, one that suggests its own insufficiency.

If the narrative structure of affirmation allows for a propitious (if ultimately unstable) solution of the problems of narrative asynchrony, so much of forties cinema stages the impossibility of such a solution: spiritual redemption through the forces of domesticity—through the imposition of a domestic space—is unavailable in an America for whom innocence is becoming a mark of a vanished past: "You know, love has ruined more business than the Sherman Antitrust law" (*Neptune's Daughter*, 1946). Desire becomes in the forties a force outside the economy of controlled production and narrativity. For example, against a text like Kitching's *Sex Problems of the Returned Vet* which, in its attempt to lock desire into a structure of postwar commitment, will declare that "masturbation is an incomplete and immature form of sexual activity," the Kinsey Report will declare confidently that "sex is a normal function acceptable in whatever form it is manifested." The report naturalizes sexuality. Indeed, the postwar importance of the Kinsey Report will lie less in any accuracy of its reporting of a sexualization of America than in the seriousness with which it is regarded by that America (indeed, so forceful will be the effect of the Kinsey Report that the president of Vassar will claim that college students are turning to sex just to make sure they meet the averages of sexual activity listed in the report). Giving statistical recognition to adolescent sexuality, homosexuality, extramarital sexuality, the Kinsey Report offers a sexualized image of America even to those critics who would want to deny the extent of sexuality.[24]

(The challenge to a traditional image of sexuality sublimated into spirituality leads to a new representation of both sublimation and sexuality alike.) On the one hand, renunciation of sexual desire becomes ever more intense, as if to suggest that any avowal of desire would exceed the bonds of sublimation: hence, a whole series of films in which religious figures (fathers and nuns especially) face a desire that they ultimately realize must be closed off to them: for example, *The Bells of St. Mary's, Come to*

the Stable, and, especially, *Winter Meeting,* where a budding relationship between a spoiled socialite (Bette Davis) and a would-be
priest (Jim Davis) is resolved by his decision to renounce romance
and her decision to reestablish her broken contact with her
mother. On the other hand, by rational norms, sexuality itself
becomes all the more extreme, entering a perverse register untouched by the demands of oedipalization; hence, an interest in
incest (James Cain's novel *The Butterfly)* and intensely fixated par-
ent-child relations (for example, *White Heat, Leave Her to Heaven* or
Christmas Holiday, where the narrator tells us about Robert Manette
[Gene Kelly] that "Robert's relations with his mother were pathological. . . . He wasn't just her son, he was . . . her everything");
a linking up of romance and a hot-blooded exoticism (hence, a
new acceptance of the positive image of the Latin or South Am-
rican lover as in *Neptune's Daughter,* which ends with the American
businessman losing the woman [Esther Williams] to a South
American [Ricardo Montalban] and conceding, "The boy got the
girl, the girl got the boy, I got the business. . . . South America,
take it away!"); infantile attachment (for example, *Claudia,* with
its title character refusing to admit adult responsibility); homosexuality;[25] a morbidity verging on necrophilia (in Waldo's words
to Laura describing Mark's love for her, "When you were unat-
tainable, when you were dead, he wanted you most"); a fascination with explicit Freudian symbolism (for example, in *Gun
Crazy,* there is a running association of weaponry and virility,
reaching one climax in a montage that cuts from Laurie and Bart
going to bed (finishing their relationship "on the level" as she
puts it) to a gumball machine shot to bits in a paroxysm of violence); and, most especially, the sense that ordinary life itself has
become the site of a new, calculating sexual enticement (told that
she's swell, the middle-class Alice in *The Cat People* replies, "That's
what makes me dangerous. I'm the new type of other woman").
     The 1950 film *Born To Be Bad* even suggests that the
mythic division of American woman into two exclusive camps—
good girl and bad girl, mother and whore—is inadequate to a new
situation in which sexuality is no longer automatically assumed
to be in the camp of the bad. The scheming adventuress (Joan

Fontaine) may first operate in contrast to the nice girl (Joan Leslie) whose wealthy fiancé is seduced away by the adventuress. That the millionaire finally returns to the nice girl can seem to suggest the strength of that "feminine mystique" of domesticity and innocent, unquestioning devotion to a man no matter how errant he may be. But the film suggests the possibility and even justifiability of a third identity for women: that of a guileless but energetic sexuality. Against the schemes of the adventuress and the devotions of the wife, there is the acceptable option of lover, as the adventuress discovers (even if she finally rejects it) when she enters into a passionate and steamy relationship (explicitly referred to as a "sex thing") with a vibrant, earthy novelist (Robert Ryan). There is no condemnation here; quite the contrary, the adventuress is wrong only when she rejects earthiness for a cold rationality that sublimates sexual desire into the most pragmatic of economic calculations (as when the adventuress gets out of sleeping with her millionaire husband by keeping her time busy with all sorts of philanthropic committees and organizations).

Similarly, a 1949 film, *Mother is a Freshman*, draws a distinction between the love of girls and of women, acknowledging that the latter may have a sexual wisdom and maturity that no longer follows the needs of oedipal progression. Like the wartime films, *Mother is a Freshman* argues that girlish love is a kind of puppy love, driven not by conscious desire but by all sorts of unconscious determinisms that mean that what one believes is love are really impulses being applied to the wrong object or in the wrong context. Indeed, *Mother is a Freshman*'s college professor will explain one of his student's infatuation for him through a long speech that is nothing so much as a dissection of oedipalism: he argues that the young girl is really transferring to him the love that she felt for her father which was itself only a transfer from her earliest emotional dependencies. Unlike the war films, though, *Mother is a Freshman* will then go on to assume that the answer to puppy love is fully expressed adult love, not the sublimation of all loves in committed duty. Arguing that oedipalism is a determination by the past, the film proposes to go beyond Oedipus to a realm where women who have already known sexuality—the widowed heroine of the film's title, for example—can follow through on their desire in a self-determined way.

"Marital hazards beset U.S. domestic life as postwar nation goes back to abnormal" (caption to two page photo spread in *Life*, January 1, 1946). To be sure, there will be endless attempts to renormalize sexuality in the forties—to suggest that sexualization is at most a temporary aberration that a firm reestablishing of sexual roles will help dissipate. Hence, as a number of writers have analyzed it, there is the rise in postwar America especially of a "feminine mystique," a whole barrage of discourse that argues woman's necessary social and biological place in the home. A graduation address to Smith College women by Adlai Stevenson can well sum up the bluntness of this discourse. "I think there is much you can do about our crisis in the humble role of housewife. I could wish you no better than that." And yet the narratives of the moment frequently register such "normalization" as a problem, even as a dismal compromise.

The interruptions in *This Gun for Hire* that pull upright Michael Crane away from Ellen and push the psychotic killer, Raven, toward her suggest a nonsynchrony in which desire and domesticity can find no easy meeting ground. Indeed, *This Gun for Hire* can suggest more generally a problem of desire in narrative. Desire is to be the target of sublimation but it is also something to be encouraged, itself an object and cause of further desire. Film narrative only partially controls a spiraling, mounting energy—narrative difference is here not a violence but a spectacular seduction.

Indeed, if musicals have seemed so typically a Hollywood art, this is not so much because they inevitably move a couple toward the finality of an ostensible productivity of an adult middle-class heterosexuality but because they propel characters toward an endless nonfinality, the spectacle as literally a show-stopper. Even a thriller like *This Gun for Hire* can be run through by spectacle: here not simply the spectacle of thrilling actions but, literally, the world of show—the song-and-dance numbers that

Ellen (Veronica Lake) performs during the film. Spectacle here is a force that combats the fall into narrative, the propulsion toward acceptance of position.

More generally, we might suggest that the forties represent a discourse of the richness of objects. Not just a discourse *on* such a richness but *of*; that is, discourse will present itself as a wonderful commodity, a vast open display of possibilities. For example, the development of advertising that cultural historians have analyzed for previous decades achieves a particularly intense amplification in the forties: an elegant, bursting parade of commodities. *Life* magazine in the forties is a visual explosion: articles and even news photos compete with color ads that entice not only through their particular contents but rather through a whole rhetoric of promise and display (such as direct address and objects that seem to leap off the page). Even during the war when certain products are pulled from the market, advertising continues its investment in visual richness and perhaps even intensifies it: the promise of the product, the ostensible referent, makes the ad all the more a show, the promise of a reality in which the promise takes over reality and becomes itself a kind of commodity. Similarly, to take another case, the mass market book becomes the site of a sort of split between display and reference: the forties will be the first big period of the low-priced omnipresent paperback and the rise of paperback cover art.[26] Where an established company like Penguin will simply advertise its books generically by stark covers with a different color for each genre, for many other companies the cover will become the place for a kind of show—dramatic images that often have only the meagerest of connections to the story inside. Moreover, the covers will form among themselves their own network of exchanges and allusions: as Piet Schreuders has noted in *Paperback, U.S.A.*, successful covers will be reworked again and again to different ends.

The forties can seem an intense moment in the development of what some sociologists have termed "The Society of the Spectacle," the possibility in late-capitalist production of a certain separation of commodities from reference to a use and even perhaps from a stable system of exchange values and, instead, their constitution as sources of show: not, that is, the show of meanings, but a kind of display for the sake of display.[27] Objects lose any necessary connection to a utility and become the possible elements of a vast permutation, commodities no longer as signifiers even but as an interweaving network of play. In Jean Baudrillard's words, "Symbolic values efface themselves behind organisational values."[28] Forties ads for kitchens, for example, talk as frequently of the possibility for endless variation and rearrangement of kitchen "utilities" as of the utility of such "utilities"—a possibility where, in Baudrillard's terms, "value resides not in appropriation or in intimacy, but in information, invention, control" (p. 30).

Mass culture here becomes a sort of postmodern culture, the stability of social meaning dissolved into one vast, spectacular *combinatoire*, a dissociation of cause and effect, a concentration on the allure of means and a concomitant disinterest in ends. Such spectacle creates the promise of a rich sight, not the sight of particular things per se, but sight itself as richness, as the possibility of experience. This "vocation of the perceptual" (as Fredric Jameson calls it in describing a historically earlier moment) works to divorce reference from sense and sensation or to make reference be no more than a vague support for an instantaneity of perception. Yet, as Jameson notes, this spectacle is not somehow a "pure" escape from the commodity, but a further confirmation of its power: "The very activity of sense perception has nowhere to go in a world in which science deals with ideal quantities. . . . This unused surplus capacity of sense perception can only reorganize itself into a new and semi-autonomous activity, one which produces its own specific objects that are themselves the result of a process of abstraction and reification."[29]

Jameson, however, may be here overemphasizing even the semi-autonomy of the spectacular moment.[30] Jameson tends to see spectacle as a refuge from the pragmatics of productive capitalism. In contrast, I would suggest that the power of spectacle comes from its ability to turn back onto other moments of the social totality and infuse them with the qualities of spectacle. Thus, in the forties, science is a functioning practice, but it is also a commodity, reported on in the mass media, converted into an image: Einstein, for example, becomes a cultural value and a value moreover that is not necessarily tied to his functions as scientist; indeed, "Einstein" will become a richness of elements—the wild hair, the eccentricity, a mathematical formula—all of which can be worked and reworked for different effects in different moments of popular discourse. Science here becomes not meaning, but the possibility of show.

In the advertisement, science, politics, work, will all become elements in display, elements that achieve a kind of synthesis in the advertisement of the commodity as a mediation of the social totality: the ad becomes a place of equivalence and exchange, a network through which values pass and become spectacular. Thus, for example, labor as everyday spectacle: "Notice how [with a Crosley Kitchen] my work flows along just like a war assembly plant" (*Life*, August 13, 1945). Thus, science as commodity, the commodity as science: "Take the T-zone test. The T-zone—taste and throat is your own laboratory" (Camel cigarettes ad, *Life*, January 7, 1946). In this spectacle, science itself will leave the stuffy confines of the laboratory and become a force of everyday life: one article in *Life* (August 20, 1945) reports glowingly on the wartime ability of engineers to construct entirely new towns in the United States (in this case, for atom bomb researchers and workers). In this world of a vast spectacle of production, even social events become only one more element in a show, in that kind of aestheticizing flow that Raymond Williams has analyzed for television[31] Here, the advertisement creates a flow between elements, a flow that culminates in the notion of the world as endless promise, rich possibility, a spectacle everywhere. For example, one issue of *Life* (January 14, 1946) moves from a reportage on "starving, ill Chinese children" (pp. 40–41) to the confident assertion (by Vicks) that "today, relieving miseries of children's colds is not the problem it used to be" (p. 71) to an article on vacations that announces that "the whole world will be used as a *playground*" (p. 79; my emphasis).

"Unlike 1937's abortive market boom which was a

professional boom for the benefit of professionals, this is a boom for everybody" (*Life*, January 7, 1946). The spectacle of the forties revels in possibility, in a world of endlessly operating, spectacular gadgets, of life itself as a parade of new sights, new perceptions. Moreover, discourse will present such experiences as easily and readily available; the forties are, on the one hand, the promise of endless loans (the G.I. education bill; the G.I. housing loans) and, on the other hand, of endless credit—the magic, for example, of possession without the necessity for immediate payment—the instantaneity of pleasure, the renunciation of renunciation.

Of course, the tendency toward spectacle—for example, the freeing of perception from the bounds of obedience to story and storytelling requirements—has always been a tendency of cinema. The forties are in one sense merely a continuation of a process: for example, the continuation with the rise of B movies and double features in the thirties of film-going as a rich experience: features, shorts, cartoons, all becoming equally part of a show. Indeed, the show can take priority over story as even the very act of entering the cinema—crossing the display-filled lobby of the movie palace—becomes itself a kind of spectacle.

And yet the forties are not only a continuation of spectacle; they are its intensification. As much as it continues telling stories, the forties cinema exists also as an affirmation and self-demonstration of itself as form, presenting itself as endless product, the film experience as rich commodity. First, there is an increased investment in techniques and possibilities of display: for example, technicolor, gliding camera movement (the exploitation of the crab dolly), all culminating in something like the 1950 movie-promotion campaign, "Movies are *bigger* and better than ever." Technicolor specifically, for example, is a technique caught between storytelling possibilities and the possibilities of display for display's sake. While somewhat approximative of profilmic colors, Technicolor will also brighten colors and de-emphasize shades, making of each object a visual block of radiant color. The display of color will become a kind of goal of films, a kind of liberation of formal qualities from representational ones. Color will take off from the story, from any simple contribution to narrative possibility, and become instead the possibility of the showing off of form for the sake of showing off form.

⌐   Similarly, the musical will enact the notion of a show that disavows or even attacks the need for story. The musical here becomes a sort of reversal of the representational project of classic narrative: form exists here not to tell a story, but, quite the contrary, the story can become a mere pretext of spectacle, a kind of alibi, what the Russian Formalists summed up in their notion of art as *device*—that is, art's use of certain subject matters not for their meanings, but for their ability to allow a maximum of formal possibilities.[32] Hence, the use of show plots in musicals as a way of bringing in show numbers. Of course, such formalism is already part of the thirties musical, the sheer theatrical unstageability of so many of the numbers in the let's-put-on-a-show musicals serving as a mark of these films' disinterest in verisimilitude. But, in the thirties, the particular moments of spectacle are generally still bound—even if loosely—to a narrative progression; significantly, the ending of many musicals is not a number but a *narrative* event: for example, the concretization of the couple, the affirmation of the characters as "people in love" and not merely as performers.

In the forties spectacle, the story seems to matter less than the possibility of what Dennis Giles has termed "the permanent show," a spectaclization of story that does not make a final return to the narrative world. Story here exists as a way of leading to a show that will forever suspend the engendering story.[33]

For example, in its opening action, the 1950 film *Summer Stock* establishes itself as in a turning point between story and spectacle. On the one hand, the enunciation itself is one geared not to story but to the instantaneity of spectacle. After the credit sequence, the camera tracks across a farmyard and then cranes up to a window that shows Jane Falbury (Judy Garland) in the shower. An opening based on display: within the frame formed by the window, the woman is here a show, an evident spectacle. Moreover, the song that Jane is singing is itself about show—"If you feel like singing, sing"—and at moments becomes pure form with lyrics like "Tra la la la la." Here, before the story proper has begun, the story is already encountering an antinarrative force: spectacle as nonprogressing show, spectacle as the utility only of demonstration, a kind of closed circuit of pleasure (thus, Jane will sing to her mirror image). Significantly, the interaction of character and actress here will also create a kind of antinarrative. Thus, the song stands as an ironic and deconstructing counterpart to Jane's later narrativized actions: her expressions of anger at show people, her declarations that the pleasure of spectacle matters less than the responsibilities of a productive farm life, are all made ironic by our first sight of her as a sort of show person. Similarly, the very use of Judy Garland would seem to run against the role of farm woman: as entertainer, Garland will be expected to sing and dance; moreover, a kind of intertextual operation will maintain a sense of Garland as the person who, in *The Wizard of Oz*, set up the world of fantasy and play precisely as an alternative to farm work. The elements of the opening, then, work together to overdetermine from the start the superiority of spectacle over the story of farm struggle.

To be sure the next scene would seem to reinvest *Summer Stock* intensely in the telling of a story. Jane's two hired hands quit, and she realizes that she will have to run the farm on her own. She decides she needs a tractor, and the simultaneous nervousness and resolve with which she goes to the Wingate store to ask for a tractor seems to set up the action as a central moment of what Barthes calls the hermeneutic code, the structuring of narrative according to dominant enigmas: here, will Jane get her tractor? Will Jane be able to make a go of her farm? Yet the film de-emphasizes the first enigma—Mr. Wingate almost immediately agrees to let Jane have a tractor on credit, and spectacle begins again (Jane drives her tractor home, singing "Howdy neighbor, happy harvest"). And Jane's arrival back at the farm— where she discovers an "invasion" by show people—will begin the complete suspension of the second question. Significantly, from this moment on, the tractor can begin to lose its value in the narrative as an aid to the resolution of the initial narrative issue. Accidentally destroyed by the show people, the tractor will first be a mark of Jane's dislike for a life of spectacle, and would thus seem to throw her back all the more onto the initial questions of the narrative (now converted into the question "What will Jane do now that she is once again tractor-less?"). But the head entertainer, Joe Ross (Gene Kelly), will sell his car to buy Jane a new tractor, and this action will cause Jane to discover suddenly the glimmerings of an admiration for such people as Joe. Yet, significantly, this moment of exchange (of tractor for car, of admiration for hatred) becomes the moment for complete suspension of the farm plot: Jane has her tractor once again but it is never referred to again (and even though the film includes several shots of the farmyard, it is never seen again).

Even more significant, no aspect of Jane's farm narrative is shown again: not so much abandoned as ignored, the initial narrative line drops out to give way to the putting on of a show. Significantly, the end number of the film replays the earlier images of farm life but now enframed: onstage, in front of painted backdrops, Jane and Joe together sing "Howdy neighbor, happy harvest." But the neighbors are no longer farmers at work, but now the audience for a spectacle. Similarly, the harvest is no longer the harvesting of crops but the success of the show; as Joe had explained earlier, the success of the play would lead to its being put on Broadway for a long run. The harvest here will be part of a path toward wealth: as the lyrics explain, "We're gonna roll in plenty. Spend a five, a ten, or twenty." What started as the independence of farm life becomes inscribed within a spectacle form offered up as endless bounty. Such an offer is moreover represented in the temporal unfolding of the film as the presentation of one number after another, as the end of the film gives itself over (with some interruptions by the story) to the presentation of spectacles from Joe's play. Moreover, though Joe had earlier described the play as a "story," the numbers that are presented have little link (other than the fact that they are all numbers in the same show), little sense as part of a single story.

The musical here serves as a kind of chain of performance, a moving on- and offscreen of one spectacle after another. Indeed, story can even give way to a parade, as emphasized by the title of the 1948 musical *Easter Parade*. If *Summer Stock* begins in a tension between story and spectacle, *Easter Parade* seems to emphasize the intensity of spectacle's triumph: the beginning of the film only faintly makes use of a narrative line as we see Don Hewes (Fred Astaire) engage in a process of spectacular accumulation and spectacular display. The very opening scene of the film, for example, shows Hewes buying items of clothing, but the motives behind such actions are submerged beneath the ways the actions encourage a display of dynamic visual options: for example, in a dress shop, woman after woman comes forward modeling an outfit (and picking up the lyrics of the opening song, "Happy Easter"). Here plot gives way to a fetish of sight, the visits to the store become an excuse on the film's part for a spectacular specularity. Significantly, the number ends not with any sort of emergence of story, but with a continuation of spectacle in a second number: entering a last store, Hewes turns the items in that store into the props for a demonstration of dance. Only after this second number does a story proper begin, but it is quickly derailed: Hewes meets his partner, Nadine Hale (Ann Miller), but she immediately announces her desire to go into a show on her own, and Hewes has to go out to find another partner, a need that becomes the source of a next number (Hewes ends up at a restaurant where a group of chorus girls including Hannah Brown— Judy Garland—are performing). Hannah and Hewes will form the possibility of a certain story—the formation of a couple—but that story is held within the limits of an emphasis on spectacle: for example, song and dance numbers separated from the narrative development. Moreover, the story is one that leads to the dispersion of story within the space of a "permanent show." The narrative trajectory, man and woman joining together, becomes part of an interest in display—especially Hannah's desire to walk along the avenue in the Easter Parade and show herself off—and the last shot of the film will show Hannah and Hewes disappearing in the immense spectacle of a crowd whose milling about fills the bottom of the screen. The couple cedes its story to a vaster display.

The "permanent show" suggests that in spectacle it is not so much a couple that is formed but, at most, a performing team. The moment of show brings male and female together, but this moment is a moment outside the forward propulsion of time, outside the impulse of a domestic desire that drives oedipal narrative along. Indeed, desires for specific objects or partners are precisely what the spectacle works against: in the words of Serafin speaking to Manuela in *The Pirate*, "You don't have to love me to be in the troupe. You don't have to love me but it helps." Love becomes not a necessary center but a useful accessory at best. This is not to say that romance isn't a concern of spectacle but merely to suggest that the couple becomes part of a less object-bound energy: as Hewes claims in *Easter Parade*, he could make *any* woman into a stage star. In a sense, the desire for woman increases, but such desire is increasingly displaced from an oedipal desire into an asexual one: the fetish of bodies for their interchangeable parts. Significantly, when specifically object-bound desires occur, they are often desires for abstract qualities related to spectacle (for example, the desire to march in the Easter Parade, or the desire to play a particular theater, such as the Palace, in *For Me and My Gal*). Or they are desires limited to lesser characters in the film or limited to early attitudes in a character who hasn't yet discovered the qualities of spectacle.

For example, in *Summer Stock* and *Easter Parade*, the musical heroes are juxtaposed against rival males who are either opposed to spectacle (Orville Wingate in *Summer Stock*, who doesn't have a single song or dance number in the film) or only peripherally connected to its world (Jonathan Harris III [Peter Lawford] in *Easter Parade*). It is in such characters that the musicals invest *narrative* development: thus, in *Summer Stock*, it is Orville, not Joe, who goes through the most dramatic changes, who is most in rivalry with a father figure, and who most explicitly announces a desire to control narrative development. Yet such narrative force is displaced, deferred, minimized, put on hold. For example, Jonathan Harris in *Easter Parade* will literally have to wait on the telephone when Hannah sees Hewes at the door. Harris' last action—telephoning with an air of resignation to Nadine to ask her if she is free for dinner—is a kind of summation of the ways that *Easter Parade* makes the narrative of sexual desire secondary. Harris' successful call here doubles his unsuccessful one to Hannah but shows romantic success to be a sort of begrudged compromise. Similarly, Orville's declaration of power actually gives him little power—Jane refuses to listen to him and Esme, the housekeeper, threatens to end their friendship if he tries to stop the show—and Orville ends up finally with a compromise love (Jane's sister, Abigail) and, moreover, even only ends up with Abigail because she has accidentally knocked him out and so rendered him helpless.

And yet, if, as I've tried to suggest, the forties suggest the breakdown of a univocal symbolic meaning through a rendering ambiguous of narrative space, time, agency, etc., spectacle doesn't so much offer a transcendence of breakdown as a confirmation of the intensity of that breakdown. That is, the art of forties spectacle is not an innocently redemptive art; the musical, for example, as some sort of efficient reconstruction of aura in an age of materialism. Quite the contrary, spectacle confirms the materialism of the modern age and renders it attractive or seductive.[34] But the seduction is an endlessly deceptive one. Spectacle works not by the delivery of that which it promises, but by the endless making of promises that are not always kept. In the musical, for example, the endless parading on- and offscreen of spectacular sights can encourage a certain sense of loss, the notion that no image can stay eternally in place. There is a tragedy in musicals: the tragedy of an art whose most spectacular moments are always moving into the past.

Furthermore, the limitations of spectacle as redemptive art become the explicit subjects of other genres. Thus, in the melodrama or in *film noir*, the full or spectacular moment is held up as incomplete, transitory, even impossible. For example, in *Letter from an Unknown Woman*, the spectacular moment is what the characters precisely cannot possess fully: Stefan cannot have his successful musical career, and the ostensible richness of cinematic spectacle itself is unveiled in Lisa and Stefan's visit to a stationary train behind which are projected mock-images of travel. The full, transcendental image is an impossible image, as Stefan himself realizes when, on the morning of his death, he finally remembers what Lisa looked like: as Tania Modleski has pointed out, in *Letter from an Unknown Woman*, accession to the order of respectability is viewed with regret and even fear (for example, in taking up the demands of Viennese society, Stefan is taking up death).[35] Lisa's fleeting image can pinpoint the fragile status of the cinematic image as representation: a fullness ultimately based on absence—the twenty-four frames per second that create an impression of motion—the cinema is not a natural image, but a construction of sight through the mechanical intercession of technology.

Some films even seem to acknowledge such a constructedness at pivotal moments where the film hesitates between creation of a story and a fall into loss. For example, the fade into unconsciousness in scenes where a detective is knocked out *(Murder, My Sweet)* not only shows a loss of consciousness but a momentary loss of cinema itself; the *fade-out* in *White Cargo* when Tondelayo first presents herself signals the danger around which the representation of this woman pivots: Tondelayo as both the object of sight but also as a kind of threat to sight. Similarly, the openings of films can suggest a kind of search by the cinematic apparatus for a possible grounding in representation: for example, the first-person fade-in that opens *Somewhere in the Night* echoes its character's rise to consciousness with a parallel rise on the spectator's part; in the credit sequence in *Guest in the House* (1944), the alternation of light and dark in various rooms can serve as a metaphor of cinema itself, and suggest its grounding in an artificiality. If, as Jean-Louis Baudry and Christian Metz have suggested, a power of cinema lies in its embodiment of the promise of a transcendental vision, the opening moments of many films imply that film may only deliver on such a promise vaguely; the fall into story is a fall into a stability always threatened by anxiety.

Moreover, music itself can, in nonmusicals, become not a redemptive path to a romantic fullness but a moment of virtually analytic self-reflexivity, the cinema's investigation of its own powers and potentials. If, in the belief of a certain aesthetic idealism, music would be the condition toward which art ideally aspires, cinematic representation of music actually can suggest the inadequacy or impossibility of such aspiration. Music first becomes the mark of dream, of a fantasy unrealizable in any possibly existing realm: for example, in the forties play *Death of a Salesman*, music is either the unnarrativized flute playing at the play's opening and unheard by Willy Loman; or, in contrast, it is the raucous music of the nightclub where Willy's sons abandon him in their pursuit of women just when they are supposed to be wining and dining him. Indeed, music can turn into the sign not of transcendence but precisely of immanence, a reassertion of inescapable materiality. In *Phantom Lady*, (1944) Kansas' descent away from the happiness of romance into the lowlife of rough sexuality will center in one scene around the carnal effects of music: her attempt to seduce the drummer, Cliff, into revealing withheld information becomes a kind of grotesque carnival of the flesh, as a jazz jam session becomes the place of a weird, dangerous energy. Similarly, music can become the sign of unconscious obsessions: George Gershwin driving himself to death in *Rhapsody in Blue* (1945) or Joe Bascom (Lou Costello) in *Mexican Hayride* (1948) finding that the playing of Mexican music sends his body off into uncontrollable spasms. As obsessive return of the repressed, music can, then, become a mark of an insistent and incessant disruption of human projects—a mark even of death: for example, the horror music that precedes each murder and each act of voyeurism in *The Spiral Staircase;* the punctuating wail of an ambulance siren that the deathly ill Rick Martin hears as a perfect trumpet note in *Young Man with a Horn* (1950); the party in *D.O.A.* that draws Frank Bigelow away from a telephone call with his girlfriend and entices him to the nightclub where, while listening to hot jazz, he will be fatally poisoned; the fantasies of Alfred de Carter (Rex Harrison) in *Unfaithfully Yours*, who, during a symphony, imagines ways to kill his wife.

The control of spectacle can thus all too easily become a loss of control. Significantly, for Baudrillard, such a loss is an inevitable part of the process of commodification: for Baudrillard, production is a unidirectional, nonreversible process that is run through with the threat of its own collapse. While we might want to disavow the predictive validity of Baudrillard's theory as the description of process that he assumes will automatically lead to the collapse of Western representation, it does seem that the representation of spectacle and commodification is an ambivalent one. For example, in the forties, the optimistic discourse of richness will as frequently be matched by a representation of richness as a vertiginous chaos, a disruptive force. Indeed, if as a number of scholars have suggested, the forties show many of the intense signs of what will come to be our modern, informational, telecommunicational society (see, for example, Marvin Harris' *America Now: The Anthropology of a Changing Culture* [1981]), the narratives of the forties already represent the complexities of a society that is caught between the production of things and the production of meanings. Against Jacques Lacan's confident sense of the symbolic order of culture as a force so much in place that communication is always effective—"A letter always arrives at its destination"[36]— we might suggest that in the forties, the surety of a system of communication and the values it is based on and supports seem often in question. Lacan's declaration can seem more appropriate for a rationalist age in which each meaning takes its univocal sense from a single, fixed, stable force (for Lacan, the phallus as signifier). As Sartre notes in his analysis of the fantastic, much of the horrific uncanniness of a new fantastic art of everyday life derives from its disturbance of systems of communicated meaning; uncannily anticipating Lacan's argument. Sartre suggests that horror can come from a letter that reaches its destination but reaches it wrongly. For example, in the forties, there is the letter that hurts (the notice of Robert's death in *Mr. Roberts*), the letter that has too many destinations *(Letter to Three Wives)*, the letter that arrives too late *(Letter from an Unknown Woman)*, the letter that kills *(The Letter)*. It is perhaps not inappropriate that one forties image of a fate that controls and turns one's projects into nothingness is the metaphoric postman who always rings twice in the film and book of that name.

Ultimately, in an age of information and commodification, objects become subjects, and humans become objects, mere supports of an absurd system that deals with them in a mechanical, arbitrary way. If, for Lacan, the force of the social system may lie oedipally in a Law of the Father, in contrast, in an age of spectacle, force lies in law of the commodity, a fetish of production that circulates through the social realm.[37] In Bob Hope's book *So This Is Peace* (1946), for example, much of the discussion revolves around Hope's sense of the postwar world as a place where, at every level from the minute of everyday life to the intensity of international endeavor, technology will decide human destiny. Hope's book is a kind of montage which contrasts accounts of his wartime tours (where he is a human agent, alone responsible for the success or failure of his gags) to the postwar world where agency has no place: "Please excuse references to the European and Pacific Theaters of Operation. They may be the last of their kind that any actor gets to play. The next war won't last long enough for us to get packed."

To be sure, narratives will still confidently try to tell strong stories of strong will. For example, like the Nash car's "Road of Mystery" or like *Uncertain Glory's* road that's "come to the right ending," the late forties film *Paid in Full* uses the image of the road to suggest the possibility for confusion to end, for the accomplishment of a perspective of confident knowledge: when the man she loves (but who's married her sister) comes to complain about his wife, Jane (Lisabeth Scott) will confidently reply, "You said you and Nancy turned off on one of those side streets, the lights few and far between but, look, sooner or later, every side street turns back into a street where the lights are bright as far as you can see." Jane's teleology binds the future into a necessity radiant with all the plenitude of full romance. And, indeed, even the title resonates with a fullness, suggesting an exchange that is complete and final. And yet, in an informational age marked by a free-floating spectaclization of everyday life, the strong narrative reveals perhaps its ultimate weaknesses, its ties to *fictions* of power and its underpinning by loss and death.

Thus, in *Paid in Full,* Jane can only bring Bill (Robert Cummings) and her sister (Diana Lynn) back together by paying *with her life;* knowing that childbirth is fatal in her family, Jane marries the divorced Bill so she can give Bill and Nancy the child they so need in their marriage and, then, she dies. A full exchange leaves out something—the couple forms on the basis of a loss. A last-image close-up of the new baby suddenly has superimposed over it an image of the dying Jane; if Nancy and Bill's road has brought them back together, the road that Jane travels (as in the opening, first-person images of a dying Jane arriving by car at the hospital) can only end in death. The superimposition of the two images at the end suggests, then, the irreducibility of the two narrative lines—their inability to become one. Every narrative has its other side, its other scene. What I have tried to suggest in the previous pages is nothing else but the force and fascination of this other scene.

Notes

Introduction

1. John Morton Blum, *V Was for Victory: Politics and American Culture During World War II* (New York: Harcourt Brace Jovanovich, 1976), pp. 64–70.

2. Michel Foucault, *Discipline and Punish: The Birth of the Prison*, Alan Sheridan-Smith, tr. (New York: Pantheon, 1977).

3. See "Human Nature: Justice Versus Power," in Fons Elder, ed., *Reflexive Water: The Basic Concerns of Mankind* (London: Souvenir Press, 1974), p. 150.

4. Hence, a certain problem with Foucault's last work—especialy vols. 2 and 3 of the *History of Sexuality*. Acknowledging the necessity to theorize the place of subjectivity within a theory of social discourse, Foucault goes on to theorize that subjectivity as a mere effect or result of particular discourses. That is, in these texts at least, Foucault seems to assume that by studying discourses that intended to prescribe behavior, one can get a full sense of the subjectivity of those social subjects addressed by the discourses. He assumes that the discourses effectively accomplish what they set out to do. There is no discussion of resistance or the possibility that any particular sexual discourse may have appeared as only one discursive choice among many. Thus, Foucault can go on to read prescriptive discourse (for example, manuals on sexuality), while bracketing out, or while assuming to be already answered, the question of the effects of such prescription on individual subjects. Far more intriguing to my mind is a study like *Discipline and Punish* which suggests both a conflict *within* official discourses of prescription (for example, different theories of incarceration) and *between* official discourses and all sorts of popular opposition and protest—a certain refusal by subjects of their prescription within dominant discourses.

5. Many studies today discuss this phenomenon. See, for example, Sheila Tobias and Lisa Anderson, "What Really Happened to Rosie the Riveter?: Demobilization and the Female Labor Force, 1944–1947," M.S.S. Modular Publications #9, 1974.

6. See Macherey's review-essay of P. F. Moreau, *Le récit utopique,* in *Revue internationale de philosophie* (October 1983), nos. 144–45, pp. 228–38; and "Histoire et roman dans *Les paysans* de Balzac," in C. Duchet, ed., *Sociocritique,* pp. 137–46 (Paris: Nathan, 1979).

7. Juliet Mitchell, *Psychoanalysis and Feminism* (London: Allen Lane, 1974).

8. See Luce Irigaray, *Speculum of the Other Woman,* Gillian G. Gill, tr. (Ithaca: Cornell University Press, 1985).

9. Carl Freedman, "Towards a Theory of Paranoia: The Science Fiction of Philip K. Dick," *Science-Fiction Studies,* (March 1984), 11(1): 17. Freedman's essay makes some particularly interesting suggestions about a political utilization of the psychoanalytic theory of paranoia elaborated by Jacques Lacan.

10. Michael Renov, "The State, Ideology, and *Priorities on Parade,*" *Film Reader* (1982), no. 5, p. 218.

11. Sylvia Harvey, "Woman's Place: The Absent Family of Film Noir," *Women in Film Noir,* E. Ann Kaplan, ed. (London: British Film Institute, 1978), p. 22.

12. See Dana Polan, "Dark Passages and Blind Insights: The Problem of Placement in Forties Film," *The Velvet Light Trap* (Summer 1983), 20: 27–33.

13. A. J. Greimas, *Sémantique structurale* (Paris: Larousse, 1966).

14. See Fredric Jameson, *The Political Unconscious: Narrative as a Socially Symbolic Act* (Ithaca: Cornell University Press, 1981); and applications of the Greimasian model in such studies of his as *Fables of Aggression: Wyndham Lewis, The Modernist as Fascist* (Berkeley and Los Angeles: University of California Press, 1979); and "After Armageddon: Character Systems in *Dr. Bloodmoney,*" *Science-Fiction Studies* (March 1975), 2(1): 31–42.

15. Fredric Jameson, "Metacommentary," *P.M.L.A.* (January 1971), 86(1): 9.

16. Rosalind Krauss provides another example of this procedure, again using Greimas, in "Sculpture in the Expanded Field," in Hal Foster, ed., *The Anti-Aesthetic: Essays on Postmodern Culture,* pp.39–50 (Port Townsend, Wash: Bay Press, 1983). Krauss suggests that the modernist theory of sculpture worked from an initial set of ideas about sculpture and a controlled combination of those ideas in such a way that postmodern sculptural forms could find no place in theoretical discourse and so were roundly dismissed by critics. Krauss employs the Greimasian rectangle to bring about a different combination of initial terms and show the possibilities for a new discourse on postmodernism. Krauss' projection thus shows the ties of ideology and logic, of the ways that they mutually interweave to enable or disable certain social or cultural possibilities.

1. Writing the Space of the Forties

1. Mikhail Bakhtin, "Discourse in the Novel," *The Dialogic Imagination,* Caryl Emerson and Michael Holquist, tr. (Austin: University of Texas Press, 1982), 259–422.

2. Roland Barthes, *S/Z,* Richard Miller, tr. (New York: Hill and Wang, 1974).

3. See Frank Kermode, *The Sense of an Ending: Studies in the Theory of Fiction* (New York: Oxford University Press, 1966).

4. See Raymond Bellour, "Symboliques," in Bellour, ed., *Le cinéma américain: analyses de film,* pp. 173–99 (Paris: Flammarion, 1980); and Daniel Dayan, *Western Graffiti:*

Jeux d'images et programmation du spectateur dans "La chevauchée fantastique" de John Ford (Paris: Clancier-Guenaud, 1984).

5. Stanley Cavell, *Pursuits of Happiness: The Hollywood Comedy of Remarriage* (Cambridge: Harvard University Press, 1981).

6. For a reading of the narrative importance of *Detour,* see Tania Modleski, "Film Theory's Detour," *Screen* (November-December 1982), 23(5): 72–79.

7. See, for example, Barry Salt, *Film Style and Technology: History and Analysis* (London: Starword, 1983).

8. Janet Staiger, *The Hollywood Mode of Production: The Construction of Divided Labor in the Film Industry,* Ph.D. thesis, University of Wisconsin, Madison, 1981. More recently, in *The Classical Hollywood Cinema: Mode of Production and Film Style to 1960* (New York: Columbia University Press, 1985), Staiger has joined with neo-formalists David Bordwell and Kristin Thompson to analyze in depth the interweavings of film style and film industry. The authors expertly demonstrate how there was a Hollywood discourse— in journals, in manuals, in the precepts of trade organizations—that worked to impose the regularities of Hollywood representational paradigms. But I think that we also need to theorize the possibility of a slippage between the discourse and its actualization in specific historical moments; in particular, as these pages will imply, the psycho-social situation of the forties poses problems to narrative in ways that narrative can't always fully contend with.

9. See Marie-Claire Ropars (with Pierre Sorlin and Michele Lagny), "Analyse filmique d'un ensemble extensible," in Jacques Aumont and Jean-Louis Leutrat, eds., *Théorie du film,* pp. 132–64 (Paris: Albatros, 1980).

10. Ropars, Lagny, and Sorlin, "Le récit saisi par le film," *Hors-Cadre* (Spring 1984), no. 2, pp. 99–121.

11. See for example, the essays collected as "Archives, Document, Fiction: Film Before 1907" in *Iris* (1984), vol. 2, no. 1.

12. See, especially, Raymond Williams' *Problems in Materialism and Culture* (New York and London: Verso/Schocken, 1981).

13. My point here is inspired by Jean Baudrillard's similar analysis of the theorization of power in his *Oublier Foucault* (Paris: Galilée, 1977). For Baudrillard, the rhetorical strategies by which Foucault announces ostensible subversions of power only to then argue how these subversions actually extend power become in Foucault's writing extensions of power themselves. In other words, Baudrillard argues that Foucault's overriding emphasis on the effectivity of power, with little more than vague reference to the possibilities of resistance to power, can actually help the continuation of power. In particular, Foucault can make one believe that things are bad in ways one had not even dared to imagine; this can easily encourage defeatism or the idealist hope that systems will change simply through purely aleatory, noninitiated, nontheorized reversals.

It is interesting to note that Bellour is aware of the choice between classicism and anticlassicism. In an interview, he notes how Roland Barthes' narrative analysis encourages a search for a potential free play beyond the constraints of codification, while Lévi-Strauss' mythological analysis encourages a search for precisely the logic of constraint. Bellour announces his decision to follow the Lévi-Straussian option. See Raymond Bellour, "Alternation, Segmentation, Hypnosis: An Interview with Janet Bergstrom," *Camera Obscura* (1979), no. 3/4, p. 75.

14. Jonathan Culler, "The Uses of *Madame Bovary,*" *Diacritics* (Fall 1981), 11(3):74–81.

15. Jeffrey Mehlman, *Revolution and Repetition: Marx/Hugo/Balzac* (Berkeley and Los Angeles: University of California Press, 1977), p. 22.

16. Pierre Macherey, *Pour une théorie de la production littéraire* (Paris: Maspero, 1966); translated by Geoffrey Wall as *A Theory of Literary Production* (London and Boston: Routledge and Kegan Paul, 1978).

17. For an attempt to open up the Machereyan model, see Terry Eagleton, *Criticism and Ideology* (London: Verso Books, 1976). As a number of critics have noted, however, Eagleton's analysis is not without its own share of potential essentialism.

18. Pierre Macherey, "Queneau, scribe et lecteur de Kojève," *Europe* (June-July 1983), no. 650, pp. 82–91.

19. Paul Hirst, *On Law and Ideology* (London: Methuen, 1979).

20. For readings of histories of wartime ideology, see Alan Clive, *State of War: Michigan in World War II* (Ann Arbor: University of Michigan Press, 1979), pp. 2–6; and Paul A. C. Koistinen, "Warfare and Power Relations in America: Mobilizing the World War II Economy," paper presented at the Tenth Military History Symposium (GPO, forthcoming).

21. Richard Polenberg, *One Nation Divisible: Class, Race, and Ethnicity in the United States Since 1938* (New York: Viking Press, 1980), p. 46.

22. George Lipsitz, *Class and Culture in Cold War America: ''A Rainbow at Midnight''* (New York: Praeger, 1981).

23. The critical literature on forties imperialism is vast. For one analysis that specifically examines wartime plans for postwar expansion, see Henry Jackson Lowe, *The Planning and Negotiation of U.S. Postwar Security, 1942–1943,* Ph.D. thesis, University of Virginia, 1972.

24. See Nelson Lichtenstein, *Labor's War at Home: The C.I.O. in World War II* (Cambridge, Eng.: Cambridge University Press, 1983).

25. See, for example, the chapter on "Models of Womanhood in the Popular Culture" in Susan M. Hartmann's *The Home-Front and Beyond* (Boston: Twayne, 1982), pp. 189–208. James Heath notes in an article on the historiography of the forties that most historians have been unable to see the domestic scene as anything other than the site of an increase in the role of federal government; the rise of bureaucracies; the interaction of science and technology. Culture can only be ignored or misconstrued in such a context. See Heath, "Domestic America During World War II: Research Opportunities for Historians," *The Journal of American History* (September 1971), 58 (2):384–414.

26. Michel Foucault, *L'usage des plaisirs* and *Le souci de soi* (Paris: Gallimard, 1984).

27. Peter Filene, *Him/Her/Self: Sex Roles in Modern America* (New York: Harcourt Brace Jovanovich, 1974).

2. Wartime Unity: The Representation of Institutions and the Institutions of Representation

1. Records of the Office of War Information, Box 177, Record Group 204, National Archives, Suitland, Maryland. All references to O.W.I. material are to this collection.

2. Archie Satterfield, *The Home Front: An Oral History of the War Years in America, 1941–1945* (Chicago: Playboy Press, 1981), p. 3.

3. John Morton Blum, *V Was for Victory: Politics and American Culture During*

World War II (New York: Harcourt Brace Jovanovich, 1976), p. 67. The whole section pp. 64–70 functions as a kind of catalogue of the narrative raw material that the war narrative draws upon. Following his necessitarian framework, Blum argues that the mobilization of images of the past prohibited any possibility for Americans to tell stories of a new and possibly different future.

    4. There is a copy of "Small Town, U.S.A." in the library archives of the United States Information Agency. I wish to thank the staff of the agency for allowing me to consult this document.

    5. It may not be inappropriate to note that labor historians like Nelson Lichtenstein have suggested that the Automobile Worker's Union was the hardest hit by labor strife during the Second World War. See Lichtenstein's *Labor's War at Home: The C.I.O. in World War II* (Cambridge: Cambridge University Press, 1983).

    6. Here the naturalization may strain the limits of its own logic. First, the whole booklet has emphasized the specifically *American* aspects of Alexandria; there is a potential dissonance between what Alexandrians and people of other countries are fighting for. Second, there is the suggestion that equality is not an automatic, inevitable, and always already given aspect of town life. Rather, equality appears as no more than something that occurs *in response* to wartime dangers. Like the Reverend Mr. Cummings' famous wartime declaration, "There are no atheists in foxholes," there is possible the sense that the normal situation before or after war is a situation of chaos and corruption. Here, I want only to note such potential tensions; the straining of war logic will be the subject of the following chapter.

    7. Walter Benjamin, *Charles Baudelaire: A Lyric Poet in the Era of High Capitalism*, Harry Zohn, tr. (London: New Left Books, 1973), pp. 40–55.

    8. See, especially, Emile Benveniste, "L'homme dans la langue," *Problémes de linguistique générale* (Paris: Gallimard, 1966), 1:225–85.

    9. Roland Barthes, "Analyse Textuelle d'un conte d'Edgar Poe," in Claude Chabrol, ed., *Sémiotique narrative et textuelle* (Paris: Larousse, 1973).

    10. See, for example, Vincent Descombes, *L'inconscient malgré lui* (Paris: Minuit, 1977). Descombes applies enunciation theory to suggest the markers of history and sociality in the supposedly neutral discourses of science.

    11. For extended discussion of the limits of the ideology/deconstruction equation, see D. N. Rodowick, *The Political Avant-Garde: Modernism and Epistemology in Post-'68 Film Theory*, Ph.D. thesis, University of Iowa, 1983.

    12. For a study of propaganda's self-constitution in an agonic and adversarial position, see Marc Angenot, *La parole pamphlétaire: typologie des discours modernes* (Paris: Payot, 1983). The operations of such a position in wartime propaganda are perhaps epitomized in the documentary work and theory of John Grierson in Canada during the war. For Grierson, the masses seemed most characterized by their vulnerability to miseducation: hence, the need for the propagandist not to show but to refuse to do nothing more than show—to refuse to leave meanings open and uninterpreted by an authoritative perspective. On this aspect of propaganda, see Gary Evans, *John Grierson and the National Film Board* (Toronto: University of Toronto Press, 1985).

    13. There are many studies of the O.W.I. Blum presents an overview of the agency's history in *V Was for Victory*, pp. 21–31 (a chapter entitled "Truth as a Handicap"). For more detailed histories, see Allan M. Winkler, *The Politics of Propaganda: The Office of War Information, 1942–1945* (New Haven: Yale University Press, 1978); Charles D. Lloyd, *American Society and Values in World War II from the Publications of the Office of War Information,*

Ph.D. thesis, Georgetown University, 1975; Gregory Black and Clayton R. Koppes, "The O.W.I. Goes to War: The Bureau of Intelligence's Criticism of Hollywood, 1942–1943," *Prologue: The Review of the National Archives*, (1974), 6:44–59; and Black and Koppes, "What To Show the World: The Office of War Information and Hollywood, 1942–1945," *Journal of American History* (June 1977), 54 (3):87–105.

14. Susan Suleiman, *Authoritarian Fictions: The Ideological Novel as Literary Genre* (New York: Columbia University Press, 1983).

15. See Robert Fyne's Ph.D. thesis, *Hollywood Fights a War*, New York University, 1976.

16. Fredric Jameson, *The Political Unconscious: Narrative as a Socially Symbolic Act* (Ithaca: Cornell University Press, 1981), p. 13.

17. Evelyn Steele, *Wartime Opportunities for Women* (New York: Dutton, 1943), p. 73.

18. See, especially, the essays "Narrative Space" and "Film, System, Narrative," in Stephen Heath's *Questions of Cinema* (Bloomington: Indiana University Press, 1981).

19. Heath, "Film, System, Narrative," p. 136.

20. The practice of representing Pearl Harbor as the end of one story and the beginning of another continues after the war. In the words of a postwar article that quotes a wife's story of her soldier-husband's war history, "After a hard struggle up the ladder to success he felt in 1941 that his dreams were coming true; the fine building that housed his automobile agency was all but paid for, and comfort and ease were almost in our grasp. Then came Pearl Harbor and the order that stopped the selling of cars and tires." Quoted in Ann G. Norelius, "War Casualties of the Home Front," *Hygeia* (August 1946), 28:584.

21. Probably most extreme in this respect is a film made late in the war, *The Master Race* (1944), which so has a faith in the writable future that it imagines a postwar world and chronicles the discovery of a Nazi plot in that world.

22. See Roland Barthes, *S/Z*, Richard Miller, tr. (New York: Hill and Wang, 1974).

23. Jean-Paul Sartre, "Du groupe à l'histoire," *Critique de la raison dialectique, vol. 1, Théorie des ensembles pratiques* (Paris: Gallimard, 1960), pp. 381–755.

24. Richard Polenberg, *War and Society: The United States, 1941–1945* (New York: Lippincott, 1972), p. 2.

25. The English translator renders this as "the pledge," but there is a necessary religious connotation to Sartre's word choice, suggesting not so much an individual initiative ("I pledge") as a kind of transcending force that descends upon the group, often without agency.

26. Colin Shindler, *Hollywood Goes to War: Films and American Society, 1939–1952* (London: Routledge and Kegan Paul, 1979), p. 9.

27. Christian Metz, "Story/Discourse (A Note on Two Kinds of Voyeurism)," *The Imaginary Signifier*, Celia Britton and Anwyl Williams, tr. (Bloomington: Indiana University Press, 1982), pp. 89–98.

28. Dana Polan, "A Brechtian Cinema?: Towards a Politics of Self-Reflexive Film," forthcoming in Bill Nichols, ed., *Movies and Methods*, vol. 2. (Berkeley and Los Angeles: University of California Press).

29. On the rewriting of generic codes (with specific reference to the gangster film) for new narrational situations, see Gregory Lukow and Steven Ricci, "The 'Audience' Goes 'Public': Inter-Textuality, Genre, and the Responsibilities of Film Literacy," *On Film* (Spring 1984), no. 12, pp. 29–36. To a large degree, the wartime films are simply picking up on a general mythology of the Nazi, one even encouraged by the government. In the

words of an O.W.I. radio show, "Our Enemy the Nazis" (January 12, 1943), "Nazism is the biggest, boldest example of legalized gangsterism the world has ever known."

30. See, especially, Raymond Bellour, "Hitchcock, the Enunciator," Bertrand Augst and Hilary Radner, tr. *Camera Obscura* (Fall 1977), no. 2, pp. 67–87.

31. I'll return to this point in the next chapter, suggesting that the war film can become caught in a tension between competing goals of narrativity.

32. David Hull, "Central Subjects and Historical Narratives," *History and Theory* (1975), 14(3):255.

33. On Roosevelt's battle with illness as a narrative of conquest that becomes part of public discourse, see Blum, *V Was for Victory*, pp. 246–47. But for the ways that the official discourse framed and minimized the illness, see the chapter on "The Best-Kept Secret" in A. A. Hoehling, *Home Front, U.S.A.* (New York: Crowell, 1966), pp. 137–51.

34. See, for example, Peter Roffman and Jim Purdy, *The Hollywood Social Problem Film: Madness, Despair, and Politics from the Depression to the Fifties* (Bloomington: Indiana University Press, 1981), p. 130.

35. In his notes to the published screenplay of *Mission to Moscow*, David Culbert discusses this: "Roosevelt did not usually permit impersonations of himself or of his voice on radio or in films. As a special concession, the White House granted an exception with the proviso that the actor remain off-camera." See Culbert, ed., *Mission to Moscow* (Madison: University of Wisconsin Press, 1980), p. 228.

36. Carolyn Ware, *The Consumer Goes to War: A Guide to Victory on the Home-Front* (New York: Funk and Wagnalls, 1942), p. 262.

37. Mauldin chronicles some of this debate in this autobiography, *The Brass Ring* (New York: Norton, 1971).

38. Office of War Information, *Battle Stations for All: The Story of the Fight To Control Living Costs* (Washington, D.C.: GPO, 1943) p. 85.

39. See also the chapter on people who are "Forty Plus" but can greatly help the war, in Shelby Cullom Davis, *Your Career in Defense* (New York: Harper, 1942), pp. 76–83.

40. On the team role in the combat film, see Kathryn Kane, *Critical Analysis of the World War II Combat Films, 1942–1945*, Ph.D. thesis, University of Iowa, 1976.

41. Myron Fagan *Red Treason in Hollywood* (Los Angeles: Cinema Education Guild, 1949), p. 5.

42. Katherine Archibald, *Wartime Shipyard: A Study in Social Disunity* (Berkeley and Los Angeles: University of California Press, 1947). The ways in which the working class could well become the scape-goat for an American populism that wanted to see itself as above issues of class is well represented in the story treatment for *Destination: Tokyo* (Box 20, Delmer Daves collection, Stanford University). In the unity-encouraging space of their submarine where everyone accepts his place in a system of hierarchies, the sailors were to hear with outrage the following broadcast: "There is little news from the fighting fronts today, but here at home 55,000 men of the Carney Corporation East Jersey plant went on strike this morning for $2.00 a day higher wages. Despite the fact that the parts manufactured by this company are essential [to the war effort], J. L. Millis, spokesman for the union, stated, 'Our men will not give up their rights as Americans to bargain collectively, war or no war.' Millis made his statement from his suite in the swank Sherry Netherlands hotel."

43. Richard Polenberg, *One Nation Divisible: Class, Race, and Ethnicity in the United States Since 1938* (New York: Viking Press, 1980), pp. 101–5.

44. For example, in a later (1950s) war film, *Attack!*, Lieutenant Costa (Jack

Palance) has all the qualities of the wartime sergeant: a brute force (but also a native intelligence), a love for his men (but also an ability to readily make them put themselves in danger when need be).

45. Since I originally wrote this section, Susan Suleiman has come out with *Authoritarian Fictions: The Ideological Novel as Literary Genre,* which has a useful discussion of the function of conversion in propaganda novels.

46. In noting the synchrony here, I don't mean to suggest any direct influence of existentialism on America or vice versa but, rather, no more than the sharing of parallel situations: faced with a moment that threatens sheer contingency, two countries come up with similar philosophies of narrative and commitment. For more specific points of comparison, see Steven G. Kellman, "Everybody Comes to Roquentin's," *Mosaic* (Winter-Spring 1983), 16(1–2):103–12.

47. See, for example, Bruce Catton's *The War Lords of Washington* (New York: Harcourt, Brace, 1948).

48. Nell Giles, *Punch In, Susie!: A Woman's War Factory Diary* (New York: Harper, 1942–43), p. 29.

49. John Berger, *Ways of Seeing* (New York: Viking, 1973), p. 46.

50. This area is explored in great depth in Michael Renov's Ph.D. dissertation, *Hollywood's Wartime Woman: A Study of Historical/Ideological Determination,* University of California, Los Angeles, 1982.

51. Howard Kitching, *Sex Problems of the Returned Vet* (Verplanck, N.Y.: Emerson Books, 1946), p. 26.

52. Portland Shipyard company newspaper, quoted in Karen Beck Skold, *Women Workers and Child Care During World War II: A Case Study of the Portland, Oregon, Shipyards,* Ph.D. thesis, University of Oregon, 1981, p. 69.

53. Keith Ayling, *Calling All Women* (New York: Harper, 1942).

54. Quoted in Frank W. Fox, *Madison Avenue Goes to War: The Strange Military Career of American Advertising, 1941–1945* (Salt Lake City: Brigham Young University Press, 1975), p. 62.

55. Quoted in Joan Ellen Trey, "Women in the War Economy," *Review of Radical Political Economics* (Summer 1972), 4(3):50.

56. Such a tactic is significant in the ways that it can suggest limits to the ostensible newfound power of women in the war. Against William Chafe's famous argument in *The American Woman: Her Changing Social, Economic, and Political Roles, 1920–1970* (New York: Oxford University Press, 1972) of war as a moment of new possibility for the American woman, recent revisionist historians have emphasized both how economic progress for women was not all that great and how economic progress was only infrequently matched by social or cultural concessions on the part of men. In this respect, it is interesting to find a warning as early as 1942 of women's new power. "The men had better beware, when they return home after the emergency, for they will find stern competition in the factories, fields and offices" (Davis, *Your Career in Defense,* p. 98). For a representative example of the revisionist critique of Chafe, see D'Ann Campbell, *Wives, Workers, and Womanhood: America During World War II,* Ph.D. thesis, University of North Carolina, Chapel Hill, 1979.

57. Quoted in Eleanor Straub's Ph.D. thesis, *United States Government Policy Toward Civilian Women,* Emory University, 1973, pp. 17–8.

58. Quoted in Fox, *Madison Avenue Goes to war,* p. 80.

59. Quoted in Fox, p. 80.

60. In *The Hollywood Social Problem Film*, Peter Roffman and Jim Purdy read *Pride of the Marines* as part of a group of films based on an optimism about *postwar* reconversion. I am treating it here as a film of the war out of a wish to not draw too sharp a line between films about the war struggle and films about immediate postwar problems; the two overlap and feed into each other. As I have tried to suggest, part of the quality of the war discourse is its ability to make claims about the future, a representation of peace. Indeed, if the war discourse suggests the interchangeability of home front and war front, so too it implies an interchangeability of war story and postwar story. For Roffman and Purdy's argument, see *The Hollywood Social Problem Film*, pp.229–30.

61. Tania Modleski, *Loving with a Vengeance: Mass-Produced Fantasies for Women* (New York: Archon Books, 1982), pp. 85–109.

62. A number of Bellour's texts deal with narrative rhyming; two in particular connect the rhyming to the narrative function of vehicles: "Le blocage symbolique" and "Système d'un fragment" in *L'analyse du film* (Paris: Albatros, 1979), pp. 131–246 and 81–122 respectively.

63. On the role of the "true" woman in forties film, see Serafina Bathrick, *The True Woman and the Family Film: The Industrial Production of Memory*, Ph.D. thesis, University of Wisconsin, Madison, 1981. The description of Ruth in the film's treatment is also explicit about Ruth as the "true woman:" "She is the sort of girl who 'steadies' her man, and who becomes a rock for him to lean upon. If the truth were told, behind most successful men of all classes in America there are women . . . who have one thing in common with Ruth: her quality of character. The men who marry the Ruths of this world frequently don't realize it but they are getting the best of the bargain." The treatment for *Pride of the Marines* can be found in Box 25 of the Delmer Daves collection, Stanford University.

64. See, especially, Raymond Bellour, "Un jour, la castration," *L'Arc* (1978), no. 71, pp. 21–41.

3. Narrative Limits: The Fiction of War and the War of Fictions

1. Raymond Bellour, "Alternation, Segmentation, Hypnosis," *Camera Obscura* (1979), 3–4:88.

2. Paul de Man, *Blindness and Insight: Essays in the Rhetoric of Contemporary Criticism* (New York: Oxford University Press, 1971).

3. The political and ideological limitations of an essentially logical reading become pronounced in de Man's analysis (in *Allegories of Reading*) of the story in Rousseau's *Confessions* of Marie's ribbon. Rousseau had stolen a ribbon from his employers, but when interrogated, he had imputed the guilt to a servant girl, Marie, who was subsequently fired and who, so Rousseau imagines, probably had to become a prostitute to get by. For de Man, it was not so much Rousseau's imputation *but* the reading by Rousseau's employers of the imputation as a referential statement that was at fault. That is, if the employers had simply understood Rousseau's declaration to be a mere case of textuality with no claim on reality, then everything would have been fine. What's left over in such an analysis is Marie herself, victim of a real power that may well be rooted in a referential reduction of language but that has a dangerous power nonetheless. De Man, *Allegories of Reading: Figural Language in Rousseau, Nietzsche, Rilke, and Proust* (New Haven: Yale University Press, 1979), pp. 278–301.

4. On such romanticism, see Stephen Heath, "Contexts," *Questions of Cinema*

(Bloomington: Indiana University Press, 1981), pp. 236–45. Nonetheless, as Phil Rosen well points out in a critique of post-structuralist critiques of agency and teleology, there may be a *provisional political expediency* in thinking of a social group as a subject or agent of history. See Rosen, "Subject Formation and Social Formation: Issues and Hypotheses," in Stephen Heath and Pat Mellencamp, eds., *Cinema and Language*, pp. 168–79 (Baltimore: University Publishers, 1983).

5. Gyorg Lukács, *History and Class Consciousness: Studies in Marxist Dialectics*, Rodney Livingstone, tr. (Cambridge: MIT Press, 1971).

6. Michel Foucault, ed., *I, Pierre Rivière*, Frank Jellinek, tr. (Lincoln: University of Nebraska Press, 1982).

7. Alvin Gouldner, *The Dialectics of Ideology and Technology: The Origins, Grammar, and Future of Ideology* (New York: Oxford University Press, 1982).

8. See, for example, Henry M. Barry's *I'll Be Seeing You* (New York: Knopf, 1952), which summarizes anecdotally much of this discourse.

9. See, especially, the discussion in Raymond Bellour, "Le blocage symbolique," *L'analyse du film* (Paris: Albatros, 1979), of the rivalry of Roger Thornhill and Philip Van Damm over Eve Kendall in *North by Northwest* (1959).

10. John Austin, *How To Do Things with Words*, rev. ed. (Cambridge: Harvard University Press, 1975). In referring to Austin, I don't at all intend any support of speech-act theory. Quite the contrary, I am intrigued by the ways this theory's image of communication meets up with certain conceits of film narrative. I argue the interest of this complementariness of two forms of discourse in my essay "The Infelicity of Ideology: Speech-Act Theory and American Cinema in the 1940's," *Iris* (Fall 1985) 3(1):35–44.

11. Constance Bowman, *Slacks and Callouses* (New York: Longman, Green, 1944), p.100.

See, among other studies, Nelson Lichtenstein, "Auto Worker Militancy and the Structure of Factory Life, 1937–1955," *Journal of American History* (September 1980), 67(2):335–54; and his book *Labor's War at Home* (Cambridge, Eng.: Cambridge University Press, 1983).

12. Nell Giles, *Punch In, Susie!: A Woman's War Factory Diary* (New York: Harper, 1942–43), p. 36.

13. Ironically, this kind of enclosing of the protest within dominant limits continues even today. Thus, A. A. Hoehling's *Home Front, U.S.A.* describes the zoot-suit phenomenon as an aberration of an unbearable sort: "The zoot-suiters were undoubtedly the most preposterous of all who defied law and order. At best, as one pundit observed, they were 'not characterized primarily by intellect.' . . . Their targets for physical harm were members of the armed forces, with a special predilection for sailors. The latter fought back with devastating spirit."

14. Dick Hebdige, *Sub-Culture: The Meaning of Style* (New York: Methuen, 1979). For analysis of the zoot suit as stylistic statement, see Stuart Cosgrove, "The Zoot Suit and Style Warfare," *History Workshop* (Autumn 1984), 18:77–92. As Cosgrove notes, the zoot suit was such an outrage that Senator Jack Tunney claimed it was actually a weapon of America's enemies and asked for investigation by the Senate Un-American Activities Committee.

15. George Lipsitz, *Class and Culture in Cold War America: "A Rainbow at Midnight,"* (New York: Praeger, 1981) p. 27.

16. Margaret Mead, "The Women in the War," in Jack Goodman, ed., *While You Were Gone*, pp. 274–89 (New York: Simon and Schuster, 1946).

17. Howard Kitching, *Sex Problems of the Returned Vet* (Verplanck, N.Y.: Emerson Books, 1946), p. 94.

18. Zbynek Zeman, *Selling the War: Art and Propaganda in World War II* (New York: Exeter Books, 1982), p. 109.

19. The best study of this is Eleanor Straub's Ph.D. thesis, *Government Policy Toward Civilian Women During World War II,* Emory University, 1973.

20. See Leila Rupp, "The Survival of American Feminism: The Woman's Movement in Postwar America," in Robert Bremner and Gary Reichard, eds. *Reshaping America: Society and Institutions, 1945–1960,* pp. 33–68 (Columbus: Ohio University Press, 1983).

21. Quoted in Charles D. Lloyd, *American Society and Values in World War II,* Ph.D. thesis, Georgetown University, 1975, p. 246.

22. Jane Gaines, *Popular Icon as Commodity and Sign: The Circulation of Betty Grable,* Ph.D. thesis, Northwestern University, 1982, p. 364.

23. Paul Koistinen, "Warfare and Power Relations in America," forthcoming from GPO.

24. Frank W. Fox, *Madison Avenue Goes to War: The Strange Military Career of American Advertising, 1941–1945* (Salt Lake City: Brigham Young University Press, 1975), p. 70.

25. See William M. Leary, "Books, Soldiers, and Censorship During the Second World War," *American Quarterly* (Summer 1968), 20(2):237–45.

26. Ed Lowry (Southern Methodist University), "Propaganda as History: Capra's *Prelude to War,*" unpublished essay.

27. See, for example, Mary Ann Doane, "*Gilda:* Epistemology as Striptease," *Camera Obscura* (1983), 11:7–27.

28. Alfred Appel, Jr., *Signs of Life* (New York: Knopf, 1983).

29. I examine *Manhunt* in greater depth in my article "*Manhunt:* Ideological Reversibility and War-time Representation," forthcoming in *Enclitic.*

30. Odile Bächler, "*Manhunt,* Film Hunt," *thèse de maitrise,* Université de la Nouvelle Sorbonne, 1982. My analysis is greatly indebted to Bächler's detailed study of this film.

31. See Jacqueline Rose, "Paranoia and the Film System," *Screen* (Winter 1976–77), 17(4):85–104.

32. Jean-Louis Comolli and François Géré, "Two Fictions Concerning Hate," Tom Milne, tr., in Stephen Jenkins, ed., *Fritz Lang: The Image and the Look* (London: British Film Institute, 1981), p. 129.

33. For Leo Braudy, see *The World in a Frame: What We See in Films* (New York: Doubleday, 1977). But for a breakthrough antihumanist reading of the Renoir image, see Noël Burch, "*Nana,* or The Two Kinds of Space," in *Theory of Film Practice* (New York: Praeger, 1973), pp. 17–31.

34. And even the casting of Sanders in the role encourages an ambiguation of the figure. Indeed, in his December 22, 1942, *New York Times* review of another film, *Quiet Please, Murder* (1942), in which Sanders plays a Nazi, Bosley Crowther expresses surprise: "George Sanders is cast, very queerly, as the villain." Alternating between the Falcon and Favell, Sanders is a mark of narrative ambiguity for forties film.

35. Raymond Bellour, "Ségmenter, analyser," *L'analyse du film* (Paris: Albatros, 1979), pp. 247–70.

36. Bellour, "Le blocage symbolique," pp. 160–232 especially.

37. Susan Suleiman, *Authoritarian Fictions: The Ideological Novel as Literary Genre,* (New York: Columbia University Press, 1983), pp. 206–33.

38. And as I've noted, it seems further to do so through the very choice of George Sanders for the role of Quive-Smith.

39. See Bächler, "*Manhunt,* Film Hunt," p. 145.

40. Bellour, "Alternation, Segmentation, Hypnosis," p. 97.

41. Reynold Humphries, *Fritz Lang, cinéaste américain* (Paris: Albatros, 1982), p. 10.

42. See, for example, the account by Howard W. Koch in "*Casablanca*": *Script and Legend* (New York: Overlook Press, 1973).

4. Knowledge and Human Interests: Science, Cinema, and the Secularization of Horror

1. Norbert Wiener, *Cybernetics, or Control and Communication in the Animal and the Machine* (New York: Wiley, 1948).

2. See, for example, Jacques Derrida's "Le parergon" in *La vérité en peinture* (Paris: Flammarion, 1978), pp.19–168.

3. Norbert Wiener, "Cybernetics," *Scientific American* (November 1948), 179:15.

4. Julia Kristeva, *Les pouvoirs d'horreur* (Paris: Seuil, 1980). For Kristeva, in other words, the power of horror is the horror of all those experiences that might suggest to the human subject the ultimate nothingness or foundationlessness of all his/her being.

5. Peter Brooks, "Virtue and Terror: *The Monk,*" *E.L.H.* (Summer 1977), 40(2):249–63.

6. Erik Erikson, *Childhood and Society* (New York: Norton, 1950).

7. Tzvetan Todorov, *Introduction à la littérature fantastique* (Paris: Seuil, 1970).

8. Michel Foucault, *The Order of Things: An Archaeology of the Human Sciences* (New York: Random House, 1970), pp. xv–xxiv.

9. For general discussion of the place of cybernetics in Asimov's work, see Patricia Warrick, *The Cybernetic Imagination in Science Fiction* (Cambridge: MIT Press, 1980).

10. For an excellent analysis of the strategy of enunciation in *Now, Voyager,* see Lea Jacobs, "*Now, Voyager:* Some Problems of Enunciation and Sexual Difference," *Camera Obscura* (Spring 1981), 7:89–110.

11. Wiener, *Cybernetics,* p. 191.

12. Similarly, see Claude Shannon and Warren Weaver, *The Mathematical Theory of Communication* (Urbana: University of Illinois Press, 1948). Shannon and Weaver's professed desire to examine only mathematically encodable forms of communication does not prevent them from filling the book with all sorts of general observations.

13. Nadia Khouri and Marc Angenot, "The Discourse of Prehistoric Anthropology: Emergence, Narrative Paradigms, Ideology," *The Minnesota Review* (Fall 1983), 19:119.

14. Carolyn Ware, *The Consumer Goes to War: A Guide to Victory on the Home-Front* (New York: Funk and Wagnalls, 1942), p. 225.

15. John Seeley, *The Americanization of the Unconscious* (New York: International Science Press, 1967).

16. C. P. Oberndorf, *A History of Psychoanalysis in America* (New York: Grune and Stratton, 1953), p. 239.

17. Karen Horney, *Self-Analysis* (New York: Norton, 1942), pp. 17–18.

18. For one expression of this battle, see F. Wertham's critique of criminal psychology in *The Show of Violence* (Garden City, N.Y.: Doubleday, 1949).

19. See Marc Vernet, "Freud: effets spéciaux—Mise-en-scène: USA," *Communications* (1975), 23:223–34.

20. Maureen Turim (SUNY Binghamton), "Psychological Melodrama in the 1940's: *The Locket*," paper presented at the Annual Conference of the Society for Cinema Studies, 1983; forthcoming in *Boundary 2*.

21. See, especially, Mary Ann Doane, "The 'Woman's Film': Possession and Address," in Linda Williams, Mary Ann Doane, and Pat Mellencamp, eds., *Re-visions: Essays in Feminist Film Criticism*, pp. 67–89 (Baltimore: University Publishers, 1984). In an essay published since I originally wrote this chapter, Doane does suggest that some of the medical films represent a sexualization of medical knowledge. See Doane, "The Clinical Eye: Medical Discourse in the 'Woman's Film' of the 1940's," *Poetics Today*, (1985), 6(2):205–227.

22. On Erikson's attempt to write himself into American life, see Steve Welland, "Erikson and America: *Childhood and Society* and National Identity," *American Studies* (Fall 1982), 23(2):5–23.

23. Robin Wood, "The Return of the Repressed," in Wood et al., *The American Nightmare* (Toronto: Festival of Festivals, 1979).

24. Jean-Paul Sartre, "*Aminidab*, ou du fantastique considéré comme un langue," *Situations* (Paris: Gallimard, 1947), 1:154–55.

25. On the ways that *It's a Wonderful Life!* naturalizes the move from a supernatural externality to an internal human psychology, see Brenda Wineapple, "The Production of Character in *It's a Wonderful Life!*" *Film Criticism* (Winter 1981), 5(2):4–11.

26. David H. Fink, *Release from Nervous Tension* (Simon and Schuster, 1943), p. 167.

5. Blind Insights and Dark Passages:
The Problem of Placement

1. The novel motivates this coincidence; Irene had deliberately cultivated Madge's friendship to see if Madge might in fact be a likely suspect for the killing. See David Goodis, *Dark Passage* (New York: Messner, 1946).

2. In saying this, I don't at all intend an acceptance of the existentialist discourse. I am more interested in the ways the films themselves attempt to promote their own existential reading. For a critique of the humanist function of the concept of fate or destiny in film narrative, see Reynold Humphries, *Fritz Lang: cinéaste américain.* (Paris: Albatros, 1982).

3. I owe this observation to Professor John Belton, Cinema, Columbia University. At least one other writer has dealt with the problems of entrapment in *Dark Passage:* in an essay that refers to an earlier version of my discussion here, J. P. Telotte agrees that *Dark Passage* is a paranoid work but argues that it is still a coherent work, organized by the figure of looking and being looked at. I would agree that there is an overriding thematics of sight and nonsight in the film, but suggest that the particular rendition of this thematics makes *Dark Passage* seem strange in relation to what we might typically expect of a Hollywood film. Whether this strangeness has a (non-Hollywood) coherence is another

question. See Telotte, "Seeing in a Dark Passage," *Film Criticism* (Winter 1984–85), 9(2):15–27.

4. See, for example, Susan M. Hartmann, *Truman and the 80th Congress* (Columbia: University of Missouri Press, 1971).

5. Truman's efforts in this respect are chronicled in William E. Leuchtenberg, *In the Shadow of FDR: From Harry Truman to Ronald Reagan* (Ithaca: Cornell University Press, 1983). As Leuchtenberg explains, "Observers did not ask what kind of president Truman was but rather whether he was comparable to F.D.R. In the first months of his presidency, a single question was heard again and again: 'What would F.D.R. do if he were alive?' Increasingly, as the new president failed to measure up to F.D.R., or at least to the heroic F.D.R. as he was remembered, the question became even more bitter" (p. 18).

6. Quoted in Alonzo Hamby, "The Liberals, Truman, and FDR as Symbol and Myth," *Journal of American History* (March 1970), 56(4):859.

7. Jean-François Lyotard, *The Post-Modern Condition: A Report on Knowledge* (Minneapolis: University of Minnesota Press, 1984).

8. See, for example, Teresa de Lauretis, "Desire in Narrative," *Alice Doesn't: Feminism, Semiotics, Cinema* (Bloomington: Indiana University Press, 1984), pp. 103–57.

9. Ernesto Laclau, *Politics and Ideology in Marxist Theory* (New York: Schocken Books, 1977).

10. Mary Ann Doane, "*Gilda:* Epistemology as Strip-Tease," *Camera Obscura* (1983), 11:7–27.

11. Vadimir Propp, *Les racines historiques du conte merveilleux,* Lise Gruel-Apert, tr. (Paris: Gallimard, 1983).

12. My original inspiration for the study of an object's instability *within a text* comes from Jonathan Culler's *Flaubert: The Uses of Uncertainty* (Ithaca: Cornell University Press, 1974). Culler's critique of univocal interpretations of Flaubertian objects—for example, the window in *Madame Bovary*—suggests a way to read the variable textual force of represented objects.

13. Kathryn Kane analyzes this aspect of the film in her Ph.D. thesis, *Critical Analysis of the World War II Combat Films, 1942–1945,* University of Iowa, 1976.

14. For one introduction to *noir's* relation to expressionism, see Foster Hirsch, *The Dark Side of the Screen: Film Noir* (La Jolla, Calif.: Da Capo Press, 1981).

15. Lawrence Alloway, *Violent America: The Movies, 1946–1964* (New York: Museum of Modern Art, 1971).

16. Tania Modleski, "Film Theory's Detour," *Screen* (November-December 1982), 23(5):72–79.

17. Jurij Lotman, "The Origin of Plot in the Light of Typology," *Poetics Today* (Autumn 1979), 1 (1–2):161–84.

18. On the comic nature of this sort of narrativity, see Hayden White's discussion of Hegel in *Metahistory: The Historical Imagination in Nineteenth Century Europe* (Baltimore: John Hopkins University Press, 1974).

19. On the inevitable nonclosure of Hegelian-like narrativity, see Pierre Macherey and Jean-Pierre Lefebvre, *Hegel et la société* (Paris: P.U.F., 1984).

20. See Walter Benjamin, *Charles Baudelaire,* Harry Zohn, tr. (London: New Left Books, 1973).

21. Marc Vernet, "Le transaction filmique," in R. Bellour, ed., *Le cinéma américan,* 2:129 (Paris: Flammarion, 1980).

22. Against notions of the classic cinematic image as offering the plenitude of a full or transcendental image, Charles Affron has argued the possibility of reading a figuration of loss in the images of thirties and forties film. See Affron, *Cinema and Sentiment* (Chicago: University of Chicago Press, 1982).

23. Jack Shadoian, *Dreams and Dead Ends: The American Gangster/Crime Film* (Cambridge: MIT Press, 1977), pp. 342–43.

24. See, especially, Raymond Bellour, "Hitchcock, the Enunciator," *Camera Obscura* (Fall 1977), 3/4:69–89.

25. See, for example, Peter Wollen, "*Citizen Kane,*" *Readings and Writings: Semiotic Counter-Strategies* (New York: Schocken Books, 1982), pp. 49–61.

26. See J. Edgar Hoover (with Courtney Ryley Cooper), "Camps of Crime," *American Magazine* (February 1940), 130:15. For a survey of the cultural image of the motel, see John A. Jakle, "Motels by the Roadside: America's Room for the Night," *Journal of Cultural Geography* (Fall-Winter 1980), 1(1):34–49.

27. In all that follows, I don't mean to imply that it is only in the forties that such a mutation occurs. Quite the contrary, the forties are only a continuation of tendencies that are present in tough-guy or hard-boiled detective fiction from the start. Moreover, we can already find a certain playing around with classicism within the heart of classic detective fiction itself; in the self-reflexive moments of such fiction (each detective's reference to all his literary predecessors) and in the plethora of parodies of such fiction's narrative optimism, we can find a certain awareness of the limits of classic detective narrativity's optimistic logic.

In discussing whether the convoluted films of *film noir* are challenges to Hollywood narrativity or not, David Bordwell (in *The Classical Hollywood Film*) suggests that much of the structure and style of *noir* comes from its inheritance of a tough-guy tradition in literature and other arts in the twenties and thirties. *Noir* takes up already established conventions, no matter how much it modifies them within its own filmic interests. See Bordwell, "The case of *film noir,*" *The Classical Hollywood Film: Film Style and Mode of Production to 1960* (N.Y.: Columbia, 1985), pp. 74–77.

I would generally agree with Bordwell about *noir's* lineage but contend that the borrowing of conventions is not enough to make an artform classical. It certainly may make it find a base in conventions of its own but all art, classical or not, is conventional; indeed, Bordwell's previous work on such directors as Dreyer or Ozu shows them to be engaged in a systematic elaboration of a film language *but* one that has little to do with the classic narrativity of the Hollywood paradigm.

It is necessary to inquire, then, about the kinds of conventions that *noir* picks up from previous traditions. I would argue that these conventions are frequently ones that take a certain distance from those in the paradigmatic range of classic narrativity: hence, a lack of interest in plot as a quest to find truth (Raymond Chandler's famous declaration that the best detective novel would be one that one read even if the last chapter were torn out); consequently, an interest in nonlinear temporalities—writings filled with nonprogressive repetition, digression and disruption of major narrative moves; consequently, too, a sense in the tough-guy fiction of the strong narrative form of classic detective fiction as something to be parodied or dismissed (hence, a novel like Hammett's *Red Harvest* where the detective solves the case he has been assigned to in the first few chapters); an image of the detective not as someone who "writes" the meaning of past events from a position of retrospective security but, quite the contrary, the detective as someone who is directly immersed in events and must either submit to those events, finding that they are "writing" him, or take things into his own hands and understand the present not as a narrative logic but as an open permutational field that one should merely experiment in (as in *Red Harvest* where the detective has no knowledge to gain and simply sets out to see what kind of catalytic function he can have in a town that various factions are warring over). Indeed, in the way that Bordwell's neo-formalism leads him to value strategies of "defamiliarization" in modern art, I would argue that new detective art (both literary and cinematic) can represent a defamiliarizing of the conventions of the action-narrative. Narrative frequently becomes a mere excuse or alibi for an aesthetic play, the detective genre as a kind of "machine" for generating mood or even poetic language with little referential function. Hence, in Hammett, there is a strong emphasis on language for its own sake, a fascination with *argot* and a fetish for a naming that goes on and on (opening line of *Red Harvest*: "I first heard 'Personville' called 'Poisonville' by a red-haired mucker named Hickey Dewey in the Big Ship in Butte"); hence, too, in Hammett, the way an expansive language intrudes into the most sudden of actions to lengthen the time of action into a kind of slow motion deconstruction of the very energies of will and narrative.

28. Steven Marcus discusses this aspect of Hammett's writing in his introduction to *The Continental Op* (New York: Random House, 1974). Of course, *The Maltese Falcon* is a preforties novel. In fact, much of the specific mutation of the detective form that I am referring to derives from the hard-boiled tradition of the twenties and thirties. The forties *films noirs* seem more indebted to the ambiance of this fiction than to the more classical gangster films of the immediate preforties moment.

29. Burton Turkas and Sid Feder, *Murder, Inc.: The Story of "The Syndicate"* (New York: Farrar, Straus and Young, 1951), p. 72.

30. Fredric Jameson well captures the symbolic import of this aspect of Chandler's writing in his essay "On Raymond Chandler," in Glenn W. Most and William W. Stowe, eds., *The Poetics of Murder: Detective Fiction and Literary Theory*, pp. 122–48 (New York: Harcourt Brace Jovanovich, 1983).

31. Willard Waller, *The Veteran Comes Home* (New York: Dryden Press, 1944), p. 13.

32. Benjamin Bowker, *Out of Uniform* (New York: Norton, 1946), p. xi; my emphasis.

33. Richard Tregaskis, "Jim Davis Comes Home," *Saturday Evening Post* (February 9, 1946), p. 106.

6. Beyond Narrative: The Space and Spectacle of the Forties

1. Janey Place and J.L. Petersen, "Some Visual Motifs of Film Noir," *Film Comment*, (1974), 10(1):30–32.

2. See Saim Nalkaya, *The Personalization of a Housing Environment: A Study of Levittown, Pennsylvania*, Ph.D. thesis, University of Pennsylvania, 1980.

3. Henri Lefebvre, *La révolution urbaine* (Paris: Gallimard, 1970).

4. See, for example, Serafina Bathrick's essay on *Meet Me in St. Louis* in Raymond Bellour, ed., *Le cinéma américain*, 2:145–61 (Paris: Flammarion, 1980); and her Ph.D. thesis, *The "True" Woman and the Family Film: The Industrial Production of Memory*, University of Wisconsin, Madison, 1981.

5. Ed Lowry well examines this aspect of the film in his M.A. thesis, *Art and Artifice in Six Musicals Directed by Vincente Minnelli*, University of Texas, Austin, 1977.

6. Andrew Britton, "*Meet Me in St. Louis:* Smith, or the Ambiguities," *Australian Journal of Screen Theory* (1977), 3:7–25.

7. In the book version by Sally Benson, the association of grandfather with the swamp is even more explicit as he takes Tootie to the construction site for one last look at one of his old stomping grounds.

8. Robin Wood, "The American Family Comedy: From *Meet Me in St. Louis* to *The Texas Chainsaw Massacre*," *Wide Angle* (1977), 3(2):5–11.

9. I examine the logic of *The Pirate* more closely in my essay " 'Above All Else To Make You See': Cinema and the Ideology of Spectacle," *Boundary 2* (Fall-Winter 1982–83), 11(1–2): 129–44.

10. Here, I should perhaps make it clear that I intend no endorsement of a natural-symbols approach to culture. I am more interested in the process by which a culture comes to participate in such symbolisms. The tie of water to romanticism in American culture is well suggested by Harold Bloom in *A Map of Misreading* (New York: Oxford University Press, 1975).

11. In all that follows, I don't mean to suggest that the forties represent the only critique in American culture of the idyllic space. The critique runs through the history of American representation. But where the earlier representations—for example, Melville's ambivalent sense of the romance of the sea—are directed toward a reality contemporary with the representation, by the forties, romanticism can only be nostalgic at best, an elegy for past ways of life.

12. Jean Baudrillard, "The Ecstasy of Communication," in Hal Foster, ed., *The Anti-Aesthetic: Essays on Postmodern Culture* (Port Townsend, Wash.: Bay Press, 1983), p. 138.

13. For a contemporary commentary on the postwar fascination with mythologies of the country, see Conrad Taueber, "Recent Trends of Rural-Urban Migration in the United States," *Milbank Memorial Fund Quarterly* (April 1947), 25(2):203–13. As Taueber notes, "To an increasing degree, there are included among the people living on farms, individuals who have little or no relation to the operation of the farm or the performance of the work on the farm" (pp. 210–11).

14. John Belton, "Film Noir's Knights of the Road," paper presented at the Purdue Annual Film Conference, 1982.

15. See Lucy Fischer's discussion of *Lady from Shanghai* in her book in progress, *Shot/Counter-Shot: Essays on Women and Film*.

16. See Mary Ann Doane, "The 'Woman's Film': Possession and Address," in Linda Williams, Mary Ann Doane, and Pat Mellencamp, eds., *Re-visions: Essays in Feminist Film Criticism*, pp. 67–89 (Baltimore: University Publishers, 1984).

17. See Tania Modleski, *Loving with a Vengeance* (New York: Archon Books, 1982).

18. For a discussion of this tactic, see Diane Waldman, *Horror and Domesticity: The Modern Gothic Romance Films of the 1940's*, Ph.D. thesis, University of Wisconsin, Madison, 1981.

19. Doane, "The 'Woman's Film,' " p. 84.

20. On the dual narrative of *Rebecca*, see D. Ranvaud, "*Rebecca*," *Framework* (Autumn 1980), 13:19–24.

21. Mary Ann Doane, "*Caught* and *Rebecca:* The Inscription of Femininity as Absence," *Enclitic* (Fall 1981/Spring 1982), 5/6(1/2): 75–89.

22. Deborah Linderman, "Terminating the Analyst: Tourneur's *The Cat People,*" paper presented at the 1982 annual conference of the Society for Cinema Studies.

23. Thomas Elsaesser, "Tales of Sound and Fury: Observations on the Family Melodrama," *Monogram (1973), 4:11.*

24. For an introduction to the cultural context of the Kinsey Report, see Paul Robinson, *The Modernisation of Sex: Havelock Ellis, Alfred Kinsey, William Masters, Virginia Johnson* (New York: Harper and Row, 1976).

25. On the generation of the representation of homosexuality in postwar cinema, see Richard Dyer, "Homosexuality and Film Noir," *Jump Cut*, (1977), 16:18–21.

26. On the rise of the paperback and its cover art, see Geoffrey O'Brien, *Hard-Boiled America: The Lurid Years of Paperbacks* (New York: Van Nostrand Reinhold, 1981); and Piet Schreuders, *Paperback, USA: A Graphic History, 1939–1959* (San Diego: Blue Dolphin Books, 1981).

27. For the theory of spectacle, see, especially, Guy Debord, *La société du spectacle* (Paris: Champ libre, 1971).

28. Jean Baudrillard, *Le système des objets* (Paris: Denoel, 1970), p. 25.

29. Fredric Jameson, *The Political Unconscious* (Ithaca: Cornell University Press, 1981), p. 229.

30. I examine Jameson's argument more closely in " 'Above All Else To Make You See.' "

31. Raymond Williams, *Television: Technology and Cultural Form* (New York: Schocken Books, 1975).

32. See, for example, Victor Shklovsky, "Art as Technique," *Russian Formalist Criticism: Four Texts,* Lee T. Lemon and Marion J. Reis, tr. (Lincoln: University of Nebraska Press, 1965), pp. 3–24.

33. Dennis Giles, "Show-Making," *Movie* (Spring 1977), 24:14–25.

34. For a study of the musical's mass-reproduction exploitation of aura, see Jane Feuer, *The Hollywood Musical* (Bloomington: Indiana University Press, 1982).

35. Tania Modleski, "Time and Desire in the Woman's Film," *Cinema Journal* (Spring 1984), 23(3):19–30.

36. Jacques Lacan, "Seminar on 'The Purloined Letter,' " Jeffrey Mehlman, tr., *Yale French Studies* (1972), 48:72.

37. To be sure, as Jean-Joseph Goux argues in *Economie et symbolique: Freud, Marx* (Paris: Seuil, 1973), the emergence of the power of the commodity can seem to parallel the emergence of patriarchal power. Yet, as Goux himself argues in his more recent *Les monnayeurs de langage* (Paris: Galilée, 1984), the parallel may break down with the emergence of a new monopoly stage of capitalism no longer dependent on the monad of the individual family as productive unit.

Name and Subject Index

Manual for the Motion Picture Industry (Office of War Information), 79
Mead, Margaret, on Frank Sinatra, 126
Meet Me in St. Louis (Benson), 325n7
Mehlman, Jeffrey, on Marx, 37–38
Merleau-Ponty, Maurice, on the body, 212
Metz, Christian: on film discourse, 62; on film vision, 304
Minnelli, Vincente, 40s musicals of, 258–61
Mitchell, Juliet, on social context of psychoanalysis, 14
Modern Woman: the Lost Sex (Lundberg and Farnham), 169
Modleski, Tania: on soap operas, 90; on *Detour*, 215; on female gothic, 277–78; on *Letter from an Unknown Woman*, 304
Motels, as 40s locale, 232
Mr. Roberts (Heggens), 119, 306
Murder, Inc. (Turkas and Feder), 243
Musicals, as spectacle, 293, 298–303
Mythologies (Barthes), 48

Nalkaya, Saim, on Levittowns, 255
Narrative, as ideological strategy, 12

Oberndorf, C. P., on 40s definitions of psychoanalysis, 176
Office of War Information, The, 54, 79

Paperback cover art, 294
Paysans, Les (Balzac), 12
Pearl Harbor, as narrative element, 57–60
Petersen, J. L., *see* Place, Janey
Place, Janey and J. L. Petersen, on style in film noir, 254
Poe, Edgar Allan, "The Mystery of Marie Roget," 238
Polenberg, Richard, on 40s politics, 41, 60; on 40s sociology, 71
"Primitive cinema," as historical concept, 34
Propaganda, in wartime discourse, 53–54
Propp, Vladimir, on components of narrative, 209, 213
Psychoanalysis: and cultural interpretation, 14; as narrative, 14–15
Purdy, Jim, *see* Roffman, Peter

Queen, Ellery, Wrightsville trilogy, 277

Red Harvest (Hammett), 323–24n27
Renov, Michael, on wartime film, 15–17, 40, 43
Riesman, David, 204–5, 255
Roffman, Peter and Jim Purdy, *The Hollywood Social Problem Film*, 34, 317n60
Roosevelt, Franklin D.: in war-effort, 62, 64; narrative function of, 66–68; contradictory representations of, 133–36; postwar legacy, 201–2, 212
Ropars, Marie-Claire, on narrative analysis, 32–33
Rose, Jacqueline, on paranoia in film, 145
Rosen, Phil, on agents of history, 318n4
Rupp, Leila, on 40s feminism, 129

Salt, Barry, on statistical analysis of film, 32–33
Sartre, Jean-Paul: on group formation, 59–61, 74; on the project, 75; on the fantastic in literature, 187, 216, 252, 306; on the body as being-in-the-world, 212
Sayers, Dorothy, *Whose Body?*, 237
Scapegoating, as community-building force, 61–62, 73–74
Schreuders, Piet, on paperback art, 294
Science-fiction, in the 40s, 166–69
Science, as narrative form, 164–66
Screwball comedy, 26–27, 217
Second-in-commands, as figure in war films, 72–73
Sense of an Ending, The (Kermode), 23, 97, 113, 198
Sexuality, wartime contradictions of, 124–32; 40s attitudes on, 290–92
Shadoian, Jack: on *The Killers*, 25; on *D.O.A.*, 240
Shannon, Claude and Warren Weaver, *The Mathematical Theory of Communication*, 320n12
Sinatra, Frank, as contradictory symbol, 124–27
Skold, Karen, on wartime women's labor force, 129
Smith, E. E. Doc, and 40s science fiction, 168, 206, 208
Spectacle, as 40s form, 294–308
Speech-act Theory, and American film, 115, 318n10

Film Index